TECHNOLOGICAL CAPABILITY AND LEARNING IN FIRMS

AF738718

For Huong, Linh and Khoi

Technological Capability and Learning in Firms

Vietnamese industries in transition

TRAN NGOC CA
Japanese-European Technology Studies Institute
The University of Edinburgh

Routledge
Taylor & Francis Group
LONDON AND NEW YORK

First published 1999 by Ashgate Publishing

Reissued 2018 by Routledge
2 Park Square, Milton Park, Abingdon, Oxon, OX14 4RN
52 Vanderbilt Avenue, New York, NY 10017

Routledge is an imprint of the Taylor & Francis Group, an informa business

Copyright © Tran Ngoc Ca 1999

All rights reserved. No part of this book may be reprinted or reproduced or utilised in any form or by any electronic, mechanical, or other means, now known or hereafter invented, including photocopying and recording, or in any information storage or retrieval system, without permission in writing from the publishers.

Notice:
Product or corporate names may be trademarks or registered trademarks, and are used only for identification and explanation without intent to infringe.

Publisher's Note
The publisher has gone to great lengths to ensure the quality of this reprint but points out that some imperfections in the original copies may be apparent.

Disclaimer
The publisher has made every effort to trace copyright holders and welcomes correspondence from those they have been unable to contact.

A Library of Congress record exists under LC control number: 98045759

ISBN 13: 978-1-138-34274-3 (hbk)
ISBN 13: 978-1-138-34275-0 (pbk)
ISBN 13: 978-0-429-43958-2 (ebk)

Contents

Tables and figures

Tables

Figures

Preface

This book is made thanks to many people from various organisations. First, my biggest thanks go to Wendy Faulkner, who helped me throughout the difficulties of scientific research, and academic writing. I would like to thank Simon Collinson for his friendly attitude and useful advice and for being both a great friend and supportive advisor.

During a long period of writing this book, I have benefited from discussions with and help of different people, whom I would like to thank: Lynn Mytelka, Bo Goransson, Mike Hobday, Arni Sverisson, Martin Bell, Norman Clark, James Fleck, John McMillan, Vu Cao Dam, Martin Fransman, Tran Ngoc Kim, Lez Rayman-Bacchus, and Hew Dundas. I would also like to express my gratitude to the staff of the Research Centre for Social Sciences at Edinburgh University, with Frank Beckhoffer as the director, for providing me with favourable and friendly working environment.

My big thanks go to the University of Edinburgh for its support without which I would not be able to do this study, as well as to organisations such as SAREC, Leche Foundation, Gilchrist Foundation and others which provided partial financial support to complete my work.

Finally, I want to thank my parents Kim and Chinh, especially my wife Huong and all my family for their endless understanding and support for me to undertake this long and difficult work.

Abbreviations

ASEAN:	Association of South East Asian Nations
CEE:	Central and Eastern Europe
CKD:	Complete Knocked Down
CMEA:	Council of Mutual Economic Assistance
DRV:	Democratic Republic of Vietnam
EU:	European Union
EA:	East Asia
FSU:	Former Soviet Union
IKD:	Incomplete Knocked Down
IMET:	Institute of Micro Electronics Technology
IOIT:	Institute of Information Technology
MOLI:	Ministry of Light Industry
MOI:	Ministry of Industry
MOSTE:	Ministry of Science, Technology and Environment
NCSR:	National Centre for Scientific Research
NIC:	Newly Industrialised Countries
OEM:	Original Engineering Manufacture
ODM:	Original Design Manufacture
OBM:	Own Brand Manufacture
SOE:	State Owned Enterprise
TC:	Technological Capability
RCGI:	Research Centre for Garment Industry
RITI:	Research Institute of Textile Industry
SKD:	Semi-complete Knocked Down
VIELIN:	Vietnam Institute of Electronics and Informatics

Map of Vietnam

1 Introduction

1.1 Technology, technological capability and learning

The question of building up technological capabilities (TC) in developing countries has been addressed by development studies as the technology dimension has become a more visible and important issue. Economic theories based on traditional factors (labour and capital) do not fully explain the phenomena of how developing countries emerge as new actors in the international technological arena. Similarly, dependency theory fails to explain why some developing countries can catch up quite successfully with the industrialised world. For the development of advanced countries in general, and for the rise of newly industrialised countries (NICs) in particular, the role of technological change in economic development has been repeatedly confirmed. There is also much evidence that the need to accumulate TC is crucial for almost all developing countries seeking to achieve more technological and economic development. The original focus on technology transfer and technical choice in technology studies of developing countries has shifted with the recognition that TC acquisition is a pre-condition for successful technology transfer. Moreover, unlike some NICs in Asia and Latin America, not all developing countries have achieved success in the catching-up process. The issue of formulating TC is even more pressing for late-comers. In academic discourse and in the policy-making process, concerned actors are asking questions like: what is the technological capability required by developing countries? what role do these capabilities play in the process of late industrialisation of a poor country? and how can these capabilities be built up?

It is not by chance that the problems of technological capability are seen as pivotal. The question of why some countries are able to create TC that helps them to achieve positive economic performances while others are not, leads the discussion directly to the specific localised nature of each country in the learning process. For each country, in their specific given conditions, the path of development has evolved in a long and painful process of accumulating experience and incremental change. Another question arises: in the same given country, with similar macroeconomics and other political and social conditions, why are some firms productive and quite competitive both locally and internationally while others are not? Rephrasing the question, why are some firms able to learn how to adopt, absorb, adapt and assimilate the processes of external technology, regardless of whether the source is foreign or local? There must be something crucial happening 'behind the gate' of the firms.

These questions suggest important sets of research issues to be investigated in this area. The first is learning process and its aim - the accumulation of TC. To understand the determinants of TC accumulation for countries and firms, it is necessary to look at the learning process and TC acquisition at the firm level with the firm as the main actor in this process. The second set of research issues concerns the firm's interaction with its environment. The acquisition of TC is influenced both by the macro level factors of the environment in which firms operate, and by the specific actions of each firm in the form of its strategic plans and behaviours and its whole learning attitude. This micro-macro interactive process is thus a central question to be examined in this book of learning and TC accumulation.

1.2 Vietnam's context

As one of the poorest countries in the world, Vietnam has recently entered a rehabilitation period after successive wars. Alongside the many radical changes in the international political and economic situation, the country is also undergoing the process of transition from being a centrally planned economy to a market economy. At this turning point in its development, it seems clear that, among other things, technology could and should play a very important role. Again, the questions facing researchers and policy makers in Vietnam are how to build up the TC of the country and how to ensure that the local efforts of a sector or firm contribute significantly to this TC.

As both a developing country and an economy in transition, Vietnam has characteristics similar to both types of country. The combination of these different features may create additional specific conditions for Vietnam's technological development. Another important question, therefore, is how all these factors are related to the learning process and TC accumulation in Vietnamese industrial firms. Examination of this will surely contribute not only to our general understanding of knowledge on learning and TC development in general, but also to a stock of knowledge on developing countries in Southeast Asia, and of transitional economies in the Asian context.

This book seeks to address the problems which Vietnamese firms have to face in the process of building up their TC. Specifically, the book has focused on the learning process of the firms as a core activity for the creation of technological capabilities. The influences of macro-environmental factors on the learning process and the reaction of the firms to these influences have also been examined. On the basis of this analysis, the book suggests some policy implications about conducive environment conditions for learning and TC accumulation.

1.3 Aims and outline

I had four aims in writing this book: first, to examine the development of TC in Vietnamese industrial companies and to look at how the learning process is related to the accumulation of TC; second, to understand the link between macro environment factors and micro internal actions of firms in shaping learning and TC accumulation; third, to address more specific issues relevant to Vietnam's context in comparative perspective with other developing countries, or with transitional economies that may have similar features of technological learning; and finally, to provide a background for elaborating some policy implications and recommendations for those organisations within and outwith Vietnam which are concerned with enhancing TC acquisition in similar settings.

The book has following structure: Chapter 2 deals with the concept of technological capabilities, learning and its characteristics. Chapter 3 presents the research questions and methodologies adopted.

The empirical material of this book starts with Chapter 4 on the country background of Vietnam in its transition. Development of two industries is given in Chapter 5. Chapter 6 addresses the issue of TC accumulation in the Vietnamese firms, their sequence and patterns. The learning process used to acquire these TCs is examined in Chapter 7: patterns, dynamics and the contribution of different learning mechanisms to different TCs. Chapter 8 addresses questions about the reasons behind the patterns of TC accumulation and learning: the influence of external macro factors and firm-level micro factors on firms' learning activities. In Chapter 9, four firm case studies are presented so as to illustrate in more depth the processes of learning and TC acquisition in the context of firms as a whole.

Chapter 10 analyses the findings of this study in comparison to relevant literature, while Chapter 11 draws some conclusions and implications for policy-making, from both firm and country perspectives. This final chapter also suggests some issues for further research concerning TC accumulation and learning in the context of both developing countries and transitional economies.

2 Technological capability of firms, learning and macro environment context

2.1 Technological capabilities (TC): concept and taxonomies

In economics studies, technology has been known as a source of growth, development and wealth for rich nations. Technology is central to regional and economic change, job-creation and job-destruction (Malecki, 1991). In the context of developing countries, until the late 1970s, the agenda of development economics and technology studies had mostly been shaped by neoclassical approaches which emphasised the choice of appropriate technology and technology transfer (Enos, 1991; Fransman, 1985). But the purchase of machinery or capital goods from industrial countries by firms does not of itself contribute to economic development. There must be considerable efforts devoted to learning the new technology, to developing the capability to produce machinery and design capability (Chudnovsky, 1986; Enos & Park, 1988; Fransman, 1986b). As Lall (1987) noted, the efficient development of industry requires a broad range of TC which can be only acquired by a long process of learning.

By the mid 1980s, the above mentioned agenda was questioned and the shortcomings of the conventional concept was criticised in a search for new ways of conceptualising technology studies (Rosenberg, 1976; Nelson & Winter, 1982; Bell & Pavitt, 1992; Fransman, 1995). In this context, technological capabilities became a central question (Fransman & King, 1984, Westphal et al, 1985). Although technology transfer is still a relevant question, particularly in the initial stage of technological development, the need to pay more attention to technological capability has come into the viewfinder of technology studies (Fransman, 1986c & 1995) and as Clark (1985) observed, there has been an explosion of literature on the subject of TC.

According to many studies, TC plays the critical role in sustaining the competitiveness of nations and firms (Hewitt & Wield, 1996). It is the central and decisive factor in creating competitive positions (Ernst & O'Connor, 1989), a key source of competitive strength (Mytelka, 1993). Key TCs are needed for sustained growth, structural transformation and continuous adjustment (UNCTAD, 1990). Especially in conditions of accelerated globalisation of trade and investment, those firms and nations that fail to accumulate their TC cannot maintain the growth, performance and rising knowledge-intensity and change-intensity of industrial production (Dosi & Soete, 1991; Justman & Teubal, 1995; Bell & Pavitt, 1993).

As a result, the concept of TC has come into consideration with increased focus on the factors influencing the acquisition and assimilation of imported technologies, and attempts to achieve progress through mastering, adapting and improving these technologies. Moreover, the efforts of developing countries to introduce new elements in imported technologies has become a decisive factor in their ability to catch up, to seek and sustain a place in a global industry, to compete in the international market (Cooper, 1995).

The questions of TC creation have been dealt with in numerous empirical studies during the 1970s and the 1980s (Katz, 1987b; Lall, 1984). These studies comprise two main types: the large and comprehensive project sponsored by different international organisations, which cover many countries and many industries at the same time, and specific cases which cover certain country, industry and concrete companies in particular. More current works include some regional-based research on the production and technology networking of Japanese firms in Pacific Asia (Baba & Hatashima, 1995), and the technological dynamism and export performance of East and South East Asian economies (Ernst et al, 1997).

Next to these programmes, there are various country studies which have concentrated on the technological development of specific countries in Asia (Lall, 1987; Westphal et al, 1984b & 1985; Enos & Park, 1988; Amsden, 1989; Fransman, 1986a; Bell et al, 1982; Teubal et al, 1986) and many others.

Studies on Latin American countries have been done by Katz et al (1987b), Teitel & Sercovitch (1984), Teubal (1984), Dahlman (1984). In the meantime, Mytelka (1985 & 1992), Langdon (1982 & 1984), and Bennell (1984) have conducted research into some African countries. More recently, there have been noteworthy case studies on Asian NICs (Hobday, 1994, 1995a & 1995b; Ernst, 1995; Ernst et al, 1998).

The purpose of these studies is to look at the technological development of developing countries in general, and/or of most NICs in particular. Different and specific features of development have been considered: industrialisation (Amsden, 1989); the acquisition of TC (its forms, content, etc.) (Katz, 1987b; Lall, 1987; Fransman, 1986a); technological innovation and its contribution to economic performance as measured by export activities (Lall, 1984; Teubal et al, 1986; Ernst et al, 1997); and the adoption and diffusion of imported technology (Enos & Park, 1988).

Most of these empirical studies have provided evidence of the importance of TC (Amsden, 1989; Mytelka, 1985; Lall & Wignaraja, 1994; Hobday, 1993). In contrast, Bell et al (1984) have shown that the majority of nascent industries never achieve maturity in large measure because of a failure to build up adequate TCs. As Amsden (1989) points out in her study on the industrialisation of South Korea, the credo of successful firms is to invest in in-house technological capability. In the World Bank's study on the export of technology by NICs, Lall (1984) noted the significance of TC for export activity.

By the end of the 1980s, many studies suggested different definitions of TC. These definitions are mostly related to the context of developing countries in their effort to formulate a basis for technical change and economic growth.

The most simplified definition of TC is the general ability to undertake a broad range of technological tasks (Lall, 1987). Similarly, TC can be described as a set (or sub-set) of abilities relating to: the understanding of specified technology-related tasks or actions; the transforming of inputs into outputs; and the activities of buying, producing and selling (Fransman, 1986c). Many other studies go further than this definition in giving more detailed and concrete divisions of TC.

In looking at the experiences of South Korea in the acquisition of TC, Westphal et al (1985) identified technological capability as the ability to make effective use of technical knowledge. This inheres, they argue, not in the knowledge that is possessed but more in the use of that knowledge and in the proficiency of its use in production, investment and innovation. The focus of these production, investment and innovation capabilities, thus, is the application of knowledge. Lall (1990, 1992, 1993a, 1993b & 1994a) grouped TC into three main functions: investment, production and linkage within the economy with three degrees of complexity: basic, intermediary and advanced. Fransman (1984a), in his overview of TC in the Third World, suggests the following categories of technological capability:

- the *search* for available alternative technologies and the selection of the most appropriate technology;
- the *mastering* of the technology;
- the *adaptation* of the technology to suit specific production conditions;

- the *further development* of the technology as a result of minor innovation;
- the *institutionalised search for more important innovation* with the development of R&D facilities; and
- the *conducting of basic research.*

Similarly, technological capability is defined by Amsden & Kim (1986) as the ability, embodied in people, to select the appropriate technology, to implement it, to operate the production facilities, to adapt and improve those facilities, and to create new processes and products. Baranson and Roark (1985), in their studies on international technology transfer processes, distinguish different kinds of transfer imparting different capabilities: operational, duplicative and innovative.

Although these definitions adopt different terms and perspectives, they have much in common in the sense that all describe different levels of complexity of technological effort for the recipient (in technology transfer) or for the concerned actors. Also, all see these complexities as increasing with the evolution of technological mastery: from the *use* of existing technologies (in the broadest sense of use), to the *change* of existing technologies (through adaptation and assimilation) and, ultimately, to the *creation* of new technologies (through technological design and R&D).

There are some notable features among the different taxonomies on TC discussed above. These taxonomies have one thing in common: their divisions are all related to abilities to undertake certain *functions* of the firm. It is not so easy to separate all these taxonomies. It seems that they overlap and duplicate each other. For example, in order to operate (or produce) successfully it is necessary to master and adapt, or, if one wants to change, one should conduct research and innovate, etc. It seems reasonable to see this as layers of functions, and as layers of abilities to conduct these functions. The point here is that the function/action of firms is seen as the focus of all taxonomies on TC.

There is another point to address here. In their latest works on TC, Bell & Pavitt (1993 & 1997) have distinguished *production capacity* and *technological capability*, because the focus of these studies is the dynamism of industrialisation and the resources necessary to generate and manage this dynamism. For them, production capacity incorporates the resources used to produce industrial goods at given levels of efficiency and given input combinations. At the same time, technological capabilities consist of the resources needed to generate and manage technical change, including skills, knowledge and experience, and industrial structures and linkages. These studies also differentiate *technical change* and *technological learning.* While technical change encompasses the ways in which new technology is incorporated into the production capacity, technological learning (or technological accumulation) refers to any process by which the resources for generating and managing technical change are increased or strengthened.

At first sight, it seems that Bell & Pavitt's taxonomy might be contradictory to other taxonomies of TC, because their TC concept only deals with technical change. However, if we adopt the view that knowledge, skills and experience are the focus of TC accumulation regardless of its purpose, TC can also include the knowledge, skills and experience used for the production function. These labour skills (operational and managerial know-how and experience) together with experience in arranging organisational methods and systems which are part of the production capacity in Bell & Pavitt's (1993) taxonomy, therefore, are also part of technological capability. This capability may be called production capability in other taxonomies. For example, Westphal et al (1985), Lall (1992, 1993a, 1993b and 1994a) or Baranson & Roark (1985) all include these elements in production capability. In other taxonomies, Fransman (1984a) describes it within the category of mastering technology, while Bell & Scot-Kemmis (1985b) give the categories of using (manufacturing) technical systems. As a result, these old and new concepts of TC are not contradictory, but merely different in focus. Depending on the purposes and emphases of the studies, there can be various names. But, in general, they all refer to knowledge, skills, and experience as a core element of TC.

One notable feature is the increasingly recognised importance of marketing capability. For instance, in earlier works on TC, Lall (1992) mentions this competence in TC taxonomy only implicitly. The significance of market linkage is only mentioned in relation to linkage capability. However, in more recent studies and more specific work on the garment industry of Sri Lanka, Lall & Wignaraja (1994) emphasise marketing as one of the necessary technological capabilities of the firms. For firms exporting from developing countries, marketing in the sense of finding or attracting customers and persuading them to place orders or buy products is almost inseparable in practice from building up the firm's supply capabilities (Keesing & Lall, 1992).

2.2 Some key issues emerging from studies of TC

Several issues emerge from existing studies of TC. One concerns the *uneveness* of TC accumulation across firms in a single country and across different countries. Various TCs are accumulated to different extents. Firms in Korea or Taiwan, for example, have developed strong capabilities for generating continuous incremental change in technologies initially acquired from industrialised countries, then for replicating technologies already developed elsewhere, and eventually for developing more original innovations (Bell & Pavitt, 1993). The findings of many studies on the software and computing industries (Ernst & O'Connor, 1993; Correa, 1995; Katz, 1987b) and the fashion garment industry (Mytelka, 1991; Lall & Wignarajar, 1994) report that compared to production and minor technical change capabilities, the investment and to a larger extent, the marketing capabilities of firms tend to be weak.

The uneveness of TC development points to the *sequential feature* of their accumulation. Firms do not acquire their different TCs at once, but step by step. The above mentioned increasing complexity of TC over the process of technological mastery implies that the accumulation of TC cannot happen simultaneously for all kinds of TC. Rather, there is a tendency to start from lower and easier levels of TC (i.e., using technology) and to progress to a higher and more complicated level (i.e., changing and creating technology). This progress can occur in a sequence of TC acquisition, over time. This sequential aspect is not new if one takes into account the notion of the progressing of TC accumulation from simple to more complex tasks/functions over time (Rosenberg, 1994). Thus, Lall (1993b) noted the attitude of "getting into production" as the first stance taken by many firms in developing countries. Empirical evidence given by Ernst (1994 & 1995) have illustrated that Korean electronics firms (even large chaebol, like Samsung or LG Group) in their first period of learning TC, tended to develop production competence first, such as the final assembly of mature and proven imported product designs. On the basis of the development of production, these firms can then further develop other capabilities. This is called reverse-sequence, which starts with production capability as the foundation for developing other capabilities such as investment and adaptive engineering (minor technical change). The Korean experience of first beginning with production capability with other capabilities coming later is confirmed by Kim (1990). Similarly, the case of other East Asian NICs suggest that firms in these countries started with simple assembly of mature products and processes for their first accumulation of production capability. Then, they moved "backward" along the path of a traditional technology life-cycle through technological assimilation such as reverse engineering (Hobday, 1993). Using the simple model of technological development on the basis of NICs experiences, Hobday (1994 & 1995b) stated that TC accumulation in these countries has gone through stages from basic production capability to minor incremental process engineering capability, then to more innovative ones.

A second important feature of TC accumulation seen clearly in the existing literature is *firm-specificity* as specified by Teece et al (1990), Coombs et al (1992a) and many other authors (Lall, 1990 & 1993b; Cooper, 1991). In most studies, the TC concept seems to imply the abilities to *use*, *change* and *create* technologies as those abilities related to concrete activities at the level of the firm.

Since most innovations are developed by firms, the abilities to select, adapt, use and transfer technology necessarily have to be developed by the enterprise itself (Katz, 1984a; Lundvall, 1992). In theories of evolutionary economics (Nelson & Winter, 1982; Dosi, 1988; Nelson, 1987), the firm is the central actor for several reasons: firms do not operate on a common production function; technological knowledge is not shared equally by firms; and the extent to which firms master transferred technologies varies according to the skills, efforts and investment mobilised. Because of this, the enterprise-level of technological effort is important (Lall, 1992; Amsden 1989; Mowery & Rosenberg, 1989). As Bell & Pavitt (1992) put it, the firm is the most important actor in accumulating technology because it learns from developing and operating specific production systems.

It has been shown by many studies that the technological behaviour of firms is conditioned by different forces including those coming from outwith the firms (Katz et al, 1987a; Lall, 1984). The firm and its technological activity are not isolated from the economic, technological, political, institutional and socio-cultural context in which the firm operates. Accordingly, these country-level (or macro-economic) factors play an important role in shaping the TC of firms and the ways firms acquire their capabilities (UNCTAD, 1990; Lall, 1992; Metcalfe & de Liso, 1995).

Although authors emphasise different factors, in general they point to certain common groups of factors which typically influence firms' activities. These consist of both supply- and demand-side factors: macro-economic government policies, market factors or structure, industrial supporting systems, physical and science and technology (S&T) infrastructure (including academic research), functioning of legal, financial, marketing, system of information and other institutions (Lall, 1993a & 1994b; Bell & Pavitt, 1993).

Many analyses have conceptualised the role of these factors in terms of the *national system of innovation* or NSI (or as some call it, the national innovation system) and its impact on the innovative capabilities of firms (Nelson, 1988; Lundvall, 1992; Freeman, 1987a & 1988; Fransman, 1990 & 1991). The main implication from this work is that it is impossible to separate a firm's technological accumulation from its operating environment. Moreover, the accumulation of TC does not depend on the impact of external factors on a passive firm but on the interaction of firms with their environment, thus, on the way firms react or respond to these factors.

The combination of micro and macro conditions shaping the accumulation of TC can be found in many different case studies of various countries (Bell & Scott-Kemmis, 1985a; Lall, 1982; Cooper, 1991; Fransman, 1984a). Recent lessons from East Asian NICs suggest that external factors, such as the education system, investment in training efforts (Korea, Taiwan) or the active role of government policy in Singapore, are all vital for TC accumulation (Hobday, 1994; Lall, 1994b). Thus, the interaction between activities at the micro level of the firms and factors at macro level is undoubtedly a key issue to examine if one wants to understand the technological behaviour of firms.

Throughout the literature available, it is clear that TC accumulation is not a single action, but a long-term and painstaking process. The technological competence of firms is *accumulated incrementally* over time mostly through slow step-by-step development (Hollander, 1965; Imai, 1986). The cumulative nature of TC accumulation has been noted by Dahlman & Fonseca (1987), Enos & Park (1988), Fransman (1985). According to Bell & Pavitt (1992, 1997), given the importance of specific knowledge, individuals and firms are not capable of learning simultaneously across diverse technological and organisational dimensions. Instead, they tend to move along the particular trajectories by which past activities shape present directions of technical change, and experience reinforces the existing stock of knowledge and expertise.

2.3 Framework for studying TC

As discussed above, the firm is the main actor in the technological development of industry and country. Different firms have different backgrounds (historical circumstances of establishment, managers' experiences and education, firm-specific practice, etc). For this reason, firms' capabilities in the forms of functional/organisational activities are the focus of this study, while interactions of the firms with their macro-environments (influences of environmental factors on changes of TC and reactions of firms to these impacts), is another dimension of the research. Following the review of TC taxonomies, another division of TC used by UNCTAD in a study of some East and South East Asian countries (Ernst et al, 1998) seems quite operationally useful. This taxonomy divides TC into six types of functions with knowledge and skills positioned as the core elements that firms need in order to acquire, assimilate, use, adapt, change and create technologies:

- *Investment capability*: the ability to undertake the functions of identification, preparation, design, setting up and commissioning of new industrial projects, or the expansion and/or modernisation of existing ones. This capability can have two sub-elements: pre-investment and project implementation.

- *Production capability*: the ability to operate plants, where shop floor experiences and learning-by-doing have an important role. This capability has elements like production management, production engineering, repair and maintenance of physical capital.
- *Minor technical change capability*: the ability to adapt engineering and organisational features, reverse engineering and analytical design, and system engineering.
- *Marketing capability*: the ability to deal with demand patterns, market trends, user needs and skills so as to collect marketing intelligence.
- *Linkage capability:* the ability and organisational competence to transfer technologies at three levels: within a firm, among firms, and between firms and their scientific and technological infrastructure (network or system).
- *Major technical change capability:* the ability to create technologies which are new in principle, design new features of products and processes (including new product ideas), and the ability to deploy scientific knowledge in developing patentable ideas.

This taxonomy is quite similar to the others. It has a functional focus. The capabilities include (or are almost the same as) those of other taxonomies (investment, production/operation/use, minor change/adaptation, major change/innovation and linkage). And it also divides capabilities into the various stages of technological development within firms: starting from the pre-investment period up to diffusion and transfer activities. Specifically, marketing capability is named, which in other taxonomies is included under the rubric of different capabilities: under the categories of production capability (Westphal et al, 1985; Lall, 1992), or capability to use a technical system (Bell & Scot-Kemmis, 1985b) so as to undertake marketing and user support. In separating out marketing capability, Ernst et al's classification acknowledges one more important aspect which is essential for successful innovation activities of firms.

The distinction between minor and major technical change capabilities is also noteworthy. In this taxonomy, although minor technical change can have quite significant gains in terms of profits and economic growth for firms, in technical terms it is less noticeable than major technical change which are a kind of breakthrough activity. This second type of technical change tends to lead to new invention, using scientific principles to create very new technologies (product ideas for patenting, etc.). One of the reasons this distinction is used is that in the context of developing countries, the technical change activity tends to be closer to minor type rather than to radical type of change which is out of reach of most firms from developing countries.

Linkage capability concerns the transfer of technology. The new taxonomy includes the technology transfer not only among firms, but also between firms and the whole industrial supporting system (R&D, training, etc.) as well as among different divisions of firms. This means the linkage capability includes technology transfer occurring not only from firms to other firms, but also from the whole S&T infrastructure into the firms which is crucial for the firms' long term economic performance and growth.

Comparing taxonomies, it can be said that Ernst et al's is an extended and updated version of Bell & Pavitt's (1992 and 1993). Production capability in the former includes those skills, knowledge and experience (and only these elements, equipment is not included for instance) which are grouped within the production capacity classification of the latter. At the same time, the distinction between production capacity and technological capability in the latter approach, in fact reflects the difference the former taxonomy makes between TC in production and TC in technical change. The reason that Bell & Pavitt (1993) did not include marketing capability in their technological capability is that they are mainly concerned with technical change as the focus of TC leading to production capacity. Nonetheless, for firms to operate and sustain their operation, sales activity is an important element, in both local and export markets. Particularly, with increasing interdependence and globalisation of economic and technological development, contacts with markets ensure that firms have constant feedback for their future innovation activities. These characteristics are certainly vital for the 'normal living' of the firms. It would be fair to say that by using this more detailed classification of TC by Ernst et al, it is easier to look at the evolution of TC and at the changes over time of a firm's reaction to outside influences.

2.4 The concept of learning

Many authors of technology studies have recognised the importance of the incremental nature of technical change. Hollander (1965) emphasises that the cumulative effect of minor technical changes upon cost reduction are no less than the effect of major technical changes. This point is similar to Enos' (1958) study of the rate of technical progress, saying that the cost reduction achieved by later improvements through minor innovations were greater than the cost reduction associated with their initial introduction. The main point here is that the economic gains from major innovation may be at least equalled by the gains from continuing improvements to the innovation during their diffusion and use (Rosenberg, 1982 & 1976). The taxonomy of innovation given by Freeman (1987b) divides innovations into three categories: incremental, radical innovation and technological revolution. The incremental type of innovation is described as a "relatively smooth continuous progress leading to steady improvements in the array of existing products and services and the way in which they are produced".

Minor cumulative developments such as modification and improvement can occur through the bandwagon effect (Mensch, 1975), which accompanies diffusion (Dosi, 1984). There can be no doubt that incremental innovation is the most important type of technical change in developing countries, at least in the first period of their technological development, where social and economic conditions do not enable them to pursue more radical technological innovation. As Fransman (1985 & 1986a) concludes, over time, incremental technical change is usually of greater significance than radical frontier-shifting change. Breakthrough technological innovation is often necessary to introduce qualitative change in the economy (such as new industries) and occurs mainly in highly industrialised countries rather than developing ones, while far more significant quantitatively are incremental changes which appear in all countries.

Empirical studies of developing countries have illustrated that their TCs have been gained mainly through incremental processes (Kim, 1990; Westphal et al, 1984; Amsden & Kim, 1986; Lee, Bae & Choi, 1988; Maxwel, 1981; Viana, 1984). Other evidence can be found in studies on the contribution of continuous improvement to competitiveness in Japan (Imai, 1986), or the petrochemical industry of Korea (Enos & Park, 1988), steel industry in Brazil (Dahlman & Fonseca, 1987) or more recent studies carried out by the World Bank on the cumulative nature of technical change (Mody et al, 1991). In the process of technical change, minor innovations are accumulated over time, not overnight.

The implication of this discussion points to the concept of learning which is an important issue for firms creating TC. Unlike a machine or a piece of equipment which can be bought, knowledge, skills and experience - as the core elements of TC - need to be learnt step-by-step. One of the first uses of the learning concept comes from Arrow (1962) where he introduces the model of learning-by-doing which argues that production costs decline as productive experience increases. This core concept regarding the possibility of accumulation of experience during the process of practising production and other related activities has been developed further by other authors. Similar findings about the automatic effects of learning in the course of production emerge from the study of labour productivity increases in the Horndal steel works, the textile mills of Lowell (David, 1975), and the unit cost decrease in a US rayon plant

(Hollander, 1965). Arrow's idea is examined by other authors who introduce the concept of a learning curve (Hirsch, 1963; Hirshleifer, 1962; Hartley, 1965; Enos, 1958).

2.5 Key features of the learning process

As argued above, learning is a complex process involving many different types of activities, it is *not costless and automatic.* In fact, learning does not come 'just so' as Arrow (1962) mentioned, but as a conscious, systematic and frequent effort made by the concerned actors. The assumed automatism of learning is criticised by many authors (Cooper, 1991; Westphal et al, 1981; Bell & Pavitt, 1992 and 1993). Empirical evidence in many studies has rejected the classical perception that learning is a costless and automatic phenomenon (Enos & Park, 1988; Bell et al, 1982). It is argued that the old concept of learning-by-doing contains nothing that leads to the idea that firms might have explicit and active technology search strategies (Katz, 1987a). Indeed the evidence for a 'reverse tendency' - that operating efficiency and labour productivity can decrease rather than increase over time - illustrates that learning cannot be automatic (Ahmed, 1981; Bell & Hoffman, 1981; Bell et al, 1980; Girvan, 1983; Maxwell, 1981; Fransman, 1985; Lall, 1987; Fransman & King, 1984; Bell & Pavitt, 1992 and 1993). As Fransman (1986c) summarises, learning requires an expenditure of effort, therefore it is a costly activity; learning does not accrue automatically as a function of output, investment or time; and the gain from learning cannot be presumed. These assumptions are in contrast to the old and classical concept of automatic learning-by-doing as used in economic literature.

Another important characteristic of technological knowledge is the *incremental cumulativeness* of its acquisition (Malerba, 1992). Nelson & Winter (1982), for instance, have identified the cumulativeness and tacitness of knowledge as crucial features in learning. The accumulation of technology is a continuous, long-term process which relies on feedback flows of information (or learning) from within the industry and from users (Baark, 1991). Experience and further knowledge can come through feedback and error correction which Alic (1995) calls artful practice. These learning activities are *dynamic* phenomena. They involve myriad improvements and changes (Boisot, 1995). For example, Lapid's work (1994) shows that the development of a product moves over time from direct learning to learning-by-doing, learning-by-using and then to cross-learning. A study by Lall & Wignaraja (1994) on how Sri Lankan firms use the foreign connection mechanism also indicates the diversity in forms of foreign involvement.

If knowledge is the main focus of the learning concept, it is necessary to mention that knowledge is tacit; it cannot be codified nor can it be embodied in a single person or organisation (Bell and Pavitt, 1993). The tacitness of knowledge was noted quite early by Polanyi (1966) and many other authors. Lall (1987) also emphasises the importance of tacit or uncodified elements. These elements cannot be bought off-the-shelf in the form of capital goods, nor through drawings or manuals. They are part of what constitutes skill, technical knowledge, experience and organisational ability.

It is important to note that tacit knowledge which is often skill-based and acquired on-the-job, makes a greater overall contribution to product development than does formal knowledge, which is acquired through research literature and education (Senker, 1992; Senker & Faulkner, 1992). More often than not, this kind of knowledge comprises specific know-how techniques that are not encoded in text books and often cannot be written down or described, and which can only be learnt through practice. Despite the importance of this specific tacit knowledge, however, Senker and Faulkner (1992) emphasise that technological innovation demands the synthesis of both types of knowledge.

This synthesis suggests that there may be a need to combine different types of learning mechanisms for effective learning (Teece et al, 1992; Bell & Casiolato, 1993; Cooper, 1995). Learning-by-doing is more associated with the acquisition of tacit knowledge (Faulkner, 1993) and it can be combined with other sources of learning such as reading literature; doing research; receiving formal training and instruction (Alic, 1995; Spender & Di Bello, 1995); learning-by-absorption (Dickson et al, 1995); or learning by foreign connection (Batchelor et al, 1995). This combined effect of learning - "integrated learning" as Bessant et al (1996) call it - can bring much more significant comprehensiveness and complimentarity of learning than reliance on just one or two types of learning.

The evidence of many empirical studies show that firms, industries and countries need time to accumulate their TC (Bessant et al, 1996; UNCTAD, 1990; Hobday, 1994 & 1995b). Among the implications of the incremental cumulativeness of knowledge such as the length of time firms need to learn and accumulate their TC, many authors have pointed out that prior accumulation of knowledge and expertise is crucial (Rosenberg, 1982; Nelson & Winter, 1982). Knowledge accumulated in the past contributes to present innovative activities and to the direction of technological change in the future. Therefore, the knowledge, skill and experience accumulated by personnel in firms elsewhere can be crucial in determining what firms learn at a later stage (i.e., that they know what to learn and they know how to learn it). This absorptive capacity of firms (Cohen & Levinthal, 1990) to recognise the value of new external information and to assimilate and apply it to commercial ends is critical to its further learning and innovative capabilities. Partly through this ability to recognise the value of new research directions, firms invest in basic research activity that can help them better understand how and where to conduct research of a more applied nature leading to potentially commercial products (Rosenberg, 1990). In any case, this cumulativeness is intrinsic to knowledge acquisition and places the incremental process of learning - especially of prior knowledge accumulation - in a privileged position. This implication is significant for identifying prior accumulation (e.g., through choosing to recruit new graduates or experienced personnel) as a distinct learning mechanism.

2.6 Taxonomy of learning

The learning process can take different forms depending on various criteria. Lall (1982) and Bell (1984) propose taxonomies of learning that are particularly appropriate for developing countries. According to Lall (1982), all progress in technology or in efficiency can be regarded as a form of learning which takes time to be realised and involves the accumulation of experience. He distinguishes technical and non-technical learning. In *technical learning*, he identifies three stages each with two sub-stages. The first stage, learning within a given technology, refers to the import of technology by developing countries (or its transfer from abroad). Learning the embodied technology is the second stage and occurs when some of the machinery required is manufactured within the country, to reproduce or improve that particular function within the technology. Between these two stages, there are some small but quite important steps: putting together imported components, doing some detailed engineering, then some basic design work which involves knowledge of the exact qualities and specification of materials, components, mechanical principles, requiring more experience, search and purposeful technical work. At a later stage, it usually requires the creation of a separate R&D unit. At the third stage, learning the entire technology or production system involves a transition from the capability to produce similar machines to being able to produce the whole technology in a functional plant with a variety of different kinds of machinery, each with its own sub-technology, and overall design. The ability to train others in the know-how needed to run the plant is also included in this stage.

Non-technical learning expresses the whole gamut of functions required for successful commercial activity: organisational, managerial, financial, marketing and political. Some of these functions can be learnt together with technical learning, and some are independently learnt. The importance of non-technical learning has been stressed since the failure of this learning may hold back or abort technical learning.

The taxonomy given by Lall can be mostly placed in the context of the production and export of capital goods by developing countries. Hence, this taxonomy seems closer to the country level than the firm level perspective. This taxonomy, however, has identified a framework for looking at learning phenomena in developing countries.

Another important aspect of the content of learning is the distinction between know-how and know-why (Bell & Scott-Kemmis, 1985a; Lall, 1985). Indeed, while know-how is a kind of practical knowledge and tends to be more useful for doing and using technical and production systems, know-why (usually theoretical knowledge) seems to be more appropriate for changing these systems. This feature of the firm's knowledge has a major bearing on the substance and the depth of the learning process (Bell & Scott-Kemmis, 1985a).

The taxonomy presented above shows the progress of learning from simple to more complex forms. The taxonomy of learning introduced by Bell (1984) categorises learning by the *functions* firms perform in order to learn. He divides learning into two kinds of process whereby technological capacity is acquired. In addition to learning-by-doing where acquiring skill and knowledge depends largely or entirely on experience, there is the acquisition of increased skill and knowledge by different means: other mechanisms that do not rest on experience accumulation. As a result, he distinguishes a number of types of learning, the first two of which are doing-based (or experience-based) activities.

Through *learning-by-operating,* the flow of experience derives from the doing of operational tasks, and is one kind of feedback mechanism. *Learning-by-changing* is generated not by operating existing plants, but by doing various kinds of technical change activity. *Learning-by-training* in which formalised training is a source of technological capacity and a kind of explicit investment in the acquisition of technological capability. *Learning-by-hiring* by which skills and knowledge may be acquired through the simple mechanism of hiring the people who embody those sources; the hiring of more or less ready-made technological capacity. *Learning-by-searching* involves looking for forms of disembodied knowledge and information rather than being (i) already embodied in hireable human capital or (ii) transferred by a reasonably explicit training process. This type of information very seldom just arrives. It has to be actively searched out and acquired by firms. It requires the prior accumulation and deployment of resources to make the search effort.

While the taxonomy of Lall (1982) is more purpose-oriented for the technological progress of a country (or a firm) through stages, the one given by Bell is more firm-level and action-oriented with the focus on the very specific core element of learning: accumulation of skill, information and knowledge. However, these two kinds of taxonomy are not alternatives, but complementary. Both are quite useful as methodological tools for research on the learning process. In a similar vein, depending on the actions involved in the learning process, other studies introduce forms of learning-by-using (Von Hippel, 1982; Rosenberg, 1982), learning-by-exporting (Teubal, 1984; Westphal et al, 1981), by licensing activity (Erber, 1986), and by R&D (Rosenberg, 1982; Katz, 1985). The main element of these categorisations is also the accumulation of knowledge, skill and experience through various activities.

Whilst Lall's taxonomy answers the question of what to learn (i.e., the content of learning) and Bell's looks at learning by various means, others have drawn distinctions which tend to reflect different facets of how learning takes place. For some authors (Amsden & Kim, 1986; Pyke et al, 1990; Nohria and Eccles, 1992; Kogut et al, 1993; Lundvall, 1993; Grabher, 1993), the *formality of learning* is the main criterion of distinction. In studies of the knitting industry in Modena, Italy (Lazerson, 1990) and of the electronics and textile sectors in Korea (Myung Rae-cho, 1994), networking among personnel of various firms and industrial supporting units was found to make an important contribution to learning. In this networks of learning (Powell & Brantley, 1992), both formal and informal learning can take place, but informal networking has an important role to play in specific conditions where formal learning cannot function and more tacit understanding of knowledge is required.

With regard to the purposes of learning, Teubal (1984) mentions two types of learning, mostly in the context of the capital goods sector: simple or process learning and more complicated product learning. *Process learning* enables the firm to produce existing equipment at lower cost, to introduce relatively minor technological improvements or to more fully exploit the markets currently served by the firm. In the meantime, *product learning* enables the firm to shift to new, but technologically-related, types of equipment which are more difficult to produce or require a design capability as well. This involves better exploitation of the existing set of sub-markets or user segments related to its areas of expertise.

From another angle of strategies of firms, Dodgson (1992) suggests a distinction between *tactical* and *strategic learning* with differences in time scale and complexity. While the former aims at immediate problem-solving activities and has a shorter time scale, the latter involves the firm developing managerial and scientific or technological skills for the long term future.

These additional distinctions, in fact, are not so different from each other, since some notions in one categorisation are used in others, depending on the purposes and focus of the studies. Most of the distinctions which focus on the formality, the aims and the time-scale of learning in this section include more concrete functional learning and different contents of learning. Therefore, for the purpose of this study, in the next section an integrated approach for using learning mechanisms is proposed.

2.7 The integrated approach

The proposed six categories of learning is an extended version of Bell's taxonomy which integrates elements of other taxonomies. The first is active *learning-by-doing* in its broadest sense, including incremental improvements made before and after technology is implemented and used. In this sense, this form of learning refers to all learning-by-doing, learning-by-operating/using, changing and trying/adapting, etc. Examples of this kind of learning are also found in studies of learning mechanisms presented in studies by Lapid (1994) and Von Hippel & Tyre (1995), where problem identification and solution finding can be done through practical tests and checking. This form of learning - called "learning by templating" by Von Hippel & Tyre (1995) as a variant of trial and error problem solving - can also be described as a form of pattern recognition. As a result of templating, problems are discovered in the course of doing. In a study on Celltech, a biotechnology firm, Dodgson (1992) presented a similar use of various kinds of mechanisms in the learning process of the firm. In the Celltech case, learning-by-doing takes the form of learning by solving technical problems. To pursue this type of learning, firms try to implement something, adjust the problems, change the configuration and learn from mistakes to improve certain targets after each test trial, etc. In short, it is much more broader and active than just passive doing. Fleck's (1994) notion of learning-by-struggling or by-trying fits into this active learning-by-doing.

However, doing-based learning is not enough and firms need to have more active learning forms for TC accumulation. Other active learning mechanisms are required. First, learning by *prior accumulation* of knowledge, skills, experience from recruitment is necessary. This way of learning helps firms to acquire knowledge and experience through their personnel *before* they start working for the firm and to increase firms' absorptive capacity for subsequent learning.

Learning by local *training*: *on-the-job* mode includes various training and supporting activities which do not require workers to leave their jobs, and these are mostly offered on-site. This also includes hiring experts to come in from outside to solve problems in firms and to share their experience with the firms' personnel. This category is close to the in-house training activities mentioned by others, and these activities are usually short-term and more frequently informal than formal in style. As Enos (1991) notes, on-the-job training can offer advantages over formal training (being quicker, more pragmatic and achievable with a minimum of overhead) and its effects seems to be substantial. The *off-the-job* mode of local learning refers to training courses whereby staff leave their job for some time to attend off-site activities. This form of training usually tends to be more formal and long-term, and is offered by outside organisations such as universities, vocational schools, training centres or other companies. The study by Bell and Scott-Kemmis (1985a) shows the value of examining both on-the-job and off-the-job training.

Learning by *searching* and *collecting information* (for instance, through documentation) and by contacting consultants is quite an important mechanism, as is networking. As an example of this way of learning, Robert (1973) mentions that the role of local consultancy is crucial to the successful transfer of turnkey projects from an external source for internal incorporation by the firm.

Last is learning through *foreign connections*: both for training on-the-job or off-the-job, as well as for other technical assistance in searching out expertise and collecting information, etc. The reason for adding one more learning type into this taxonomy lies in the context of developing countries, where, in many cases, foreign connections are the most important initial input to starting up a business, either through technology transfer or through direct investment. In a broad sense, foreign connections may already be implicated in many other mechanisms such as forms of training and information collection which are foreign-related. However, in many cases, a firm's success or failure in using foreign connections for acquiring TC can be so substantial (Lall & Wignaraja, 1994) that it remains necessary to consider this mechanism separately from the other forms of learning.

As can be seen here, the proposed taxonomy has a function-based focus, although it includes other distinctions. It can involve both technical and non-technical contents, product or process learning purposes and long-term strategic or short-term tactical learning perspectives.

2.8 Macro-level factors and micro-level responses

Learning, as the process leading to the acquisition of TC, is necessarily affected by macro factors. Much of the literature addresses the conditions which must pertain if learning is to be successful, and catalogues the reasons for failure. The rate and direction of technical search efforts (one form of technical learning) of the firms in developing countries are affected by four major sets of factors: (i) micro-economic determinants, (ii) the competitive climate, (iii) macro-economic determinants, and (iv) new technical knowledge as international technological frontiers expand (Katz, 1985). The impact of macro determinants on learning in the firm is examined from different angles in many studies (Porter, 1990; Patel & Pavitt, 1992; Nakaoka, 1987; Ozawa, 1980; Hobday, 1994 & 1995a; Lall, 1994b). Depending on government policies, firms may face harsh competitive pressure in the external macro environment or, alternatively, may be protected from this competition. The notion of competition versus protection is reviewed in many studies (Fransman, 1985; Dalum et al, 1992; Bell & Pavitt, 1993). This debate has important implications for learning.

A similar debate occurs in the context of developing countries where the importance of some degree of government intervention is often noted (Lall, 1993b; Wong, 1992). It is argued that effective learning in developing countries requires some intervention involving preferential financing and various measures of protection (Kim, 1980; Wade, 1990).[1] Moreover, intervention (for instance, by creating some protective measures through taxation and other incentives) needs to be selective to support capability building in different developing countries (Lall, 1993a). Next to the macro policies of government, the learning process is becoming increasingly dependent on factors like the training and education system, the networks of R&D activities and other industrial services, which, in turn, require enormous investment and effort both from the state and from individual firms. These factors are embedded in the external environment in which the learning of firms takes place, and from which learning activities at the firm level cannot be isolated (Kline & Rosenberg, 1986; Dosi, 1995).

Besides external factors, learning by firms also depends on their internal action and on the behaviour of their personnel. For example, the maximisation of learning potential depends on firms' behaviour in defining exactly what technology is wanted; in identifying potential suppliers and selecting the best; and in preparing negotiations and contracting the core of technology while subcontracting peripheral technologies (Mytelka, 1985). An important implication of firm-specificity mentioned above is the impact of firms' strategic behaviours on learning activities such as on human resource development (Saviotti, 1992). Having (or not having) different strategies for doing business, firms may have different needs for learning and adopt different measures and behaviours to learn. As a result, the interaction between macro factors and micro actions have jointly shaped the learning of TC by firms (Cooper, 1995; Malecki, 1991). Coombs et al (1992a) see the interactions of the constraining effects of the external environment, and the internal actions of firms as complementary and not mutually exclusive. The macro-micro link becomes a crucial determinant in examining the learning activities of firms.

The influence of macro environmental factors on learning and acquiring TC is important in all economies. In the context of countries in transition from centrally-planned to market economies, the role of the state discussed above has been actively debated (UNIDO, 1994; Balazs, 1995). The traditionally strong role of the government in a centrally-planned economy is challenged by the transition to a market mechanism. However, the role of the state in introducing intervention measures is emphasised as still vital for firms' activities in the transitional period (McMillan, 1995). This role can be crucial in supporting the building up of TC (Radosevic, 1993), in reorganising the national R&D system (Shaw, 1995; Zhang & Reeve, 1995) and in influencing activities at firm level (Bell & Pavitt, 1993; Gourevitch et al, 1994; Gu, 1996). It is impossible to review all relevant studies on transitional economies (and there is no need to do so in the scope of this thesis), but taking into account the fact that Vietnam is the focus of this study, it is both a developing country and an economy in transition, so this issue has specific significance.

2.9 Learning and TC: some issues of research interest

The first problem observed from existing studies concerns the separation of learning and TC accumulation activities. Although some authors specify that learning is the process of TC accumulation (Bell & Pavitt, 1993), most studies indicate this relationship more implicitly. The strand of management and business-related learning studies tends to deal with learning activities only in firms of developed countries, and only for the purpose of improving competitiveness (Von Hippel & Tyre, 1995; Fleck, 1994; Lapid, 1994 & 1995). A shortage of sufficient detail also colours certain studies.

Another strand of studies deals with TC accumulation in the context of developing countries, but this strand tends not to discuss learning mechanisms explicitly (Enos, 1991; Lee et al, 1988). The majority of these studies discuss the accumulation of TC at the national level with little examination of concrete learning mechanisms used (UNCTAD, 1990 & 1991). Other studies examine learning activities a bit more while discussing TC accumulation, such as studies of garment export in Sri Lanka (Lall & Wignaraja, 1994), learning in the Indian context (Lall, 1987) or in African countries (Mytelka, 1985 & 1992; Mlawa, 1983). But they are not explicit enough in addressing learning's relation to TC. In the framework of other country or sector studies, authors tackle the problems of accumulation of TC and therefore, relate themselves to issues about learning, but they do not directly indicate the concrete forms of learning they encounter, nor do they examine which forms of learning contribute to which kinds of TC.

As can be seen in both strands, there is not enough examination of the various forms of learning mechanism used to accumulate these TCs.

Assuming the six types of TC and the forms of learning, the role that each form of learning plays for each type of TC may differ. In other words, the way each TC is acquired by learning might be different or similar, depending on various factors internal and external to firms. However, it is difficult to find studies that address this relationship in a comprehensive and systematic way, although some studies have moved in this direction (Bell & Scott-Kemmis, 1985a & 1985b; Hobday, 1993; Frischtack, 1994). Although these studies discuss very well the learning activities in firms, it seems that the more specific discussion of the learning-TC relationship remains to be done.

One aspect of previous learning studies concerns the sector perspective of learning. So far, not many studies have been done on sectors' similarities and differences in terms of learning mechanisms and TC accumulation as a follow-up to the concept initiated by Pavitt (1984) on sectoral innovation patterns. Moreover, studies on learning in developing countries tend to concentrate on one sector (or one firm) and there is no possibility to look at the sector perspective.

The examination of macro-micro interactions is another point of discussion. The process of TC acquisition through learning is subject to influences of macro environmental factors. These macro elements can be grouped in the following categories:

- *Policies of the government.* These can include macro economic conditions, policies on financial, banking, monetary, labour, investment, trade and management issues. These policies, as shown in the review of other literature, have a significant impact either on creating a conducive environment for the operation of firms or on hindering their technological efforts.
- *Market practices:* These include structure, regulations and pressure. It is well known that markets create the necessary competitive pressure for firms in their innovative activities. The market-pull needed for technological development of firms is unavoidable if firms want to upgrade their technological competence and sustain their performance.
- *Supporting system:* This includes education, R&D, training, information, documentation and all other industrial services such as consultancy, quality control, standardisation, etc. In short this group of factors include all elements of the national system of innovation surrounding the firm's activities which, as supply-side factors, can create a push for technological innovation in the firm.
- *Other socio-cultural factors:* These include cultural tradition, social context, specific political and historical circumstances and advantages/disadvantages which have influences on the process of TC accumulation by firms.

Two issues emerge from this. First is the lack of examination of the interaction between macro environment factors and internal micro level factors on firms (structure, behaviours, background, historical circumstances of establishment, etc.). Although most existing studies recognise the importance of this interaction for TC accumulation and learning, not many of them examine this issue in sufficient detail. Moreover, studies in this area tend to point out how macro environment factors influence firms in their activities, but provide little data on how firms react to those factors over time. This weakness has been recognised by authors in some studies (Hobday, 1995b).

The second issue is related to the question of strategies of firms and their impact on the learning process to accumulate TC. Although in the context of developed countries this issue has been addressed vigorously, it is far less well explored in developing countries (Bell & Pavitt, 1992). A more systematic examination of this issue could bring great value to our understanding of a more balanced view of the interaction between macro and micro factors.

An understanding of TC accumulation and learning in the context of developing countries is in short supply, especially when it comes to learning activities at firm level (Cooper, 1991; Hobday, 1995a). Most available studies are of the East Asian NICs of Korea or Taiwan, with less on other countries in different parts of the world (see Bell & Pavitt, 1993 for a comprehensive review). With regard to transitional economies, the majority of studies are on economic reforms and restructuring whilst R&D activities, technological accumulation are less well studied. A study of technological learning and TC accumulation in the case of South East Asian countries such as Vietnam may contribute to remedying this deficit in our knowledge. The experience of Vietnam (a developing country and at the same time an economy in transition) can belong to both categories.

Up till now, and in general, studies of Vietnam are scarce and have been undertaken by international organisations concerned with economic reform (World Bank, 1993; IMF, 1991; UNIDO,1991) or with politico-economic change (Beresford, 1989; Fforde & de Vylder, 1989 and 1996; Vo Nhan Tri, 1988; Gourevitch, 1994). Few studies have been done on its technological and industrial development (UNIDO, 1989 & 1990) or its S&T activities (APCCT, 1988; Vu Cao Dam, 1992; UNIDO/UNDP, 1994). Firm level studies on technological learning and TC accumulation are virtually absent with the exception of few studies (Tran Ngoc Ca & Le Dieu Anh, 1998).

One more reflection is that studies in other developing countries tend to consider the technical side of learning more diligently than the non-technical side. But, in the conditions of economies in transition like Vietnam which lacks market-oriented entrepreneurship and other management skills, it seems that non-technical learning must play a great, if not greater, role and this aspect should be addressed more explicitly. This emerging issue adds another dimension to the purpose of this study.

Note

1. The anti-interventionist position is strongly criticised most clearly in Lall's (1994b) study on industrial policy. He criticises the World Bank study on the East Asian miracle which failed to address the important role of the government in tackling market failures. Similar points criticising anti-intervention arguments and advocating a governmental role can be found in a range of studies of Dalum et al (1992), Amsden (1994) and Ranis (1995).

3 Research design and methodology

In the last chapter, I presented the concepts of TC accumulation and learning. Some problematic issues have emerged from the discourse on the study on learning and TC. This chapter addresses the research questions and the methodology adopted for this study.

3.1 Objectives and research questions

The overview in last chapter identified some key questions that emerged in studies of TC and learning which require further examination. The overall aim of this research is to address these questions by looking at the experiences of firms in two Vietnamese industries: textile/garment and electronics.

More concretely, there are several reasons for doing this study. The main one is that learning activities and TC accumulation have not been investigated sufficiently at the firm level. In particular, little is known in detail about the relationship between concrete learning mechanisms and types of TC. A second reason is that the interaction between macro environmental factors and firm-level micro factors in shaping TC accumulation and learning has not been examined much. A third reason to do this study, is the dearth of research work on Vietnam, a developing country in transition from a planned to a market economy. Finally, it is hoped that as well as contributing some insights to fill this knowledge gap, this research will point to policy lessons both for Vietnamese policy-makers and firms wishing to pursue learning efforts. These lessons may also have implication for other countries with similar development or transitional conditions.

The research examines the TC accumulation process in the practices of Vietnamese firms focusing on the use of various learning mechanisms for TC creation, and the interaction of firms' strategic behaviour and environmental factors in shaping their learning efforts. Six

TCs and types of learning mechanisms proposed in Chapter 2, are used for this examination. Within this framework, the study aims to answer the following research questions:

What TCs existed or are being accumulated at the firms over time? Proposition (1), associated with this research question, is that the patterns of TC accumulation (level, sequence) are different across different contexts: sectors or firms. This well-accepted argument is examined in the context of Vietnamese industrial firms.

The second question is *how do firms accumulate their TCs by different learning mechanisms?* Specifically, the study looks at (i) how important and dynamic learning is in TC accumulation, (ii) how different learning mechanisms individually and in combination contribute to the accumulation of various TCs; and (iii) how learning patterns differ for different backgrounds of firms and/or sectors.

Proposition (2), associated with this research question, suggests, in order to accumulate different TCs, a firm needs to use different learning mechanisms in combination. In general, the firm has to rely on much more active learning forms than learning-by-doing to acquire their TCs. At the same time, different firms and sectors have different patterns of learning. Again, this proposition is examined in relation to other studies mentioned in Chapter 2, with more detail in the case of Vietnam.

The third research question is *why do firms have the modes of TC accumulation and learning they have?* The purpose is to explain similarities and differences between firms in their TC acquisition and learning patterns. In doing this, it seeks to answer more specific questions: (i) what are the external environmental factors shaping firms' learning, and how do they influence this process? (ii) how do firms interact with these external environment factors and how does this interaction jointly shape their learning and TC accumulation patterns?

There are two propositions underlying this research question. Proposition (3) is that the macro environment can have different rates and ways of influencing specific firms, depending on the firm's nature and characteristics and, as an outcome, different ways of shaping how firms use learning for accumulation of TCs. Proposition (4) is that the plan of actions and learning behaviour of managers of firms play an important role in the TC accumulation process and can help to remedy some constraints created by the external environment. This proposition suggests that only those firms having conscious strategies, costly expenditure and long-term vision in their active learning efforts can acquire TC relatively successfully: those who lack these elements will usually fail to do so, despite passive learning-by-doing.

In this study, the hypotheses are not tested in terms of statistical data, since it is not feasible to do that kind of research solely on quantitative basis. But by combining some quantitative data where it is available, with qualitative interpretation of case studies, it is hoped that some conclusions can be drawn concerning these propositions. Thus, the case study material, to a large extent play quite an important role in this qualitative research.

3.2 Overall research design

The research was designed to be conducted in three stages, each using different methods and sources. The first is based on a survey of the macro socio-economic context, using general material available from existing literature and reference sources. The second and largest stage uses interviews with firms in two industries, plus some observations and firms' data (archive, reports, etc.) to examine the main questions concerning TC and learning. Third, case studies of selected firms are used as illustration.

Following the research questions mentioned in the previous section, this study contains the following working blocks, each designed to examine a theme:

- to identify TC in the firms of two Vietnamese industries: textile/garment and electronics;
- to examine what kind of learning mechanisms these firms used to accumulate their TC;
- to analyse the influence of external factors on the general activities of the firms and on their learning processes in particular, then, the interactive responses of the firms to these influences and their impact on different patterns of TC accumulation and learning are examined.

After the examining which of the six suggested forms of TC exist in firms, patterns of TC accumulation are identified in terms of the extent of TC development and the sequence of accumulation.

The next research question is examined by putting together two categories: the use of learning mechanisms as the means to accumulate TC and the TC which resulted. The interactions between learning mechanisms and types of TC are represented in the matrix below. Along the horizontal axis are types of TC while the vertical columns represent forms of learning mechanism. Symbols (+) or (-) express the contribution of particular learning mechanisms to various kinds of TCs. For instance, (+) means the firm used this learning mechanism for the corresponding TC and (-) means it did not use this mechanism. By putting findings in this tabulate format, the study aims to identify the frequency of use made of particular learning mechanisms by the firms for their various TCs.

The trends of learning mechanisms used in accumulating TC are the main findings of this section of the examination.

Types of TC	1	2	3	4	5	6
Learning mechanisms						
By doing	-	-	+	-	+	-
By prior accumulation	+	-	-	+	+	+
By training	+	+	-	-	-	+
By foreign contact etc.	-	-	-	+	+	-

The influence of the external environment are grouped into four main categories for the purposes of this study: (i) government-related policy factors; (ii) market factors; (iii) factors supporting systems like R&D, education and training, etc.; (iv) other socio-cultural factors. Details of these factors are provided in Appendices. The influence of various environmental factors on different modes of learning in the firms, such as incentives and constraints, is represented in the table below.

Groups of environmental factors	1	2	3	4
Learning mechanisms				
By doing	+	+	+	-
By prior accumulation	+	+	-	+
By training	-	-	+	+
By foreign contact etc.	+	-	-	-

Again, the study aims at identifying patterns of influence by external factors on learning, by looking at the frequency of responses of firms to external stimuli. A (+) means this group of factors has had an influence on a corresponding learning mechanism and a (-) means that it did not influence the mechanism according to firms. The immediate findings of this table reveal the firms' perspective on whether specific external factors tend (or tend not) to affect specific internal learning mechanisms. The findings should have significant implications from both firm and government perspectives in adjusting their actions so as to reduce the constraints on (or increase the likelihood of) deploying various learning mechanisms.

In the concluding part of the study, interpretation and analyses are provided to answer research questions and propositions.

3.3 Methods of data collection and analysis

The study had three stages each using different research techniques to examine propositions and research questions.

Stage 1: Survey of Macro Socio-Economic Background

This part of the project served as an introductory background for the subsequent research on companies. The method used was mainly bibliographical search, using material on the general development of the Vietnamese economy and the technological development of two industries - the textile/garment and electronics sectors. In addition, interviews with some external organisations (ministries, research institutes, universities, schools, associations, etc.) were conducted to map out the general context of the relevant industries. In this stage, the important milestones in Vietnamese development that have impacted on TC accumulation in Vietnamese industries were identified, an overview of the two industries was produced.

This stage of the research was important for drawing a general picture of Vietnam's social and economic development, with the focus being on those factors which are having an impact on the process of TC accumulation and learning in the targeted industries. Specific industrial surveys provided more detailed sectoral background, covering features of the two industries such as ownership, production capacity, technological level of equipment, management issues, size and location of firms, R&D and training and education activities. These factors are discussed to show how they might influence the technological development of firms in these industries.

Stage 2: Survey of Interviews and Questionnaires

I selected candidate study firms on the basis of several criteria. First, that the firms should have pursued some technological accumulation activities with different levels of success. Second, that these companies were usually known for some years by my contacts. These contacts, initiated through other research projects, have helped to establish good relationships with those firms, increasing my chances of gaining access to their data and to their personnel for the purposes of interviewing. Twenty four firms in total were chosen and approached (14 in the textile/garment industry and 10 in electronics)[1] and interviews were arranged with various people in these firms: directors, technical staff, personnel in the financial, planning and sales divisions as well as shop-floor workers. For each firm, interviews were repeated through several visits over a 5 to 7 month period. Each firm has been interviewed at least twice, and not more than five times. A list of the firms, and the number and date of interviews, are given in Appendices. Some firms have been studied over a much longer period, thanks to prior access I had gained to their data through other projects I have been involved in. I was thus able to observe some firms' development over a period of almost 7-8 years.

Basic data on the firms selected for interview are given in Tables 3.1 and 3.2. These firms are mainly state-owned (11 in textile/garment and six in electronics). Five are private companies (two in textile/garment and three in electronics), and the data set also includes two joint ventures between Vietnamese and foreign partners, one in each sector. The companies in the textile/garment industry are predominantly big employers (ranging from 1,400 to 6,158 staff) with only a few smaller companies (90 to 600 staff). In electronics, almost all companies are small (less than 400 employees). The products of the companies are very diversified. In textiles, they range from upstream products like spinning, weaving to knitwear to more downstream products such as various types of garment. Electronics companies produce both consumer electronics and smaller non-consumer products (for various industrial and telecommunications uses). Computer companies mostly concentrate around computer assembly and the production of some related software products or services. Fourteen textile/garment companies have different backgrounds of establishment and development. Five companies were founded before 1975. In the third period during the 1980s, three firms were set up. Three cases were established in South Vietnam during the 1960s and 1970s and were later transformed into SOEs after unification. By the end of the 1980s, three companies were set up. Seven electronic firms were created before the reforms, when most private and joint venture firms were born with the liberalisation period after the reforms.

To conduct the interviews, a check-list of questions was used (see Appendices) which addressed the three main research questions about TCs, the learning-TC relationship and the impact of macro-micro factors interaction on learning. These firm level interviews are intended to give an *inside-out* perspective on the issues, i.e from the firms' point of view.

In order to gain an *outside-in* perspective, and to supplement the bibliographical material collected in Stage 1, an additional round of interviews was conducted with relevant actors from organisations in the external 'environment'; these organisations include ministries, government agencies, R&D units, universities and other education organisations, that is, the whole supporting system for industrial development (concerned with issues such as standardisation, quality control, consultancy, information services, industrial association, etc.). The full list of these organisations, and the date and number of interviews is available in Appendices. This round of interviews was mostly conducted after the interviews with the firms so as to provide for some cross-checking of information given by the firms relating to their collaborations. A second check-list of questions was used for this group of respondents, and it can be found in Appendices. For some organisations, my long-term relationship with them proved useful for conducting several interviews and for using their own data sources (e.g., annual reports, reviews).

Stage 3: Company Cases

Based on the results of interviews, a few further in-depth case studies were conducted. By pursuing this task, I was able to clarify more concretely what happened in these firms, and how and why. The choice of firms was based on the available contacts with particular firms which allowed me to have greater access to their activities than others, and hence ensured that a greater richness of material could be gathered from interviews and other sources.

The firm case studies show in fine detail what happened in terms of their use of learning mechanisms to accumulate different TCs; what kind of TCs they acquired; what elements of the external environment most influenced their business; what kinds of response they adopted; and how this came to influence their learning processes and their TC accumulation. As a result, the case studies helped to clarify some issues more lucidly than would have been possible by Stage 2 interviews alone. Moreover, this stage of the study gave the sense of a 'whole firm' picture by linking all three research questions together within the context of a few chosen firms. In this way, the study could more easily show the interaction between the different sets of issues: TC, learning and micro-macro interactions.

The case studies were done in different ways. First, direct interviews were conducted which built upon Stage 2, by means of upgraded and expanded interviews with relevant staff. In addition to the interviews, a study of the firms' archival material such as documentation, reports and statistical data was carried out and proved helpful. In some firms with which I have rather good contacts, I was able to do some on-site observation of production lines, technology implementation, and of sales and marketing activities. For this stage of study, questions similar to those given in the check-list for TC accumulation, learning and external factors were used, although in finer detail and spending more time at the firms.

As I mention above, the first stage of study gives the general macro level background of the country and of the chosen industries' development. Through this study, I have found some sector strengths and weaknesses which may influence the learning activities and TC accumulation of industrial firms. The form of the data is mainly a description of tendencies. In addition, stage one data was analysed to produce descriptions of the historical development of the industries.

For the second stage, using the check-list in Appendices, I have tried to present the data in tables showing the extent of TC accumulation (for each of the six TCs) in the 24 chosen firms. TC development in firms is divided roughly into three levels (strong, weak and non-existent) judged by criteria of systematic regularity and autonomy of its own personnel laid out in Appendices in accordance with activities that the firms could perform in the corresponding TCs. For example, a firm can have strongly developed TC if it is able to perform all technological tasks (functions) related to this corresponding TC by its own staff on a regular basis. At the other extreme is non-existence of TC. The rest, which did not fall into either of these levels, belong to the middle level of weak TC. Because firms are working in different product areas using different kinds of technology, the assessment of their TC accumulation was made in accordance with their specific areas. Therefore, the division of TC accumulation into levels was useful in elucidating differences in the extent of TC accumulation. The main purpose of this assessment is a mapping of what kinds of TC are accumulated in firms. This mapping is used for the main focus of the study which is to examine the learning mechanisms used for their TC accumulation. By finding out the time at which firms became able to perform various tasks, I was also able to establish the sequence of their TC accumulation. Data on learning mechanisms concerned what learning mechanisms firms used, and for gaining what kinds of knowledge, skill or experience. The uses made of learning mechanisms are also presented in tabular format. For each TC, the number of firms using one or another learning mechanism was counted against the existence (or not) of a TC in these firms. Then, by linking the frequency of using learning mechanisms to the total number of firms having the various types of TCs, I tried to see whether there was a relationship between learning use and TC existence in the firms. Thus, the results of the interviews are first presented as a description of activities, then converted into tabular format for identifying and partially codifying emerging trends and patterns.

A similar method of data analysis was used for the next research question. The interviews with firms yielded descriptions about the influence of macro factors on the firms, together with their responses to those external influences. Then, by counting firms' references to each of four groups of macro factors, the relation between these factors and business activities and learning are recorded. To tease out details which did not emerge sufficiently clearly from the previous steps, the firm case studies provide more detailed descriptions of data.

The first two chapters of this book have dealt with the theoretical background of studies on TC accumulation, learning and presents the design of the research and the methods used for the study. The study sought to examine TC accumulation, the learning process leading to this accumulation and the relationship between them in the case of 24 industrial Vietnamese firms. In addition, the joint impact of external macro factors on firms and of their responses to these factors with respect to the learning activity of the firms was another important research question. In order to conduct this research, the dominant data collection method has been to conduct interviews with personnel working in the textile/garment and electronics industries, supplemented by a macro level survey and other firm-specific archival materials. The study involved a two-way process: first focusing from macro material onto firm-specific material; then focusing in reverse for a generalisation of the arguments.

Now, I move on to the next part of the book which presents the empirical material of the study, using the methods and research framework outlined in this chapter.

Note

1. Cases TG11 and E6 declined to be interviewed.

Table 3.1 Main characteristics of textile/garment firms

	Date of estab.	Own.	Products, types of activities	Empl. (USD)	Turnover	Export (%)	Main export market
TG1	1958	state	shirts jackets jeans blouses	2,300	6 mln.	100	Japan, Sweden Germany Korea Holland
TG2	1959	state	knitwear coats sportwear underwear	2,500	5.6 mln.	60	Japan, Switzld. Holland
TG3	1984	state	yarns knitwear	2,300	11 mln. (export only)	20 (yarn) 70 (knit.)	Taiwan, Japan
TG4	1968	state	poloshirts fabrics	2,200	9 mln. (export only)	-	Japan, Sweden Korea
TG5	1987	state	shirts embroidery lingeries	6,518	7 mln.	83	Germany Japan France Hong Kong
TG6	1982	state	yarns poloshirts	2,150	9 mln.	60	Taiwan, Japan Singapore Hong Kong
TG7	1989	joint vent.	sewing threads	90	1.5 mln.	30	Australia Middle East

TG8	1991	privt.	jackets embroidered garment	600	400,000	100	Japan Canada Belgium France Australia
TG9	1990	privt.	sportwear jackets coats	3,500	5 mln.	100	Germany Czech Republic Korea FSU
TG10	1968	state	garment	3,000	4 mln.	100	Japan EU
TG12	1960	state	fabrics knitwear	1,400	1.4 mln	80	FSU EE
TG13	1959	state	knitwear garment	2,000	2.2 mln	n.a	EU FSU ASEAN Japan
TG14	1972	state	garment	6,000	15.9 mln	98	EU Canada FSU Japan Taiwan
TG15	1973	state	poloshirt fabrics	1,400	n.a	n.a	Japan South Korea EU

Table 3.2 Main characteristics of electronics firms

	Date of estab.	Own.	Products, types of activities	Empl.	Turnover (USD)	Export (%)	Main export market
E1	1980	state	consumer electronics (TV, cassetes)	200	6 mln.	0	No
E2	1984	state	TV sets, parts of industrial robots	320	100,000	15	Japan South Korea
E3	1989	privt.	PCs software	50	3 mln.	100 (before 1990)	FSU
E4	1989	privt.	PCs software	115	2.1 mln.	60	FSU Czech Japan, France
E5	1988	joint.	PCs other related products, software	55	2 mln.	100 (before 1990)	FSU
E7	1984	state	industrial electronics services	100	21,800	0	No
E8	1986	privt	speakers	200	1.2 mln	0	No
E9	1986	state	computer appliances consumer electronics (TV)	100	4 mln.	5	Australia
E10	1974	state	consumer electronics TV, cassetes	-	12 mln.	0	No
E11	1974	state	consumer electronics TV,cassetes	450	17 mln.	0	No

4 Historical milestones: Vietnam in transition

This chapter examines the socio-economic context in which the industrial firms of Vietnam began their development and continued it over time. Also, the chapter will give some specific historical circumstances for Vietnam which are important for the analysis in the following chapters. This development evolved over time through four main periods: colonial (before 1945), war time (1946-1975), pre-reform crisis (1976-1986) and reforms (after 1986). The milestones presented in this chapter have important impact on the TC accumulation of the firms in the two industries studied. The periods given in the chapter are turning points in the history of Vietnamese industrial development and therefore influence very much the ways industries acquire their technology, learn competence and react to external factors.

4.1 Colonial impact before 1945

The first industrial activities in Vietnam occurred in the period of French colonialism. Among the different industrial facilities set up by the French, textiles were one of the most important. For example, a textile factory set up in Namdinh province had already 2,000 workers in 1920 with a profit of about 52 millions francs (Buttinger, 1982: 65). The areas around the North delta of Vietnam were centre for the spinning of imported raw cotton and silk into yarns and fabrics (Beresford, 1989: 19). The French contributed somewhat to the education and training system in Vietnam, but these activities contributed little to the general development of the colony. Serious learning was not encouraged by the authorities. The most characteristic feature of this period is that the French contributed to some industrial activities and infrastructure establishment, but industrialisation was almost negligible in terms of training local human resources. Among the earliest industrial activities, the textile sector acquired some industrial experience and technological skills.

4.2 Two Indochina wars and Vietnam divided: 1946-1975

The Democratic Republic of Vietnam (DRV) was born in September 1945. Due to the first Indochina war starting in 1946, the newly born government of Vietnam had to withdraw from the cities and evacuate to mountainous and countryside areas. From that time, the DRV government began to build up its industries. In 1947, expansion of industries occurred and by 1949-1950, there were about 40 national factories, four of which were textile mills set up in areas held by the DRV (Fforde & Paine, 1987: 87-88). By that time, there there had been established the first industrial management system. Immediately after the establishment of the DRV, President Ho Chi Minh declared a nation-wide campaign to eliminate illiteracy. By the end of 1958, 93.4% of the lowland population aged 12-50 could read and write (Marr, 1981: 186-187). In the regions controlled by the DRV, university level education and the first S&T research were undertaken as well as other manufacturing activities (APCTT, 1988: 10). Also, after the recognition of the DRV by China and then by the Soviet Union, foreign experts from these countries came to assist with industrial management. At the same time, in the urban area occupied by French forces, certain industrial facilities (most were light industries including textile plants) existed to serve the limited needs of the population and army. There was a limited trade in textiles mostly among the different provinces of the country.

Following the Geneva Peace Agreement of 1954, Vietnam became divided. In the *North*, the DRV started its socialist construction. The need for building up a strong technological base for socialist construction was recognised by the leadership of the country. The first period of this development was a three-year plan (1958-1960) devoted to the rehabilitation of certain industrial activities to commence the first stage of socialist construction and prepare for the first five-year plan (FYP) to begin in 1961. Foreign trade and other foreign economic relations also started to develop, mostly with the Soviet Union, China and socialist countries in Eastern Europe. With the help of these countries, Vietnam began to build up its first large scale industrial facilities. The aid received from these countries during the first FYP was evaluated as 1 billion USD (Duiker, 1983: 105) and Vietnam could then already export certain products to these countries, including natural resources, light industrial products and handicrafts.

A new education system was introduced with free, compulsory education for children aged from 6 to 15. Teaching was undertaken in

Vietnamese, while that literacy campaign which had started even before 1954 continued quite successfully. More informal training for technical skills and industrial competence was also taken into attention by supplementary technical training. Because only a few thousands workers could receive training in some special schools, the rest was being taught in schools attached to enterprises or directly in these enterprises under supervision of more senior workers. For example, by the end of 1960, 79% of workers in heavy industry were in spare-time classes. In 1961, the Office of the Prime Minister issued an instruction on the organisation of "on-duty" studies to raise the technological qualification of workers.

Alongside these positive trends for technological accumulation, industrial development in the North also experienced some setbacks in this period. Due to the division of the country, there was a massive migration of North Vietnamese to the South, especially of businessmen, bourgeois and intelligentsia with the knowledge and skills necessary for business and industrial development. Those who stayed in the North, faced a socialist reform campaign. After 1954, the new government encouraged private enterprises to form joint private-state enterprises. By the beginning of 1961, capitalists no longer existed as a stratum in society. During 1961, there were further attempts to re-educate capitalists and small bourgeoisie such as the movement to turn them into state employees or members of co-operative organisations (Post, 1989: 39). These activities contributed to the destruction of the emergent group of industrialists and business people including many private textile producers with rather good entrepreneurial spirit and technological management skills. In spite of training campaigns and programmes, the acquisition of technological competence still remained big problem due to the passive work habit of newly recruited workers (most of whom were peasants, military personnel, poor urban population).

It can be said that there were ambitions and awareness among the leadership of the DRV to build up industrial Vietnam with a modern and technologically advanced economy. However, the Soviet model and other limitations of economic management did not contribute positively to this ambition. Among several limitations, one was the lack of an explicit national policy for technological development. There were different implicit measures, but these were inconsistent and even contradictory sometimes. Economic development in the North had been interrupted in 1965 by the start of air-raided by the US airforce. Dispersal of industrial plants to rural area began and this severely affected not only the general performance of industries, but also the industrial mentality of the work force. This situation continued up to the Paris Peace Agreement in 1973 and the start of the second FYP.

Development in the *South,* after 1954, had taken another direction. The Saigon government started the capitalist development of the South on the basis of relatively good industrial infrastructure facilities left by the French. One of the main features in the development of South Vietnam was large aid received from the US. During the period 1955-1960, US economic aid to South Vietnam was 220 million USD per year (or 22% of South Vietnam's GNP) (Dacy, 1986: 3). During the war, annual aid increased from 230 M USD in 1964 to 800 M USD in 1966. In contrast to development in the North, the private sector played a significant role. The rate of private investment in industry was 88% of total investment for 1968, 86% and 71% respectively in 1969 and 1971 (Nguyen Truong, 1974: 16). Almost all manufacturing, commerce and financial activities were in the hands of private sector.

With the period of "Vietnamisation of war" commencing in 1968, a massive influx of foreign technicians as well as technical advisors for civilian purposes came to support economic development and reconstruction. Thousands of foreign experts came under USAID programmes together with substantial investment to build up manufacturing industries. There was an advisory desk run by foreign experts for almost all the activities of South Vietnamese government (Dacy, 1986: 197). However, managerial and labour skills were never abundant to industry, due to the fact that most qualified people were in the armed forces. Technical and professional education was not fully integrated into the system of higher education. Industrial productivity was low and industry was not evolving in such a way to be competitive and self supporting. The share of manufacturing industry was always small (including for textiles) with limited potential for industrial development. The economy was totally dependent on US assistance since the late 1960s (Duiker, 1983: 101). The withdrawal of the US involvement from 1972 brought recession. Only 200,000 persons were employed in industry and, by the end of the war, in 1975, the economy was in a state of collapse (Dacy, 1986: 73).

Nonetheless, conditions in the South were more favourable for technological development compared to that in the North. South Vietnamese industrial companies had more advantages for their technological development such as access to much better physical infrastructure (roads, harbours, airports, storage facilities) thanks to large investment by American aid. The industrial workforce had acquainted itself with the management style of a market economy and access to a more advanced technological equipment in manufacturing. As a result, by 1975, South Vietnam had accumulated a technological base of sorts, with different industrial, commercial and managerial skills. There was also evidence of the birth of an entrepreneurial class and the emergence by that time of a corps of technocrats in South Vietnam (Hoang Ngoc Nguyen, 1990).

For all their differences, North and South Vietnam both faced unstable conditions for development between 1945-1975. Except only for some short periods of peaceful conditions, Vietnam's development was shaped by the very specific conditions and requirements of a war economy. The instability was even more economic than political. Inflation, budget deficits, trade deficits, foreign debt, dependency on aid from big donors, difficulties related to frequent changes of economic conditions were characteristic features for the economy.

4.3 The planned economy and economic crisis: 1976-1986

In 1976, the Socialist Republic of Vietnam (SRV) was created by the unification of two regions and the second FYP (1976-1980) started for the whole country. The SRV continued process of socialist transformation in the South, which may be called socialisation (Spoor, 1988: 113) or northernisation of the South (Vo Nhan Tri & Booth, 1992). During this period, the financial system, the state budget, the currency and the banking system were unified and the state launched a second battle against the bourgeoisie which led to even further destruction of Southern capitalist entrepreneurship and loss of production management skills.

The first foreign investment code introduced in 1977 failed to attract foreign investors. Industrial output increased in the period 1976-1978, then fell during the years 1979-1980 due to poor management, hastened socialist transformation, lack of capital and a shortage of energy, raw material and spare parts for enterprises. As a result of these economic difficulties, the government recognised the seriousness of the situation and the need for some reforms.

The first reform measures were introduced in 1979 and included the devaluation of the Vietnamese currency (dong) and greater autonomy of planning by locally-managed industries. In foreign trade, more exporters were allowed to deal directly with customers and make arrangements to import raw material and other goods. In industry, a new system of enterprise management was introduced with wages now paid according to a piece-rate system. Enterprises got more freedom in their production, finance and trade.

Exports for this period were tied solely to market of CMEA countries (Council of Mutual Economic Assistance - the economic organisation of socialist countries in the Soviet block). Trade relations between these countries were regulated by long-term goods exchange agreements signed by governments. Due to a general shortage of commodities, the export-import quotas among the member countries of CMEA were not designed to protect the importers' market, but to guarantee the importer country that the goods agreed in the agreement will be supplied sooner or later. In this context, product quality was not a main concern of export.

In 1981, the third FYP (1981-1985) started. As a result of the first tier of reforms introduced in 1979 and 1981, many economic activities could gain certain benefits. However, many state enterprises still received subsidies from the state to operate regardless of their efficiency and no enterprise was allowed to become bankrupt (Beresford, 1989: 205). At the same time, the rate of inflation increased again. The currency reform in 1985 was a big failure resulting both in a drastic increase in shortage of goods in urban market and in an inflationary surge in prices (Beresford, 1989: 211). Inflation rate rose from 50% per annum to 700% and then to about 1,000% in 1987-1988 (Beresford, 1989: 211; Tornquist, 1991). The results of this currency reform were disastrous. By 1985-1986, Vietnam was in a state of economic crisis.

To sum up, before the first tier of reforms in 1979-1981, the economic system of Vietnam had some main features such as:

- a monopoly of the state sector in economic production; private sector did not exist or was destroyed (at least temporarily) by different socialist transformation campaigns;
- all production and management decisions were decided by plans given from above like from a command centre; enterprises did not have autonomy for their production and business activities; plan implementation was more important than the other criteria of production efficiency;
- economic policy gave priority to heavy industry;
- the monopoly of the state in foreign trade; reliance on the Soviet Union and Eastern European markets only; isolation from Western markets; no foreign direct investment;
- the inability of the banking system to lend to productive units on a commercial basis, lending being restricted to fulfil lending plans designed by the state; high state budget deficit; high rate of inflation.

In addition, for almost two decades (1960-1980), Vietnam had had a more inward than outward looking development. The self-reliance idea of development of big countries such as the Soviet Union, China or India was applied in Vietnam for rather a long time and had a significant impact on its economic structure. Officially, the economy of Vietnam (and society as well) was not closed to outside world. But, in fact, for some decades it related itself only to one economic and political block of the Soviet Union and other socialist countries and due to some well known reasons, it had no normal links with the Western world as most other Southeast Asian developing countries had.

The unification of North and South had some impacts on technological development of the country. On the one hand, it led to the combination of strengths of two regions in terms of natural resources and technical labour forces. On the other hand, the effort to adopt the development model of the North in the South has not worked. The unification gave the North some pressure coming from the South for its changes towards a more dynamic economy, and more business oriented attitudes of the whole society. During 1985-1986, many managers of state owned enterprises (SOEs) in order to keep their companies alive, did not follow official regulations on production activities such as input supply, sale of products, use of labour force and material incentives, etc. They merely broke these rules or *"pha rao"* (broke the fences - as it was called in Vietnamese) by adopting their own new rules. These fence-breakers are the first group of reformists among managers of SOEs, and created strong pressure for the government to take further reform steps when the fourth FYP (1986-1990) started in 1986. Concerning the legal framework of industrial development, one of the main characteristics is that Vietnamese legal system is not appropriate to foster private sector, laws are still influenced by ideology to maintain an inherent bias in favour of the state sector and collective ownership. This situation caused an extra problem for private ownership in addition to those anti-private attitudes exercised by the state during the 1960s and the 1970s.

4.4 The reforms and transition to market economy: after 1986

The code word for pre-reform economic status is "centrally planned bureaucratic subsidised system". New crises by 1985-1986 created stronger pressure for more reform. Standing on the edge of much more serious crises than previous years, the leadership of the country tried to seek measures for more radical reforms. In 1986 the renovation policy *(doi-moi)* was officially announced. The major features of reforms, some of which started even earlier than 1986 included:

Structural change of investment priorities

- a shift from heavy industry to three more specific orientation: food production, consumer goods and export.
- the role of private sector has been recognised and private sector could come back to participate in the economic life of the country.

Decentralisation of economic management of state-owned enterprises (SOEs)

- the move away from a strict planning system to giving state enterprises more autonomy in their decision making for production, management and other activities.
- experiment with equitisation of SOEs by making them a share-holding companies.

Radical change and development of financial and banking system

- by the middle of the 1980s: introduction of new tax system. Structure of revenues and expenditures had also been changed to reduce budget deficit.
- in the banking and monetary system, there had been new changes to reorganise and expand the formal sector. The banking system was commercialised in 1990 with a two-tier banking system: the state bank and other commercial banks. The activities of banks also relied more on efficiency criteria than before. Private companies now can borrow from the bank, although there are still many disadvantages in comparison with SOEs.
- in 1989 interest rate and exchange rate were adjusted and the interest rate level was increased, leading to sharp increase of saving (Dau Hoan Do & Svensson, 1992: 53).

Diversification and liberalisation of external economic relations

- with the radical changes in Europe (CMEA was dissolved in 1991), Vietnam receives no more aid from these countries. All trade had been converted into hard currency settlement. Facing difficulties, the government tried to react quickly to the situation in two directions. With the old market of former CMEA countries, Vietnam tries to maintain relations and continue trade. Relations are now based more on bilateral contracts and company-company level than the governmental ones. The orientation of export to convertible currencies area was a big shift.

In addition, the more regional integration of Vietnamese economy with Asia-Pacific and EU countries made it less dependent on the economic relation with the former CMEA countries.

- domestically, there were some significant changes in foreign trade management mechanism. Many enterprises now got the right for direct doing business with foreign partners. For them, export-import activities are now much less cumbersome than before, including the right to travel abroad and having contacts with foreign companies.

- in 1987, the new Foreign Investment Law was promulgated by the State Council. In addition, different decrees on technology transfer from abroad to Vietnam as well as those concerning industrial property rights, patenting, etc. also have been promulgated.

Concerning the open door policy characterised for this period, there is one more observation. Technologically speaking, sole trading relations with CMEA countries had been a big disadvantage because the country has to rely on only one source of technological competence which may not be the best in the world. There have recently been possibilities of opening up the country to the "other side" of the world which would clearly bring more conducive conditions to develop a technological base for the economy.

4.5 The system of research and development (R&D), education and training

The system of *R&D institutions* in the country is divided into 3 parts, until recently:

- laboratories and other R&D institutions operated by the various sectoral ministries.
- research departments and specialised R&D institutes at universities and other units of higher education (in fact, they are laboratories to serve mostly teaching purposes).
- specialised R&D organisations at the national level, including the National Centre for Scientific Research of Vietnam (NCSR), the National Institute of Technology and others.

Also, there are some smaller R&D units functioning as the subordinate departments within large enterprises in various industries. Similar to other communist countries in Central and Eastern Europe (see Balazs, Faulkner & Schimank, 1995), this system of R&D institutions had specific features as follows:

- science and technology (S&T) activities were treated as state monopoly. Private activities in S&T did not exist and were not allowed. All S&T activities were planned and directed from the higher level such as ministries. Universities had mostly teaching functions, but not R&D.
- R&D activities were not formulated by market requirements but by subjective plans. Enterprises themselves did not have a need for technological innovation due to lack of market pressure.[1]

- weak linkages between academic research and higher education, between engineering research and industry. The direct horizontal contacts between R&D units and industrial enterprises were not allowed. In order to do some services for industry, R&D institutions had to go up vertically to their leaders through very cumbersome procedures.

Together with changes in economic policies, during the 1980s various reforms were introduced to open up S&T system to the use of economic activities. The major measures of reforms in S&T were:

- recognition and implementation of the right of R&D institutions to get direct contracts from the industry.
- diversification of activities of R&D institutions. Now they can participate in a wide range of activities such as research, development and technology transfer, S&T services, which included experimental and pilot manufacturing, other kinds of small scale production, etc.
- diversification of financial resources for R&D: next to the state budget sources, now budget for R&D activities can come from contracts and bank credit.
- privatisation of R&D activities and protection of intellectual property rights. It goes together with the privatisation tendency of the economy. Private initiatives and involvement in R&D activities now are recognised. The intellectual property rights (including industrial) which were considered as socialist state properties for a long time, now are recognised and protected by laws (Vu Cao Dam, 1992: 5-10).

These reforms had been crucial to free the potential of R&D institutions to serve the need of industrial firms in their technological capabilities accumulation. It is thanks to these changes that many companies can have access to information, consultancy and training sources provided by scientists. In addition, it enables many scientists to work closer with industries, or even to move out to create their own firms.

Next to the R&D institutions, *training and education organisations* constitute an important part in the supporting system for industrial companies. The relatively high literacy rate of Vietnamese population gives an important advantage (88% for 1990). Good primary and secondary education systems (some are compulsory), which existed up to very recently, prepared quite good basic education for the Vietnamese work force, including industrial workers.

Higher education and training system has been developed by the state since the 1960s. In total, there are currently 103 state colleges and universities in the country (9 universities and 94 other colleges). Among these 94 institutes and colleges, there are 13 engineering institutes and colleges and 6 economic institutions which can offer training and education necessary for industries. Although these organisations have contributed significantly to the education of graduates who had been recruited to the industries during three decades of the 1960s-1980s, they still have serious problem in their capacities to support the learning process of the students. One survey showed not only that merely 13 institutes and colleges had laboratories for their training activities, but also that the laboratories were poorly equipped and in backward conditions (with machines and instruments from the 1960s). A gap was recognised between the technological sophistication of the equipment in these institutions and of other organisations in industry. Similarly, libraries and information centres as sources of learning also were poorly developed and of little use (Nguyen Thi Tri, Pham Quang Sang and Sloper, 1995: 185-187).

The numbers of students that 103 institutions produced have been quite stable despite changes in social and economic conditions. Figures for 1989-1990 academic year are: 17,312 with bachelor degrees (14,916 for 1980-1981 year), 2,689 postgraduate degrees (1,409) and 680 in professional secondary education (1,267). The number of the last category has radically decreased over the last ten years which has created a big problem in providing industries with middle level professionals (managers, masters of workshops, technicians, etc.). Throughout the 1960s and the 1970s, the higher education and training system produced a rather good stock of graduate and R&D labour force comparatively to similar developing countries (in 1985 Vietnam had 11,500 bachelor degrees graduated per million of inhabitants compared to 3,329 in India, 11,472 in Brunei and 1,220 in Indonesia)(Dang Ba Lam, Nghiem Xuan Nung & Sloper,1995:141).

After the move to the market economy, many new hurdles arrived with less subsidies of the state. The inability or unwillingness of the government to increase significantly the rate of expenditure on higher education among other social welfare commitments is one cause (Le Thac Can & Sloper, 1995: 18). The massive training of Vietnamese students abroad for undergraduates and postgraduate degrees (mostly in the Soviet Union and East European countries) had ended by the end of the 1980s. The move to a market economy also created more difficulties for higher education institutes in organising their technical experimental activities that are crucial for students' technological learning. Research and experiment facilities were obsolete (established 20-30 years ago), poorly equipped, inadequate and satisfied only 30% of hours required in the curriculum. In many cases, facilities of higher education institutions were more obsolete and less developed than that of industries. It became more difficult to send students to practise their knowledge at production enterprises since most enterprises did not want to accept students. All these factors contributed to the lack of practical knowledge and experiences by students to work for industries.

At the same time, vocational training has also had some problems. Most of the facilities were supplied to the public sector and very few to co-operative and private sectors. Also, the training of foremen or middlemen has been neglected as training for specific category of industrial labour forces. The same weakness, either quantitatively or qualitatively can be said for training of maintenance staff, managers of the enterprises. By the end of 1980s, a number of efforts were made by provinces, local governments, big companies, social groups to change this situation to provide vocational training for those who will work later in co-operative and private sectors, and a number of "complex training centres" were organised like training courses on tailoring provided by garment co-operatives, computer application or TV repair provided by Hanoi Polytechnics, etc. (Vu Cao Dam et al., 1991: 20). Also, as the measures to fight unemployment some training programmes are being undertaken to enhance workers' skills. Still, these have rather short-term orientation (ILO, 1994).

In spite of these shortcomings, in general, rather high rate of literacy in Vietnam and a large core of academically trained people are main advantages of the industries for learning. Although the quality of education can not match Western standards, this is a positive factor for formation of a technological labour force in the country.

It can be seen that Vietnamese industrial activities began even in the French period before 1945, then developed further during the second and third periods. But these periods were characterised by very specific conditions, not very conducive for industry to accumulate their technological capabilities (wars or overall social-economic crisis during the 1980s). However, certain factors (positive measures adopted by the government, foreign assistance, etc.) during these periods had brought to the industries some level of technological expertise, production management knowledge and skills that are ready to be upgraded in the fourth period after 1986.

With reforms, particularly the "open door" economic policy, the fourth period has created new opportunities for industry to acquire new technological competence. This acquisition in particular came with the liberalisation of the S&T infrastructure and relatively effective education and training systems existed throughout the socialist construction period. At the same time, the current period has brought new challenges: deterioration of education and training facilities, unavailability of state subsidies for innovation and learning activities, tougher market conditions for industries to maintain their export performance and large, but still disorganised domestic market. All these factors have strong impact on the development of TC in the studied industries, to which I now turn: textile/garment and electronics.

Note

1. One striking fact is that in the structure for profit calculation of enterprises by the state, profit was added automatically as certain percentage upon the cost of production, hence, the higher cost of production the higher profit they will get from the state. This specific phenomenon of a centrally planned economy is one of the main obstacles for enterprises in building up their technological capability.

5 Development of two industries: textile/garment and electronics

5.1 The textile/garment industry

5.1.1 The periods of development

The textile/garment industry had gone through four main periods of development: limited initial activities (pre-1945 under French rule); start-up and consolidation (1946-1975); expansion (1976-1986) and export-oriented growth (post-1986). The textile industry began under the French regime, but that early heritage is only evident in a few nationalised spinning plants in urban areas, and in some skills and experience of workers who were involved in the textile industry. Most of this analysis, therefore, will deal with the last three periods.

The start-up and consolidation period took place between 1946-1975. After the end of the first Indochina war in 1954, there were very few textile plants left in a good condition. The biggest one, the Namdinh textile plant, which was used to produce cotton thread yarn to supply artisan weavers (Fforde & Paine, 1987: 85), had been dismantled and brought down to the South including the migration of its owner and its technical labour force. Facilities set up by the DRV government before 1954 were small-scale and handicraft-oriented. By the beginning of the 1960s, a few spinning, weaving and knitting plants were installed around the big cities. Textile equipment and facilities were erected with aid from China, the Soviet Union and other socialist countries, and the equipment was of a 1950-1960s vintage. During the war (1965-1973), these facilities were either evacuated to rural areas, or were severely damaged by American bombing. In the South, the textile industry concentrated around the big cities, its equipment was of the 1960s-1970s, and was imported from Japan, the US, Germany, France, etc. The textile industry in both regions relied on imported material and spare parts and mainly served the domestic market.

As for garments, during the war period involving the French, some small workshops were set up to serve the needs of the army in regions held by the DRV. In the North, by 1956-1958, there were only two factories producing some hundred thousand pieces of simple clothes for the domestic market and some for export. In the South, the garment industry began in 1971 with six factories producing for the domestic and export market.

In the third period (1976-1986), industry was spurred by two stimuli to upgrade and acquire new production facilities. First, modern spinning plants were purchased with loans from France, Germany, Japan and Italy to produce cotton and polyester yarn. Second, some of the large spinning, weaving and garment plants left in South Vietnam were nationalised by transformation campaigns after 1975.

In the reform period after 1986, production was expanded further with a shift to consumer goods and export programmes. In the conditions of a more open economy and of more diversified linkages with foreign investment sources and markets, many enterprises had initiated business relationships with foreign partners so as to expand their production activities. In addition, those private entrepreneurs who had survived the different transformation campaigns and were encouraged by multi-sectoral economic reforms, started to use their own resources and personal links with foreigners to create new production plants. The garment industry also witnessed a boom in the setting-up of new plants and workshops, utilising both state and private funds, to produce for export. Important milestones of textile/garment industry are provided in Figure 5.1. The macro data of the industry is given in Appendices 5.1 to 5.7, most of which refers to the 1980s.

5.1.2 Ownership, size and location

Anti-private attitudes and priorities for large-scale industries were well known features of the old DRV model of socialist construction. Although officially, up till the reforms of 1986, there was no private sector in Vietnamese industrial activities, private activities in textile and garment existed throughout the period of socialist transformation, mainly in the form of small co-operative handicraft industries.

These co-operatives serve as a network of production units in implementing certain orders from the state enterprises and in fulfilling their production plans in a domestic subcontracting relationship. In the South, private companies in garment manufacture mushroomed during the reform period of the industry's development, some of them becoming quite large. As for the size of the firms, most SOEs are medium- to large-scale (with some thousands of workers). Besides these, there are many medium- and small-scale enterprises in the co-operative sector.

The geographical locations of the textile and garment industry are largely concentrated around Hanoi and HoChiMinh City (formerly Saigon) - the two big industrial centres of the country. An educated labour force and an appropriate infrastructure are more available in these areas.

5.1.3 Export activities

Vietnam began to export textile and garment products in the 1960s. However, this kind of activity was small-scale and on a trial basis. Before 1975, in the South, the textile industry mostly served the domestic rather than the export market .

Serious exporting began in the mid 1970s, mostly to CMEA countries. Contracting relationships with the former Soviet Union started in 1976: Soviet companies supplied cotton and, in return, Vietnamese companies produced fabrics and garments for them. At this time, the export activities of Vietnamese textile/garment companies were mostly based on passive subcontracting relations with CMEA countries. Vietnam, in addition to being a supplier of primary agriculture products and tropical natural resources, was a subcontractor for these countries in simple products. These countries supplied Vietnam with equipment, input material and bought back the output. There was no active role for Vietnamese companies to develop technological expertise, or to improve the quality and design of products. This passive mentality towards export made companies quite comfortable with simple types of co-operation, poor quality and a limited range of products.

In 1986, Vietnam and the Soviet Union upgraded their relationship in a large subcontracting garment programme. Soviet buyers supplied designs, patterns and materials and received clothing products. The fee for subcontracting was paid in the form of sewing machines and equipment as well as with other goods. Thanks to this programme, Vietnam received 5,600 new Soviet-made sewing machines and, more especially, the technical expertise of Soviet experts who came to each enterprise to give guidance and technical assistance in the garment business. Products for export were cotton and mixed cotton/polyester yarns, clothing of various kinds (shirts, underwear, knitwear, baby cloth, work overalls, etc.). Between 1986 and 1990, Vietnamese companies supplied more than 60 million pieces of garment to the Soviet Union in the subcontracting programme framework.[1]

However, the difficulties of this intra-CMEA system (e.g., not all deliveries were ensured by parties, there was a low probability of getting desirable products in exchange, etc.) and the need for hard currency encouraged Vietnamese companies to embark on trial export to non-socialist countries. Japanese trading houses supplied Vietnamese companies with technologies (mostly in spinning) during the 1980s and later they initiated a modest exporting business to Japan and other non-socialist markets.

This development of trade with market economies got a strong stimulus from the reform period post-1986 and after the collapse of the Soviet and East European markets. Those companies which had been involved in trial trading with Western countries got a chance to go further. Those which were not ready had to face a tough choice: to shift quickly to new markets or to collapse. These conditions shaped the unavoidable shift of Vietnamese companies to new export markets.

A exporting surge came by the end of the 1980s and the beginning of the 1990s, with more clothing exports (including jackets, coats and some high quality products such as suits) going to countries like Japan, South Korea, Australia, the EU, etc. Currently, more than 30% of total clothing production is for export. Change in the reform period happened not only in the form of market orientation, but also in the types of product produced, the forms of export contacts (or linkages), and the modes of doing business. In order to enter totally new kinds of markets, companies had to be more careful in their product choice. Many companies had previously concentrated only on upstream products (as spinning, weaving) but they now moved to downstream products like knitwear, garments and high fashion products. At the same time, the domestic market became more attractive to producers. Previously, the output of the industry had been distributed via networks of wholesalers. Liberalisation of the economy, a competitive atmosphere, and the autonomy of companies led to the opening of shops and showrooms by almost all textile and clothing plants.

Opportunities for foreign direct investment after 1987 created a rush of companies looking for new forms of co-operation with foreign partners. Instead of continuing their passive subcontracting relations - which, in fact, is still quite an effective form for many companies starting in the export business - some enterprises moved into joint venture, mostly in garment manufacture. Private companies also took advantage of the new situation by trying to conduct business more consciously and by devising more efficient operations.

5.1.4 Management practice

In general, enterprises belong to the Ministry of Light Industry[2] or to local governments. Recently, the Association of Vietnamese Garment Enterprises was set up, which includes not only the SOEs but also private companies as members. As an attempt by companies to concentrate their resources and efforts on the common purpose of producing and exporting garments, this Association meets several times a year to discuss general tendencies, and to consider strategies for developing the sector. It set up some funding to support the necessary activities of its members, as well as undertaking some lobbying of government organisations.

The changes in foreign trade concerned not only the market destination of exports, but also the mechanism for managing foreign trade. Although the Ministry of Trade is responsible for export/import management, companies are now allowed to make contacts and forge import/export transactions more directly, provided they satisfy certain conditions on volumes of export and business experience. The Ministry deals more with the general management of trade, and in order to link foreign trade more closely with production, two trading companies - Textimex and Confectimex (which for a long time belonged to the Ministry of Trade and monopolised the export/import of textiles and garments) - were transferred to the MOI.

5.1.5 R&D, education and training activities

In MOI's structure, there are two main research units for the textile industry: the Research Institute for the Textile Industry (RITI) and the Research Centre for the Garment Industry (RCGI) in Hanoi, with filial units in HoChiMinh City. The industry was supplied with its educated technical labour force and with information from the textile faculties of various polytechnic institutes in Hanoi and HoChiMinh City, as well as from the information centre of MOI.

Although these activities proved useful for the industry's development particularly during the initial phase, many problems remain. Before 1986, these activities were far from the actual needs of the companies and provided little help with the day-to-day operation of enterprises. Due to the old style of R&D management, there was no link between research and industry. After the reforms, these research institutes became more associated with production. Research organisations now rely more on contracts signed with enterprises.

Many problems remained and new constraints arose. The activities of the mentioned *R&D institutions* are not very effective (see Box 5.1). R&D expertise in the industry is neither innovative nor dynamic enough to support the needs of the companies.

Training and education organisations are in a similar situation. Until recently, the Vietnamese higher education system was only able to produce engineers for the textile industry (through the textile faculty of Hanoi Polytechnic, for example). In addition, the industry received newly graduated engineers from the Soviet Union and other East European countries until the end of the 1980s. As for garment activity, the industry relied entirely on graduates coming back from abroad. Only in the last 3-4 years has Hanoi Polytechnic begun to offer courses in the garment business to engineers, designers or production managers. At lower educational levels, two vocational schools (one in the North and one in the South) train garment workers. Still, the number of trained people only amounts to 200-300 workers per year - far less than is required by the industry. More seriously, these schools only provide training for workers. There is no training for managers or for workshop headmasters. This weakness in the training and education system has caused major problems for companies in their efforts to secure the necessary labour force at all levels, a problem which is especially acute at the level of skilled garment workers. Other institutions serving the industrial infrastructure like those which provide information sources, documentation or consulting, and related industries like mechanical or chemical engineering, have similar problems in supporting the industry.

Box 5.1 R&D in the textile/garment industry: RCGI & RITI

In the clothing industry, the only research unit is the Research Centre for the Garment Industry (RCGI) which aims at designing new collections of garment products, researching the production organisation of garment workshops, and dealing with standardisation issues for the industry. When having intensive business with the Soviet bloc, this Centre produced some models for the market. When moving to new markets, the Centre has problems in satisfying the needs of new and more demanding customers. The Bulletin of the garment industry - an information newsletter published by the Centre - had to cease for lack of finance. Although the Centre had a staff of 50, only a few worked as designers producing new collections (recently, this number has been reduced to only one person). With less and less financial resources from Confectimex (its parent organisation), the Centre became quite weak and the sources of information and expertise necessary for supporting companies became more scarce. The prospect that this Centre may become a research institute, as many would wish, is unlikely.

The Research Institute for the Textile Industry (RITI) has also many problems. The Institute has 125 employees, of whom 90 are engineers or with university degrees, and about 10 of whom possess postgraduate degrees (masters and doctors). During the 1970s and 1980s, the Institute engaged in considerable research, training and consulting work for the industry. However, for the last couple of years, it has became less necessary for firms. Research projects are not very relevant to the recent needs of the industry, and the findings from these projects do not seem to be have been taken-up and applied by the companies.

5.1.6 Some notable features of textile/garment industry

The textile/garment industry has enjoyed significant evolution over the 1960s-1980s period. The first advantage of the industry was the abundance of relatively cheap labour and a long tradition of Vietnamese artisans engaging in small-scale textile activities. Second, during the period of dominance by state enterprises, small-scale and family-based production units constituted an important part of a subcontracting network which served the needs of the large SOEs. Third, the large domestic market of more than 75 million people, and their increasing purchasing power over the last three to four years, is a good basis upon which the industry can develop locally.

At the same time, there are some critical weaknesses in the industry. First, the main feature of the industry's technology is its obsolescence. The industry received its first technology at the end of the 1950s and during the 1960s from China, East Germany, the Soviet Union, etc. During the 1980s, some modern plants were imported - spinning technology, especially - from Japan, Germany and Italy. However, this expansion has only partly reduced the obsolete technological level of the industry. In the clothing industry, the situation is better than in textiles. About 20% of the sewing machines in use by centrally-managed SOEs are less than 10 years old, with 10% older than 15 years. In SOEs under local management, only 10% of machines are less than 10 years old, due to the fact that less investment resources are available to local than to central government (UNIDO, 1991). Post-1986, however, there has been a boom in the garment industry and more new sewing machines, both ordinary and specialised (like automatic embroidery machines, stone-washing machines), are being imported to serve the needs of the export market. Not only SOEs but also private companies are actively participating in this equipment and technology innovation activity.

A lack of consistent investment policies by the state, a dependency on technologies stemming from one source of CMEA (up to the beginning of 1980s), and constraints on capital investment are causes of the elderly technologies found in the firms. Moreover, the lack of incentives, or competitive pressure, from markets has made company managers passive about innovation activities. Phenomena like normative profit as a percentage of production cost have not encouraged companies to innovate technologically in order to reduce their production costs. The abolition of this old management system during 1976-1986, and subsequent reforms since 1986, are radically changing companies' attitudes towards technological innovation.

A second weakness in the textile and garment industry has been its resource base of supplies of raw materials. The range and volume of domestically-produced raw materials are rather limited. Only some cotton is produced domestically, whilst synthetic fibres are not available. Almost all raw materials have to be imported for the textile industry (e.g., cotton yarn, viscose, polyester). In addition, other supplies like chemicals and spare parts for operating the plants also have to be imported (about 15 million rubles & USD in 1989) (UNIDO, 1991: 78). The processing equipment for domestically-produced raw cotton is obsolete and also leads to a low quality of cotton supply. Thus, up till now, the spinning industry has had to rely on imported raw materials like cotton and synthetic fibres. Because high quality fabrics cannot be produced by the textile industry, garment companies have to import their material from foreign partners (about 90% of input for the industry) if they are to produce top quality products.

The third problem of the textile/garment industry has been that despite changes, the policy of foreign trade management remains inconsistent. It has changed rather frequently and created difficulties for companies. Also, this policy has not been effective in preventing smuggling. With the normalisation of relations with China, control of the northern border has relaxed and since 1991, Chinese fabrics and yarns have been increasingly smuggled into Vietnam. Fabrics are also being smuggled from Thailand. For example, 50% of the domestic fabric market consists of material smuggled from other countries, and companies simply cannot compete with traders.

At the same time, due to a long period of reliance on one market and a passive attitude towards doing business, the industry has quite poor international experience in doing business. Lack of competitive pressure has generated a dearth of interest in, or knowledge about, marketing activities. Firms are not forced to become technologically innovative to upgrade their product quality. The private sector of the industry has not existed until recently, and the main players of the industry are the SOEs.

Following the reforms of 1986, the industry is exploring new opportunities through co-operating with new foreign partners for export markets. Thanks to these opportunities, the industry can obtain new resources (capital, technology) for its technological innovation and learning activities. For the first time, firms are being forced to become interested in marketing activities.

5.2 The electronics industry

5.2.1 The periods of development

The electronics industry has evolved through only three periods: start-up (pre-1975), rehabilitation (1976-1986), and liberalisation (post-1986). During the 1950s, electronics activities were mostly engaged in as a mean for radio broadcasting. Systems of radio receivers, broadcasting and wire transmission were developed. Television broadcasting started around 1960 in black-and-white with a small system of transmission and a studio. TV sets were few and were mostly imported from Poland.

Before 1954, there were some small workshops in Hanoi and other big cities to take care of maintenance services and trading activities for foreign firms. Since 1956, together with the development of radio broadcasting, workshops for repair and maintenance were developed in all provinces. By the end of the 1950s and the beginning of the 1960s, the government had set up some small factories to assemble amplifiers and transformers and to produce loud speakers. Main components like condensers, resistors, vacuum tubes, etc. were imported from abroad (the Soviet Union, East Germany, Hungary). In the South, the assembly of black and white TVs and radio cassettes from imported parts and components began before 1975. Four plants with Japanese technology from Sony, Sanyo and Matsushita started operations when the war ended in 1975.

Colour television broadcasting began in 1982 though the number of TV sets was limited and mostly relied on imported Soviet and Polish technologies. In the South, using American technology, TV broadcasting was undertaken to serve American troops and the urban population in the 1970s. Television broadcasting began using satellite facilities in 1980 with Soviet satellite earth stations.

As for computer use, the first computer system was imported and installed in 1967 in Hanoi and was run by Vietnamese technicians and specialists. Some early units for teaching computer science were also initiated by that time (APCTT, 1988: 54). In 1966, the first IBM-360 was installed by the IBM Vietnam company in Saigon. American experts played an important role in guiding Vietnamese staff in the maintenance of these systems. After 1975, almost all Southern technical personnel who had worked in the computer industry had left the country.

By 1977-1979, some production plants were set up for the small-scale production, repair and maintenance of radio electronics parts. In 1977, a plant was set up with French assistance outside Hanoi to produce transistors and other parts at a simple technological level. Unification of the country in 1976 brought in Southern assembly facilities, physical infrastructure and some technical personnel who had previously been involved in production. The government sent many engineers from the North to the South to take joint responsibility (with old workers and technicians) for rehabilitating those plants which had had to cease production due to a lack of materials and components. These companies, together with those in the North, formed a group of enterprises under the Union of Enterprises for Electronics and Informatics (Viettronics).

By the end of the 1970s, a few Viettronics enterprises purchased equipment from abroad to produce new products like printed circuit boards. Unfortunately, due to economic difficulties, these technologies just stood idle. During 1984-1985, these factories got technical assistance from East European countries and either continued to produce simple products like electronic parts and components or to assemble TVs from imported Polish components. In 1986 some Southern firms established relations with Western companies which enabled them to import Japanese components for assembly work. However, by 1986, the Vietnam electronics industry was still underdeveloped. Industrial activity had mainly involved the assembly of consumer products, producing simple parts and components for the domestic market, together with a few exports activities. A computer industry did not exist.

The next period (1986 to the present) was characterised by some changes. The first was the more active production of consumer electronics and the emergence of computer firms. While electronics companies (most are in the Viettronics group) continue to produce simple consumer goods (loud speakers, amplifiers, radio cassettes and TV sets, both in black and white and colour), there has been a shift of highly-educated labour and of material resources in computer works, towards business from R&D and higher education institutions. This move happened during the middle of the 1980s (1986-1988). Computer companies have sprung up, most of which have been occupied with trading and consultancy. They provide small-scale services, mostly in hardware. Due to the many extra costs of business start-up (for example, where companies need to install assembly lines), some prefer to occupy the niche of simple trading or to rely on assembly facilities abroad. Assembly of PCs in Vietnam is still very rare. Companies mostly import parts and assemble them without adding much value. Most machines still keep the brand name of the foreign firms which supplied the parts. Concerning software products, only a few companies can sell a number of copies tailored for very specific customers.

Since 1990, both electronics and computer companies have developed quite fast in terms of the quantity and quality of their products and services. The private sector has emerged as a significant factor in the industry's development (especially in computers). As the main actor in the state sector, Viettronics re-grouped as the Vietnam Electronics and Informatics Corporation (VEIC) and it now has 15 member-companies:

12 consumer electronics companies, two computers companies and a trading company, Vietronimex. Both computers and consumer electronics products are now being reoriented to serve the domestic market more systematically than before. Types of products and services have become diversified, such that electronics companies not only produce TVs but also audio-visual systems. Computer companies not only sell PCs but also software-related products and they provide package solutions for customers (including hardware, software, related office equipment, installation, training and maintenance, etc.). Many companies have diversified their activities to other sectors: real estate, tourism, hotel, construction, biochemical, garment, etc. This is described as a 'complex diversification of business' and it is one of the main features of the most recent phase of development of the electronics industry. Figure 5.2 presents the milestones of the electronic industry.

5.2.2 Ownership, size and location

Most consumer electronics companies are SOEs (VEIC members are the main actors in the industry). Private companies are mostly small and provide repair and maintenance services but do not engage in production. In computers, the number of companies is even smaller, but the situation is different. SOEs are not very active in computing. In contrast, it is private firms (set up by technologists) who are the main players in producing computers and in providing services in this business.

Most companies in the consumer electronics and computer industry are quite small, ranging from around 50 to 400 employees. For obvious reasons, these companies mainly concentrate around the two big cities, Hanoi and HoChiMinh City, where they have easy access to information and R&D expertise, more skilled labour and a good infrastructure.

5.2.3 Export activities

In consumer electronics, Vietnamese firms first began exporting in the middle of the 1980s. Some Czechoslovakian companies (e.g., TESLA) supplied Viettronics with materials and technological training in return for the production of electronic parts like resistors, condensors and transistors which were sent back to Czechoslovakia on a trial export basis. However, after a few years it became apparent that this success was to be short-lived since the enterprise lacked the back-up of necessary policy incentives. In the computer industry, the export of PCs to the Soviet market assembled in co-operation with foreign partners (e.g., through joint venture or contract manufacturing) started around the end of the 1980s and was mostly undertaken by private firms. This form of export activity declined after 1990 as a result of the difficult situation in the markets of the Soviet Union and East Europe following the collapse of the old regime. By now, most companies have begun to reorient themselves to the domestic market.

Still, some firms continue to export to the former Soviet Union and East Europe. In order to continue exporting, these companies try hard to find new partners and opportunities to produce new products. A few SOEs have started assembling electronics parts for industrial robots and for telecommunications equipment for small-scale export to Japan or other Western countries. Those who still operate in the old and familiar market of the former Soviet Union have changed their way of doing business: they can sell on credit, look for tripartite partnerships, arrange payment for buyers, or use a barter system, etc.

Some computer firms are exploring niche products for high-tech developments. For example, some design software (for cartoon film-making) for sale to targeted markets in France or Japan. However, the revenues from these sales range from just a few thousand to tens of thousands USD at most. There is no large-scale export of software products.

5.2.4 Management practices

Although electronics and computing have always been considered as one of the development priorities of Vietnam, the industry is seen merely from the research and training perspective. The country lacks a national policy for electronics and computer production and lacks the necessary levels of state investment. Measures to promote this sector are only temporary and they fail to take a long-term view (Phan Dinh Dieu, 1992: 11). This is the main reason why the industry has developed in such an unstable fashion, characterised by rapid growth and equally rapid decline over a very short period of time. It is only very recently that a policy for the national development of informatics technology has been approved by the government. Many companies continue to develop in an uncoordinated way through launching their own initiatives and finding their own opportunities. The development of production and export is fragmented, and is mostly achieved through the effort of individual companies.

A second problem is that changes in institutional and organisational structures have caused much confusion. In 1983, in order to give greater priority to the industry, the government set up the General Department of Electronics and Informatics to oversee the industry's development. Then, in 1988, this Department was dissolved and was replaced by Viettronics run from the Ministry of Machinery Engineering and Metallurgy. The reason for this change was a move to replace a formal ministerial structure (the General Department had functioned with a Ministry status) with a body directly oriented to production. Changes of this kind have caused much disorder and difficulties for companies in organising their activities.

In January 1989, the Association of Informatics of Vietnam was established and its members consists of state-owned and private organisations and individuals. The Association acts as a bridge between its Vietnamese members and other similar international organisations, and Vietnamese experts in computer science living abroad (in France, the US and Canada) who have competence, expertise and resources in IT development (Nguyen Quy Son, 1992:35). A similar association for microelectronics also exists and plays a similar role in the consumer electronics industry.

5.2.5 Training, education and R&D activities

Training in radio electronics was first undertaken in 1958 in the Hanoi Polytechnic while other students were sent to train in Eastern Europe. For technicians, a two-year training programme has been in operation since 1960. A number of workers in the industry have also been trained, since the 1950s, through short courses in radio electronics. Some Vietnamese expatriates, who came back from France after 1954, were actively involved in the initial organisation of these establishments. Up to 1975 most teaching of radio electronics was undertaken by the polytechnics. At the same time, research activities were limited.

After 1975, electronics subjects were taught more widely in universities and colleges like the polytechnics in Hanoi and HoChiMinh City. Some other economics and statistics colleges, and the vocational school of the General Department of Statistics, also offered courses on computer programming. Higher degree courses (graduate and postgraduate) in computer science and electronics were organised, to a limited extent, in some research institutes like the Institute of Computer Science and Cybernetics (now the Institute of Information Technology - IOIT) which belonged to the National Centre for Scientific Research (NCSR). Simple courses on computer use and applications for administrative work, and for electronics assembly, repair and maintenance work were organised mostly on a part-time and self-study basis through evening classes offered by various universities, colleges and companies, both state and private.

With the privatisation tendencies in social and economic life of the 1980s, some private and semi-state organisations were set up at the end of the 1980s to offer formal education towards university degrees. At present, all colleges and institutes annually train about 200 persons for university degrees in electronics and computer science, and many more as computer programmers, technicians and related workers. If we include the Vietnamese who have been educated abroad in electronics and informatics, the number of persons with university graduate and postgraduate degrees amounts to a few thousand.

R&D activities are carried out in some national institutes. The IOIT is the strongest in computer science. However, research programmes at national are inefficient in terms of serving the needs of the industry for several reasons: the absence of a coherent and co-ordinated policy for the development of the whole sector, the lack of necessary investment resources, and weakness of market pressure.

At international level, research has also been carried out in co-operation with the CMEA, which offered its members a programme of informatics development and application (PIDA) to develop and diffuse electronics and information technologies. According to some assessments, some Vietnamese participants felt frustrated because very little, if any, information technology was transferred into Vietnam within the framework of this programme (UNIDO, 1990: 45).

During the 1970s and 1980s, some research institutions also conducted research on electronics. Examples are the Laboratory for Semiconductors in the Institute of Physics (also of the NCSR); the Institute of Microelectronics Technology (IMET) and the Information System Centre (both belonging to the National Institute of Technology); some laboratories of the Ministry of Defence; and the Vietnam Radio and Television Broadcasting Commission. The Ministry of Heavy Industry (now MOI) also created the Vietnam Institute of Electronics and Informatics (VIELIN) in 1985. These institutes have carried out various kinds of research in solid state physics, optics, electronics, telecommunications and other informatics projects. There were some attempts to link all research activities into a state co-ordinated programme. The latest programme for 1991-1995 is for electronics, informatics and telecommunications. Many participants in these programmes argue that the project targets have been too fragmented, with some projects being too theoretically-oriented.

As can be seen here, the electronics sector enjoyed a rather early start-up in R&D and training to run in parallel with application activities and these activities helped in the establishment of the first institutional framework for the sector. In both electronics (consumer and industrial) and computing, quite massive state-run R&D institutes have been created, although they do not serve well many companies in the industry (see Boxes 5.2 and 5.3).

With the liberalisation of economic activities and the tendency to commercialise R&D results in the 1980s, many scientists - frustrated by their wasted efforts on useless R&D activities conducted under state co-ordination - moved out and grasped opportunities to set up their own companies so as to commercialise their technological expertise. This heralded the set-up of many new computer firms (for more data on the development of the electronics industry, see Appendices 5.8 to 5.10).

Box 5.2 VIELIN

The Vietnam Institute of Electronics and Informatics (VIELIN) in the Ministry of Industry has 81 employees. It engages in various research projects in industrial electronics (control equipment for production processes in industrial projects), computing (computing applications and designing software for industrial use) and communications technology (research on switching systems and the transmission of data by teletext or videotext). All these projects sound quite impressive, but they are not linked to similar activities in industrial enterprises. The Institute acts as an isolated research unit monitored by the Ministry. Although VIELIN also co-ordinates the state research programme on automation technology (code KC-02), it only links various similar activities very loosely. From time to time, it also provides training in co-operation with Hanoi Polytechnic (graduate and postgraduate courses), but offers nothing that serves the immediate needs of companies. The only resource that VIELIN offers companies is some consulting and problem-solving, but even this is not on a regular basis (Interview with VIELIN director, 1994).

Box 5.3 IMET

Although the aim of the Institute of Micro Electronics Technology (IMET) in the National Institute of Technology (set up in 1986) was to foster closer links between industry and technological innovation, it still has not brought its research activities closer to industry. With 40 employees, IMET specialises in high-tech areas like research on electronics materials and components, equipment and ASIC. It also has a division engaged in research on computing software applications. These projects of the institute cannot be commercialised since they are far removed from the consumer electronics activities most firms are involved in, and almost no industrial enterprise can apply their work. As with VIELIN, IMET and its mother National Institute of Technology are in charge of another state research programme on electronics, informatics and communications (code KC-01). Strikingly enough, IMET itself sees this programme as being too formal and ineffective, lacking co-ordination between and co-operation amongst the institute's participants, and without making a real impact on the industry (Interview with IMET director, 1994).

5.2.6 Main features of the electronic industry

Originating with R&D, training and education activities, and application of consumer electronics, the Vietnamese electronics and computer industry is still in its infancy. Consumer electronics is the most developed part of the industry, but the computer industry has started to emerge over the last couple of years. Reforms in R&D management together with the liberalisation of the economy has created many new opportunities for researchers to set up their own private computer companies. Moreover, these computer businesses tend to start exporting almost immediately to the very unique market of the former Soviet Union. However, the volume of production and of export is small and, more importantly, export activities are still conducted on a trial basis rather than systematically. Assembly work is simple, using complete-knock-down (CKD) and semi-complete-knock-down (SKD) components, particularly for computer products.

The two electronics sub-sectors started under different conditions, and with different initial knowledge and experience, to develop further their technological competence. While the consumer electronics industry shares some general features with other manufacturing industries in the country (e.g., most firms are SOEs, created and supported by the state), the computing industry has had a very different background, relying more on private initiatives which are commercial spin-offs from R&D activities.

One of the problems faced by the industry is a weak domestic market. The purchasing power of the population is increasing but this only enables them to afford some consumer electronics. As for computers, some of the first consumers have been state organisations which buy computers for small-scale administrative and office use rather than for industrial purposes. In general, Vietnamese society remains information-poor, and this is one of the main reasons for the weak domestic market for computer products (Phan Dinh Dieu, 1992: 11).

A second set of problems relates to Vietnam's poor physical infrastructure, the after effects of the trade embargo imposed by the US until 1994, and a lack of efficient international co-operation in the high-technology industries. Foreign investors hesitate to invest in electronics; it is only recently that a few Japanese firms have launched initiatives in this direction (Ostry & Harianto, 1995). A few companies have just begun joint ventures with foreign companies to produce TVs and parts. However, it has only been possible to find opportunities to engage in international co-operative endeavours in electronics since the very recent lifting of the embargo and the establishment of full diplomatic relations with the US.

A third problem points towards the most distinctive difficulty faced by the sector: the lack of a long-term, coherent and co-ordinated state development policy. This not only affects over-arching strategies to develop the sector, but also any concrete measures introduced to support the industry.

5.3 The industrial background

The brief history of industrial development in Vietnam can be divided into several periods which have an important impact on the technology establishment of concerned industries. The transitional reforms from a centrally planned economy (some main features of which are the monopoly of the state sector over economic production; all production and management decisions were planned from above; the reliance on the Soviet Union and Eastern European markets only; isolation from other Western markets; and no foreign direct investment) to a market economy in the middle of 1980s are the most significant change of the Vietnam political economy. The major reforms included structural change of investment priorities; decentralisation of economic management of state-owned enterprises (SOEs); radical change and development of financial and banking system; and diversification and liberalisation of external economic relations. These features of both pre-reform and reform periods are crucial as the external factors in having impact on the TC acquisition and learning process of firms.

This chapter also presented the overall picture of development in the two industries. The evolution of these industries over time show that they have moved from very limited abilities in the 1950s towards rather active production and export in the 1990s. Comparing the development of two industries, some main points can be observed.

Although the two sectors share some features such as the negative attitude towards development of private ownership, and the influences of unification after 1976 and of reforms after 1986, there are some distinct differences. The textile/garment sector began much earlier than electronics. The electronics sector's initial activities were mainly in the areas of training, education and R&D rather than for industrial purposes. This factor is proving decisive in shaping the different ways that electronics firms have begun operating and learning technological capabilities. The phenomenon of spin-off companies is specific to the electronics sector (especially computing) and is not shared by textile/garment firms. As a result, electronics firms have a more R&D-based origin than textile/garment firms.

In the textile/garment sector, firms are mainly SOEs, they tend to be large, and private companies play a less active role. In the electronics sector, private ownership is more significant although firm size is generally small. As regards export activity, although both sectors began with CMEA countries and then re-oriented themselves to the local market and to some new markets of Asia-Pacific or the EU, electronics firms commenced their exporting activities in a more targeted manner, with single types of product destined for specific niched markets. Management practice in the two sectors show that the electronics industry is less guided by a consistent and coherent state policy for the development of the whole sector. As a result, it has had to face more confusion, and its development is more unstable than that of the textile/garment industry.

These main features of development at the sectoral level influence the activities of firms' TC accumulation and learning. These issues are examined in more detail in Chapters 6 and 7, where I look especially at the sequence of TC accumulation, the extent to which TCs are accumulated and the patterns of usage of different learning mechanisms to build up these TCs.

Notes

1. A similar system of co-operation was also used with other East European countries. Hungary, for example, supplied equipment, materials, technological documentation and technical supervision for Vietnamese companies and received 4-5 million pieces of clothes in return. Czechoslovakia and East Germany also held similar contracts. These subcontracting programmes helped Vietnamese companies to significantly upgrade their production expertise and technological competence in garment-making activities.

2. Now this Ministry merges with Ministry of Heavy Industry into the new Ministry of Industry (MOI).

Years	Events
1945	First simple textile plant built by the French.
1954	Division of the country. Migration of technical personnel and textile facilities to the South.
1959	Construction of new textile plants: Chinese and Soviet technologies in the North, American and Japanese technologies in the South. Garment plants set up in the North.
1970	Garment industry began in the South. Large new textile plant built in the North.
1976	Unification. Taking over Southern plants. First export to CMEA.
1980	Purchase of new modern turn-key plants from Japan, France, etc. Subcontracting agreement in garment with the Soviet Union, Eastern European countries.
1986	Reforms. FDI: joint venture. Private sector re-emerged.
1992	Boom in garment export. Export to new markets of EU, Asia-Pacific countries.

Figure 5.1 Textile/garment industry: milestones of development

Years	Events
1950	First radio application. Service workshops: maintenance and repair.
1960	First factory to assemble consumer electronics: amplifiers, etc. in the North: technologies imported from Soviet Union, EE countries.
1965	First black & white TV broadcast. First computer use.
1970	First assembling of black & white TV and other audio products in the South: American and Japanese technologies.
1976	Unification. Taking over Southern plants. Migration of Southern technical personnel. First trial production of components and parts.
1980	First colour TV broadcast. Subcontracting for export of parts to EE countries.
1982	First colour TV assembling with Polish and later Japanese technologies. Upgraded assembling of radio-cassettes, etc.
1986	Reforms.
1988	Spin-off companies from R&D. Private sector emerged. First computer assembling and services. First export of PC.
1993	First industrial production of electronics and computer software. First trial export of industrial parts and software. Diversification beyond electronics.

Figure 5.2 Electronics industry: milestones of development

6 Patterns of building technological capabilities in firms

6.1 Technological capability building in textile/garment companies

The main findings of the firms' studies reveal that the existence of TC differs between firms within the industry. The mapping of TC accumulation for this sector is presented in Table 6.1. This mapping is made possible according to the taxonomy and check-list of TC for the textile/garment industry (the criteria for TC accumulation given in Appendices). The firm has strongly developed TC if it has highest level of autonomy, regularity and extent of tasks performing and is ranking with (2). Another extreme is non-existence of TC and ranking as (0) with the lowest level of these three criteria. Weak TC is in the middle between these two positions and ranking as (1). Using this assessment, results of mapping for each TC are discussed below.

6.1.1 Production capability

Ten companies have strongly developed production capability ranking as (2) in Table 6.1, while this capability is weaker in four companies, ranking as (1) in the table. Firms with strong TC are those able to master all activities in production management, production engineering, repairs and maintenance. Weak firms in this capability are only able to conduct some of these activities. Some production capability exists in all cases surveyed:

- In *production management*, there are three areas of capability. First, the firms knew how to operate rather modern machines and equipment in weaving (TG4), spinning (TG3 and TG6) or sewing. Almost all of them (TG1, TG10, TG9, TG5) were able to use automatic embroidery machines with computer-aided design (CAD) as well as other specialised equipment like stoning for making jeans, brushing, etc. without serious problems. Second, the firms knew how to organise and control textile/garment production processes for different products. Many textile firms (TG3, TG6, TG4) were able to organise production of downstream products like garments, while some garment companies were doing the same for knitwear. Third, firms knew how to interact with suppliers of raw materials (cotton/yarns for textiles, fabrics and other materials for garments), and with suppliers of other supplementary activities in mechanical engineering or chemical (for dyeing), etc.

- In *production engineering*, first, the firms were able to adjust their textile or sewing machines for different products. This was particularly strong in garment firms which adjusted certain mechanical parts to suit the requirements of new products when moving from simple products like trousers and shirts to more skilled operations like jackets (TG1, TG5, TG9, TG10 and TG14). Second, companies substituted raw materials and did various kinds of trouble-shooting and test products to meet quality standards. Technical personnel of the firms handled small trouble-shooting activities, or they knew whom to invite from outside to solve more serious problems.

- Third, companies maintained equipment and did repairs when necessary on modern technologies like combing and carding together and open-end in spinning (TG3 and TG6), jet loom in weaving (TG4) or vertical sewing (TG14).

In general, all these companies were able to run their production facilities using their own staff and without reliance on outside personnel. Their managers, technicians and workers were capable of dealing with all production activities. The fact that companies produced not only for domestic markets but also for export - with four companies TG1, TG8, TG9 or TG10 producing only for export - is evidence of their production competence.

Although the companies achieved this using their own staff, in some specific production activities a few companies still relied on the involvement of foreign partners in order to achieve their best performances. For example, quality control in TG2 has been jointly supervised by its Vietnamese staff and experts coming from buyers like Sanshin of Japan. Sanshin's staff also took part in the supervision of some production lines, and provided technical guidance when it was required. Similarly, Korean experts participated in activities of TG1's special workshop which produced for export.

6.1.2 Investment capability

All but four companies have some levels of the capability. Five firms - TG2, TG5, TG6, TG9 and TG14 - possess a strong capability as they can carry out investment tasks confidently on a regular basis for both pre-investment and project execution phases. Others firms involved in only some selected activities are deemed to have a weaker status. SOEs like TG3 and TG6 made their first investment in new technologies during the 1980s. TG2 and TG10 started their production facilities earlier in the 1960s. They played a rather passive role in the first investment efforts initiated by the state, with technologies coming from Japan (TG6), Germany, Italy (TG3) as turnkey plant projects. The staff only participated in some construction and installation activities.

By the end of the 1980s and the beginning of the 1990s, real investment capability came with SOE efforts to expand the range of production. From these activities, the following levels of investment can be seen:

- In the *pre-investment phase*, the firms were able to organise and prepare various investment studies: pre-feasibility and feasibility studies, and site selection. Weaving companies TG4 and TG15 prepared their investment studies when moving to polo shirt production. The same happened in TG2 when it reorganised its production planning to upgrade the quality and range of its knitting products. TG10 upgraded its production facilities by purchasing and investing in new projects and equipment in order to export to new and more demanding markets in Japan, and the firm did almost all its own studies in this phase.

- In the *project implementation phase*, two types of expertise were found. First, firms themselves choose the plant design and type of textile/garment equipment - as TG10 did with Japanese CAD embroidery machines and with Korean leather processing equipment. TG3, in its new phase of expansion from spinning to knitting had chosen knitting equipment better suited to its own yarns material. Second, firms organised designing, sourcing, construction and erection start-up activities.

- In starting *new ventures* at home or abroad, the firms were rather active in moving either from upstream to downstream (textile to knitting and garment) or vice versa, and in take-over and merging activities, etc. TG4 took over a spinning plant nearby in HoChiMinh City in order to ensure its supply of raw materials. Similar new expansion can be seen in TG6, TG5 and TG14. TG5 began new production of kimonos for export to Japan and suits to European countries in 1992. TG14 purchased new workshops for producing suits for export to France, using new vertical sewing technology from Japan.

The two private companies TG8 and TG9 were very active in new investment. As a private family business, TG8 began all its investment and pre-investment preparation with its own staff, including choice of technologies, design of the plant and production planning. In order to implement their investment plans, they hired local construction companies to build their new premises for production. Similar capabilities can be seen in TG9, formed from a group of co-operatives and private businesses.

Four cases (TG1, TG7, TG12 and TG13) did not have any investment capability. TG1 acquired its investment, new sewing and other specialised machines, and expertise and technological training from foreign sources. All pre-investment and investment feasibility studies were done largely by a foreign consultancy firm. TG7 is a joint venture with British Coats Tootal. Its investment activities, including choice of technologies, sourcing of materials, installation, erection and start-up all relied on British expertise. By participating in some activities requiring specific knowledge and skills (like construction activities under Vietnamese conditions), the staff of these companies partly improved their investment skills, so that they could do some new small investment in expanding production facilities. But this is still far from being capable in investment activities. The investment activities of TG12 and TG13 were usually run by external consultants and experts assigned by the Hanoi City which owns the company, or from experts in ministries. This passive reliance has continued even through the 1970s and 1980s up till the present, when the firms took part in some new investment ventures.

6.1.3 Minor technical change capability

Seven firms developed minor technical change capabilities, while this capability was weaker in five firms. Only companies which have done minor change activities in all categories can be considered as acquiring strong capability (TG1, TG2, TG3, TG4, TG12, TG13 and TG14). Some other firms like TG7, TG9 and TG10, can be regarded as being very active in one or two types of minor change, but since they have done very little in others, their overall capability is weak. In many companies staff were involved quite successfully in various kinds of minor technical change.

First, firms carried out improvements to existing *process technologies* (or added new elements to them) to make the equipment or machine more suitable for the needs of production. For example: TG2 introduced changes to create new equipment for printing labels, flowers and other images onto its clothing products; TG3 had changed the specification of spinning equipment (reducing the angle of the spinning gears to increase the quality of yarns or replacing imported spare parts and components by locally made trolleys, metal and non-metal gears, etc.) to save on foreign exchange. Some attempts to improve technologies to suit the lower quality of local raw cotton (to replace imported material or to supply yarns through the tube system, etc.) were taken by TG13.

Second, some companies have improved *product specifications*: modification of foreign models taken from catalogues; improvement of quality and design of products by changing minor details; and prototype production of new industrial fabrics by using new weaving techniques. Based on these improvements, some companies introduced their products with new designs, colours, or other details for trial offer to customers. For example: TG7 introduced on a regular basis a more diversified range of threads (its main product) by changing the colour mixture of raw material; and TG14 offered customers new models of polo shirts and suits.

Third, companies made minor improvements in the *organisation of production* (the arrangement of technological schemes), to achieve more optimal variants. A new organisational pattern for cutting operations, for example, had been introduced at TG2 to save millions of Vietnamese dongs and increase the productivity of workers. The technical unit at TG14 and TG15 adapted the technology by combining the best variants of existing production lines to produce new products.

The *organisation of change activity* in most firms varies but is quite active in many cases. Some firms have created special units for dealing with technical problems in production. For instance, TG2 has one small group attached to its technical division for model design. Most companies have assigned their vice-director to take care of these technical divisions and allocated to them regular amounts of money for R&D. Receiving money from Hanoi City's S&T Department to carry out technical development projects, TG12's technical division has one group specialising in supporting technical initiatives and improvements.

Two companies, TG4 and TG10, developed their organisations to support minor change activities more seriously. TG4 has a special R&D unit (10 persons) responsible for the preparation of feasibility studies for new investment plans, and studies of improvements in technological processes. This activity contributes importantly to more major technical change in TG4 in the use of microfibre material for its new products. The technology and engineering division of TG10 is responsible for technical improvement and development.

Box 6.1 Minor technical change in TG3

Minor technical adjustments and improvement in TG3 range widely from sample use of Vietnamese raw cotton material to replace imported cotton, to changing the consumption rate of other materials. The company has introduced some technical changes to improve its production performances and save production inputs. It has:

- replaced imported spare parts with locally-produced ones (some plugs, carriages, gears, etc.)
- introduced flexible optimisation of production processes to suit local conditions;
- improved certain parts and technical details of spinning technology to upgrade the quality of products;
- re-equipped electrical supply facilities using local materials and parts.

Improvement activities also include reorganisation of production plans and working conditions, such as measures to ensure hygienic conditions for industry on the site; management structure of the company and of each workshop, etc.

The company has a special unit for designing new models, mostly in knitwear products (underwear, outerwear, towels, etc.). Each month it produces about five new models of products which have sold well. Up to now, about 70% of knitting products have been produced from the designs of the company itself and only 30% from the designs of buyers. The rate of export of knitwear has also increased: 70% of total production in 1991, 80% in 1992 and 87% in 1994. In the near future, the company plans to use computers in its design activities. In general, these minor technical change activities are handled actively and entirely by the staff of the firm. Clear vision and conscious improvement programmes designed by the firm's managers are very important factors contributing to this minor change capability. One reason for this attitude is that its top managers and most middle level staff are technologically highly-educated. The General Director of the enterprise is a textile engineer, almost all directors of workshops or mills are engineers, and one of them has a PhD degree in engineering from Eastern Europe. Also their average age is rather young by Vietnamese standards: top managers are in their 40s and 50s; middle level managers of workshops or production lines are in their 20s and 30s. As a result, this company enjoys higher levels of dynamism, pragmatic motivation and education than most Vietnamese companies. Working for this company is considered prestigious amongst many new graduates from universities and polytechnics which, in turn, contributes to attracting a higher quality of new recruits.

Companies having no special units relied on a 'soft' structure (ad-hoc groups created by the director of the company which recruit people from different divisions) to deal with minor change tasks as in the case of TG6. In TG7, all responsibilities for technological improvements or model changes belong to the production division. Box 6.1 is an illustration of how minor change activity takes place at one firm, TG3.

Two firms, TG5 and TG8, did not have any minor change capability. Although both have made some changes, these were quite disorganised and any accumulated knowledge and experience cannot be developed further into sustainable competence. Initial activities at TG5, for example, were impressive. The firm tried to cooperate with foreign designers to set up a fashion centre for designing its collection of garments. Due to lack of resources this attempt was unsuccessful and, with a recent change of the firm's managers, these activities have ended. TG8, as a small private company, has introduced some initiatives in making embroidery for Japanese buyers, but these are no more than simple and individual fragmented actions. Accordingly, both firms are not yet capable of initiating and sustaining technical change.

6.1.4 Marketing capability

All in all, marketing capability is generally still absent in the textile/garment companies. Only two firms - TG5 and TG9 - have some weak marketing competence. The first aspect of this capability concerns the ability of firms to regularly gather marketing intelligence on market structure, trends in fashion design, information about other competitors and buyers, suppliers of cotton, materials, machines and equipment, etc. Up to the end of the 1980s, the firms had no need for, and no intention of doing, marketing. Recently, they began some limited marketing activity. In terms of the organisation of marketing activity, there are few special units in these companies. This function is usually assigned to sales and distribution or production divisions (TG4, TG6, TG12 and

TG7). TG3 and TG14 have a unit for marketing but this is aimed at the domestic market only.

The second aspect is the setting up of firms' own distribution channels, and the supply of both sales and after-sales services locally. Most companies have opened shops or transaction centres in big cities in order to target the domestic market. TG8 did not have any marketing activities even for local markets because all of its products were exported; for this it relied entirely on foreign buyers.

The third aspect is the setting up of representative offices, show-rooms, fashion centres or shops abroad to promote sales of garments, yarn or fabrics. In almost all companies, the ability to penetrate foreign markets, and to establish distribution channels or sale representative offices abroad is not developed. The companies have to rely on contacts with foreign partners to sell or export their products (through subcontracting or OEM relationships). By the end of the 1980s, in moving towards a market economy, some firms have become aware of the necessity for marketing, and have begun to explore foreign markets more actively: e.g., TG10 (by becoming a member of the Chamber of Commerce of ASEAN countries); TG12 (by sending people to be based in the Ukraine market); and TG13 (by taking part in market intelligence gathering at presentation seminars held by foreign companies doing business in Vietnam). So far, this awareness is just beginning and had only led to limited results.

Box 6.2 Marketing in TG9

In May 1990, as a private company, TG9 began garment production for export. Products such as sportswear, jackets, coats and wind-breakers are exported to Germany, the former Soviet Union, Hong Kong, South Korea and Czechoslovakia. When TG9 received orders for simple shirt production, it gave these orders to its small subsidiary production co-operatives having about 6,000 employees so the company could concentrate its efforts on high-quality products like jackets. TG9 opened sales offices in Moscow to take care of business in Eastern Europe. The company intends to open a new office in France or Belgium to serve the EU countries. It also has plans to export to the North American and Scandinavian markets. During the first trip organised by the Vietnam Chamber of Commerce to the US in April 1993, the company got acquainted with the regulations, demand and potential opportunities in the US market. Also it has begun to explore new joint business possibilities with American companies in Vietnam in exchange for opportunities to export Vietnamese textile and garment products to the US market. In doing this, in 1994, TG9 concluded preliminary contracts with some US companies (for 4 to 5 million USD) to buy US technology in textile/garment and to organise an exhibition of American textile/garment equipment in Vietnam.

TG5 and TG9 are the only two firms with a marketing capability developed to any significant extent. TG5 has a special marketing unit. In co-operation with foreign partners, it has opened representative offices in Moscow and France (as a joint venture company Lega-Scavi with Scavi.S.A, a company of a Vietnamese expatriate living in France which produces lingerie and women's underwear for export). TG5 has also sold some of its products directly at various international exhibitions and trade fairs in Thailand, Hong Kong and Eastern Europe. Through these channels, the company has gained insight into fashion trends and market dynamics abroad; as a result, it has adjusted its production plans accordingly. Interestingly, the market division of TG5 also has responsibility for R&D activities which, according to them, should be guided by market change. This capability has helped TG5 to increase its exports to the high-demand markets of the EU. For the TG9 case, see Box 6.2. Although these two companies have made some marketing efforts, they still face many difficulties in trying to enter the more sophisticated markets of Japan and the EU.

6.1.5 Linkage capability

Overall, 10 companies have this linkage capability to some extent. However, only six firms (TG2, TG3, TG10, TG12, TG13 and TG14) develop all of these linkage types (with S&T infrastructure, inter- and intra-firms) and can be regarded as having strongly developed this capability. Although the majority of firms have this capability, the types of, and partners in, linkages are not the same. The most common link is co-operation with state-owned *R&D institutions* for solving technical problems for the companies, or for repair services. For example, TG2 co-operates with Hanoi Polytechnic to solve technical difficulties in operating Japanese knitting machines. TG4 co-operates with a branch of the Research Institute of Textile Industry in HoChiMinh City to improve the quality control of yarns. Other firms have had close contact with the National Centre for Standardisation-Metrology-Quality Control of MOSTE to set up technical standards (TG12), or with R&D units in other industries for different services (TG13 contacted the Institute of Industrial Construction for water treatment services). This linkage can sometimes be seen to be at more technologically sophisticated levels, as when TG14 relied on HoChiMinh City polytechnic for using computers for pattern design and garment stitching.

Linkages with *universities* and *colleges* for the training of staff occurred in a number of subjects: technical, managerial and in economics. Most firms look to training and education organisations as a source of training for their labour force. In the North, TG1, TG2 and TG3 relied on Hanoi Polytechnic and the Garment Vocational School No.1 or on the Chamber of Commerce. Southern firms TG4, TG5,· TG8 and TG14 used links with HoChiMinh City polytechnic and the Garment Vocational School No. 2.

A third form of linkage is between companies and local *enterprises.* Many companies have signed contracts with other firms to provide raw materials in exchange for training and technical assistance, or for sharing job opportunities and/or sales and distribution channels (TG12, TG10, TG14, TG4, etc.). Some companies have created a network of small subcontracting units (or subsidiaries) for which the large firms provide technological assistance and parts of their contracts. For example, in addition to co-operating with other companies in HoChiMinh City to execute those contracts which are too large to be done alone, TG8 had four subsidiary small companies in other provinces. It held a part of their assets (as share-holding companies) and shared with them production contracts and forms of technical assistance. TG5 and TG14 had a similar network of small units to implement contracts that require neither very high quality of products, good delivery time nor high technical standards. This kind of domestic subcontracting was important for companies because it allowed them to organise their business more flexibly and dynamically. Moreover, firms usually transferred some of their technological expertise, skills and experiences to other firms in the same subcontracting network.

A few companies also have links with local *consultancy companies* which help them create economic and technological information databases, as in the case of TG4 and the Technology Development Company (TEDCO) of HoChiMinh City.

Internal linkages between divisions within the firms were variable. In some firms, these links were stronger and were organised more systematically than in others. In general, most firms know how to circulate information and staff, how to link activities across different units (such as the link between production and sales), and how to relate improvement activities to market trends.

Four companies are considered as not having any linkage capability. As a joint venture, TG7 relied very much on the strong network of linkages provided by its British partner and it became passive in seeking other linkages (especially local links). TG9 did not have strong enough contacts with the R&D and education system and therefore, is considered as not having this capability. TG15 is the weakest firm in this dimension, not having good enough relations with either the S&T infrastructure or the industrial network.

6.1.6 Major technical change capability

This capability is absent in nearly all cases. Although some firms claimed that they have some radical R&D and design activities, these remain as plans only. Some firms were able to introduce design modifications in order to launch new products (mostly in garments) but without using a new type of machine or equipment. So in the taxonomy adopted here, these changes count as minor improvements to, and adjustments of, existing models. No new process technology was developed by the firms. Some attempts were found to substitute components by using local sources. So far, these attempts have been either small-scale, unsystematic or unsuccessful. At the highest level of major technical change, no patentable technological breakthroughs as a result of R&D activities were introduced. Most R&D activities carried out by companies were below this level and therefore are classed as minor change. In my view, the only company with a major technical change capability is TG4 presented in Box 6.3 below.

Box 6.3 Major Technical Change in TG4

The company has 2,433 employees, of whom 180 received higher education from the Polytechnics of Hanoi and HoChiMinh City, the universities and other financial and economics colleges. The company was involved in weaving, spinning and garment assembly and began exporting in 1986 indirectly to East Europe. In 1988, it started to export polo shirt products mainly to Japan (90% of total current exports).

For R&D activity, the company set up a division with eight staff which is mostly responsible for modification to, and improvement of, products. Expenditure for this type of R&D in 1992 was more than 1 billion VND (about 100,000 USD). The company also used a system of incentives by increasing salary and other bonuses for improvement activities. Staff in the R&D unit receive a salary 15-25% higher than that of other staff. The R&D unit co-operated with technical staff in other divisions and workshops to introduce some minor technical changes in designing models for garments (polo shirts). The company introduced a digital control system instead of an electrical control system and produced new materials like polyester/wool mix, etc.

It has also set up a special library of textile/garment documentation for its use and has a regular expenditure on journals and reviews of about 100 USD per month.

Lately, the R&D unit carries out research on the application of a new principle using microfibre in the production of fabrics. Up to now this kind of material has been monopolised by a few Japanese and German companies. According to TG4 staff, if successful, this attempt will open opportunities to compete equally with the Japanese in entering the EU market.

Since 1993, TG4 has been producing fabric made from this fibre and the products compete with imported materials for the garment industry. In addition, the R&D division conducted feasibility studies for new investment projects when the company moved both to upstream (spinning) and downstream (garment) activities, including the choice of equipment and machines from catalogues. Exchanges of experience and skills with other spinning companies were quite common practice in this firm. The company offered weaving and garment expertise to some spinning companies and, in return, received their expertise on spinning for expanding its new Khanhhoi spinning plant in a suburb of HoChiMinh City. Also, the R&D division together with some garment companies studied the possibility of producing fabrics as material for their export products.

The existence of TCs in the 14 textile/garment firms is summarised in Table 6.1, following the ranking of points in TC development (two for strong TC, one for weak and none for non-existent), the TC landscape in textile and garment firms can be crudely mapped. Production capability has received 24 points out of a total 28 available. Similarly, the points ranking of other TCs appear as follows: minor technical change (19); linkage (16); investment (15); marketing (two) and major technical change (one).

As can be seen from the table, only three capabilities are most evident in the companies studied: *production, minor change* and *linkage*. The *investment* capability is less developed, although almost all companies seem to have engaged in various new investment activities recently. *Marketing* and *major change* capabilities are the least developed. Companies were involved in developing these TCs to various extents but, lacking one or two types of activities as set by suggested criteria, they cannot be considered to have strongly developed TC. The ranking of TC also allows for a crude whole firm assessment: out of a total 12 points available for each firm, firms range from eight in the most competent firm (TG14) to three in the weakest ones (TG7, TG8 and TG15).

6.2 Building technological capability in electronics companies

6.2.1 Production capability

Among nine firms having production capability, the extent to which they acquired production competence differs. While six firms (E1, E2, E4, E5, E10 and E11) strongly developed their production expertise, E7, E8 and E9 still have difficulties and their capability is still rather weak. In these nine firms, production activities were run quite actively, and mostly, by their own staff. Companies were capable of handling all the mentioned production functions as we now see.

In *production management*, they were operating machines and equipment to assemble TVs, cassettes, VCRs (for consumer electronics) or PCs (for computing) without major problems; and they knew how to organise the assembly line and to monitor its link with other supporting activities (supply of materials, sourcing components and provision of other inputs).

Consumer electronics companies such as E1 started by simple assembly of CKD components and moved to higher SKD and IKD (incomplete-knock-down) assembly. The firm is capable of handling various sources of input material (locally-made plastics and stereophore packaging in combination with imported CKD from Japan Victor Co. (JVC) to produce its Viettronics TV. Other firms increased their rate of colour TVs per total TV production (up to 45% in E10) or moved from TV production to other audio-visual products like CDs (E11).

In *production engineering*, electronics firms knew how to change plant organisation, to plan the operation of assembly lines, and to carry out tests ensuring the high standards of products. They also systematically carried out arrangements necessary for the maintenance and repair of equipment and machines. For example, in E4, a three-round test (function test, burn-in test and final test before packaging) was applied to ensure high quality standards of PC assembly equal to that of others produced in the region. To ensure quality, the company had a test card for each machine and a sales engineer took care of monitoring quality assurance with buyers after sales. E9, having started as a SOE producing calculators for the East European market, produced power supply systems for PCs in a subcontracting agreement for export to Australia. The quality of these systems is ensured by the firm to mesh with the PCs produced by an Australian firm.

6.2.2 Investment capability

This capability in the majority of firms remained underdeveloped. Only four firms have some investment competence while the rest do not yet have this capability. Among these four firms, investment capability was more developed within E2, E10 and E11.

Consumer electronics companies E1 and E7 - having received initial investment from the state - were only recently involved in investment. At the initial stage of assembling consumer electronics, these firms participated in investment studies in a rather passive way. Despite certain skills and experience in investment activity, only few consumer electronics firms have acquired any investment capability. Both E10 and E11 enjoyed initial Japanese investment during the 1970s (E10 as Matsushita Vietnam, and E11 as Sony Vietnam). These firms had gone through many difficulties in the post-unification period and began to receive new investment from the state during the 1980s. At that time, they still had a passive attitude to doing business.[1] For their latest ventures, however, these firms were more entrepreneurial and active in their investment. When E10 wanted to expand its production, it got both design input and an offer of financing from Matsushita for a new turn-key process. This was too expensive and the firm decided to install a new facility by itself, using only designs acquired from Matsushita. E10 bought only the core element - a CKD assembly line 34 metres long - from Matsushita for 200,000 USD. For the rest, it bought cheaper Chinese components, through a Hong Kong-based trading firm. Combining these two sources, the firm commenced the new production line, having saved a large sum of money. This example shows how E10 became more self-determined and confident in new investment. This confidence can also be seen in E11 where the firm has invested in many new facilities since the beginning of 1990s (300,000 USD for an assembly line for JVC products, including a centre for broadcasting and test facilities; another line of 770,000 USD to specialise on Sony products; and a take-over of some other electronics assembly facilities in HoChiMinh City).

Among the computer companies, the private firm - E4 - engaged in investment efforts from the firm's inception, but these were limited and its export success was temporary. In the later period of 1990s, the firm's investment stagnated and this capability was not developed further. The joint venture - E5 - has also not obtained this capability due to all investment activities being done by its foreign partner which has more experiences and skill. E3 is the only computer company with investment experience (see E3 in Section 9.5).

6.2.3 Minor technical change capability

Among seven companies involved in minor technical change activity, six firms (E2, E3, E4, E1, E10 and E11) have developed this competence more strongly than E7 by engaging in all types of change activities on a regular basis. Companies have made various improvements to their *product specifications*. Consumer electronics companies replaced some components in radio cassettes (E2) or improved the design of TV sets to make them more suitable to tropical conditions (increasing the range of brightness and colour) and produced a better quality of loudspeaker (E10). E11 created new plugging sets to replace imported ones and saved hundreds of USD per set. Similarly, E1 modified TV sets by adding some small components to make products more multi-functional than before, or to make them more appropriate for a hot and humid climate. Computer company E4 has introduced a new model of computer (modified from a Taiwanese model) as a specific product which is sold to the Russian market. The machine, with the brand name of KB (Knowledge Base), has got a rather good response from buyers.

Another effort at the firms is to change *process technology*: the way of assembling TV sets or altering the production arrangement to suit the conditions of less productive Vietnamese workers (E2). When starting a new production line, E1 adapted an old principle of assembling new equipment and so designed a new one.

In the *organisational aspect,* electronics firms had set up divisions responsible for technical change activities. All SOEs in the study have R&D or technical divisions which organise and co-ordinate technical change in the firms. Three electronics companies did not perform modification and adaptation activities. E8, as a small company based on a family business, did not have any resources (financial, human and intellectual) to organise its very limited change activities into more systematic efforts. E9 was passive and only able to engage in certain technical improvements with the help of outside experts. As a joint venture with a French company, Bull S.A., to assemble Bull computers, E5 has not developed this minor change capability because production is fixed strictly by its foreign partner and all models, components and parts have been kept exactly as they were supplied.

6.2.4 Marketing capability

The two sub-sectors have reached very different levels in their development of marketing capability. While in consumer electronics this capability is almost absent, in computer companies it has become one of the most important factors ensuring their continued existence. Overall, only three computing companies - E3, E4 and E5 - can be said to have developed marketing capability to some extent (for one market and one product only). Other firms, having tried to export and to do some marketing, remain very weak and their marketing expertise is nearly non-existent.

Consumer electronics companies engaged in some export activities on a very limited scale during the 1980s, when they had to rely on using the channel of foreign partners for marketing intelligence and for sales. For example, E10 had a subcontract with a Czechoslovakian electronics company, TESLA, to produce simple electronic parts and components like condensers. Technology and training were provided by TESLA and it bought back all products. These relations were passive, relying on the planning and foreign trade experts of each of the governments, and the firm had neither the intention, nor the resources, to develop marketing activity. In the local market, all consumer electronics firms developed a network of organisations to take care of marketing. They have shops, showrooms and service centres around the country, both to provide services and to collect marketing information. Still, these activities were limited to the domestic market only.

By contrast, computer companies have been more active. Three companies - E3, E4 and E5 - have entered the former Soviet market and sold their products quite successfully since the end of the 1980s. For example, E5 got this capability through many years of having relations with, and experience of, the Soviet market in terms of knowing the structure of the market, the trading relations, the procedures of foreign trade payment, banking and other aspects of external economic relations between Vietnam and the Soviet Union. Moreover, it has a specific know-how in using convertible currency and transforming it into hard currency through goods and services. Similarly, E3 and E4 have entered the Soviet market with products designed specifically for this market. Later on, E4 acquired a market foothold in France and Japan, where it sold some software products for cartoon movie-making (although it was not very sophisticated and of limited volume), and for multimedia use in education. Thanks to the development of this capability, companies sustained some level of export performance for several years. But because this marketing know-how was so specific (tied to the Soviet market and to PC products), companies had difficulties using this strength in other markets and for other products, once the Soviet market collapsed in the beginning of the 1990s. At present, all three firms have returned to the domestic market quite vigorously, offering their products and services to meet the emerging demand at home.

6.2.5 Linkage capability

This capability is quite developed in electronics companies. Eight out of ten firms have acquired this competence to a reasonable extent. Among eight companies with linkages, only five (E2, E3, E10, E4 and E11) belong within the range of possessing a strongly developed capability. They were able to develop all three types of linkages (with the R&D, training and education infrastructure; with industrial enterprises; and having intra-firm links) and these linkages became routine activities. Meanwhile, three other firms (E5, E7 and E9) developed just one or two types of linkage, and did so on a less regular and systematic basis.

First, they knew how to - and did - cooperate with various *R&D institutions*, and *universities* in Hanoi and HoChiMinh City to share information and to solve their own problems. E11 was among the firms having the best relations with S&T and education institutions. It has asked the Institute of Television and Radio Broadcasting to help with the creation of a radio signal generation station for its TV test. It also received regular assistance from HoChiMinh City polytechnic. Similar links with the R&D and education network also occurred in E7 and in the computer firms E9, E3 and E4.

Computer companies have also developed linkages with their collaborators in *industrial enterprises*. As a joint venture with a foreign company, E5 has less need to link with domestic partners. With the reorientation to the local market once exporting became difficult, it began to develop domestic links with other computer firms to supply each other with services and to use technical facilities jointly. Consumer electronics firms linked with each other through the VEIC, where they exchanged and co-ordinated their production and business plans.

Linkages were also developed *internally among divisions* of the companies. In E4, the R&D division was responsible for maintenance and repair activities - something which typically belongs to the production division in other companies. This factor enhanced the company's chances of getting feedback information on defect rates and customers' needs for its R&D. This circulation of information among sales, production and technical divisions was also common in E7, E10 and E11.

Linkage capability is absent in E1 and E8. Although E1, as a SOE, tried to establish various connections with R&D institutes, these connections were not very effective for the firm. Relations with other organisations were very formal, even within the framework of state research programmes. As a small family company, E8 could not build linkages with any external R&D organisation.

6.2.6 Major technical change capability

This is the weakest capability of electronics firms. In all companies, there were no radical changes to their production technologies or major improvements in the design of their products. A few companies were involved in certain R&D activities, trying to develop skill by investing in R&D units (like the software centre of E3 or the R&D unit of E4). Their scale of activities, while contributing significantly to the profit-making of each firm, still remained in the category of minor technological modification and improvement rather than representing the achievement of any more radical change. As a result, no company has got this capability. However, judging by the current minor technical change activity which is quite strong in some firms, it is likely that some of them (E2 and E3) - depending on their future investment in new resources and learning efforts - might become capable of acquiring more expertise in undertaking major technical change.

Table 6.2 presents the result of TC acquisition in the electronics firms. Using the ranking system adopted, the table shows that out of a total 20 points available, *production* capability existed in nine firms (E3 had deliberately not developed this capability). It is the most developed TC with an overall 15 points, and six firms have strongly developed this capability. Next is the *linkage* capability (with 13 points) and only two firms do not have this; five companies have strongly developed linkage capability. *Minor technical change* (also 13 points) and *investment* (seven points) capabilities come next, with six and three firms respectively having these capabilities at a developed level. *Marketing* capability is very weak in electronics firms; only three computer firms have this experience, and none have developed a strong competence. No companies have competence in handling *major technical change*. As for the whole picture of all the firm, out of a maximum 12 points, the three most developed firms in terms of technological capability (E2, E10 and E11) have got eight points, while the least developed firm, E8, has one point.

6.3 Patterns of TC accumulation

6.3.1 Patterns in textile/garment firms

The first observation concerns the sequence and dynamics of TC creation. Most textile/garment companies have a similar sequence of TC accumulation. Following the inception of the companies, they first acquired production capability after some years of operation. Then, minor technical change and linkage capabilities were added during the

1970s and the 1980s. Investment capability only became evident at the end of the 1980s when the companies became more active and started to expand their production facilities by themselves. At the stage of initial start-up accomplished through aid programmes or joint ventures, most had a passive attitude, relying on the state or their foreign donor. Marketing capability was absent throughout the 1970s and the 1980s in the planned economy, and only began to be accumulated through the companies' increased integration into international markets in the 1990s. Major technical change capability is not yet evident in companies' development.

Different sequences of TC acquisition occurred in the firms depending on their *ownership* and the *date of their start-up*. The sequential feature of TC building mentioned above does not apply to all the firms, but is common among SOEs. Two private firms which set up during the early 1990s - TG8 and TG9 - had different backgrounds to the SOEs. According to interviews with these firms, they had commitment to 'seize the opportunity' to make money in a more open and liberalised economy. As private firms, they could not have afforded the long waiting and struggling periods experienced by the likes of the SOEs. They needed some investment experience in order to start the business, and this capability was developed almost simultaneously with their production capability in the early 1990s, while the other capabilities of minor technical change, linkage and marketing expertise appeared a few years later. The difficulties of starting up stimulated these private businesses to develop this capability, while the SOEs were more-or-less able to rely on state resources (aid programmes, credit) to start-up. Because of these more favourable conditions for SOEs, there was a more relaxed attitude to investment issues among the latter.

As is shown in Figure 6.1, there is no significant difference between textile and garment companies in the sequence of their TC building. The main difference in the sequence of TC building is more related to ownership of the firms and their date of establishment. Second, the extent to which textile/garment firms developed their TCs and the types of TC acquired is uneven across the firms. The ranking of TC acquisition is as follows: production, minor technical change, linkage, investment, marketing and major technical change. At the same time, the number of firms deemed to have strong TC produced the same ranking: production (10), minor technical change (seven), linkage (six), and investment (five). Table 6.1 also outlines a pattern of distribution of TC creation among firms. Nine firms (TG2, TG3, TG4, TG5, TG6, TG9, TG10, TG12 and TG14) are among the best; TG14, in particular, has four strongly developed TCs.

6.3.2 Patterns in electronics firms

The study reveals different sequences of TC building between firms in the two electronics sub-sectors, as presented in Figure 6.2.

In *consumer electronics* companies (E1, E2, E7, E10 and E11), production capability came first accompanying the start-up of the operations process. Minor technical change capability arrived later when the companies had a need for, and became involved in, various improvements, adaptations, and modification activities to increase production proficiency. Linkage capability came about simultaneously with minor technical change because the companies needed to interact with potential collaborators. Investment capability has been developed through companies' recent attempts to handle expansion activities, while marketing is still almost absent.

In the *computer* companies (E3, E4 and E5), minor technical change and marketing capabilities existed from the outset, as their primary assets for starting up the business. They had been accumulated even before the companies were established, through previous training and work experience in other organisations. Production and linkage capabilities emerged shortly afterwards to strengthen the companies' minor technical change capability. Investment capability was only evident in E3. So far, no firm has achieved a major technical change capability.

The ranking of the extent of TC building is as follows: production, linkage, minor technical change, investment and marketing with no firm having major technical change capability. Electronics firms with strongly developed TC show nearly the same ranking as given in the Table 6.2: both production and minor technical change capabilities are strongly developed in six firms, as is linkage capability in five firms, and investment capability in three firms, while no firms have developed strong marketing capability. Concerning the development of whole firms, E2, E4, E10 and E11 appear to have developed their TC much more vigorously than the rest, with eight and seven points out of total 12 available.

6.3.3 Overall patterns

These patterns of TC acquisition among the studied firms in the two sectors may be examined at three levels. First, looking at both sectors, there is a *similarity in the overall extent of TC development*. In both sectors, the areas in which firms are more capable are production, linkage and minor technical change activities - although different patterns can be seen to operate between particular firms. Marketing and major technical change activities are virtually absent in most firms. One of the main reasons is that state support during the 1960s and 1970s focused entirely on helping firms to begin production and to maintain it at a reasonable level. Campaigns to promote production and minor technical change activities were common in the pre-reform period. Linkages in this period were developed both by formal systems of organisation and by informal networks of contacts. Also, during the pre-reform period, there was little new investment expansion. Moreover, relations with CMEA countries, a lack of competitive pressure and a low demand for quality products resulted in Vietnamese companies having no need to develop marketing and major R&D activities. For them, the main concerns of this period were to operate production facilities, to produce standardised and simple products and to implement some minor technical changes (mostly in their process technologies).

The reforms have brought new demands on companies to gather intelligence on new markets, introduce new products and engage in new ventures. Therefore, investment and marketing activities were less developed before reforms and only began to assume importance in the 1990s. Hence, the patterns of TC development in these two industries is the outcome of the previous planned economy, when there were few incentives for product innovation and marketing, and the focus was more on the quantity than on the quality of products.

Second, there are *differences between the two sectors* in their *sequence* of TC building. While in textile/garment firms, the sequence of TC building varies by ownership, in electronics it varies among sub-sectors (the kinds of activity and products). This difference in TC creation is, in part, illustrative of wider sectoral differences in technological innovation (Pavitt, 1984; Bell & Pavitt, 1993). As a more mature technological sector, the textile/garment industry requires less research-based activity than electronics. Thus, the patterns of TC accumulation in the two industries were shaped both by the characteristics of the planned economy in the pre-reform period, and by the specific features of the technologies and products of these industries.

Ownership is the most important factor differentiating firms in the textile/garment industry in terms of their TC building. The pattern seen in Figure 6.1, starting with technical experience of production, minor technical change and linkage capabilities then later moving on to the non-technical skills of investment and marketing, is rather common for the majority of SOEs in both Vietnamese industries. Compared to private firms, SOEs in textile/garment were more protected (in terms of their quota allocation for export, their access to financial and information resources, etc.). The starting conditions were, however, very different in the 1990s for private firms like TG8 and TG9, who needed more technological skill and experience from the outset. They also faced more restrictive regulations and tougher competitive pressure than their state-owned competitors. In electronics, the differences between private firms and SOEs are less marked. Electronics firms under different kinds of ownership still operated in rather similar conditions: lacking long-term policy and specific support from the state for sectoral development, but at the same time, enjoying a more strongly developed R&D, training and education base than the textile/garment firms. The more important differences between electronics firms relate to the historical features of the two sub-sectors. In the 1970s and 1980s, the computer sector as such was hardly developed while most consumer electronics firms were already in existence. Computer firms only sprang up in the 1980s and 1990s, on the basis of existing TCs (namely minor technical change and marketing). These two capabilities helped firms to establish themselves as export businesses. The unique context in which Vietnamese computer firms emerged is the main reason behind the different sequences of TC accumulation between the two electronics sub-sectors.

Another difference between the two industries is the *level of TC acquisition in marketing*. Although the overall development of marketing is weak, marketing seems more developed in electronics than in textile/garments. This is especially the case for computer firms. This is again explained by the unique start-up conditions characterising computer firms, and their consequent learning activities.

Third, within these general patterns of similarity and difference, there are some firm-specific tendencies. As can be seen from Tables 6.1 and 6.2, the study falls broadly into three groups in terms of the overall level of TC accumulation: average (with six points), above average and below average. In the textile/garment firms, average TC development tends to be evident among medium-size SOEs. Firms with above average TC are all SOEs, and those firms with weak TC development include a private one, a joint venture and some smaller SOEs. What does this suggest? Large SOEs (TG5, TG6 and TG10) with more resources may partly explain their superior TC development as compared with private companies. As for joint ventures, the passive reliance of the local firm on its foreign partner is the reason for this weakness. However, the size of firms is just one factor. Some SOEs of the same size still exhibit very different rates of TC accumulation (comparing TG10, TG12 and TG1, for instance). A similar phenomenon can be observed in electronics firms. Private firms have a rather spread-out distribution among the three levels of TC development. Most of the firms with stronger TCs are SOEs, with one private firm as the exception. This suggests that those firms with higher levels of TC accumulation tend to be SOE, in both industries. Private and joint venture firms tend to be weaker.

In this chapter, the book presented material from interviews conducted with 24 firms in two industries, regarding their TC accumulation. The first notable finding is the uneven development of

TC, which is also reported in the literature on TC acquisition (Bell & Pavitt, 1993; Katz et al., 1987). Across different sectors, patterns of TC accumulation follow different sequences, and firms differ in the extent of their TC development. So this chapter has confirmed proposition (1) that modes of TC creation are different in different sectors and firms. The main similarity is that most firms first acquire production capability, with the exception of computer firms which possess some minor technical change and marketing capabilities from their inception. In addition to sectoral differences, the impact of the historical context of firms' establishment on sub-sector characteristics appears to have had a strong influence on patterns of TC accumulation. This is what the concept of external environmental factors (Fransman, 1986c; Lall, 1987) has emphasised.

In addition to these findings, some firm-specific tendencies are found which relate to the firms' attitude to learning, and to issues of ownership. These issues will be explicated more clearly in the presentation of findings on external factors and firms' practice in Chapter 7 and 8.

The ranking of TC accumulation among firms and across different TCs is not in itself the end purpose of the study. Rather, this mapping of the technological landscape was used as a step towards addressing the next research question, on learning activities. Using this mapping, the interactions between the use of learning mechanisms and the emergent trends of TC accumulation identified in this chapter can be analysed. Accordingly, I now move to examine the second research question about the contribution of different learning mechanisms to various types of TC acquisition. The aim is to identify how this learning process has led to the accumulation of TC and, in this way, partly to explain the patterns of TC accumulation outlined in this chapter.

Note

1. Experiences based on previous visits to E10 and E11 in 1981 and then in 1984.

Table 6.1 Mapping of TC in textile/garment firms

	Investment	Production	Minor change	Marketing	Linkage	Major change	Total
Firms							
TG1	-	2	2	-	-	-	4
TG2	2	1	2	-	2	-	7
TG3	1	2	2	-	2	-	7
TG4	1	2	2	-	1	1	7
TG5	2	2	-	1	1	-	6
TG6	2	2	1	-	1	-	6
TG7	-	2	1	-	-	-	3
TG8	1	1	-	-	1	-	3
TG9	2	2	1	1	-	-	6
TG10	1	2	1	-	2	-	6
TG12	-	2	2	-	2	-	6
TG13	-	1	2	-	2	-	5
TG14	2	2	2	-	2	-	8
TG15	1	1	1	-	-	-	3
Total	15	24	19	2	16	1	

Key: (2) indicates strongly developed TC; (1) indicates weak TC; (-) indicates non-existence of TC

Source: this study

Table 6.2 Mapping of TC in electronics firms

Firms	Investment	Production	Minon change	Marketing	Linkage	Major change	Total
E1	-	2	2	-	-	-	4
E2	2	2	2	-	2	-	8
E3	1	-	2	1	2	-	6
E4	-	2	2	1	2	-	7
E5	-	2	-	1	1	-	4
E7	-	1	1	-	1	-	3
E8	-	1	-	-	-	-	1
E9	-	1	-	-	1	-	2
E10	2	2	2	-	2	-	8
E11	2	2	2	-	2	-	8
Total	7	15	13	3	13	0	

Key: (2) indicates strongly developed TC; (1) indicates weak TC; (-) indicates non-existence of TC

Source: this study

	Ownership	
	SOEs	Private firms
Time		
1960s	Production	Firms did not exist
	Minor change	
1970s	Linkage	Firms did not exist
1980s	Investment	Firms did not exist
1990s	Marketing (little)	Production
		Investment
		Minor change
	Major change (little)	Linkage
		Marketing
		Major change: none

Figure 6.1 Sequence of TC accumulation in textile/garment firms

	Sub-sectors	
Time	Consumer electronics	Computers
1970s	Production	Minor change (before)
1980s	Minor change	Marketing (before)
	Linkage	Production
1990s	Investment	Linkage
	Marketing: little	Investment: little
	Major change: none	Major change: none

Figure 6.2 Sequence of TC accumulation in electronics firms

7 Learning mechanisms and TC building

7.1 Patterns of learning in textile/garment companies

This section presents the learning patterns of textile and garment companies in relation to each specific TC.

7.1.1 Learning production capability

Since production capability is the first capability to be acquired by textile/garment firms and is also the most developed TC, I will begin by examining the learning mechanisms leading to this capability. Patterns of using learning mechanisms for production capability in textile/garment firms are shown in Table 7.1.

Three learning mechanisms are used by all companies. *Learning-by-doing* is used by all 14 cases. By operating machines and engaging in production activities, personnel learn in informal ways how to run industrial production in its simple forms. Learning-by-doing activities - such as self-study forms of learning, sharing experiences amongst workers, and the guiding of new workers by the more experienced - were mainly accomplished through the firms' own staff. Young and new workers were taught by those in the firm who had more skill and experience. Knowledge and experience were mostly informally diffused through working together, rather than by means of organised classes or courses. Sometimes, learning-by-doing activities significantly increased the experience of personnel, especially with respect to dealing with routine production tasks. At TG14, for example, through the increased knowledge and experience gained by just doing the work, some workers and technicians were even appointed as the heads of production groups within one workshop. At the same time, there was no firm that only used this learning-by-doing mechanism without supporting it with other more active forms of learning.

The use of *prior knowledge accumulation* was also active in all 14 cases. Companies hired people who had been educated in polytechnic institutes and who thus brought ideas to the firms on how to run production facilities. In addition, the firms recruited many Vietnamese graduates of Soviet or Eastern European universities whose degrees were predominantly in technical subjects such as textiles, mechanical engineering, energy and electrical systems. The companies also received some assistance from the MOI for training their workers as technicians. With some knowledge and work experience accumulated prior to joining the firms, these kinds of recruit brought learning elements to the firms, not only at the graduate level, but also at the level of workers and technicians who were trained in vocational schools for the textile industry.

All 14 firms used *foreign connections* as a learning mechanism for production capability. First, the firms received equipment, machinery and technical assistance from China and Eastern Europe during the 1960s and the 1970s. Contacts with foreign partners took different forms, ranging from simple subcontracting to more advanced OEM relations, by which companies gained access to markets and became involved (to differing extents) in exporting. For example, TG2 first received its knitting machines from China. From 1965 to 1970, it got some more knitting, dyeing and cotton-processing machines from East Germany. The company also received guidance and instruction for workers and technicians from those foreign experts who came with the equipment. Later, while upgrading their knitting facilities with foreign technologies, TG2 received technical assistance and guidance from the Japanese supplier, Sanshin. When TG2 linked up with the Japanese buyer, Kutakura, this firm transferred knitting technology into TG2 and included in that transfer was the Japanese way of organising production. To assist TG2, Kutakura sent two experts each year to Vietnam for six months and helped the local personnel to run the new production facility. This contract has continued for ten years. The Japanese also took part in discussions on production plans and other operative issues like quality control and the normative use of materials.

In all companies, foreign experts visited for various lengths of time (about six months to a year) to help Vietnamese staff in the installation and early maintenance activities of the project. Italian and German technology suppliers worked with TG3 and this firm sent six people to train for six months in Italy and Germany on how to run a turn-key project. Through these projects, Vietnamese staff gained production skills and knowledge from their foreign contacts. Similarly, TG4 received foreign technical assistance from a French partner which had supplied technology to the company. More than foreign expertise, technical documentation and information were also supplied as part of the framework of these turn-key projects. These sources were quite valuable to companies in learning elements of production capability like how to run new turn-key projects, how to deal with supplies of raw materials and other technical trouble-shooting, maintenance and repair issues.

Many firms used mechanisms like *on-the-job* (13 cases) and *off-the-job* (12 cases) training. On-the-job training was organised within firms by their own staff. For example, TG5 regularly organised activities where managers, technical employees and foremen met and discussed their experience of running the business. Subsequently, the lessons approved by the leadership of the plant, were widely communicated to all employees. After taking part in these activities, many workers were able to improve their qualifications in later exams. These activities were called "experience lessons" and they significantly raised the grade of employees' skills.[1]

The re-training of workers by dint of their employers sending them to schools and to attend courses organised by other firms, were popular in most of the companies. Almost all firms sent their personnel to various kinds of training course lasting from a couple of weeks to some months.[2] TG3 had a systematic training programme for hundreds of workers every year. TG10 set up a long-term plan to train their garment workers through courses ranging from 18 months to three years. Its goal was to upgrade the skills of all workers to a minimum skill level of Grade 3. Similarly, TG2 had a massive re-training programme for workers when it shifted from knitting to garment production. It had also organised special training programmes for about 300 newly-recruited workers. This programme had handled about 3,000 workers by 1995. Similar on-the-job and off-the-job training sessions were held at TG14 and TG13. Even private companies like TG8 - in spite of limited funding - organised courses on-site to train their workers, albeit on a smaller scale. Interestingly, at TG7, the joint venture could not organise its own training but depended on the foreign partner to do so.

Only seven companies used *searching information* and documentation sources, as well as consultancy services from R&D institutes and universities, for acquiring their production capability. The use of both official and informal linkages with R&D institutions and with other domestic companies received a strong impetus from the need to co-operate in problem-solving; material incentives were used (e.g., high fees for consultancy work) to promote such contacts.

As can be seen from Table 7.1, firms' use of learning mechanisms for acquiring production capability is very active. For this TC, accumulation of prior knowledge and foreign connections were the two most used learning mechanisms, in addition to learning-by-doing.

7.1.2 Learning investment capability

The overall pattern of learning investment capability is given in Table 7.2. The use of *foreign connections* occurred widely: 10 firms used this mechanism to get investment knowledge. At TG14, thanks to a subcontracting agreement with Hungarian buyers, the firm learned from them not only production, but also investment knowledge, e.g., how to purchase equipment, start up facilities and implement subcontracting. In garment company TG10, the subcontracting programme with the Soviet Union and East European countries brought a new foreign source of learning. This programme and its experts helped the firm to learn not only about production but also, and more importantly, about how to start a new venture. TG10 also gained insights into the international dimension of exporting on a large scale.

As private companies, TG8 and TG9 also relied heavily on their initial foreign connections for their start-up. TG8 was supported by the Japanese trading company, Nisho Iwai, on issues of technology supply, training, guidance and quality control. German and Hong Kong companies were active in the case of TG9. By working with these foreign partners, the firms learned how to prepare investment studies for new ventures.

Nine companies acquired their investment TC through *prior accumulation*. Graduates from institutes and universities brought investment knowledge to their new employers. Also, managers from other organisations have been recruited. TG10, for example, invited the help of an expert from the Institute of Design for Light Industry, who had extensive knowledge of pre-investment and investment studies, and of cost/benefit and other financial analyses. As head of the planning/financial division, her experience and knowledge were extremely valuable to the firm in its new investment activities.

On-the-job and *off-the-job training* were used quite actively by nine and seven companies respectively. These were mostly high-level training programmes for those managers, engineers and directors who had higher education degrees. These courses lasted from three months to 3-4 years of distance learning for university degrees. In some cases, senior managers - like the director of TG14 who had an engineering degree - took second degrees (in his case, economics). This training, augmenting their former backgrounds, enabled managers to learn new skills in management and investment. Sometimes, to save working time, instead of sending people to outside courses, the firms held in-house workshops and provided short-term intensive training on how to prepare investment application documents, feasibility studies, etc.

Only five cases used *information sources* such as expert advice and consultancy services for their investment learning. Some firms had access to documentation libraries, seminars and exhibitions which upgraded their knowledge and widened their information pool for engaging in investment activities. Concerning *learning-by-doing*, 13 out of 14 firms were engaged in some investment activities and thus learned from their various experiences of that process. By participating in the investment phase of projects, they increased their knowledge and experience of how to deal with investment problems. TG14, for instance, by repeatedly investing in and expanding its production facilities, have created a favourable environment for its managers to learn investment skills through doing. Particularly after the firm lost almost all its facilities due to a fire in 1979, TG14 engaged more actively in new investment to rehabilitate the firm during 1984-1985; it bought the whole street where the firm is now located as the new site for its production workshops. Through this learning-by-massively-investing, TG14 dramatically increased its competence at handling investment activities.

Three firms have done some learning-by-doing but still could not acquire investment capability due to either a lack of other mechanisms to support learning-by-doing (TG1 and TG13) or because as a joint venture (TG7) Vietnamese staff passively relied on their foreign partner to handle investment activity. TG12 did not have any investment capability due to lacking almost all learning mechanisms including learning-by-doing, training or using information. A foreign connection was the only mechanism used and this was not sufficient for the firm to acquire investment capability. Thus, these findings show that learning-by-doing has to be complemented by other more active mechanisms, especially training and foreign connections. In the case of TG13, even the use of information search was still not sufficient, since there were no training activities at the firm. This factor may indicate the importance of training and foreign connections over that of information search.

7.1.3 Learning minor technical change capability

The learning patterns for minor change capability are presented in Table 7.3. All 14 firms engaged in *doing* various minor technical improvements and adaptation. One example is TG3, which changed its production technology by replacing foreign imported spare parts with locally-produced ones (bolts, plugs, carriages, etc.). This was mostly accomplished by being involved in the technical improvement campaigns of the government.[3] Learning-through-doing minor change can also be seen in many other firms, in their process technology activities as well as in their (re)development of product specifications. Through repeated 'trial and error', firms became increasingly confident about initiating minor technical change activities.

Prior accumulation of knowledge and experience made an important contribution to minor change capability. With the exception of TG8, the 13 other companies gained the technical knowledge necessary for their minor improvement activities, knowledge that was embodied in recruited personnel.

About half of the firms used *on-the-job* (seven cases) and *off-the-job* (six cases) training. Co-operation with people from R&D institutions, universities (whether through formal contracts or informal contacts) brought the companies training courses and research and experimental facilities which they used for problem-solving. These activities were either organised on-site or they took the form of short courses to which firms sent their people.

Information collection and accessing consultants were used in seven cases. In TG2, for instance, competitions were organised annually or quarterly among personnel to increase skills and to identify "the most experienced workers". They also used the *CKT* movement (*Chat-luong:* good quality, *Kieu-dang:* beautiful design and *Tiet-kiem:* economy and reduction of cost) to promote suggestions on new initiatives. MOI and other management organisations helped the company to introduce this kind of campaign and thus to acquire some additional information. Then, the directorship and the company's trade union kept this activity going. Although this activity has not taken the form of a formal training course, it has proved crucial in augmenting the firm's capability at handling minor technical change.

One of the most notable features in minor change capability is the minimal use of *foreign connections*: only three cases have benefited from this mechanism. One of the few examples is TG1 (see Section 9.1). Usually, companies found it difficult to learn technical change expertise from their foreign partners, simply because the foreign contacts do not provide any of these. In majority, they did not see any experience, or skills applied by foreign partners in technical change activity. It is clearly evident in many cases of this study that foreign connections are not always a helpful source of learning technical change.

Table 7.3 also shows that TG8 had learning-by-doing as the only mechanism for learning how to manage minor change. It seems that this mechanism is not sufficient if a firm is to accumulate this TC. In the case of TG5, in addition to learning-by-doing, the firm only used one additional mechanism (prior accumulation). A sole reliance on the experience and knowledge previously accumulated by the firm's employees appears to be insufficient when no further training is available to develop the required knowledge and experience.

7.1.4 Learning marketing capability

The overall picture of learning patterns for developing marketing capability is provided in Table 7.4. Very few firms were able to learn marketing capability by any mechanism. The most frequently used mechanism was simple *by-doing* associated with some recent initial marketing activities. One of the firms with marketing capability, TG9, has tried to learn through increasing the rate of its OEM mode of production in total exports, as well as by opening an office in Moscow to market itself in the former Soviet Union. By 1990, the company had 10% of its production based on OEM for market economies, and 80% for Eastern European markets. Moreover, 10% of its total production began to bear its own trade label - a first step towards an OBM (own-brand manufacture) mode. These deliberate attempts to enter foreign markets gave the firm first-hand experience of success and failure in marketing.

TG1, TG3, TG4, TG10 and TG14 have all done some marketing activities, but this learning-by-doing was either unsupplemented by other mechanisms (TG1) or received little back-up from other mechanisms. At TG3, in addition to very limited by-doing, the firm uses information collection at trade fairs and exhibitions to gain marketing skills, but this activity has only recently been initiated. Even off-the-job training courses, like the one run by the Hanoi Economic University, are very new and are not systematic enough to bring marketing competence to the firm. A similar situation pertains at TG14, where the firm is quite a novice at marketing.

As for *prior accumulation*, few training institutions could provide graduates with knowledge and experience of marketing. *On-the-job training* and *foreign connections* were used by only two firms. The private firm, TG9, sent two people to South Korea to study international payment and finance. The reliance of this firm on foreign sources for marketing, in combination with other mechanisms, has proved crucial for their accumulation of marketing capability. However, examples like this are very rare.

Off-the-job training was used to some extent by six firms to develop marketing capability. Some companies sent their people to attend courses on business administration or marketing offered by universities and colleges. TG5 trained its staff through a specific course on marketing offered by the HoChiMinh City Council, and its director attended a short course given by the World Bank in Vietnam. TG9 sent its staff to attend courses offered by Vietnamese and international organisations on banking, economic management and marketing. These courses were short, but they gave the firm a more systematic knowledge of marketing to Western customers. *Information sources* were used by five firms to gain some knowledge of marketing: sending people to trade fairs, exhibitions, study tours, etc., both locally and abroad. Through attending these events, the firms got access to the latest sources of information about market trends.

Two cases displaying marketing capability were TG5 and TG9 which had combined learning-by-doing with other mechanisms in a systematic way. Next to learning-by-doing (through exporting to Japan), TG5's relations with its foreign partners moved from simple subcontracting to OEM. It also sent people on marketing courses, and gathered information through trips to the US. All these activities had a complimentary effect, bringing the firm confidence in marketing as well as relevant knowledge and experience. TG9 went further in acquiring this capability. What these two firms hold in common is the use of foreign connections to learn about marketing. Although a foreign connection did not necessarily lead to marketing capability, all cases which lacked this learning mechanism also lacked this capability. This is an indication of the importance of a foreign connection for acquiring marketing capability.

7.1.5 Learning linkage capability

As Table 7.5 shows, *prior accumulation* has been most helpful for developing linkage capability, while other mechanisms were used to a much lesser extent. Firms mainly acquired their linkages thanks to the relations of their staff with university colleagues, etc. These personal relationships became very important for firms in organising and using linkages with R&D institutes, universities and other firms. Other managers were assigned from MOI, where they had accumulated knowledge of the industry and forged external links with R&D units. These MOI personnel contributed to the accumulation of firms' capabilities, not only in technical but also in investment and linkage experience. In total, 10 firms used this mechanism to accumulate linkage competence. Thirteen companies were developing links with different organisations and institutions and so gained direct experience of how to get, and maintain, contacts effectively.

Four firms used *information search* and documentation as a learning tool - a mechanism that was used to a lesser extent than in the building of other capabilities. Just two or three firms made use of *on-the-job* or *off-the-job* training, and *foreign connections*. Some companies (e.g., TG2) used their personal contacts with Vietnamese living abroad (in France and the US) to establish foreign links.

7.1.6 Learning major technical change capability

Little can be said about the learning of major technical change capability since only TG4 has this capability to some extent. The experience of doing R&D has given the firm a better idea on how to organise R&D and how to deal with difficulties.

7.2 Main features and dynamics of learning in textile/garment firms

Some general points can be drawn on patterns of learning as shown in Tables 7.1 to 7.6. First, learning-by-doing is a must for all firms in all areas of TC. The examples of TG12 in investment, TG1 in linkage and many other firms in marketing confirm that, despite pursuing other active learning activities, these firms could not acquire TCs without learning-by-doing.

Second, however, learning-by-doing is not sufficient for the firms to acquire TC. This is illustrated by the cases where learning-by-doing was the only learning mechanism in use, for example investment in TG1 and TG7, minor change in TG8, marketing in TG1, and linkage in TG7. Moreover, even when learning-by-doing is supported by other learning mechanisms, some firms have still failed to build up the necessary TC. The evidence suggests that companies need more than one supplementary active form of learning to support learning-by-doing.

The third point is the tendency for certain combinations of learning mechanism to be associated with the acquisition of particular TCs. For each TC, there were differences in both the combination of mechanisms and in their ranking. More concretely, in addition to learning-by-doing, the general tendency to combine learning mechanisms can be seen as follows:

- For production capability: prior accumulation, foreign connections and on-the-job training.
- For investment capability: foreign connections, prior accumulation and off-the-job training.
- For minor technical change capability: prior accumulation, on-the-job training and information search and documentation.
- For marketing capability: off-the-job training, information search and prior accumulation.
- For linkage capability: prior accumulation and information search.
- For major technical change capability: prior accumulation and information search.

The patterns of learning presented here, however, did not appear all at once. The use of learning mechanisms - in terms of their type and source - is not static but changes over time. It took decades for these firms to come to their present situation.

The dynamics of this learning process can be seen through periods of industrial development. As the first period of industrial development did not have any significant impact on this industry, the last three periods will be examined. As seen in Figure 7.1, over these periods, the learning mechanisms that firms have invoked have changed in their contents and sources and in their contribution to acquiring different TCs.

7.2.1 Before unification: 1946-1975

Companies TG1, TG2, TG12, TG10 and TG13 were set up in this period (mostly between 1960 and 1975). They received investment from the state and engaged in the planned production that implied. Some initial export of simple garments (TG1 and TG10) was arranged by subcontracting agreements between Vietnam and socialist countries. In this period, the only capability the companies began to acquire was production and only by very simple means of learning: by-doing and on-the-job training such as courses organised by ministerial organisations. These learning mechanisms, in addition to production experience, introduced basic technical knowledge that proved useful for technical change activities. Prior to 1975, the firms' main learning sources were their first foreign suppliers or buyers, coming from China, the Soviet Union and Eastern Europe. Prior accumulation also came through the assignment of managers from outside the firms. Off-the-job training and information collection were almost non-existent in this period.

7.2.2 Pre-reform period: 1976-1986

This period witnessed the expansion of many new production facilities. Companies TG3, TG5 and TG6 set up in this period and TG4, TG14 and TG15 were established after the unification of the country in 1976. These companies mostly received new investment through technology transfer from industrialised countries, as well as technical assistance from their foreign connections. The format of connections shifted from simple subcontracting to more active relations such as OEM, where companies received materials and designs from buyers and sent them back their products. Sources of foreign contacts became more diversified. Using new technology supplied from Western countries, many firms began to work in Eastern European markets, particularly through subcontracting agreements for garment products. In addition to production knowledge, early investment experience became available to the firms through their foreign connections. Prior accumulation through massive recruitment from universities and polytechnics brought to the firms the technical knowledge crucial for their production and minor technical change capabilities, together with an increased ability to link with academic institutions. In some firms, like TG12, recruiting from universities became a strong tradition and has continued each year since the firm's inception.

On-the-job and off-the-job training were actively used in this period. Direct contact with R&D institutions - permitted since 1981-1982 - further contributed to the ability of companies to carry out minor technical improvements and production activities. However, these courses contributed primarily to mastering technical issues and the same technical orientation of this period can be seen in the use of information sources. In addition to production, firms found more opportunities to engage in minor change, linkage, and investment activities within the context of learning-by-doing.

7.2.3 The reforms: after 1986

The reforms of 1986 heralded many radical changes for companies, including the emergence of non-SOEs such as private firms (TG8 and TG9) and joint ventures (TG7). This period has been characterised by companies making much more conscious efforts to acquire TCs. The means they have used to achieve their aims are also wide-ranging.

Although foreign connections continue to be an important mechanism throughout this period, earlier connections with the Soviet and East European markets are being replaced by connections with the Asia-Pacific economies and the EU. Further, the form of foreign connections is moving from simple subcontracting relations to more active participation by Vietnamese firms in producing value-added through OEM and ODM relations. In some cases, the move is even to an OBM mode of production for the less sophisticated markets of the former Soviet Union and Eastern Europe. This mechanism has helped firms to learn modern production technology, new investment skills, ways of organising linkages and even, in some cases, marketing knowledge.

On-the-job and off-the-job training mechanisms appear to have both new advantages and disadvantages. Thanks to changes in the R&D system, firms have easier access to new sources for their training needs. Following reform, the need to re-train staff has shifted from a concern with merely technical matters to non-technical fields like business administration and economic management. Although firms now require non-technical knowledge like investment more than they previously did, it is still more difficult to access support from the S&T, training and education infrastructure for help in non-technical as opposed to technical affairs. Training courses are provided on a smaller scale, and more selectively focused in terms of subjects. The training of workers has become more difficult than before due to a loss of subsidised funding. Nevertheless, firms now enjoy more favourable conditions for tapping into new learning sources such as collecting information and documentation. Contact with R&D and other supporting organisations is becoming more flexible and business-oriented, allowing for easier circulation of information.

The main difficulty of the reform period is in recruiting personnel who can contribute through their prior accumulation of TC. Because of funding shortages, recruitment is small-scale, cautious and selective. The shift to a more non-technical focus in recruitment has also strengthened in this period and thus some additional investment and marketing expertise has been gained. Learning-by-doing in this period has extended to newer activities such as developing new ventures and engaging in R&D and marketing. Thus, the radical changes of the reform period are having a significant impact on the use of different learning mechanisms.

7.3 Learning patterns in electronics companies

7.3.1 Learning production capability

The overall pattern of using learning mechanisms for production capability is provided in Table 7.7, where we can see that three companies - E1, E2 and E9 - used all the learning mechanisms in their accumulation of this capability. Foreign connections and prior accumulation were the two mechanisms most used by firms. Nine out of 10 cases used *foreign connections* to accumulate their production capability.

The first time Vietnamese electronics companies (E10 and E11) used foreign connections as their learning source for production was in the 1970s with the setting up of subsidiaries of Japanese consumer electronics firms in what was then South Vietnam. Some technical assistance was provided together with equipment to guide Vietnamese technicians and workers on how to use the technology and organise production. Later other firms received guidance from Japanese experts in installing and starting-up assembly lines. Foreign connections were crucial for firms in acquiring knowledge on how to operate the technology and how to deal with various production issues such as materials supply, operating routines, maintenance of equipment and quality control.

In the 1980s, Czechoslovakian experts came to the companies providing technical guidance, quality control, and maintenance of the technology to produce condensers. At E10 and E11, two different Czech companies of the same group, TESLA, supplied them with input materials and other technical assistance for producing electronics components. Polytechna - a Czech training service company - at the request of TESLA, provided training programme for the staff in these two companies. Hundreds of people were sent to Czechoslovakia for training.

E11, through its most recent foreign connection, again learned from the Japanese firms, Sony and JVC. Each year, the firm has sent several groups of personnel to Japan (three or four people at a time for trips lasting up to a fortnight) to learn the organisational skills needed for producing Japanese TVs. At the same time, both JVC and Sony seconded experts to E11 on a regular basis to assist with the production and management of assembly (Sony sending people every month, and JVC once for a couple of months). These experts stayed from two to three months each time to help supervise production, using Sony's procedures on inventory and quality control and JVC's sales techniques to advise on local marketing. With the help of Sony, E11 has adopted the system of daily checking in combination with flexible personnel management. By doing so, the productivity of the firm in assembling TVs has increased six fold: before using Sony's method, the firm could only produce 50 TVs per day over two shifts; afterwards, it assembled 300 TVs per day. To ensure the quality of the product, some products were chosen randomly to be sent back to Japan for higher quality testing. As a result, E11 also gained experience of quality control.

Among the computer companies, E5 acquired production capability in a joint venture with Bull. E4, in order to start assembling PCs, relied on the foreign technological expertise of Taiwanese suppliers. Although the suppliers did not take any direct part in assembly activities, their advice and knowledge were available to E4 through discussion and exchange of information. E8 was the only case that did not have foreign connections and it had to rely on local experience gathered through prior accumulation or through its network of informants.

Prior accumulation was used by nine firms to develop production capability, through massive recruitment of graduates from the polytechnics and universities. In addition, managers coming from other organisations have introduced valuable knowledge and experience of production activities. E1, E2 at their start up, E11 after rehabilitation and E10 have all received support from the Ministry (see VEIC) or the local city councils in terms of personnel. They received many radio electronics and mechanical engineers for jobs in various divisions and workshops. Many key managers of the firms (directors, heads of divisions) came from R&D and education organisations. Similar prior accumulation of knowledge and experience occurred at other computer firms through recruiting people from IOIT and other research institutes (E3, E4, E5 and E9).

Learning-by-doing occurred in nine firms. At E10 and E11, after standing idle for a couple of years at the end of the 1970s, the production of components came back in a subcontracting agreement with TESLA. Growing through this activity, unlike the previous situation of working for Japanese firms as their subsidiaries, managers of E10 and E11 have learnt more about running a business independently, especially in relation to exporting. Workers and technicians who acquired knowledge and experience as former employees of the Japanese subsidiaries were able to learn the new activity of producing components. Assembly activity at the Northern firms E1 and E2, and electronics services at E7 opened up the opportunity for these firms to practice their operational skills. At first, E1 and E2 only learned how to produce with CKD components - the easiest mode of production. After three or four years, they moved to undertake more complicated production operations like SKD component assembly. The same 'trial and error' process was evident in computer firms dealing with PC assembly, particularly in maintaining quality through various kinds of product testing.

For production capability, between six and eight cases used *on-the-job* and *off-the-job* training, and *information search.* Courses were offered by R&D institutes and polytechnics, mostly on technical topics related to radio electronics and computer science.

7.3.2 Learning investment capability

The companies gained less investment knowledge and experience as compared with production and this pattern is shown in the Table 7.8. Non-technical learning has been implemented widely at many firms through *doing* (nine out of 10 cases). Experience was gained by staff through investing in various new ventures (E2, E3, E11 and E7). Almost all firms have recently expanded their production facilities, thus providing them with a chance to experience some of the difficulties of investment, and to learn how to solve problems and avoid mistakes.

Five cases (E1, E4, E7, E8 and E9) have done some learning-by-doing but could not acquire this capability due to a lack of other supporting mechanisms. Besides learning-by-doing, E7 and E8 only collected some information and documentation for investment knowledge and did not offer or avail of any training. Similarly, E9 had some minimal off-the-job training to support its by-doing mechanism.

However, this mechanism was too formal (some seminars, a meeting at the directors' club, etc.) to be effective for acquiring this capability. E5 as a joint venture with a French company did not have investment capability due to lack of learning-by-doing and other training measures, in spite of its foreign connection.

Only five firms accumulated investment knowledge through *prior accumulation* (E3, E2, E4, E10 and E11) where their managers had worked and studied before joining those firms. For example, E3's managers accumulated their investment knowledge while working for a joint venture firm (see E3 in Section 10.5).

The companies have also gathered investment knowledge by cooperating with foreign experts in their new investments (assembling Japanese and Korean TVs in E1, and new sample production of industrial robotic parts for Japanese companies in E2). Most commonly, they acquired this knowledge through discussion with foreign technology suppliers, and by sending a few people abroad for short study tours financed by the foreign partner. Similarly, E5 learned how to start a joint venture from its French partner (although this connection was not sufficient for the firm to acquire its own investment capability).

Off-the-job training was used by six firms. Thanks to recent opportunities offered by economic institutes and universities, the firms sent some key staff to take part in these courses. This was easier than organising courses on-site, where they would have had to take responsibility for organising the whole programme. These courses were on import/export procedures (E7), investment studies (E9 and E10) and financing (E11). In order to learn about investment and purchasing, E1 sent some of its Hanoi staff to work for periods in other Southern firms in HoChiMinh City (E10 and E11), which have experience of expanding production facilities.

In contrast, no firm could use *on-the-job* training to learn about investment and only four firms used *information search*. For example, E1 acquired its investment knowledge (planning, cost-benefit analysis, etc.) by co-operating with local consultants.

Table 7.8 again reveals that learning-by-doing is the first and necessary condition for acquiring investment capability, but it is not sufficient in itself. In addition, looking at a combination of learning mechanisms, the firms with this capability share one thing in common: the combination of prior accumulation with foreign connections.

7.3.3 Learning minor technical change capability

The pattern of acquiring minor change expertise is rather similar to that of learning production capability. Table 7.9 shows that eight companies used *learning-by-doing*. In these companies, participation in R&D

programmes organised by other institutions, state organisations or by themselves significantly increased the skill base of the companies. Almost all companies engage in R&D activities, either in specialised R&D units, or as part of a technical division.

The *prior accumulation* mechanism was used by nine cases. As mentioned earlier, a specific feature of electronics firms is that they first began as research and teaching enterprises, especially in computing. When these firms began commercial activity, they had immediate access to R&D and technical expertise through the personnel of universities and R&D institutions. For example, E1 started in 1970 as a laboratory doing research on electronics technologies. When this laboratory was transformed into a firm in accordance with the change of the whole Viettronics group, E1 was able to use the laboratory's personnel as its first prior accumulation of technical expertise. In E10, the director was educated in electronics in Hungary. After graduation, he stayed in Hungary to work for a year in the electronics industry, and spent another two years in a group of electronics trade service companies. On his return to Vietnam, he worked for the first electronics laboratory of the Ministry of Heavy Industry (now MOI). When E10 began its rehabilitation in HoChiMinh City, he was placed in charge of this company where he continued his accumulation of knowledge by reading documents left by Matsushita, and by co-working with its former employees.

In computer firms, technical personnel, scientists and lecturers working in R&D organisations accumulated both theoretical and practical knowledge of computing. This knowledge was one of their most important assets when they became managers dealing with the technical aspects of a computer business. Almost from the start, these manager-scientists knew how to deploy their pre-existing knowledge of minor technical adjustments to create new computer models. Managers of these firms were all educated abroad in Eastern Europe. After graduation, they stayed in these countries and worked in R&D institutes or computer firms before going back to Vietnam. This prior accumulation has been augmented by their work experience gathered in Vietnamese R&D institutes (NCSR, the laboratory of Ministry of Defence, etc).

Unlike textile/garment companies, some electronics firms were able to utilise their *foreign connections* to learn about technical change. Although only five companies used this mechanism, it is second only to prior accumulation in importance.

Other mechanisms like *on-the-job*, and *off-the-job* training were used to a lesser extent (only four cases used each mechanism). In training activities, R&D institutions and universities played an important role. Hanoi Polytechnic and its Radio Electronics Faculty has regularly supplied instructors for courses at E1, E2 and E7. These courses are for both large classes of workers and technicians, and for small short-duration classes (one or two days). For example, E7 has sometimes held classes for only two people so as to tackle very specific technical problems. In the South, E10 and E11 relied on the courses of HoChiMinh City polytechnic for knowledge on the technical aspects of electronics such as radio frequencies and how to adjust different functions of audio-visual equipment. These courses were more useful for production and minor change activities than for other TCs. *Information search* was only used by four companies.

As presented in Table 7.9, E8 was unable to acquire minor change capability since it did not invoke any other mechanisms beyond learning-by-doing. Two firms (E5 and E9) did not even do any learning-by-doing in respect of this TC. Although they had some prior accumulation and even had support of foreign connections (E9), this was not enough for them to acquire the minor change capability.

7.3.4 Learning marketing capability

The patterns for learning marketing are given in Table 7.10. Interestingly, all companies were able to gain their first experience of marketing through *doing* various marketing activities. After 1986, all firms expanded or organised networks of sale points (shops and showrooms) which proved useful to their learning of marketing. For example, E4 in this period tried to sell its products (PCs and software) not only in the former markets of Russia and France, but in some new ones such as neighbouring Cambodia.

Firms made little use of other learning mechanisms. *Prior accumulation* was only used in three computer firms (E3, E4 and E5). Some of the would-be managers of computer firms have worked in various state trading and financial organisations, and have acquired a sound knowledge of the Soviet market, and of its strengths and weaknesses, and some financial know-how on how to do business in this specific arena. E4's director was educated and worked in France for many years before coming back to Vietnam. His expertise encompasses not only technical knowledge, but also knowledge of the French market which is important to the company as they produce software for French users.

This kind of prior accumulation played a very important role in these computer firms' acquisition of marketing capability. This factor explains why these computer firms saw from the beginning how to exploit the Soviet market for computer products successfully.

Four firms used *foreign connections* to learn about marketing. While selling software products to French and Japanese customers, E4 learned more about how to overcome the standardisation barriers against entering these markets. Further, the company has strong support from the Chamber of Commerce and the Industry of Versailles (through its director's long-term French network) to advertise its products and promote sales activities in France. In addition, the use of contacts with Vietnamese expatriates is an effective way to gather knowledge and information, as in the case of E4.

Not surprisingly, given the lack of marketing expertise in R&D, training and education institutes, training mechanisms were not used very much for acquiring this capability. Only two firms used *on-the-job* training, while three used *off-the-job* training.

Five firms used *information search* and consultancy sources to develop their marketing capability. Initially, the main market for computer firms was the former Soviet Union, so they needed knowledge about how to operate in this market. The role of internal linkages was very important: companies either have their own or external groups of experts working in the Ministry of Finance, the Vietnam Foreign Trade Bank, export-import companies, the Ministry of Trade and Ministry of Industry, etc. In interview, companies were reluctant to talk about the activities of these financial, monetary and maybe even political networks. One of the likely reasons was the competitive need to keep this marketing know-how secret. Information collecting about marketing also comes from customers who provide rapid feed-back on defect rates, market trends and specific requirements.

In sum, in all three cases having marketing expertise (E3, E4 and E5), this capability was acquired thanks to combining learning-by-doing with other learning mechanisms, of which prior accumulation was the most effective. Although the use of foreign connections and information and documentation mechanisms was more in evidence than prior accumulation, these two mechanisms did not help firms to acquire marketing competence if they lacked prior accumulation as was the case in E9 and E11. This factor may indicate that prior accumulation was the most important mechanism for marketing in electronics firms. Even some training in E1, E7, E9 and E10 was not enough for these firms to obtain marketing capability.

7.3.5 Learning linkage capability

Patterns for this capability are shown in Table 7.11. *By-doing* and *prior accumulation* were used by most firms (10 cases). Prior involvement in laboratories was crucial for firms' managers to develop linkages as well as to acquire production and minor improvement TCs. For instance, the directors of E1 and E11 were senior staff in the first national laboratory of electronics. Relations between E7's director, and his former classmates and teachers (the director of E2 had been his professor at Hanoi Polytechnic) had a similar effect on linkage development.

In contrast, no firm used any training to gain this capability. Hence, the general tendency is for linkages to be learned mostly through work experience and through contacts that firms developed during their activities. The use of *foreign connections* and *information sources* occupied the mid-ground. The active involvement of foreign partners in the firms' activities helped them gain experience in developing international linkages.

As for *information sources*, informal and personal contacts among academics (people still doing research and teaching, and former academics who are now managers in business) were the most effective means for acquiring and developing linkage capability (in addition to minor change). This informal network of scientists in electronics has kept co-operation alive. Activities undertaken under the auspices of the Association of Informatics and Microelectronics also contribute to co-operation in the context of the quite small community in this field. This personal network of contacts became even more important in three computer firms - E3, E4 and E5 - which started up on the basis of their accumulated capability.

An interesting feature of developing linkage capability is that all 10 firms had very similar ways of using four mechanisms: all have used learning-by-doing and prior accumulation, while none have used training activity for linkage competence building. Thus, the main difference was in the use made of foreign connections and information sources. Eight firms with this capability used one or both of these mechanisms. However, the foreign connection seems to be more important than the use of local networks of information and consulting. Again, this points to the significance of combining various learning mechanisms as we saw in the accumulation of other TCs such as prior accumulation and foreign connections in investment capability.

7.3.6 Learning major technical change capability

Table 7.12 shows that firms hardly used any mechanisms to learn this capability. Only two cases (E3 and E10) used learning-by-doing, even though no cases have this capability. E3 was the only company to have an information and consulting network to support learning-by-doing in this area. Although this firm has still not acquired this capability, it is progressing rather actively from minor change towards more major technical change activity. To a lesser extent, thanks to active minor technical change, E2 might also develop a major change capability.

7.4 Main features and dynamics of learning in electronics firms

The patterns of learning in electronics firms confirm some of the findings for textile/garment firms. First is the necessity of learning-by-doing without which some firms were not able to obtain TC, even where other learning mechanisms were used (e.g., investment in E5, minor change in E9). At the same time, the learning patterns of electronics firms also confirm the need for other learning mechanisms to support learning-by-doing. This point can be seen in investment in E7, E8 and E9; minor change in E8; and marketing in E2, E7, E8, E10 and E11. In general, learning-by-doing must be supported by several other learning mechanisms.

The second finding supported by evidence from electronics firms is the need for particular combinations of learning mechanisms to build up TCs. In general, the combinatory tendencies are as follows:

- For production capability: prior accumulation, foreign connections and on-the-job training.
- For investment capability: prior accumulation, off-the-job training and foreign connections.
- For minor change: prior accumulation, and to a lesser extent, foreign connections.
- For marketing capability: foreign connections, information search and prior accumulation.
- For linkage capability: prior accumulation (relations, connections), foreign contacts and information search.
- For major change: nothing was used.

Figure 7.2 shows the dynamic use of learning modes in electronics firms during the three periods of Vietnamese industrial development. Depending on the specific conditions and circumstances of each period, learning mechanisms changed in terms of sources, technical foci and their differing contributions to various TCs.

7.4.1 Before unification: 1946-1975

In this period, there were no electronic companies in the North. Most electronics activities were in training and in applying technological equipment. In the South, only two firms were set up in 1974 as subsidiaries of Japanese consumer electronics giants: E10 (Matsushita Vietnam) and E11 (Sony Vietnam). Both firms got their technological equipment from Japanese suppliers to assemble black-and-white TV sets and radios for the local market. For a short time, they acquired some production experience. Unfortunately, after the war ended in 1975, the owners and most of the technical staff left the country. Thus, in this period, any production experience of former employees at E10 and E11 was limited and was gathered mostly through their first foreign connections and their learning-by-doing operations. No other mechanisms were used for learning.

7.4.2 Pre-reform period: 1976-1986

Most Northern companies such as E1, E2 and E7 were created in the 1980s. As SOEs set up by Hanoi City (E2) or by the Ministry of Heavy Industry (E1 and E7), these firms got their technology through agreements with Japanese suppliers to produce TV sets (black-and-white and colour), radios and amplifiers, mostly for the domestic market. For many firms, JVC was the main supplier of equipment, input materials (CKD components) and technical assistance.

After unification of the country in 1976, E10 and E11 became SOEs and received some support from the state to reactivate their production. Eastern European experts supported these companies in building up their production expertise and in exporting to Eastern European markets. Although the first attempt at exporting turned out to be short-lived (the firms ended their subcontracting relationship with TESLA in 1987), foreign connections had helped them accumulate technological experience, which was then further developed through production activities. The connection with the Japanese suppliers of assembly facilities for TV and other consumer goods continued.

Training activities at the firms in this period have been held both on-the job and through sending people to off-the-job training courses offered by other organisations like the polytechnics and universities. Reliance of the companies on information search, documentation collection and consultancy services was not very marked up to the middle of the 1980s. Most sources of information used by companies such as conferences, workshops and seminars were organised by the Ministry and the VEIC and were mostly geared to addressing the technical problems of the consumer electronics industry. Literature sources like journals, books and blueprints obtained by companies concentrated on a few issues like radio electronics, and the production of consumer products. These sources of learning were only useful for production and minor change capabilities of the firms.

Learning-by-doing activity increased in this period, however, and was not limited to production skills, but also was evident in minor technical adjustment activities. Various minor improvements have been taking place in almost all firms, mostly thanks to supporting campaigns organised in SOEs.

7.4.3 The reforms: after 1986

Five companies were created in this period (E3, E4, E5 and E9) specialising in computer business and related services, and one - E8 - set up as a small firm producing simple consumer electronics. The creation of these firms reflects a very special feature of this period: the more active appearance of a private sector and of foreign investment. E8 originated as a family business doing some subcontracting jobs in simple electronics like PCB or loud speakers assembly. E3 and E4 were also share-holding private firms set up by scientists who formerly worked in other companies or state organisations. E5 was a joint venture between VEIC and a French company.

The learning dynamics of computer firms appear to be somewhat different from those of consumer electronics. Research and teaching in computer science and application activities have been developed widely in R&D institutes, universities and polytechnics. Through working in this environment, or in other companies before setting up their own firms, the managers of E3, E4 and E5 accumulated strong background knowledge and experience. This prior accumulation continued in the reform period through selective recruitment. Although consumer electronics did use prior accumulation, computer firms used it much more extensively. In this period, many scientists working in R&D institutions and universities moved out and set up the first industrial basis to the sector. They took with them experience and knowledge (in marketing and in minor technical change) accumulated prior to setting up the firms, and these became the earliest assets of the computer firms.

The use of foreign connections by firms occurred first in the assembly of simple consumer electronics, then moved to industrial and service businesses, and later computer assembly came into play. Sources of foreign learning moved from mainly Eastern European countries and the Soviet Union to Asian firms in Taiwan and Korea, while Japanese firms continued to be an important source. In addition to production knowledge, foreign connections helped electronics firms to learn investment, linkage and to a lesser extent marketing activities. This suggests two points. One is the significance of foreign connections for all the TCs except the technical change capability. Second, it shows the important impact of the reforms which exposed Vietnamese companies to new external learning sources.

There was not much change in training mechanisms. Although off-the-job training switched from technical to non-technical content, no change happened in on-the-job training. The move from technical to non-technical experience can also be seen in the use made of the learning-by-doing mechanism. While firms continued to learn by doing technical exercises, they obtained greater opportunities to gain experience of doing new things in investment or marketing.

In the reform period, the use of the information, documentation and consulting learning mechanism became more intensive, and relied more on the informal network of personal contacts among scientists, researchers, lecturers and managers of the firms. This mechanism also brought new expertise to the firms in investment, linkage and marketing affairs.

The overall picture of electronics firms in this period shows the expansion of the scope and content of technological expertise, and the knowledge and experience of firms. Expansion and diversification also occurred in the use of various learning mechanisms and firms began to combine mechanisms more intensively.

7.5 Findings and comparisons

7.5.1 Learning mechanisms

The first issue concerns the learning mechanisms and their formats and sources and the difficulties or ease of their use. Evidence of firms show that learning-by-doing is vital to TC acquisition in all areas. This learning-by-doing usually gave firms a chance to engage in 'trial and error'. It is the making of mistakes, and the lessons learnt from these mistakes, that are the most important ingredients in a firm's learning-by-doing. The knowledge and experience gained through learning-by-doing is not a systematic or codified knowledge, it does not exist in a training textbook. Just by repetitive doing (mostly through routines) firms could identify patterns worth repeating and habits best avoided. Moreover, the by-doing actively occurred in firms both before and after the technological and production systems of the project were installed. As Bell & Pavitt (1993) and Fleck (1991) have emphasised, this learning-by-active-doing is the starting point for learning, and it continues to be significant thereafter .

It might be argued that this learning-by-doing is passive and just happens anyway whether firms promote it or not. In fact, to be able to learn something from this simple by-doing, Cohen and Levinthal (1990) suggest the importance of a firm's absorptive capacity. In order to identify a pattern, or draw a conclusion from mistakes, the firm must first have had a certain basic level of accumulated knowledge, both technical and non-technical, before they can solely rely on learning-by-doing. In some cases this knowledge may even be highly-sophisticated and science-based. In computer firms E3, E4, and E5, doing minor change activity in designing software and organising R&D depended very much on their prior knowledge of computer science. Similarly, for TG4 to carry out research on microfibre it had to have a sound knowledge of chemistry and materials science. Without this previously accumulated knowledge, these firms could not do any simple R&D, nor upgrade it later. However, in these cases, prior accumulation mostly referred to their technical knowledge. This factor is explained by the weakness of the training and education environment in Vietnam, which failed to provide firms with sufficient non-technical knowledge and experience. For a long time, the courses and activities necessary for developing non-technical knowledge in investment and marketing did not exist.

The technical orientation of other mechanisms like on-the-job and off-the-job training as well as information sources is also evident. Training courses usually provide knowledge in systematic ways (through reviews, theories and summaries) and give firms some basic know-why types of knowledge. Know-why knowledge is not usually gained through learning-by-doing. Firms' experience shows that these training activities reflect strong technical biases, as was the case in training courses for learning minor technical change in the textile/garment industry. Similarly, information sources had a predominantly technical content. The above mentioned weakness of training and education institutions is observed in the use of information for investment capability, and the use of training for marketing in both industries. In the context of a planned subsidised economy, knowledge such as market economics, business administration and marketing were neglected and, when reforms came, this system was not in a position to offer firms the required knowledge. In order to compensate for the lack of formal training in non-technical knowledge, firms had to rely more heavily on their experience of doing things and on very ad-hoc training and education opportunities. For example, the textile/garment firms used ad-hoc off-the-job courses in the marketing of textiles and garments, and electronics firms used learning-by-doing to gain some investment competence.

The network of personal relations and contacts plays a significant role for both kinds of firm in how they use information. This was particularly strongly emphasised by many firms using connections previously accumulated (in universities, R&D institutes, polytechnics, etc.) for developing linkages and receiving information. In some cases, like marketing in electronics firms, these personal contacts proved crucial. In order to substitute for the weaknesses of formal training, they relied on the experience and information informally supplied by their colleagues and friends (E3, E4 and E5 are examples).

The foreign connections mechanism helped firms to learn about topics related to foreign sources: technologies, markets, financial payment procedures, investment skills, etc. So, this learning can be both technical and non-technical. However, this mechanism was used rather more actively for learning production and investment capabilities than for learning other TCs. The reasons for this were quite simple. In technology transfer agreements, foreign partners were keen to help Vietnamese firms handle their production operations in order to ensure a good supply of products for the foreign partner's markets. Later, they wanted to support their Vietnamese partners in acquiring some investment skills to further develop business in a local market from which they might also benefit. To maintain a good business relationship with local partners was another reason for foreign firms to cooperate with Vietnamese firms in activities other than production. But at this point, foreign involvement stopped. The evidence from the majority of companies in the study reveals little involvement from foreign partners in helping them learn technical change knowledge and skill, even at the minor change level. The same can be said for marketing. Although the firms in both industries confirmed that they knew how important foreign contacts were in learning marketing, it was difficult for them to forge contacts and use them effectively to learn marketing. This tendency contributed heavily to the weak level of marketing capability in both industries. There is not sufficient evidence to conclude that this weakness is caused by the deliberate unwillingness of foreign partners to help firms learn these two capabilities. However, the lack of foreign assistance in learning technical change and marketing is so overwhelming in most cases that the suggestion remains that this is very likely the case.

In addition to the unwillingness of foreign partners to help Vietnamese firms develop their relationship beyond simple subcontracting, there may be two further explanations for the weakness of using foreign connections to learn the above mentioned capabilities. One explanation for this unbalanced use of foreign connections may be that for a long time Vietnam only had access to one group of foreign learning sources: the CMEA countries. As has been emphasised earlier, because the relationship between Vietnam and the CMEA countries was based on central planning, this limited Vietnamese firms to quite poor sources of learning about the marketing skills most suitable to exploiting new types of market. Another reason is the inability of Vietnamese firms to absorb the technical assistance offered by foreign companies. The use of foreign connections as a learning mechanism, however, is not identical for the two industries. Electronics companies were able to use their foreign contacts to greater effect than textile/garment companies were. This different pattern of using learning mechanisms can be understood more clearly in the context of sectoral differences.

Examining learning mechanisms, one can see the inter-relatedness of these mechanisms. For instance, prior accumulation of knowledge in a foreign university can equally be understood as prior accumulation of a foreign connections mechanism, as was the case with

E10's director. Thus, distinctions made between learning mechanisms should only be seen as relative distinctions.

In sum, some learning mechanisms appear to be more difficult to deploy than others. As can be seen above, this difficulty is explained by weaknesses in the training, education and R&D system; by Vietnam's historic specific market orientation; and by the types of relation pertaining between Vietnam and its foreign partners. The impact of factors relating to the external environment in which firms operate will be looked at in Chapter 8. The learning mechanisms used also varied somewhat according to which TC was being acquired, as is discussed below.

7.5.2 Relationship between learning and T C accumulation

There has been observed the tendency to combine different learning mechanisms for acquiring each type of TC. However, in order to identify a relationship between learning mechanisms and TC accumulation within the firms, it is necessary to examine only those firms having the relevant TC. This closer examination shows the contribution (i.e., the frequency of use) of various learning mechanisms in generating specific TCs and these patterns are presented in two tables, 7.13 and 7.14, for textile/garment and electronics firms respectively.

Tables 7.13 and 7.14 reveal that all TCs are accumulated in some measure as a result of learning-by-doing. No firms having TCs omit to use learning-by-doing. However, this learning mechanism is necessary, but not sufficient, for the acquisition of a TC. As emphasised above, not all cases which use the learning-by-doing mechanism emerge with TCs. Concerning other learning mechanisms, the following can be seen:

- In both textile/garment and electronics firms, prior accumulation is the most important mechanism for *all TC*s, but less so for *marketing* and *major change*. This mechanism contributes to all cases having investment, production, minor change and linkage capabilities. This is understandable since new recruits (whether new graduates or experienced managers) bring previously accumulated experience and knowledge and thus help firms to begin production, expand investment, and initiate minor improvements. This prior accumulation is very useful for developing linkages; contacts (often personal) between alumni play a rather important role. This feature is even more significant for electronics firms which sprang from the teaching and research environment. All their experience is accumulated in large part through various kinds of training and working in other organisations before moving into the industry.

- On-the-job training is more important in both textile/garment and electronics firms for acquiring *production*, and to some extent *minor change* capabilities, but is less significant for the acquisition of other TCs. One reason is that instructors invited to the firms offer courses (mainly technical in content) which are more useful for production and minor change although, more recently, course contents have shifted to non-technical topics like management and investment studies. When it comes to marketing, the R&D institutions, universities and training schools lack the expertise to provide firms with the necessary teachers and curricula.

- The pattern of using off-the-job training is rather similar across the two sectors. This mechanism is important mostly for *production*, and less so for the *minor change* capability. For non-technical learning, off-the-job training seems to be somewhat used for *investment*, but very little for *marketing*. The situation is quite similar to that of on-the-job training, where the weakness in the R&D and training infrastructure means that it cannot serve the learning needs of firms on non-technical matters. A further similarity between these two training mechanisms is that they do not contribute significantly to linkage and major change capabilities. Despite the overall weakness of training and education institutions in offering non-technical knowledge, of the two training mechanisms it seems off-the-job training tends to be more frequently used than on-the-job training for learning the non-technical topics related to investment and marketing.

- In textile/garment firms, foreign connections proved to be very useful for *production* and to a lesser extent for *investment* and *linkage* capabilities. This mechanism only makes a small contribution to both minor and major technical change capabilities. Only a few firms which had close relations with a foreign buyer (TG14) or a partner (in joint venture TG7) used this mechanism to gain some experience in technical change. The experience of the majority of firms is that foreign partners tend only to share knowledge of routine operations. They offer support on using existing production facilities, but do not extend that support to teaching firms how to change those facilities. In electronics companies, the same situation pertains. The assistance of foreign partners is more evident in TCs like *production*, *linkage* and to a lesser extent *investment*, and is not so effective for learning minor technical change and marketing capabilities. As argued earlier, it is quite understandable that foreign companies are ready to help local firms build and expand their production facilities, but are less ready to help in changing technology and in becoming more competitive in the international market.

- The use of information search, documentation and consulting varies across the two sectors. In textile/garment firms, it contributes mainly to *production* and *minor change* capabilities, less to *linkage* and *investment* and hardly at all to the rest. In electronics firms, this mechanism contributes to *production*, *linkage* and to a lesser extent *marketing* and *minor change* capabilities.

The patterns given in Tables 7.13 and 7.14 reflect two main factors regarding TC accumulation. One is the content of knowledge learning, i.e., technical versus non-technical. Mechanisms such as prior accumulation which are closer to technical knowledge contribute more to the group of TCs which need technical background like production, technical change (minor and major) and linkage. Vice versa, non-technical knowledge suitable for investment and marketing can be learnt through mechanisms like off-the-job training.

However, this factor seems specific to contexts like Vietnam where prior accumulation tends to be weaker in non-technical than in technical subjects. In a different national context, this situation could be different and the same learning mechanism could be useful for acquiring non-technical expertise as well. This suggests a second factor: the availability (or not) of various learning mechanisms within the supporting infrastructure (R&D, training and education, etc.). When production facilities became commonplace in textile/garments, prior accumulation was more available to firms than was information search. The off-the-job mode of training and foreign connections with CMEA countries were also readily available for a long period. As a result, for the production capability in textile/garment firms, the general pattern was to use these three mechanisms more than the others.

It seems that the two above mentioned factors are more common in countries which lack experience of doing business in a market economy, but which have well-established systems of training and education as is the case in the former planned economies. It may be fair to say these features of the learning-TC relationship are more contingent than universal for all developing countries.

The analytical way presented above is relied on Table 7.13 and 7.14, which aggregate firms having TC, regardless they are strong or weak. To go further than this, the division of firms into two groups with strong and weak (plus non-existence) TC can give somewhat different focus on the rate of use and importance of learning mechanisms. For example, Tables 7.15 (which is in fact an upgraded version of Table 7.2) provides the picture of learning mechanisms in contributing to investment capability in two groups of textile/garment firms: low level (non-existence and weak) and high level (strong). In this Table, there can be observed two tendencies. First, the contribution of learning mechanisms to TC in firms with high TC is much more than those in firms with low TC. Average ratio of learning mechanisms in 'low' group is 2.9 per firm, while in 'high' group it is 5.4. Second, in group of firms with 'high' TC level, these firms used nearly all learning mechanisms in combination. By using Tables 7.1 to 7.3, 7.5, 7.7 to 7.9, and 7.11, similar analysis can be done where there is a group of high level TC with ranking (2). The average ratio of use of learning mechanisms per firm is presented below.

	Textile/garment		Electronics	
	Low TC (0 and 1)	High TC (2)	Low TC (0 and 1)	High TC (2)
Production	5	5.5	4.25	5.17
Investment	2.9	5.4	2.3	3.75
Minor change	2.7	4.4	2.25	4.2
Linkage	1.9	3.3	2.8	3.2

No firm has strong marketing and major technical change capabilities and Tables 7.4, 7.6, 7.10 and 7.12 are not applicable. The results have shown that in accumulating strong TC, the firms have to use at least more than three learning mechanisms on average. For some TC, the average ratio of use could even reach higher.

Another issue to be discussed is the rate at which the various learning mechanisms are combined. The learning-by-doing mechanism is not sufficient for the acquisition of TCs and there is a need to combine it with other mechanisms. The evidence suggests that the more learning mechanisms firms deploy the more TCs they may acquire, and the stronger TCs are. In the case of textile/garment firms, the tendency is to use more than one additional learning mechanism beyond learning-by-doing, and more than two additional mechanisms in electronics firms. In addition to this general tendency, when it comes to firms having strong TC, as seen above, the numbers of additional learning mechanisms in use are much higher.

Still, there is some deviation from this general pattern. One example is in how TG3 went about learning marketing (see Table 7.4). In addition to learning-by-doing, this firm used off-the-job training and information sources, but it still does not possess a marketing capability. The reason can be found by looking beyond the ranking. At this firm, off-the-job training was very simple and was only recently embarked upon by the Institute of Economic Management and by the Hanoi

Economic University. Teachers from these organisations had themselves little experience of international marketing and could only offer courses on the basis of curricula translated from foreign textbooks. Without practical knowledge, these courses were too theoretical and too remote from real experience. Information sources provided by MOI were mostly oriented to the local market. Consequently, the firm could not acquire enough knowledge of international marketing. Similar examples of deviation can be seen in other cases. The discussion here suggests that ranking the rate of use of various learning mechanisms is not in itself sufficient to explain why certain firms do not acquire their TCs. In order to understand this, it is necessary to look at the particular conditions of each specific firm. Moreover, a learning mechanism, set within the very particular context of any given firm, may emerge as being more or less useful for that firm's TC accumulation. An examination which concentrates on the firm and on its interaction with the operating environment, is perhaps the appropriate way of examining why certain firms fail to acquire TCs, and this is discussed in following Chapters.

7.5.3 Cumulativeness and dynamics of learning

Figures 7.1 and 7.2 reveal that, over time, firms move from simple to more complicated uses of learning mechanisms; from one source of learning to more diversified sources; and from one to many types of knowledge. This step-by-step movement shows a tendency for firms to begin with technical knowledge in production and/or minor change, utilising simple skills (like subcontracting) and usually deploying codified types of knowledge (in courses given in schools and thus acquired by firms through prior accumulation). Then, firms move on to acquiring non-technical knowledge (investment and marketing), utilising more complicated skills (OEM, ODM) and, at the same time, deploying less codified technical knowledge. In the next phase, codified knowledge can again reappear at a more formal level in the form of training courses, programmes and workshops. This step-by-step move provides clear evidence of the cumulativeness of learning; some things have to be learnt before others can be learnt. This particular trend is rather similar to a common pattern found by Hobday (1994) in East and South-east Asian latecomer firms, whereby they move gradually along the path of learning. Hence, we may suggest that this pattern is more or less universal for most developing countries. However, there may be some exceptions (as with the computer firms E3 and E4) where - given their specific conditions - expertise in the several technological areas of minor change, marketing and production may be acquired almost simultaneously, and almost from the outset.

With respect to cumulativeness of learning, the question presents itself as to what kind of knowledge must precede what. The experience revealed by this study points to the most simple prior expertise: *to use* technology for producing a product. Expertise of how *to improve* the technology (both product and process) by changing it comes later. Without first learning to handle technology and master it, firms tend not to progress to the more difficult task of changing and improving it. In the case of Vietnamese companies, the evidence suggests that they are still far from the high ground of *innovating* in technology. However, one firm (TG4) which is moving in this direction is doing so on the basis of an established and relatively strong capability in handling minor change. It seems that the sequence of TC accumulation (starting from production capability) is caused by this need for learning more simple knowledge first. This pattern may be quite universal for firms in developing countries.

Another issue in the cumulativeness of learning is the order of using learning mechanisms. Certainly, there are no clear-cut universal patterns, but Figures 7.1 and 7.2 indicate a general trend towards using prior accumulation and learning-by-doing as the first steps (between 1946 and 1975). In this period, almost no on-the-job training or information collection occurred. Off-the-job training was only evident in textile/garment firms. Before 1986, in addition to learning-by-doing and prior accumulation, more training and information sources came to be used by the firms. In the reform period, all learning mechanisms were used.

Concerning the use of foreign connections, this mechanism was invoked during 1946-1975 and has continued to be used throughout all subsequent periods. It is also cumulative in terms of advancing in learning complexity. In format, it moved from simple subcontracting to more sophisticated OEM and ODM modes. As for sources, with the prior accumulated knowledge of the technologies acquired from China, the Soviet Union and Eastern Europe, textile/garment firms are now able to learn about the more sophisticated technologies of Japan and Germany. Similarly, without any prior accumulation, the private firms TG8 or TG9 tend to be weaker than the SOEs in using and mastering modern technology and they rely more heavily on their foreign partners. Among electronics firms, the assembly of industrial robotics hands in E2 was an obvious outcome of previously mastered technology in TV assembly and in other more simple products. In the case of E8, it is moving towards producing complicated products on the basis of its experience of simple printed circuit board production.

Among factors mentioned in interviews, some are the outcome of the specific historical context of Vietnam as a planned economy such as the availability (or not) of learning mechanisms, and their usefulness (or not) for various TCs given the weakness in non-technical learning and, thus, the technical bias surrounding TC acquisition. These factors are more common among former planned economies than in developing economies as a whole.

At the same time, features like the sequence of TC acquisition and the upward progress in the complexity of what can be learnt are more universal for developing countries. These issues will be examined again when discussing Vietnam's features as a transitional and developing economy in Chapter 10.

7.5.4 The comparison

Textile/garment and electronics firms

There are may similarities between the two industries in the pattern of use of learning mechanisms: the necessity for learning-by-doing; the need to support it with other learning mechanisms; and their combination, are all present. Also, the particular strengths and weaknesses of each learning mechanism are rather similar for both sectors. For example, the technical orientation of mechanisms such as information sources and training (both on-the-job and off-the-job) are evident in both sectors. The overall order of importance puts learning-by-doing and prior accumulation at the top, followed by foreign connections and others mechanisms. Both sectors have used most of their learning mechanisms for building production capability, followed by minor technical change and linkage. Similar combinations can be seen in both sectors for creating four capabilities: investment, production, linkage and major change.

Next to these similarities, there are some differences. The first is in the combination of mechanisms for minor change, marketing and linkage capabilities. For minor change capability, while textile/garment firms use prior accumulation, on-the-job training and information search, electronics firms mainly use prior accumulation, foreign connections and off-the-job training. The more active use of foreign connections for minor change by consumer electronics firms such as E1, E2, E10, E11 (see Table 7.9) provides the exception to the general pattern whereby foreign connections were not deemed helpful for learning technical change. Interviewees reported that the reason behind this divergence is the ability of managers at these firms to build up very close contacts with their foreign suppliers, to learn by hearsay from different partners and to recombine them into more systematic forms of knowledge (E10, or see E2 in Section 10.4). In the case of E11, the firm even informed its Japanese partners of intended technical changes, first discussing proposed improvements with them and only then implementing adaptations. This factor indicates the crucial importance of managers' ability to create this exceptional relationship so as to more effectively utilise foreign connections.

In marketing capability, textile/garment firms use more off-the-job training than do electronics firms. Instead, the latter use more foreign connections and information sources. Again, this difference can only be explained by looking through the case material. The personal relations of managers with their foreign partners at the four electronics firms helped them to work closely with them, learning from them some marketing know-how - as illustrated by the relations of E4's director with his French partner. In E11, JVC even sent an expert to the firm to assist with organising local marketing activity. Usually, this kind of relationship is not often seen in textile/garment firms. One of likely reasons for this difference lies in the background of firms' managers. Managers of electronics firms usually come from a research and academic background and are mostly educated abroad. They have stronger connections with information sources and foreign institutions than do their colleagues in textile/garment firms. It seems that if textile/garment firms want to utilise their foreign contacts as effectively as do the electronics firms, they might have to devise suitable strategies or techniques for building closer relations with foreign partners.

The lack of off-the-job training for marketing capability in electronics firms can be explained by the fact that R&D, training and education institutions could not offer marketing courses suitable for the more knowledge-intensive sector of electronics as compared with the textile/garment sector. This weakness leads to the low rate of use of the off-the-job mechanism for other TCs as well.

State and private ownership

The difference in ownership of the firms is particularly strong among textile/garment companies. Two private firms - TG8 and TG9 - share some features which differentiate them from the SOEs. Lacking necessary connections with local authorities, these two firms are keen to seek assistance in investment and production activities from foreign contacts. Due to its limited resources, and without state support or connections with the S&T system, TG8, as a small private company, cannot afford training courses to develop technical change expertise. The firm does not engage in marketing activities and relies heavily on its foreign partners. TG9, although bigger than TG8 and having more resources, also has no close relations with domestic S&T organisations and is not able to develop its linkage capability. These two nascent firms are trying to expand their activities over a shorter period of time and with fewer opportunities and advantages than SOEs. Besides investment and production, these two firms have less experience in technical change and linkage. As for marketing in TG9, the role of its director is important: thanks to his unique vision and decisive actions, the firm pursues very vigorous strategies to develop marketing, using almost all learning mechanisms.

Unlike TG8 and TG9, private electronics companies E3 and E4 originated within S&T organisations and they enjoy very close contacts with the supporting infrastructure. Because of this advantage, the difference between private firms and other SOEs in electronics is not as marked as in the textile/garment industry. Therefore, the main difference among electronics firms is not between private and SOE firms, but between two sub-sectors: the consumer electronics and computer firms.

Consumer electronics and computing

The four computer firms - E4, E3, E5 and E9 - differ from the consumer electronics firms in how they use learning mechanisms. Most of them were set up by scientists or enjoy close relations with scientists. Managers of these firms are dynamic and have a long-term vision for developing their competence (except for E9 which is less active). The prior accumulation mechanism in E3, E4 and E5 has been useful in acquiring minor change and marketing capabilities. These three firms have been only recently established, and so must upgrade their capabilities very quickly as compared to the SOEs. Thus, the starting conditions and backgrounds of these firms make them different from other consumer electronics firms which share a more typical background.

To sum up the overall comparison, the main factors shaping the different patterns of using learning mechanisms to accumulate TC are the origin of the firms (i.e., their start-up conditions), and their managers' subsequent actions and strategies. Springing from the S&T system, the computer firms became unique in the electronics industry as technical change-driven firms. In the meantime, a lack of any close relationship with the S&T system has left the two private firms - TG8 and TG9 - without the training mechanisms and information sources necessary to develop technical change capabilities. Actually, because the majority of consumer electronics firms are SOEs, they share many features with the SOEs in the textile/garment sector, including early state support and a more relaxed attitude towards doing business.

Emerging trends presented in this chapter show that some learning mechanisms appear to support the acquisition of some TCs over others. Between the two sectors, electronics firms seem to have more science-based learning activities than textile/garment firms. Also, differences exist in terms of ownership, sectors and sub-sectors.

Still, the general question of why certain patterns exist in the learning and accumulation of TC - and of whether such patterns are universal or contingent - demands further research. It looks as if some of these features are quite universal to many developing countries (e.g., the sequential and cumulative features of learning, and the general weakness of the R&D system). Others, however, may only be characteristic of former planned economies which are now in transition (e.g., the lack of marketing awareness and competence, and the bias towards technical learning), or may even be specific to Vietnam. Further, questions such as which external factors (including state policies, the efficiency of the S&T supporting infrastructure and market changes) have the greater impact on the learning process, and why, remain to be answered in Chapter 8.

Notes

1. In the system of labour management suggested by the Ministry of Labour, there is a seven grade system for workers. These grades are given not by the number of years of working in the industry, but by the level of skill workers achieve. In order to get to a higher grade (and by that to earn a higher salary), workers have to pass exams in theoretical knowledge and in tests of their practical skill in doing certain functions related to their specialised field. These exams and tests are organised every year at all SOEs. A worker starting at a company may be a grade 2, while grade 7 is the top level which a few workers might reach before their retirement.

2. Northern Vietnamese firms like TG10, TG12, TG2 and TG13 relied mostly on the training courses of the Hanoi Polytechnic and the Vocational School of Garment Workers No. 1. In the South, the HoChiMinh City Polytechnic and the similar Vocational School No. 2 have contributed to learning sources for TG4, TG5, TG14 and TG15.

3. Various campaigns promoted by the state to support minor technical improvements have helped firms to begin engaging in minor change activity. There was a movement of "technical initiatives and rationalisation of production" supported by the Vietnam Trade Union, the ministry and the companies which became a core element of the so-called socialist competition activities which have been very popular since the 1960s.

Table 7.1 Learning mode for production capability in textile/garment firms

Firms	TC	By-doing	Prior acc.	On-t-job train.	Off-t-job train.	Foreign connect.	Information document.
TG1	2	+	+	+	+	+	+
TG2	1	+	+	+	+	+	+
TG3	2	+	+	+	+	+	+
TG4	2	+	+	+	+	+	+
TG5	2	+	+	+	+	+	0
TG6	2	+	+	+	+	+	0
TG7	2	+	+	0	0	+	+
TG8	1	+	+	+	0	+	0
TG9	2	+	+	+	+	+	+
TG10	2	+	+	+	+	+	+
TG12	2	+	+	+	+	+	+
TG13	1	+	+	+	+	+	0
TG14	2	+	+	+	+	+	0
TG15	1	+	+	+	+	+	0

+: use of learning measure for TC accumulation; 0: this learning measure has not been used by the firms; 1: weak TC; 2: strong TC

Table 7.2 Learning mode for investment capability in textile/garment firms

Firms	TC	By-doing	Prior acc.	On-t-job train.	Off-t-job train.	Foreign connect.	Information document.
TG1	No	+	0	0	0	0	0
TG2	2	+	+	+	+	+	+
TG3	1	+	+	+	+	+	0
TG4	1	+	+	+	+	0	0
TG5	2	+	+	+	+	+	0
TG6	2	+	+	+	+	+	+
TG7	No	+	0	0	0	0	0
TG8	1	+	+	0	0	+	+
TG9	2	+	+	+	+	+	0
TG10	1	+	+	0	+	+	0
TG12	No	0	0	0	0	+	0
TG13	No	+	0	0	0	0	+
TG14	2	+	+	+	+	+	0
TG15	1	+	0	0	+	+	+

+: use of learning measure for TC accumulation; 0: this learning measure has not been used by the firms; 1: weak TC; 2: strong TC

Table 7.3 Learning mode for minor technical change capability in textile/garment firms

Firms	TC	By-doing	Prior acc.	On-t-job train.	Off-t-job train.	Foreign connect.	Information document.
TG1	2	+	+	+	+	+	0
TG2	2	+	+	+	+	0	+
TG3	2	+	+	+	+	0	0
TG4	2	+	+	+	0	0	+
TG5	No	+	+	0	0	0	0
TG6	1	+	+	+	0	0	0
TG7	1	+	+	0	0	+	+
TG8	No	+	0	0	0	0	0
TG9	1	+	+	0	0	0	+
TG10	1	+	+	0	+	0	0
TG12	2	+	+	+	+	0	0
TG13	2	+	+	+	+	0	+
TG14	2	+	+	0	0	+	+
TG15	1	+	+	0	0	0	+

+: use of learning measure for TC accumulation; 0: this learning measure has not been used by the firms; 1: weak TC; 2: strong TC

Table 7.4 Learning mode for marketing capability in textile/garment firms

Firms	TC	By-doing	Prior acc.	On-t-job train.	Off-t-job train.	Foreign connect.	Information document.
TG1	No	+	0	0	0	0	0
TG2	No	0	0	0	0	0	+
TG3	No	+	0	0	+	0	+
TG4	No	+	+	0	0	0	0
TG5	1	+	0	0	+	+	+
TG6	No	0	0	0	+	0	0
TG7	No	0	0	0	0	0	0
TG8	No	0	+	0	0	0	0
TG9	1	+	+	+	+	+	0
TG10	No	+	0	+	0	0	0
TG12	No	0	0	0	+	0	0
TG13	No	0	0	0	0	0	+
TG14	No	+	+	0	+	0	0
TG15	No	0	0	0	0	0	+

+: use of learning measure for TC accumulation; 0: this learning measure has not been used by the firms; 1: weak TC; 2: strong TC

Table 7.5 Learning mode for linkage capability in textile/garment firms

Firms	TC	By-doing	Prior acc.	On-t-job train.	Off-t-job train.	Foreign connect.	Information document.
TG1	No	0	+	0	0	+	0
TG2	2	+	+	0	0	+	+
TG3	2	+	+	0	0	0	+
TG4	1	+	+	0	0	0	0
TG5	1	+	+	+	+	0	0
TG6	1	+	+	0	0	0	0
TG7	No	+	0	0	0	0	0
TG8	1	+	+	0	0	0	0
TG9	No	+	0	0	0	0	0
TG10	2	+	+	+	0	+	0
TG12	2	+	+	0	0	0	+
TG13	2	+	0	+	+	0	0
TG14	2	+	+	0	0	0	+
TG15	No	+	0	0	0	0	0

+: use of learning measure for TC accumulation; 0: this learning measure has not been used by the firms; 1:weak TC; 2: strong TC

Table 7.6 Learning mode for major technical change capability in textile/garment firms

Firms	TC	By-doing	Prior acc.	On-t-job train.	Off-t-job train.	Foreign connect.	Information document.
TG1	No	0	0	0	0	0	0
TG2	No	0	0	0	0	0	+
TG3	No	0	0	0	0	0	0
TG4	1	+	+	0	0	0	+
TG5	No	0	0	0	0	+	0
TG6	No	0	0	0	0	0	0
TG7	No	0	0	0	0	0	0
TG8	No	0	0	0	0	0	0
TG9	No	0	0	0	0	0	0
TG10	No	0	0	0	0	0	0
TG12	No	0	0	0	0	0	0
TG13	No	0	0	0	0	0	0
TG14	No	0	0	0	0	0	0
TG15	No	0	0	0	0	0	0

+: use of learning measure for TC accumulation; 0: this learning measure has not been used by the firms; 1: weak TC; 2: strong TC

Table 7.7 Learning mode for production capability in electronics firms

Firms	TC	By-doing	Prior acc.	On-t-job train.	Off-t-job train.	Foreign connect.	Information document.
E1	2	+	+	+	+	+	+
E2	2	+	+	+	+	+	+
E3	No	0	0	0	0	+	0
E4	2	+	+	0	+	+	0
E5	2	+	+	+	0	+	+
E7	1	+	+	+	+	+	+
E8	1	+	+	+	0	0	+
E9	1	+	+	+	+	+	+
E10	2	+	+	+	+	+	0
E11	2	+	+	+	+	+	0

+: use of learning mechanism for TC accumulation; 0: this learning mechanism has not been used by the firms; 1: weak TC; 2: strong TC

Table 7.8 Learning mode for investment capability in electronics firms

Firms	TC	By-doing	Prior acc.	On-t-job train.	Off-t-job train.	Foreign connect.	Information document.
E1	No	+	0	0	+	0	+
E2	2	+	+	0	+	+	0
E3	1	+	+	0	0	+	0
E4	No	+	+	0	+	0	0
E5	No	0	0	0	0	+	+
E7	No	+	0	0	0	0	+
E8	No	+	0	0	0	0	+
E9	No	+	0	0	+	0	0
E10	2	+	+	0	+	+	0
E11	2	+	+	0	+	+	0

+: use of learning mechanism for TC accumulation; 0: this learning mechanism has not been used by the firms; 1: weak TC; 2: strong TC

Table 7.9 Learning mode for minor technical change capability in electronics firms

Firms	TC	By-doing	Prior acc.	On-t-job train.	Off-t-job train.	Foreign connect.	Information document.
E1	2	+	+	+	+	+	0
E2	2	+	+	0	+	+	0
E3	2	+	+	0	0	0	+
E4	2	+	+	0	+	0	0
E5	No	0	+	0	0	0	+
E7	1	+	+	+	0	0	+
E8	No	+	0	0	0	0	0
E9	No	0	+	0	0	+	0
E10	2	+	+	+	0	+	+
E11	2	+	+	+	+	+	0

+: use of learning mechanism for TC accumulation; 0: this learning mechanism has not been used by the firms; 1: weak TC; 2: strong TC

Table 7.10 Learning mode for marketing capability in electronics firms

Firms	TC	By-doing	Prior acc.	On-t-job train.	Off-t-job train.	Foreign connect.	Information document.
E1	No	+	0	+	0	0	+
E2	No	+	0	0	0	+	0
E3	1	+	+	0	0	+	+
E4	1	+	+	0	0	0	+
E7	No	+	0	0	+	0	0
E8	No	+	0	0	0	0	0
E9	No	+	0	0	+	0	+
E10	No	+	0	0	+	0	0
E11	No	+	0	0	0	+	0

+: use of learning mechanism for TC accumulation; 0: this learning mechanism has not been used by the firms; 1: weak TC; 2: strong TC

Table 7.11 Learning mode for linkage capability in electronics firms

Firms	TC	By-doing	Prior acc.	On-t-job train.	Off-t-job train.	Foreign connect.	Information document.
E1	No	+	+	0	0	0	0
E2	2	+	+	0	0	+	+
E3	2	+	+	0	0	0	+
E4	2	+	+	0	0	+	0
E5	1	+	+	0	0	+	0
E7	1	+	+	0	0	0	+
E8	No	+	+	0	0	0	0
E9	1	+	+	0	0	+	+
E10	2	+	+	0	0	+	0
E11	2	+	+	0	0	+	0

+: use of learning mechanism for TC accumulation; 0: this learning mechanism has not been used by the firms; 1: weak TC; 2: strong TC

Table 7.12 Learning mode for major change capability in electronics firms

Firms	TC	By-doing	Prior acc.	On-t-job train.	Off-t-job train.	Foreign connect.	Information document.
E1	No	0	0	0	0	0	0
E2	No	0	0	0	0	0	0
E3	No	+	0	0	0	0	+
E4	No	0	0	0	0	0	0
E5	No	0	+	0	0	0	+
E7	No	0	0	0	0	0	0
E8	No	0	0	0	0	0	0
E9	No	0	0	0	0	0	0
E10	No	+	0	0	0	0	0
E11	No	0	0	0	0	0	0

+: use of learning mechanism for TC accumulation; 0: this learning mechanism has not been used by the firms; 1: weak TC; 2: strong TC

Table 7.13 Contribution of learning mechanisms to TC in textile/garment firms

	Invest.	Prod.	Minor change	Marketing	Link.	Major chang.
Cases have TC	10	14	12	2	10	1
By-doing	10	14	12	2	10	1
Prior accum. experiences	9	14	12	1	9	1
On-the-job training	7	13	7	1	3	0
Off-the-job training	9	12	6	2	2	0
Foreign contacts	9	14	3	2	2	0
Inform. consult.	4	7	7	1	4	1

Table 7.14 Contribution of learning mechanisms to TC in electronics firms

	Invest.	Prod.	Minor change	Marketing	Link.	Major chang.
Cases have TC	4	9	7	3	8	0
By-doing	4	9	7	3	8	2
Prior accum. expereince	4	9	7	3	8	1
On-the-job training	0	8	4	1	0	0
Off-the-job training	3	7	4	0	0	0
Foreign contacts	4	8	4	2	6	0
Inform. consult.	0	6	3	3	4	2

Learning mechanisms	1946-1975	1976-1986	1987-now
By-doing	Dominant: for Prod. only	Continued: for Prod. Minor change Investment Linkage	Continued: for Prod. Minor change Investment Linkage Begin for Marketing Major change
Prior accumulation	First-tier: first assignment for Prod.	Second-tier: massive recruit. for Prod. Linkage Minor change	Recruitment: less, selective take over for Prod. Marketing Link., Invest.
On-the-job training	Almost none	Technical: for Prod. Minor change	Nontech.: for Invest. Marketing
Off-the-job training	Simple: for Prod. Minor change	Technical: for Minor change Linkage	Non-tech.: for Invest. Marketing
Foreign contacts			
Format:	Subcontract	Subcontract/OEM	Move to OEM ODM, OBM
Sources:	China, SU	SU, EE	EU, Asia Less:EE, SU
TC type	For Prod. only	Production Investment	Production Investment Linkage Marketing
Information	Almost none	Limited technical only: for Prod. Minor change	Diversified: for Invest. Linkage Minor change

Figure 7.1 Dynamics of learning in textile/garment firms

Learning mechanisms	1946-1975	1976-1986	1987-now
By-doing	First, simple: for Prod. only	Upgraded: for Prod. Minor change Linkage	Continued: for Prod. Minor change Linkage Investment Marketing
Prior accumulation	None	First-tier: Recruitment massive: for Prod. Linkage Minor change	Second-tier: selective for Prod. Minor change Linkage Investment Marketing
On-the-job training	None	Technical: for Prod. Minor change	Technical; for Prod. Minor change Non-tech.: Marketing
Off-the-job training	None	Technical: for Prod. Minor change	Non-tech.: for Invest. Marketing
Foreign contacts			
Format:	Subcontract: assembling B-&-W TVs	Subcontract: assembling TVs components	Subcontract: assembling industrial computers
Sources:	Japanese	SU, EE, Japanese	Japanese NICs, France
TC type	For Prod. only	Production	Production Investment Linkage Minor change Marketing
Information	None	Limited technical only: for Prod. Minor change	Informal network: Investment Linkage, Marketing

Figure 7.2 Dynamics of learning in electronics firms

Table 7.15 Average ratio of using learning mechanisms for investment capability in textile/garment companies

Firms	TC	By-doing	Prior acc.	On-t-job train.	Off-t-job train.	Foreign connect.	Information document.
Firms with LOW TC: 9							
TG1	No	+	0	0	0	0	0
TG7	No	+	0	0	0	0	0
TG12	No	0	0	0	0	+	0
TG13	No	+	0	0	0	0	+
TG3	1	+	+	+	+	+	0
TG4	1	+	+	+	+	0	0
TG8	1	+	+	0	0	+	+
TG10	1	+	+	0	+	+	0
TG15	1	+	0	0	+	+	+
Sub-total		8	4	2	4	5	3
No. of learning channels used: 26							
Average per firm: 2.9							
Firms with HIGH TC: 5							
TG2	2	+	+	+	+	+	+
TG5	2	+	+	+	+	+	0
TG6	2	+	+	+	+	+	+
TG9	2	+	+	+	+	+	0
TG14	2	+	+	+	+	+	0
Sub-total		5	5	5	5	5	2
No. of learning channels used: 27							
Average per firm: 5.4							

+: use of learning measure for TC accumulation; 0: this learning measure has not been used by the firms; 1: weak TC; 2: strong TC

8 External factors and learning activities

External factors are divided into four main groups:

- *macro-economic policies* of the government: financial and taxation policies; monetary, banking and investment policies; policy of labour and management; and trade policy.
- *market factors*: both domestic and international.
- *supporting infrastructure*: R&D, education and training; activities of other organisations which have a bearing on factors such as information, documentation, consultancy, standardisation, quality control, industrial property rights, etc.
- other *social and cultural factors*.

These four groups of factors will be the main influential categories to exercise impact on the business and learning efforts of firms. At the same time, the transition from a planning to a market economy system is the most significant feature of Vietnam, which in turn, has decisive influences on all four groups of factors. Therefore, these influences will be examined more closely, in terms of both positive and to a larger extent, negative aspect.

8.1 Influences of external factors on firms' business activities

The ranking of influences of external factors on firms' business activities is given in Table 8.1: most of the firms indicated that macroeconomic policies and the supporting system were the most influential factors. In the interviews, firms' managers tended to argue more about the problems they faced rather than overall influences, whether positive or negative. Therefore, in addition to these arguments, the positive influences of external factors on learning and TC accumulation are also discussed, although to a lesser extent than the chapter's concern with negative influences.

8.1.1 Macro-economic policies

Thirteen (out of the 14) textile/garment and all the electronics companies reported that they have problems with macro-economic policy factors, divided into four main lines as follows:

Financial and taxation policy

Financial difficulties pose the most severe constraints on companies. They have to pay too many different taxes for one complete product life cycle (e.g., import duty for imported material, turnover tax, commercial tax, income tax, etc.) which results in a higher cost of production. This phenomenon of 'tax after tax' when applied to electronics companies means import tax for parts and components, followed by turnover tax and then income tax. As noted by Nguyen Ngoc Ngoan (1992), in order to produce a TV set, a company has to pay out 40.9% of their total profit in the form of taxes. Typically, the total cost of producing an electronics unit from within Vietnam is higher than the cost of importing the whole unit. Some firms, like E5, reported that taxes levied on production can be as high as 8% of total turnover, while tax on imports is only about 2%.[1] This practice is a strong disincentive for firms to attempt more complicated technological manufacture, and has led them to concentrate on simple - but more profitable - trading activities. E4 and E5 reported that they are not motivated to try to do new things and cannot afford to accumulate technological experiences by experimenting, because they risk higher financial losses.

Another aspect of financial policy is inequality of tax rates across firms under different forms of ownership, noted by E2 which argued that foreign-owned enterprises enjoy greater tax incentives than local firms to produce the same product for the same market. Restrictive regulations on the financial budgeting of SOEs also make it difficult for them to do business. As for private companies such as E3, E4 or E8, financial policies discriminate against the private sector and discourage them from using their own resources as freely as they would like.

Monetary/banking and investment policies

With the long time lag involved in producing for export and its cumbersome procedures, many companies have to borrow from banks to pay their taxes on the expectation of getting their money back later. Due to the high lending rate of the banks, companies see their money being eaten away by tax and interest payments. This, in turn, reduces the revenues available for investing in various other activities, including technological development.

Companies in the textile/garment industry argue that the lending rates of bank are too high for them and that they cannot bear the high cost of banking services (interview with S&T department, MOI). Despite the reforms, banks still treat customers differentially within the various sectors, giving priority to unprofitable state-owned companies. Most privately owned firms have to turn to informal means of raising working capital such as borrowing from friends, family or collective financial groups. One study revealed that only 8% of private business in Hanoi and 18% in HoChiMinh City are able to get credit from their banks (Hiebert, 1993). TG8 pointed out that banks discriminate against private companies by imposing more complicated procedures for raising credit, and imposing higher interest rates, etc. Electronics firm E8 also experienced a similar problem. As a joint-venture, TG7 has not been allowed to open accounts with foreign banks in Vietnam, while the services offered by Vietnamese banks are very slow and ineffective.

TG4 and TG13 see government investment policy as being fragmented and lacking a long term vision. As SOEs, they depend on the state for planning their long-term expansion in terms of material incentives, access to financial credit and other assistance. Because of this weakness, they do not have a clear enough orientation towards planning future investment. Long-term development policies in the electronics sector are even less elaborated than in textiles. The electronics SOEs - E1, E2, E7, E9, E10 and E11 - all felt that the state did not have clear enough idea how to develop the electronics sector. Because of the lack of guidance and support from the state, companies have to fight for survival by themselves, each in their own way depending on their particular circumstances, and they lack the basis for designing long-term business strategies. Besides the incentive provided by the state, another factor which explains why SOEs tend to look to the state for their long-term planning is their inability to think strategically and to operate independently in a new market context.[2]

Labour and other economic management regulations

Management practices still differ between SOEs and private firms, both local and foreign. These differences create a very unstable and unequal business environment for firms. Generally speaking, SOEs have the most favourable conditions for getting funding, sourcing information and forging connections for doing business. As E3 stressed, the preference given to SOEs continues to reproduce unequal competitive conditions for private enterprise. This strongly discourages many private firms from doing business since it reduces their credibility in creating co-operative ventures with foreign companies. In contrast, for SOEs, state ownership poses another kind of problem. E2 argued that state ownership encourages passivity and an unwillingness of employees in those companies to work harder or to be innovative, adding to the firms' general inertia and lack of long-term strategic thinking.

Also, the limits on the freedom of SOEs prevents them from implementing flexible recruitment policies, and wage regulations cause them difficulties when they need to change staff. For E2, labour policy is not consistent between different management bodies such as Ministry of Labour and Social Security and the trade union. This inconsistency creates confusion within the company's recruitment activities, particularly with respect to graduate recruitment. In the case of E9, rigid wage and salary structures together with low material incentives (which are less flexible and attractive than those of private companies, for instance) have caused a brain drain from the firm.

Trade management policy

The majority of firms criticised the absence of a coherent and consistent trade policy (including quota allocation), especially for foreign trade. For them, the government does not, as yet, have a clear policy to protect domestic production or to promote exports. Customs regulations are unstable and usually cause confusion for the firms. Smuggling is a serious problem and it badly affects the performance of companies. So far, the government has not devised sufficiently effective measures to protect the domestic market from smuggling. For those companies which rely on the domestic market to supplement their exports, all of their efforts are seriously hampered by (untaxed) smuggled trade.[3] This undermines companies' motivation to produce and to engage in technical experiments. As E10 mentioned, "we sometimes feel hopeless about improving our technological competence, because of the mass of cheap products which of sufficiently good quality coming from outside to beat our products". This comment provides evidence for the argument that the state still lacks the means to intervene selectively (and so to protect) domestic industries.

8.1.2 Market factors

Market factors are critical in the transition to a market economy. All in all, eight textile/garment and seven electronics companies complained about market factors. Problems of the pre-reform period - such as low market expectations about the quality or range of products - are serious. Companies, as argued by TG3, TG10 and TG12, are not motivated to upgrade their product quality or design. A comfortable attitude to low product quality, an orientation to just one market (CMEA), and a state monopoly on foreign trade had rendered marketing, and the need to provide incentives, unnecessary. The reform period post-1986 marked a turning point in both the attitudes and actions of companies. They can no longer rely on the state and so must take care of everything themselves. The changes in this period are working to generate a market-pull for technological innovation in SOEs, whereby they face increasing competition.

Thanks to the emergence of a domestic market and the diversification of a multi-sectoral economy, companies increasingly exploit new sales opportunities. The textile/garment SOEs (TG1, TG2, TG10 and TG14) see strong competition coming from the private sector and from other countries. Consumer electronics firms, like E1, argue that the domestic market is still rather weak and fragmented. Most consumers are country-dwellers and can only afford to buy products at the low-end of the range, like black-and-white TV sets. While few can buy colour TVs or VCRs, the number of city-dwellers customers, who potentially have more to spend, is increasing. A disorganised and very fragmented market also makes it difficult for computer companies to forecast future business trends.

The collapse of the CMEA makes future relations between Vietnamese companies and this foreign market uncertain. In general, the need to augment product quality, to diversify the range and design of products, and to find new delivery mechanisms for products and related services increases the pressure on companies. But, changing orientation to meet the conditions of market economies is not simple.[4] Textile and clothing firms like TG1, TG3, TG4, TG5, TG10 and TG12 have been particularly affected by market factors.

Computer firms like E3, E4 and E5 did enjoy some initial export success at the end of the 1980s, but then they suddenly lost the market of the former Soviet Union after 1990. According to them, the heavily-protected markets of other countries and the fast-changing life-cycle of computer products contribute to a very difficult situation for firms who are trying to enter Western markets. In the meantime, continuing to do business in the old market of the CMEA means dealing with new competition from other countries, and with a very uncertain payment capability of buyers.

8.1.3 Industrial supporting infrastructure

The number of cases that mentioned factors related to industrial infrastructure are second to policies factors (12 out of total 14 textile/garment and nine out of 10 electronics firms).

Training and education system

Training institutions for workers are very weak, especially for the garment industry. TG1, TG4, TG9 and TG14 all complained that although the training system worked rather effectively prior to the transition to a market economy, companies now have to rely on their own efforts; certain advantages of the socialist construction period, like free education and training, are no longer available to them. This factor seriously affects the supply of workers possessing a secondary education and other relevant skills.

The higher education system contributes more to firms' activities than vocational training does but training programmes are still very theoretical and fail to ensure that students learn practical knowledge, especially in areas like business administration, marketing and economics. TG2, TG4, TG14, TG10 and TG12 and almost all electronics firms (nine out of 10 cases) highlighted this as a serious problem, e.g. the dearth of potential recruits with garment and design engineer degrees.

R&D institutes

The weakness of R&D institutions is reported by the firms. Neither their physical facilities nor their research activities are sufficient to provide firms with the services they need. Many firms cannot benefit from the help of R&D organisations. For example, according to TG4, the branch of the Textile Research Institute (of MOI) in HoChiMinh City has very weak capabilities, is short of research funding, and its projects are remote from the needs of industry. Consequently, the only support that the company gets from its laboratories is some simple testing services. Before the reforms, contacts amongst industry, R&D institutes and universities were weak; direct company-company, and company-institution linkages were not allowed formally. Thus, de facto problem-solving led to the creation of informal networks between and amongst companies and R&D institutions. Through these informal networks, companies can still rely on domestic R&D sites to sort out problems acceptably well at a reasonable cost.

Physical Infrastructure

Due to poor electricity provision in the South, many companies in both sectors in HoChiMinh City must limit their operations to certain days of the week. The prevailing state of other physical facilities, like telecommunications, also cause problems for firms when collecting necessary information or obtaining consultancy services. The weaknesses of other industrial support organisations were mentioned by the companies, for dealing with affairs such as information-documentation, industrial property rights, standardisation, quality control, consulting bodies, and professional associations. In the experience of E1, the National Office of Invention (now the Department of Industrial Property Rights), the National Centre for S&T Information and Documentation (NACESTID) and the library system do little to provide the firm with information. Poorly-developed standardisation of both PC applications and software developments is most obviously a hindrance for high-tech electronics activities, particularly for computer companies E4 and E5. Computer companies see this lack of standardisation as inviting chaotic development standards in computing.[5]

In the textile sub-sector, the lack of a domestic source of raw materials (like cotton and chemical spare parts), and the obsolescence of their technologies, pose serious problems. In garments, the lack of provision from domestic sources (the weaving industry) of high quality fabrics hinders companies' efforts to be more independent and active in business planning and expansion. TG10 sees the domestic shortage of high-quality fabrics and of other parts (zippers, buttons, colouring) as a serious hindrance to its ability to export garments. Similarly, the electronics industry depends heavily on the development of other related industries (such as mechanical engineering, plastics, and the chemical industry) none of which are well advanced.

Legal and institutional infrastructure

TG4, TG8 and TG9 pointed out that the weak and non-transparent legal system has a very serious impact on their ability to protect their industrial property rights, and to settle labour and business disputes. The underdeveloped system of industrial property rights is also critical for electronics companies E1, E3, E5 and E10, in terms of enforcement regulations. The more actively the firms try to learn sophisticated technological activities (like software design in E3 and E5), the more problems they encounter with property rights issues related to their own or foreign products.

As Table 8.1 shows, macro-economic policies and failings in the supporting infrastructure present the most serious problems for companies in doing their business. Although they tend to complain about the difficulties they have to face they all agreed that they enjoy certain advantages from the external environment. The existence and functions of the R&D, education and training facilities (despite their problems) are among the most noteworthy positive factors affecting firms in their evolution throughout the 1960s, 1970s and 1980s.

Although the firms complained less about market factors than about other groups of factors, it is obvious that market factors are critical to the firms' continued activities. The fundamental shift of Vietnam's economy and society from being centrally planned to being driven by market forces, and its new orientation to the wider international market as opposed to its old reliance on CMEA, marks a turning point in

Vietnam's industrial history. Although companies face more competition in domestic markets, or experience great difficulty in entering export markets, the overall benefits which accrue from adopting a market economy are enormous in terms of new technology supplies, sales opportunities and business contacts. As a result, the companies see this market change as having a positive rather than a negative impact, and so offer little criticism of market factors. Indeed, market changes have quite positive influences on general business and learning activities.

The influences of socio-cultural factors are not very distinctly visible. These influences and the firms' responses are discussed in section 8.2.4

8.2 The firms' strategies in response to external factors

8.2.1 Responses to policy factors

Among 13 cases having problems with government policies, only nine said they had found some way of dealing with these issues. TG5 and TG7 have not yet found effective measures for tackling banking and labour problems. According to TG9 and TG14, solving the difficulties of foreign trade management procedures and customs regulations, (these are obstacles to learning and to using the foreign connection mechanism), must remain a government responsibility.

Textile/garment companies have responded in several ways. Nearly all firms have diversified their business in order to secure more sources of income, and to use these additional financial resources to overcome the problems caused by financial constraints and monetary/banking policies. This diversification is reflected in their ways of doing business, and in types of product they make. In particular, many companies have expanded their traditional production to include new products: moving from textiles to garments, or vice versa. TG8 and TG9 have even diversified their activities beyond their existing production field of textile and garment, moving to other more profitable businesses such as construction, tourism, property development, and seafood products to capitalise on the greater income-generating capacity of these businesses.

In order to be more successful after diversifying, some companies have chosen to produce sophisticated and higher value-added products which leads to intensive specialisation. For example, TG4 has invested a lot of money (from the limited financial resources available to them) to develop new garment products using new kinds of fabric, i.e., microfibre.

Electronics companies have also been diversifying their businesses. As a state company assigned to work on calculators and computers, E9 has tried to do business in consumer electronics (assembling TVs) to generate new revenues and become more independent in planning future investment. Due to restrictive regulations on joint ventures, E5 cannot diversify into other non-computer businesses but can still diversify by providing a greater variety of computer services, i.e., packaged software and mainframe networking. By serving diversified customers, the company can accumulate financial and technological resources. To overcome financial and monetary difficulties and secure more business, firms E3, E4, E7 and E1 have tried to get involved in activities other than electronics.

To react to difficulties caused by labour and other management policies, the electronics firms have tried to avoid rigid salary structures or restrictive regulations by using more flexible modes of labour management such as exchanging personnel and information without paying fees in a kind of barter agreement.

8.2.2 Responses to market factors

The disorganised domestic market and the weakly developed labour market pose substantial problems for many companies. Increasingly, they are side-stepping the problems of economic isolation by market diversification and by seeking out foreign partners across a wide range of businesses. Concerning export activity, as a response to market problems, many firms are pursuing the following gambits:

- seeking new markets in the industrialised countries of Europe, Canada and Asia-Pacific by increasing quality and improving design and other product criteria.
- maintaining established business in the former Soviet Union and East European markets, while changing their way of doing business there.

Going in this direction also, garment companies are adopting some different approaches, one of which is to avoid quota markets and enter non-quota ones such as Japan. This is reducing the difficulties of meeting cumbersome foreign trade regulations and also avoids the industrial heritage caused by export embargo to the US market. However, the non-quota market demands very high product quality which, in turn, poses new challenges.

A few textile/garment companies have clear and explicit strategies for investigating niche markets. For example, TG10 targeted the Japanese market with two kinds of product: low-end products like cotton underwear and high-end products like hand-made woollen coats. By identifying and satisfying niche markets, companies can get a better deal from their new foreign sales. Electronics companies are also adopting a niche approach by trying to identify those activities that are under-exploited by others or that still offer opportunities for further economic exploitation. Electronics companies (E1, E2, E3, E4, E5, E10 and E9) now engage in one or another kind of business specialisation. E5, for example, has diversified to the more technically difficult area of PC networking, and has specialised in local area network (LAN) services for big customers like banks and oil companies, hoping to dominate this market in the long run. E7 specialises in control equipment for industrial manufacturing. Although this business is less profitable than consumer electronics, the firm avoids competition and saturated markets due to the limited numbers of firms involved. E8, a private firm, has also found its own niche: producing cheap audio products (e.g., loud speakers) for poor rural customers. Relying on economies of scale in mass production, the firm has also established for itself a certain stable market share in this niche.

Many companies started from simple subcontracting work (assembly) on behalf of foreign partners in order to obtain production technology and marketing skills, and at the same time to avoid the restrictions of the US embargo. E1, E9 and E10, for example, started from CKD and SKD assembling, and hope to go further with IKD products using foreign inputs. Increasing supplier-buyer links with neighbouring countries in Southeast Asia, and offering more flexible sales conditions for customers in the former Soviet Union market (as E3 has done), are some ways that companies are keeping old markets while entering new ones.

8.2.3 Responses to problems in the supporting infrastructure

To solve problems related to the shortage of training facilities and in order to rely more on their own training, companies are now developing new forms of training and education. These courses mainly provide the specific or new knowledge that official training programmes of education institutions cannot or do not teach. Companies increasingly rely on foreign partners or personal linkages with people working in universities, research institutes or other companies to act as their teachers. Barter agreements for training courses among companies (in TG13, for instance) are also a common way to reduce the cost of training. Increasing the recruitment of personnel with prior knowledge and experience is another option. Companies also try to recruit engineers with more diversified competences (possessing not only technical but also economic, management and foreign languages skills). TG2, for example, requires new graduates to have two university degrees (engineering and economics).

Private companies which survive the various anti-private actions of the state, adopt different approaches. For them, the first concern is to get a company started. TG8 and TG9 are willing to depend on a foreign partner initially in order to get contracts, to produce and to earn income from exports. This is why simple exporting subcontracting relations have been preferred by private companies from their outset. Also, the lack of any support from the state has made them more conscious and active in gathering knowledge by relying more on their foreign partners. By doing so, they are able to redress the unequal situation of competing with SOEs for training facilities and access to the R&D system. TG9, for example, instead of relying on state-owned training and R&D organisations, is using its Hong Kong and German partners for providing staff with knowledge of investment activity.

Electronics companies also increasingly rely on foreign sources for their technology and technological expertise. E1 co-operates with large Japanese and Korean firms. E10 and E11 also rely more on foreign firms, not only for technical knowledge but also for management and business administration know-how, to address the insufficiencies of the domestic supply of labour force and expertise. An example is the use of Sony's management practices by E11. It is clear that many firms (E5, E3, E2 and E11) are trying to enter the networks of transnational companies in order to ensure that they have market access, that they can keep up-to-date and that they can guarantee strong technological back-up.

New ways of gathering information and documentation for business are being used by many firms. Close and long-term co-operation with suppliers and buyers (mostly foreign) can ensure that companies have a regular supply of new designs, and new knowledge about the management of production (the organisation of garment workshops, for example). Increasing their connection with each other companies, both foreign and domestic, is seen as important by firms. The exchange of staff and information and the mutual supply of input materials by various textile and garment companies provides an example. Grouping themselves around various organisations, like the Vietnam Garment Association or less formal groups, also helps companies forge more interconnections for accessing information sources.

However, redressing the problems of the infrastructure and supporting system largely remains beyond the capabilities and resources of individual firms. No one firm can tackle the inability of related industries to supply parts; the imperfect legal and institutional infrastructure; and the weaknesses of supporting institutions over the regulation of industrial property rights.

8.2.4 Influences of socio-cultural factors and firms' responses

Five textile/garment firms - TG1, TG2, TG4, TG6 and TG10 - and two electronics companies - E3 and E9 - complained about socio-cultural factors. They mentioned the generally poor quality of the labour force - in that sense that workers and other technical personnel tend to think and act passively - as a hang-over mentality from the planned economy period. The absence of incentives during the pre-reform period has led to passivity, lack of initiative, and unmotivated industrial habits among workers. Some cases (E9) even mentioned poor discipline and community spirit among workers (it may be call a *'tu duy bao cap'* - subsidised mentality). This specific situation has had a negative influence on the prevailing working habits of employees.

To overcome the passive attitude and unmotivated behaviour of personnel, the firms now use economic incentives. Workers and technical staff who perform well or who seek higher qualifications or better skills get higher wages and other material benefits and bonuses. At the same time, other administrative measures are being applied. Regulations in some firms (like TG10) are getting tougher, especially for those staff who have not upgraded their competence and qualifications. A more strict regime of work discipline is being implemented to deal with irresponsible personnel. Change of jobs, some sanctions and even dismissal are being used against them. Still, these measures only partially help to overcome inertia among Vietnamese personnel within two electronics firms which still encounter such problems (E3 and E9).

Summary of business strategic responses

For both the textile/garment and electronics sectors, the general business strategies of the companies can be broadly divided into three types. The first type of strategy is the tendency toward *diversification* and *flexibility* of firms' business in terms of products, markets and types of business linkage. The second type of strategy is *specialisation* and increasing *competitiveness* aimed at niche areas. This response is based on moving up to higher value-added products or trying to enter a niche market. Due to the high cost of all these activities, and other factors such as the high level of personal commitment and skill and expertise required from the companies' managers, only a few companies are able to move in this direction. While the first type of response is widely used by all companies, only a few large companies with firmly committed leadership and good accumulated resources (like TG4, TG9 or to some extent E2) have been attempting the second approach. In the context of structural turbulence of transitional economies, the distinction between diversification and specialisation could be difficult. However, in this study, the diversification tends to happen in firms which are trying new things ranging quite widely, from one to another type of activity. In the meantime, the specialisation of firms tends to focus narrower in a few selected range of activities. For example, firms avoiding to expand to too many kinds of products, or businesses could have a specialisation response, while in contrast, diversified firms explore as many as they can opportunities of new business and products.

In order to put some pressure on the government (which has a decisive role in introducing policies), most companies have deployed a third type of response that can be called *co-ordinating actions*. By creating Associations like those in garment and informatics, companies try to group themselves around an organisation which can protect their interests and co-ordinate actions. The use of local domestic networks is also important to companies in the sense expressed by E5's manager: "competition through co-operation".

The three types of responses mentioned above seem to help the firms to a certain extent to deal with the difficulties posed by external factors. Still, many problems remain which still have no solutions. Firms' future activities depend significantly on more radical changes from the state concerning its macro-economic policies and on an overall performance of the industrial supporting infrastructure. Also, in order to pursue different strategic approaches, firms need to acquire new capabilities, which in turn require learning efforts. In that way, the need for learning is caused by the demand to acquire different TCs in pursuing various business strategies. The interactions between external factors, learning efforts and TC acquisition are examined in the next section.

8.3 Influences of external factors on learning behaviour and TC acquisition

8.3.1 Business strategies and TC acquisition

In the pre-reform period, the lack of motivation for TC and innovation was well-known. The main concern in this period was to produce according to plan. There was little incentive to develop marketing activities. Products were simple and technical change was mainly aimed at producing more (but not necessarily better or higher quality) goods. In this context, the firms mostly needed production and some technical change capability. Investment and business linkages were required on a very ad-hoc basis. Marketing did not need to exist at all. Hence, up to the middle of the 1980s, the firms mostly acquired production, minor change and some linkage capabilities.

The reforms have changed the conditions for doing business. To respond to changes in external factors, the firms needed different TCs for each of their strategies. First, in order to diversify businesses or products, the firms now need to know new technologies of production and product design. For instance, a textile firm moving into garments has to know how the garment business operates, know the design skills of clothing, etc. In short, the firm needs production competence for new products. There is a similar need to acquire capabilities for investment activities in diversified business areas. The firms' experiences show that many have been able to acquire these diversified competencies. The move to exporting activities has created a strong stimulus for firms to learn knowledge and skills in producing new products, in investing into new ventures or in entering new markets. This has required firms to significantly upgrade their competence, not only in production, investment, linkage and marketing, but also in minor technical change which helps to improve product specifications and, thus, enhances their range and saleability.

A similar observation can be made for the specialisation approach where a few firms have moved into niche areas. In order to produce niche products, and to increase the competitiveness of the firms, they need some specific technological competence. For example, technical change activities must be done at a more sophisticated and advanced level in order to move from ordinary products to more competitive products. This was the case of computer firms E3 and E4 when they wanted to produce a specific package of software to sell abroad. Their minor technical change was carried out more vigorously and in some cases, they moved closer to major R&D activity. Production of niche products (microfibre at TG4, high fashion garments in TG5 and TG14, software in E3 and E4, robotics electronics in E2) all required the firms to articulate more specific production skills. More exact and sophisticated knowledge was required not only in production, but also in investing in new niche activities, and in marketing niche products. Experiences of the firms show, however, that not many firms are able to acquire this specific knowledge. Only a few textile/garment (TG4 and TG14) and electronics (E3, E2 and E4) firms have obtained the expertise to deal with niche products to some extent. As a result, although many firms want to follow a specialisation strategy, only a few have been successful.

To support their businesses, all firms need to develop their linkages and the co-ordination approach is widespread among them. They have different measures to develop their connections, and to maintain effective relationships, with the R&D, training and education system, and with industrial organisations.

Comparing the TCs that the firms need and those they have acquired so far, one conclusion is that most firms possess the TCs needed for diversification activity. However, even among these TCs, non-technical knowledge (of investment or marketing) is much less developed than technical knowledge (of production or technical change), as a consequence of specific historical circumstances. In order to co-ordinate their businesses, most firms develop linkage capability. As for the more specific and sophisticated capability required for specialisation, very few firms have been able to enter this area.

8.3.2 Influences of external factors on learning activities

The number of companies reporting on the impact of various groups of external factors on each learning mechanism is presented in Table 8.2.

Macro-economic policies

Macro-economics policies strongly influence firms' business activities and, in consequence, also strongly influence specific attempts at technological innovation and learning. The difficulties posed by financial and taxation policies create overall funding shortages for the firms which prevents them from investing more heavily in learning activities, such as hiring experts for on-the-job training, buying information or sending people to off-the-job courses. The cumbersome banking procedures also produce a similar effect when the firms need to borrow money from the banks to invest in these activities. Due to an absence of coherent and long-term investment policies, the firms do not have a clear enough vision of their future investment plans and so it is difficult for them to set up training programmes, especially those which meet long-term objectives. Consequently, the firms experience great difficulty in using prior accumulated knowledge (not knowing whom to recruit, nor how many people, nor from which educational backgrounds) and in organising off-the-job training courses. In TG2, labour regulations (rigid wage and salary structures and limited freedom in recruitment) has discouraged workers from upgrading their knowledge or from embarking on further study to gain higher education degrees as engineers. For the joint-venture TG7, the minimum wage of workers is guaranteed (currently it is increased up to 35 USD monthly) which has had the effect of making them less motivated about upgrading their skills. Consequently, the self-learning efforts of by-doing and on-the-job courses have been affected. At the same time, because of the brain drain problem, long-term planning for on-the-job and off-the-job training is severely jeopardised. In both cases, labour policies have caused insecurity about the future of any learning efforts that the companies may pursue.

The firms also found that trade regulations and mechanisms were not effective enough to help them deal with smuggling. Because of this, companies are now losing their motivation to produce new things, and so, to learn by-doing and by on-the-job training.

Passivity, confusion and hesitancy in doing business caused by ownership problems also have an impact on learning activities. Due to weak credibility caused by their lack of state support, private firms such as TG8 and E8 have greater difficulties in attracting new foreign connections and this also discourages learning-by-doing. For example, E8 complained that because of its private status, it experienced difficulty in developing a connection with a Korean partner to expand its PCB production for export, despite its ability to do so. At the same time, lack of incentives in SOEs have created problems for on-the-job and off-the-job training and by-doing mechanisms.

As for learning-by-doing, it should be noted that not all companies could concretely specify the influence of external factors upon this learning mechanism. However, three textile/garment cases mentioned the impact of macro-policies on this mechanism. For example, TG6 specifically pointed out that the policy of foreign currency management prevented the firm from having reserves for maintenance and repair activities and, because of this, self-learning by workers and technical personnel in dealing with the technical services of the plant have been severely affected. As shown in Table 8.2, on-the-job (for TG firms) and off-the-job training were most influenced by policy factors.

Market factors

The fragmentation and weakness of the domestic market, especially for electronics products, caused firms difficulties in forecasting sales and in launching production plans. Accordingly, investment in learning efforts have been affected. Attempts by some electronics firms to move from low-end assembly products like CKD or SKD to more sophisticated products like IKD do not have sufficiently strong support from the domestic market. E1, E10 and E2 find little incentive to learn more complicated competences in production, particularly involving learning mechanisms such as by-doing, on-the-job and off-the-job training.

Due to increasing competition in a more open domestic market, E3 has found difficulty attracting people from other firms to act as teachers in their on-the-job training endeavours. E4 and E5 have had problems getting necessary information from competitors. Concerning learning-by-doing efforts, many companies complain that the domestic market is not conducive to them increasing their knowledge sophistication or skills by doing production locally. Instead, they have to consider other business options, such as trading or moving away from computer assembly.

Almost all firms engaged in exporting need to change their technological base and to learn new knowledges. Hand-in-hand with the positive influence of entering international markets, there are also some serious problems. The loss of the familiar CMEA markets, and the embargo imposed by the US until 1994 have made the acquisition of foreign connections - and the consequent learning through these connections - quite difficult, whether it be with foreign buyers or technology suppliers. These difficulties were encountered by most textile/garment, all computer and some consumer electronics firms.

Supporting infrastructure
The companies admitted that thanks to the training, education and R&D system provided by the pre-reform structure, they have been able to use prior accumulation of knowledge and experience very actively in technical areas. This has helped in recruiting technical graduates from polytechnics and universities, as well as in tapping valuable information sources. Through technical improvement campaigns, companies are able to use learning-by-doing or on-the-job training for enhancing their production and minor technical change capabilities. Still, the technical bias and the overly theoretical orientation of courses has seriously distorted the quality of the training mechanism.

With the move to a market economy and less state subsidies for education, this system has become less useful to firms and has especially hindered their use of on-the-job and off-the-job training, and prior accumulation of knowledge and experience by recruitment activities. The weakness of R&D organisations is an obstacle for many firms in using on-the-job and off-the-job training (due to a poor supply of expertise), and as a source of information.

Due to poorly-developed areas of the legal system (e.g., industrial property rights), the use of foreign connections is difficult when foreign products have not been protected from piracy. Similarly, the intention of Vietnamese computer firms to learn by-doing by dint of expanding their software development (like E3's VietWind - a Vietnamese version of Window) is negated once those products are pirated without any legal redress. Garment firms TG14, TG5 and TG9 also face difficulties in co-operating with foreign designers in developing high fashion models. Weak standardisation and quality control have created hurdles for forms of co-operation between Vietnamese and foreign firms. In electronics, the disorder of standardised development for both hardware and software products makes it difficult to use foreign connections as a learning mechanism, and undermines firms' attempts to integrate with international networks of producers, suppliers and buyers. As E4 put it, the firm has to deal with too many different foreign standards for PC assembly [6], while there is no single and unified standard format for the Vietnamese market. This causes the firm a great deal of difficulty in trying to learn through co-operating with foreigners. The use of foreign connections is also affected by the shortage of information back-up, both technical and business. In this respect, E7 encountered a problem in dealing with Control Technique Singapore (CT - a subsidiary of a British firm). Initially, co-operation seemed to go smoothly until the Singaporean office wanted to take over some business from E7. E7 did not know what to do and tried to contact the headquarters in Britain. However, poor communication facilities and a shortage of information in general (about relations between Control Technique Singapore and its UK parent, or about any other potential technology suppliers and collaborators that might replace CT) exacerbated the dependency of E7 on CT.

Companies in both industries complained about the weaknesses of related industries which are not able to support their learning, especially when they want to experiment with something new through learning-by-doing or through inviting experts from outside. According to E10 and E11, their efforts to augment their technological skills either through by-doing innovation or by getting information have suffered from the poor input from industries like mechanical engineering, chemicals and plastics. Some of their attempts to experiment have been abandoned due to a lack of support from these industries. Table 8.2 shows that the use of information sources has suffered more from the inadequacies of the supporting infrastructure than from either policy or market factors. Similarly, on-the-job and off-the-job training have been seriously affected because of these factors.

Socio-cultural factors

Two main difficulties for business stemming from this group of factors are the passive mentality of personnel and an uncooperative attitude among R&D staff. Due to these problems, some firms have experienced difficulties in their learning activity. The use of simple by-doing and on-the-job training courses have suffered most, as can be seen from Table 8.2.

Summary of influences of external factors on learning

Using the number of complaints given by firms in interviews when referring to the influence of external factors for each learning mechanism, some trends can be identified. These are mostly related to negative rather than positive influences. Still, the trends serve to sketch the difficulties faced by firms and so may act as a template for those issues which need to be addressed by policy measures.

Except for the mechanism of collecting information (over which most pressure is exerted by supporting system factors), all other mechanisms were chiefly influenced by macro policy factors. This is followed by other factors in a descending order of importance: the supporting system, market factors, and socio-cultural factors. Comparing this ranking of importance with the ranking of external factors' influences on general business (given in Table 8.1), they follow the same order. More specifically, financial, taxation and banking problems (which contribute to the shortage of capital available to firms) are more serious than other policy factors. As for the supporting system, the deterioration in the quality of training in the post-reform period - especially for the vocational training of workers and the deficiencies in the general knowledge pool (both before and after reforms) - is the main obstacle.

As mentioned above, depending on which group of external factors is being considered, different learning mechanisms can be influenced to varying degrees. However, the picture is not exactly the same for all the capabilities concerned. For example, in textile/garment firms, *off-the-job training* and *foreign connections* mechanisms face less pressure from external factors than *information* and *on-the-job training*. However, the former are less useful in accumulating both major and minor technical change capabilities, compared to the latter. It seems that although companies have access to, and contacts with, foreign partners and external sources of learning, the knowledge and experience that they can learn from foreigners only amounts to simple operating knowledge. Knowledge of technological change lies beyond the range of these connections. Only those companies which are in a position to pursue more vigorous strategies and efforts can utilise their foreign connections to facilitate more advanced learning.

As can be seen from the above, external factors influence the learning process in two ways. First, the transition to a market economy is a strong stimulus for firms to change their business approaches, and thus, the transition creates a need for learning new technological knowledge and expertise. Second, this transition has changed the overall context of other factors to do with the supporting infrastructure, market conditions and even the mentality of the work force. As a result, the learning process of the firms occurs in the context of new incentives to develop and new conditions (which are not always necessarily easier to negotiate) within which that development must be situated. The impact of external factors on the learning process is quite similar to the impact of those influences on general business activity. In the next section, the learning behaviour of the firms is examined.

8.3.3 Learning behaviour in TC accumulation

The acquisition of TC in the firms depends on the impact of external factors and also on the ways they respond to these factors in order to learn. Since the sorts of difficulties posed by external influences on business activity and on learning processes are similar, in most cases, the ways that firms deal with learning difficulties are not very different from their general business responses.

Facing the constraints of financial policies - and in order to fund their technological innovation and learning activities - the firms look for additional financial resources, or they seek out new mechanisms of learning that do not require payment. They use barter agreements with other companies to exchange training programmes and courses in order to save resources, and to diversify the capabilities of their existing personnel. For example, textile workers are sent to learn garment skills, while garment people learn knitting activities at other firms without any fees being paid. Some companies hope that by diversifying into new areas they can accumulate extra financial income not only for other commercial purposes, but also for supporting learning efforts in familiar activities. Diversification can be seen as the most common response by the firms to accumulating more resources for learning, both financial and technological. However, this response does not always work. Not all firms know how to diversify as successfully as they would hope for. The shortage of funding to finance their business needs in general, and their technological learning in particular, is always a problem. This factor has recently reduced the use of on-the-job and off-the-job training and firms' ability to buy information.

As presented earlier, the market system in the pre-reform period produced a situation where firms had no incentive to learn marketing competence. As the reforms unfolded, among the responses of the firms to market challenges, the diversification of market connections and a return to domestic markets (by exporting firms) has had effects not only on doing business, but also on learning. By means of these responses, the firms have had more access to new sources of learning through link-ups with diverse foreign connections. Having realised that learning technology is a process of incremental accumulation, the firms moved from simple to more complex relations with foreigners. Many firms reported that they have had to start from low-end products (production of black-and-white in combination with colour TVs at E1, or E2's early reliance on consumer electronics which was followed by a switch towards industrial electronics and computing business), and then later progress to more sophisticated products in order to learn step-by-step. This cumulative move can also be seen in textile/garment firms, shifting from simple and passive subcontracting agreements towards more active OEM relations for garment products.

To deal with the weaknesses of the supporting infrastructure - whereby access to learning facilities has became more difficult in recent times - sources of learning are being made more flexible by the firms. Companies are trying different ways of obtaining expertise, including new forms of recruitment; combining methods of training; using personal and informal contacts; and taking people from other firms. By not relying on just one or two learning mechanisms, the firms try to ensure that, in conditions of a less efficient training, education and research system than obtained previously, they can nevertheless still have access to the right people to provide them with the necessary information and training. The knowledge and information that firms now try to acquire is also economic and managerial as much as technical in content. In E8, the knowledge which the firm has acquired through its informal contacts is proving more crucial than that acquired through training courses, especially since the firm cannot avail of much support from state-run off-the-job training programmes. Thanks to these efforts, some firms have began to learn not only technical knowledge but also the non-technical knowledge necessary for investment and marketing TCs.

The new learning sources that market changes have brought in their wake usually support diversification strategies. New foreign learning sources assist the firms with knowledges useful for changing products and markets, rather than for special and more competitive products. This factor also contributes to the reason why most firms are following a diversification strategy, while not many firms make a conscious effort to specialise in new products or markets.

8.4 Micro-macro interactions: the firms and their external contexts

As discussed above, the influences of external factors on doing business in general, and on learning processes for TC accumulation in particular, are almost the same. The firms respond to these influences by adopting different strategic behaviours (such as diversification) which support their way of doing business at the same time as supporting their efforts at technological innovation and learning. However, some firms focus primarily on diversification as the means for financial accumulation and only secondarily on using that as the means for accessing new sources of equipment and expertise. In this case, new technological learning sources are being traded off against more general business strategies. Thus, the firms' responses to influences of external factors in order to secure funding for new business activities, is the same as those that the firms use for learning purposes.

Looking at the wider influences of external factors on the activities of the firms and their learning processes, the problems and opportunities of the transition from a planned economy to a market economy have emerged as central. Throughout the historical evolution of the two industries, the change that took place towards the end of the 1980s and the beginning of 1990s was the most important factor in deciding the behaviour and status of the firms, not only in their business performance, but also in their technological development. This move has shaken all the firms in their activities and subjected them to conditions very different from previous ones. In order to survive in this new environment, the firms have had to struggle and become more mature in terms of experience and knowledge. Technologically speaking, the firms have become more skilful and experienced. Hence, the macro environment has shaped the behaviour and growth of the firms in their technological development and learning. It can be seen through these firms that the trend noted by Rosenberg (1980) and others that macro-factors provide the context for micro-action is indeed the case.

The *role of the state* is important in this macro-micro interaction. During the pre-reform period, the Vietnamese government had a central role in deciding all business plans for the SOEs. The cases' experiences have confirmed that even in the present transitional period to a market economy, the state still has a crucial role to play in introducing conducive policies, and creating a favourable environment, not only for SOEs as before, but also for private companies. In particular, many firms have emphasised the need for state assistance in maintaining the supporting infrastructure. This task is beyond the resources of any individual firm. In many cases, the firms want state subsidies for training, education and R&D. The importance of interrelated industries and the whole industrial supporting system (Rosenberg, 1982; Pavitt, 1984) can also be clearly seen in the case of Vietnamese firms. It is important that the state maintain its role in developing the general business environment within which firms may learn and acquire TCs.

However, as the experiences of firms in this study suggest, the involvement of the state in the technological development and learning of the firms to date is both excessive in some respects and inadequate in others. This interesting phenomenon occurs as the state intervenes too strongly and deeply in activities that firms want to control (e.g., financial, taxation and other regulations in labour and foreign currency management, etc.) In this area, the role of the state is considered to be unnecessarily intrusive. At the same time, with respect to activities such as providing a more efficient supporting infrastructure, the state has left the scene and firms now have to address their training, education and R&D needs using only their own very limited resources. Comparing this situation with other Southeast Asian countries such as Singapore (Hobday, 1994 & 1995a), it seems that Vietnamese firms are both overly regulated and insufficiently supported by the state.

The *ownership of firms* is also a noteworthy issue. The attitude of the state towards industrial firms is unbalanced as mentioned above. Private firms suffer most from the unequal practices of the state in enforcing almost every single policy. Many private firms argue that, due to this factor, mere survival is their biggest concern; they cannot afford to allocate resources for the purposes of learning and TC creation. Even for the SOEs which have benefited from state support, problems remain. Theoretically, the directors and managers of SOEs are free to do business. In reality, many of them still have to wait for the state to decide on many practical issues.

The firms' experience also suggests that their strategic response is very important in shaping how they acquire expertise and sustain competitiveness. The firms in this study are not mere passive recipients of the forces which define their external environment. They also react to this environment in several ways. This interaction has created both new demands for TCs, and new conditions for learning to occur. There is no doubt that learning and TC acquisition in these firms is the outcome of the firms' interactions with the influences of external factors.

Still, these external factors do not always explain firms' behaviours. In some cases, a deviation from general trends might occur (as the concrete company cases in the next chapter show) and may only be understood by looking at specific firm-level factors such as managers' backgrounds.

Notes

1. Since February 1994, taxes on assembly have been reduced and taxes on imports have been increased by up to 5%. Still, this is not enough for companies to recover the expenses of production.

2. Interestingly, many compared their situation as being like chickens who are used to being fed in industrial farms and who are then made free-range and expected to find their own food. This is called *'ga cong nghiep'* (industrial chicken) syndrome in Vietnam.

3. The retail price of fabrics produced locally turn out to be higher (due to old equipment, lower productivity, many taxes) than the retail price of smuggled products. Domestic production is unable to compete with foreign made products, whether imported officially or smuggled from neighbouring countries like Thailand.

4. Lack of quotas for EU markets, high pressure from non-quota markets (like Japan on subcontract prices), and very severe and rather chaotic competition in the domestic market (without co-ordination by the state) are just some of the problems.

5. Among the more than 5,000 sets of computers in use in 1990, there were about 1,000 different types and sources of supply. Although they are compatible they are not standardised (VAI, 1990: 6).

5. Among the more than 5,000 sets of computers in use in 1990, there were about 1,000 different types and sources of supply. Although they are compatible they are not standardised (VAI, 1990: 6).

6. FCC of the US, TUV of European countries and CSA of Canada.

Table 8.1 Influences of factor groups on firms' business activities

Factors	*Policies*	*Market*	*Supporting system*	*Socio-cultural*
Textile/garment firms				
TG1	+	+	+	+
TG2	+	0	+	+
TG3	+	+	+	+
TG4	+	+	+	0
TG5	+	+	0	0
TG6	+	+	+	+
TG7	+	0	0	0
TG8	+	0	+	0
TG9	+	0	+	0
TG10	+	+	+	+
TG12	+	+	+	0
TG13	+	0	+	0
TG14	+	+	+	0
TG15	0	0	+	0
Total	13	8	12	5
Electronics firms				
E1	+	+	+	0
E2	+	+	0	0
E3	+	+	+	+
E4	+	+	+	0
E5	+	+	+	0
E7	+	0	+	0
E8	+	0	+	0
E9	+	+	+	+
E10	+	+	+	0
E11	+	0	+	0
Total	10	7	9	2

+: influences
0: no influences

Table 8.2 Frequency of factors' influences on learning mechanisms

Factors	*Policies*	*Market*	*Supporting system*	*Socio-cultural*
Learning mechanisms				
		Textile/garment firms		
By-doing	3	1	1	3
Prior accumulation	7	1	5	0
On-the-job training	9	3	5	5
Off-the-job training	7	2	6	1
Foreign connection	7	5	3	0
Information	7	4	12	0
		Electronics firms		
By-doing	5	3	3	1
Prior accumulation	2	0	2	0
On-the-job training	7	2	5	2
Off-the-job training	8	1	5	0
Foreign connection	6	6	6	0
Information	3	4	7	1

9 Detailed case studies of four firms

The 24 study firms were investigated through interviews and the firms' archival material. More detailed case material on four firms is presented in order to build up a picture of the wider context of the firm, within which TC accumulation and learning take place.

In the textile/garment sector, TG1 is above average in its garment-exporting performance among Vietnamese companies. Its pattern of TC accumulation is common to most firms in the sector, including substantial foreign influence. As a foreign turn-key project, TG6 is among the modern spinning companies of Vietnam and is actively moving into the garment business. E2 is among the best performing electronics state-owned firms in Vietnam and is moving from consumer electronics to industrial electronics. E3 is a private firm set up by scientists and is unique in having established production activity abroad. Looking at this firm can shed some light on very interesting patterns of learning and TC accumulation in the context of recent changes within the electronics industry in Vietnam.

In general, the four chosen firms are above average in terms of performance and TC building. In some respects, they could serve as a model for other companies for learning and accumulating TCs. At the same time, compared to some other firms in the study (for example, TG14 or E11), these four companies are not the best at some kinds of TC like marketing, or major technical change. An examination of the chosen firms can thus also help to understand why some expertise and experience cannot be easily learnt.

9.1 Garment company TG1 (TLG)

9.1.1 Company profile and business context

The company was set up on May 8, 1958 as an export garment company and produced different products for export: shirts, jackets, jeans, trousers, baby clothes, blouses, etc. Shirts were and remain the main product.

At the start, TLG had only 25 sewing machines (non-electric), mostly supplied from the Soviet Union, East Germany and China. Now, it has about 800 modern electrical sewing machines of different makes (Juki, Singer, Amato, Kanshai, etc.), mostly supplied from Japan. Besides, the company increased its facilities from 200 square metres up to 13,000 square metres of office space and stores in Hanoi and some other facilities in Haiphong city on the east coast.

The company began with 50 employees and now has more than 2,500, among them 68 are engineers and persons with higher education degrees having graduated from local and foreign institutions. For the last 8 years, its employment numbers were:

1985: 3,000; 1986: 3,000; 1987: 3,000; 1988: 3,000; 1989: 2,968
1990: 2,750; 1991: 2,183; 1992: 2,300; 1993: 2,500; 1994: 2,410

Since the beginning of its establishment and up to the end of the 1980s, the company exported products mostly to the former Soviet Union and East European countries. Today, it exports to the EU, Japan, South Korea, etc. The company's rate of production is given below:

Year	1958	1985	1988	1992
Pieces	421,261	n.a.	4,403,000	5,730,000

Figure for turnover (in VND millions) is:

Years	1985	1986	1987	1988	1989	1990	1991	1992
VND	25	195	372	1,852	5,498	6,203	14,464	60,000

Share of export to hard currency area has increased overtime from 2.2% in 1988, to 8.5% in 1989, 10.4% in 1990 and 100% in 1993.

TLG started its production in a rather simple way: it received cut pieces from Soviet contractors, sewed them together and sent them back. All jobs were carried out in the framework of Vietnam's trade agreements with Soviet buyers at governmental level which planned everything: prices, sales conditions, production volumes, etc. The company had neither the incentive nor the possibility to develop its capabilities, except for simple subcontracting production.

By the 1970s and 1980s, the company produced simple garments to serve both limited export and local markets under plans. In the middle of the 1980s, MOI began a subcontracting programme with East European countries and the former Soviet Union. TLG also participated in the programme and so was able to upgrade its technological facilities. Although the company exported through this programme, its products were still limited in quality and range. There was no possibility to enter new markets. Before reforms, and till the end of the 1980s, TLG had relations only with CMEA markets and no chance of accessing diversified sources of technology and information. The company did not have any idea of how to do business with market economies. Activities were planned by the government, and the firm had little motivation to change the situation.

After the reforms, TLG gained new market opportunities in EU and Asia Pacific countries. Through new foreign contacts, new business opportunities became possible and new knowledge and information on production were acquired. 1989 saw a turning point in the company's activities. With the industrial rehabilitation programme supported by SIDA (Swedish International Development and Co-operation Authority), TLG received aid in the form of new sewing machines and modern equipment for garment production. At the same time, it also received some support from the state in terms of new personnel: line managers and heads of workshops or divisions. Most of them began as junior assistants to other earlier appointed managers, then began to climb up to higher positions. These were young, energetic people with degrees from universities or polytechnic institutes. More importantly, they were more pragmatic and business oriented than existing managers. One of these is Mr. Du Duc Thin, Vice-Director of TLG who was educated in Hanoi Polytechnic Institute in textile engineering, and now is in charge of technological innovation activities.

After being technologically upgraded by the Swedish aid, the company considered expanding its export activities. With the opening up of the Vietnamese economy, many foreign customers were introduced to the company. Following a 'trial and error' process of negotiating and establishing business contacts, they started to do business with TLG more seriously. In 1989, GunYoung Trading Co. Ltd of South Korea began business with TLG. It provided all material, design for production of high quality jackets (three layers) and blouses. In order to implement this contract, TLG set up a separate workshop for GunYoung, with its own staff of foreman and workers. The physical infrastructure of this workshop was the best in the company. Many from other workshops called this workshop 'Korean house' with some envy: it became one of the first modern facilities in the whole garment industry of Vietnam with the comprehensive involvement of foreign partners. Not all companies in the clothing industry were able to enjoy this advantage. The workshop used mostly TLG sewing machines but GunYoung also provided some machines that TLG did not have (stitching and patterning machines, dotting and zipper equipment, etc.). It also sent experts to supervise the organisation of production lines, and quality control, and took part in discussion of production plans with TLG. All products of this workshop were bought by GunYoung for export to Japan.

Between 1989-1991, many other foreign companies developed co-operative relations with TLG. For example, Shilton (Japan), Quell (Germany) and Hennes&Maurice (Sweden) provided their sample designs and TLG implemented the production of these models using its own machines, material and other inputs. These companies then bought the products for export to different countries. Currently, the main export market of TLG is Japan (80%) and EU countries (Germany, the Netherlands and Sweden account for the remaining 20%).

At the same time, TLG now has difficulty in adjusting to new markets which require quotas for export. After the abolition of subsidies, the free supply of trained workers ended. Current sources of competence are not very useful: technical schools, universities and polytechnics do not produce graduates specifically for the garment industry. In this context, the overall response of TLG to changes caused by external factors has been to diversify its business activities and products to serve new market opportunities. There is little evidence of it pursuing other types of response. The firm diversified its product range by producing more sophisticated products for export. It searched for new partners in Germany and Sweden, bought new sewing equipment from Japan, entered the new market of the EU, and also began to look seriously at the domestic market.

More recently, TLG started to introduce its own design by modifying foreign designs (old collection taken from the previous season or from a catalogue). Also, in some cases it discussed with customers the possibility of minor design changes to their models (counter-sample). After three years of doing business with new customers, the share of simple subcontracting is decreasing and the share of more active participation by TLG (e.g through OEM or ODM agreements) is increasing as presented below.

Although more and more products carry the label of TLG, it does not as yet manufacture any branded products (OBM type of manufacturing). The growth of TLG depends on a range of capabilities which are presented in the following section.

Type of relations	1990	1994
Subcontracting	80%	50%
OEM	20%	40%
ODM	0%	10%
OBM	0%	0%

9.1.2 Building technological capabilities

Investment capability

For the period before the rehabilitation programme in 1989, TLG did not have the capability to change or invest in any new expansion of production. The 'May 19' programme created opportunities for the firm to gain first hand knowledge of new investment. However, at this stage pre-investment activities (like preparation of technical-economic feasibility studies, or choosing the partners who will take care of all pre-investment studies), were carried out by personnel of MOI in co-operation with foreign experts. TLG personnel were passive in the next phase over the choice of machinery and equipment, designing the production processes and sourcing activities. All sewing machines and input sources were provided by the contractors from East European countries and the Soviet Union, the company simply accepted these plans given to them from MOI.

With SIDA support, feasibility studies for TLG's rehabilitation programme were carried out by experts from HIFAB International AB, a Stockholm-based consulting firm in project management and construction. Vietnamese personnel from TLG only participated in those parts of the programme which required specific Vietnamese skills or experiences. For example, TLG's personnel clarify and suggest appropriate arrangement for ventilation and lightning for dealing with hot and humid working conditions of tropical weather. Preparation and implementation of feasibility studies and project management were assigned to HIFAB.

Although in the construction of new houses for workshops, the Vietnamese side had the main responsibility, due to lack of information on technology sources, TLG depended on HIFAB for technology purchase, or on the list of suppliers given by the consultants. Some technical re-arrangements of sewing machines were carried out jointly as were machinery installation and start-up activities.

After the completion of the SIDA-supported project, TLG has not taken much part in new investment activities. Although recently, TLG was more active in the co-operation with GunYoung, it still relies rather heavily on the initiatives of foreign partners. So far, there is no evidence of the existence of investment capability in the firm.

Production capability

Until now, the production activities of TLG have gone through 3 main phases: (i) simple subcontracting for export to East Europe during the 1970s and up to the mid 1980s; (ii) production upgraded technologically with SIDA assistance, to the end of the 1980s; (iii) since the beginning of the 1990s, direct foreign investment with Korean and other involvement. After each of these, the company personnel became more confident in running sewing workshops. In the first phase, the firm's managers were dealing mostly with ensuring smooth production without the necessity of changing the arrangement of production lines or workshops which were fixed by plans. With the coming of new partners, TLG's personnel learned how to operate more sophisticated and specialised equipment, including computer-added embroidery machinery. They also became more able to re-arrange the production organisation. In short, TLG now has production management skills such as how to operate a range of equipment and organise production lines.

In the area of production engineering skills, TLG has become quite knowledgeable about dealing with raw material control or trouble-shooting in very unstable conditions of production (poor physical infrastructure, low supply and lack of long-term perspective in business contracts, etc.), and to adjust production lines to tropical conditions. Repair and maintenance is now totally handled by TLG after it received guidelines from foreign personnel. Issues of quality control are more difficult to handle. In order to ensure quality of export products, foreign partners first sent their sample design to TLG for trial production, and provided their technical support. After four to six months, the foreigners responsible for quality control left, and the buyers signed more contracts with TLG to produce these models, with all production issues taken care of by TLG staff. Now, based on one model or part of it, TLG can implement and develop the rest of the contract (all cutting, grading and stitching operations).

After about one year of working with Western companies (during 1989 - 1990), TLG improved the quality of its products significantly. According to the company, this is why foreign partners are now ready to give TLG a more active role in their contracts. In terms of production efficiency, all workshops have a longer time lag than the joint workshop with GunYoung, from the order to delivery of products. Based on the upgrading of skills and general production performance figures, it is clear that the company has a strongly developed production capability.

Minor technical change capability

In TLG, there were few changes in product specifications until the mid 1980s. The company tried to fulfil the contract exactly in terms of quality, product range and design, as agreed upon with the contractors; a non-change attitude towards the product range had remained from the planned economy period. However, the company had organised different campaigns to encourage its employees to be more active and to take the initiative in introducing minor technical improvements. One example is of changes made to the production layout of a big long hall in a workshop, in which workers had to carry cut pieces a very long distance between operations. This was inconvenient and time consuming. Workers also felt tired and isolated from each other. They have suggested replacing the linear line of operation with a round line to have shorter distances between operations. This change has improved both productivity and the working environment. However, under conditions with few incentives, the firm's employees were not very active in proposing change like the one mentioned here.

A more positive attitude toward change emerged towards the end of the 1980s and the beginning of the 1990s when the company introduced some changes in process technology. For a long time, TLG's ironing equipment was too heavy for many workers to use causing the burning of some fabrics. To solve this problem, workers in the workshops, together with technical personnel, adapted these irons to allow more air-blowing to come in. The new ironing equipment is lighter, uses less energy, is safer for workers to use, and has greatly reduced the incidence of fabrics being burnt.

After two years of passively implementing orders of foreign buyers, by 1992 TLG was able to introduce some changes to product specifications:

- minor adjustment to existing foreign designs, or models taken from catalogues;
- development of new designs based on one sample of foreign buyer;
- introducing some totally new designs by combining knowledge.

By making such minor changes, TLG could offer new models or collections of clothes to new buyers. Some of these new products (shirts, pullovers, jackets) have been accepted by foreign buyers. In this way, TLG can create designs with its own label for sale trial in other markets. All these tasks are carried out by a technical unit of the company which has existed since the 1970s. But in the pre-reform period, it was passive and its functions were mainly maintenance and repairs activities to support production plans. Its relations with other production units in the company were formal, but lacking close co-operation to achieve highest production performances. Recently, the unit has been expanded, it now has about 60 people, of which half are engineers or those with higher education degrees from universities. The unit's functions are:

- to study samples given by foreign buyers and develop them further;
- to design new models;
- to implement these new models in sewing workshops, by preparing concrete standard specifications for each stage of production.

Now, this unit also sends its staff to different workshops of the firm to take part more actively in production activities to help maintain the quality of products. Judging by these activities and the performance of the firm, it can be said that TLG has developed quite a strong capability in minor technical change.

Marketing capability

This activity is the weakest at TLG. Almost all of the firm's marketing and sales has depended on the foreign buyers. When the company relied on East European markets, TLG participated in some trips organised by MOI to trade fairs and exhibitions (Leipzig in East Germany or Varna in Bulgaria) but these trips did not have any real commercial orientation. Although TLG is now exporting more, it still depends on the sales channels and distribution of the foreign buyers. Hence, TLG's marketing capability can be considered as non existent, and without involvement in international sales and market research.

Linkage capability

The linkage among the company's different workshops and production units is developed in TLG but inter-firm linkages with other Vietnamese companies are less developed. TLG's technical personnel, who gained skills and experiences through contacts with foreign companies, are considered more experienced in garment production than staff in other companies. Indeed they are regularly invited by other local firms to give training courses or guidance in garment production.

The linkages with R&D and training organisations is least developed. The company makes very little use of government research institutions, universities or other local firms. Only in some specific technical areas like energy system, has it received assistance from some specialist units of MOI. Without the most important form of linkage with S&T and training system, TLG cannot be considered as having linkage capability.

Major technical change capability
All technical change activities at TLG are on a very minor scale without any new development or design of technology. Those new products designed by the firm have been only modifications of existing products, requiring no new technological equipment. Therefore, major technical change capability is absent at the firm. The prospects for TLG developing more major technical change activity on the basis of its minor improvements remains unclear. Among senior managers, only the vice-director has enthusiasm for undertaking more radical technical improvements. Besides, the limited facilities and resources do not allow the firm to pursue more R&D activities in the near future.

9.1.3. Learning mechanisms

Prior accumulation
Formal training provided the firm with basic knowledge on industrial production in general and textile/garment technological issues in particular. Engineers and graduates with higher education received degrees from different universities and polytechnics in Vietnam (Hanoi Polytechnic, Hanoi University) and abroad (Russia, East Germany, Poland, Czechoslovakia).

With the need in the recent years to increase knowledge of production and doing business, TLG has recruited personnel to join the first intake of managers. The number of engineers was increased from 47 to 68 (2.8% of total employees) when the firm got SIDA support. The proportion of technical workers (who can perform simple jobs and more skilful operations) and technicians with vocational education are 83.9% (2,062) and 0.9% (24) respectively. From their formal training, engineers learned both concrete operational techniques and more general knowledge about production organisation.

The training of garment workers in sewing techniques and industrial garment production was provided in a special vocational school located in a small town north of Hanoi. This school had a formal contract to provide TLG with certain numbers of workers every year (regulated by plans). Before training, most workers gained knowledge from family based activities.[1] In the vocational school, they learned to use electric industrial sewing machines, and simple techniques like cutting, stitching and grading patterns. More importantly, they also learned about industrial work organisation, standardisation and quality control.

This preparation of the work force by formal training and education prior to coming to work at the firm is significant. It prepared staff in the basic principles of production, and of operating textile/garment equipment. Thanks to this prior accumulation, production skills were acquired rather smoothly and quickly when people joined the firm.

Prior accumulation makes an important contribution to minor change as well as production activities. Technical knowledge accumulated in the universities and polytechnic institutes permit engineers to know not only what is going on in textile/garment production in general, but also why certain technologies work. This knowledge is crucial for employees when they need to change or adapt technology, especially in engineering. Knowledge of physics and mechanics, for example, has helped technical staff to deal with changing some mechanical parts of sewing machines like rolling mechanisms. Similarly, thanks to chemical knowledge, people are more confident in dealing with colouring, mixing designs, and patterns of clothes. However, this contribution of prior accumulation to minor technical improvements is limited to those from higher education institutions. Workers' training has been too simple for them to learn knowledge necessary for change.

Not only formal training, but working experiences accumulated somewhere else before joining the firm can also be useful, although to a lesser extent. Managers brought with them knowledge and experience of how to organise production in general which has been helpful in the planned economy period of simple assembly. In addition, social connections of the personnel could be used for the firm to develop its linkages with colleagues or classmates.

In spite of this usefulness, the prior accumulation mechanism did not help much for acquiring other TC like investment or marketing. The reason for this is quite simple. In the universities and schools, the employees of TLG did not get training in the relevant knowledge like investment studies, economic analysis, and marketing principles or business administration. This kind of knowledge was rarely, until recently offered by training organisations.

On-the-job training

TLG has organised various formal and informal courses and guidance programmes for its employees. The company holds short term courses annually (ranging from 3-5 days to 2 weeks), with teachers invited from outside: local universities, research institutes, consultants from MOI or other companies. At these courses, TLG's staff have gained knowledge and experiences ranging from garment skills to electrical, mechanical engineering, mostly for daily routine production operations or technical improvement.

Training is not always formal. Sometimes, consultants are contracted to solve a specific problem, in the course of which they share knowledge and experiences with TLG staff assigned to work with them. For example, when TLG changed the material for shirt production, it had difficulties in maintaining the same quality of products using the different types of fabrics. The firm signed a contract with experts from a southern company who had dealt with these fabrics before. These experts visited TLG for some weeks, discussing the problem with the firm's staff and guiding them on how to deal with changes of material by adjusting the ways of cutting, ironing and sewing. After that TLG's staff were able to use these experiences to handle quality control problem of shirt production.

TLG has also used its own staff for on-the-job training. One example is the production of fashionable Western vests for export in 1993. Before this, the production of such items with high enough quality for export was not possible for Vietnamese garment firms. The most difficult thing was to upgrade the pattern and then stitch them accordingly. To learn this kind of specific production knowledge, TLG has invited old tailor men who used to sew Western vests during the French time (before 1960s) to teach young technicians and workers about the technique. But this was not sufficient since current Western fashions are quite different to the old days. TLG combined this learning from old men with the use of more modern cutting and patterning techniques (automatic specialised equipment for cutting sophisticated patterns like pockets or pressing machines for chest and shoulders pads, etc.). The technical unit of the firm was responsible for combining these old experiences with the use of modern technology imported from Japan. In September 1993, TLG was able to begin this new export to France. As the case shows, on-the-job training was mostly related to technical and engineering knowledge. So far, few training courses are organised at the firm, nor the sharing of experiences by local consultants on other non-technical issues. Therefore, this way of knowledge learning is mainly geared to production or minor technical change activities.

Off-the-job training

This way of training has been quite popular up to the mid 1980s. Technicians graduating from vocational schools, or workers who passed entry exams, could be sent to study part-time at the Hanoi University or polytechnic for degrees in textile, mechanical or electrical engineering. For more simple garment assembly skills, workers were sent from time to time to the training centre for garment workers of MOI. Similarly, TLG has sent its technical staff to short courses on new issues like environmental regulations in production.

More useful off-the-job training came recently (during the last 3-4 years) with the pressing need for managers at divisional level with knowledge on market economies and business administration. They began to take courses in marketing or foreign trade management. For more specific knowledge such as quality control, TLG sent its people to courses or seminars organised by the General Department of Metrology-Standardisation-Quality control (belonging to Ministry of Science, Technology and Environment) on the new standard system of ISO 9000.

Off-the-job training has been helpful mainly for production and minor change rather than for other capabilities, since most off-the-job courses are concerned with engineering issues. Non-technical subjects were not available until recently.

Foreign connections

This mechanism is the most used by TLG to learn recent knowledge of business practice and more modern production technology. This learning through foreign connections can be divided into tiers. The first tier of foreign contacts came before the end of the 1980s, most foreign experts, technical assistance, and sewing machinery came from the Soviet Union and East European countries, especially during the 'May 19' programme. Soviet experts came and stayed at the firm to look after the implementation of production plans, quality control and export business. By discussing relevant matters with foreign buyers during this period, managers of the firm could, for the first time, learn about the organisation of production plans for export on a large industrial scale. Technologically, TLG learned more about the use and specifications of industrial garment machinery, not only sewing but also finishing operations such as zipping and putting buttons, pockets, etc. Still, due to the subcontracting nature of these connections and the passive Vietnamese attitude of doing business, the technological sophistication of the learning was not high. Also, TLG was only able to learn knowledge appropriate for doing business in a centrally planned economy.

The second tier of foreign connections occurred at the end of the 1980s with the SIDA programme. During this programme, TLG received assistance from consultants (Swedish HIFAB International), mostly in pre-investment and investment studies. But, again, due to the passive position of TLG in this programme, it did not learn much, except for simple knowledge of how to choose new technology, and to deal with equipment purchasing which they could use later for new local investment efforts. The passivity of TLG was only one reason for it not learning much. Another reason was that the SIDA programme was the first time that TLG heard about Western style analyses like feasibility studies. They did not have any experiences of doing this kind of analysis before. Without prior basic knowledge, the absorption of new knowledge remained limited. The discussed absorptive capacity (Cohen & Levinthan, 1990) of TLG was absent in this case. Thanks to SIDA assistance, TLG learnt how to use new Japanese sewing machines and how to organise production workshops.

The most significant learning that TLG gained through foreign connections came with the third tier of foreign involvement when it gained opportunities to cooperate with new buyers from the EU and East Asian countries. The Korean company GunYoung has been among the most important sources of learning for TLG. By providing TLG with the whole workshop, 'Korean house', GunYoung gave the TLG managers a living on-site example of a modern workshop for garment production, which enabled TLG to have a full picture of what standards are needed for export business. Korean experts visited 4-5 months each year during two years, and took part in almost every activity of the workshop: supervision of production lines, quality control, organisation of work division. In addition to ordinary sewing machines owned by TLG, GunYoung provided the firm with some specific equipment like buttoning, pressure ironing to produce high quality products to be exported to Japan (like three layer jackets and coats). Technical assistance was also attached to equipment provision. GunYoung organised special training courses for workers and technicians working in the workshop and regularly provided them with guidance or shared experiences. First, the Korean experts taught a special group of workers on how to use semi-automatic ironing and buttoning machines. Then other workers received general guidance on how to use sewing machines to produce jackets. These workers learnt many techniques from the Koreans: how to put fabrics in, how to link different cut patterns and stitching them together, how to deal with finishing problems like cutting threads or sticking decoration outlay.

At a higher level of management in this workshop, the heads of production lines or groups learned from the Koreans how to deal with quality control checking, supplying and circulating semi-finished products within the workshop, and organising workers on routine daily checking. Thanks to these intensive learning activities (by working with GunYoung for about 2 years), employees of this workshop became the most competent in the firm compared to those working in other workshops, in producing highly sophisticated garments for export.

The assistance of GunYoung was not restricted only to this workshop. TLG invited GunYoung experts to take part in general discussion about planning, organisation, and improvement of performance of the whole company's activities. Although the final decision was always left to the TLG director, GunYoung experts played quite an active role in providing business advising to TLG. According to TLG's staff, the reasons for GunYoung being more involved with TLG's business was to foster goodwill and mutual confidence. GunYuong might then, consider expanding its business relations with other workshops of TLG. Both interviews with TLG employees and the performance of the Korean workshop show that this learning has improved production and technical change capabilities.

TLG had also quite active and close connections with other foreign companies like Quell (Germany), Shinton (Japan), Hennes&Maurice (Sweden), which are based on an OEM or ODM agreement. Foreign companies provided TLG mostly with specific equipment or design, and the firm had to develop the product prototype. The most intensive way of learning from these new buyers was through discussion (on how to start a new design, how to change and improve each specification, and about the fashion trends of each season), and co-design of new collections. By working with many different buyers from different markets at the same time, TLG managers learned the different techniques (or business know-how as called by Mr. Du Duc Thin, vice director) used by different buyers. German and Swedish buyers provided knowledge with fashion trends and market orientation, while Korean or Japanese buyers gave more experiences on production issues: how to economise on material, how to rationalise labour division; and how to deal with the labour force and system of incentives.

Clearly TLG appreciated this way of combining knowledge. Furthermore, its diffusion of some experiences to other parts of the company is clear evidence that they learned a lot by this mechanism for TC building. For instance, after the staff of the Korean workshop became more confident in handling all production operations, TLG decided they should circulate their experiences to other parts of the firm. Every month, an internal meeting of director, heads of other workshops and personnel from the Korean workshop was held where they discussed experiences learned in the Korean house and how these experiences can be applied to other workshops. From time to time, TLG also negotiated with Korean partners to second some Korean-trained staff to work for a short period at other workshops. By doing this, the whole firm can be in touch with changes and learning at the Korean workshop.

However, while TLG worked with various foreign partners, most of the knowledge they learned was concerned with production and minor change activities. Experiences of investment or marketing activities were shared more reluctantly by foreigners and at the same time absorbed more passively by TLG itself. Indeed TLG was passive not only in the first and second waves of foreign contacts, but also in the third. This passiveness of TLG is explained partly by the lack of absorptive capacity (knowledge and experienced staff who can work alongside and learn from GunYuong). In addition, GunYuong assisted TLG mostly with production techniques and organisation. Investment preparation for setting up the workshop was done by GunYuong without much involvement from TLG. As for marketing, TLG relied on foreign partners for sale of its products, and involved no active learning.

An exception is GunYuong's contribution to TLG's linkage activity. Within one workshop, Korean advisors have arranged close exchange of tasks and information among different operative groups (supply, patterning, cutting, sewing, stitching and finishing). This helped TLG to have a better idea of what are the internal linkages within the firm. Also, this internal linkage was developed between the technical unit and other production units within TLG, partly thanks to advice from GunYuong's experts.

Information
TLG made little use of this mechanism. Information comes mainly through technical specifications and standards given by outside consultants or buyers. This information is used by the company mainly to improve its production performance. TLG has more difficulties in obtaining marketing or technology information from international trade fairs, exhibition, seminars and workshops.

Learning-by-doing
Learning-by-doing first occurred in production and minor technical improvement. Through the long period of doing various kinds of production tasks since the beginning of the firm, TLG's managers have been able to learn through many experiences, especially in changing and upgrading types of technology to be used (from Soviet-made to a more sophisticated Japanese sewing machines, and German specialised equipment). These experiences can also be related to products to be produced (from simple products for Eastern European markets to higher quality clothes for Japanese and EU customers) and relations with foreign partners (gradual shift from subcontracting to OEM and ODM). After each of these changes, TLG's staff became more familiar with new ways of doing business, new products and markets. One of the managers, Mr. Nguyen Van Thanh in the planning division, said:

> Before, we knew nothing about market economy. We simply are not able to have any business with Western countries. Now we know how to produce products good enough for these markets. Perhaps, it is the most important intellectual development for us in the last five years.

TLG gathers the same learning-by-doing experiences through initiating technical improvements at the firm. Over time, difficulties, problems and mistakes of this by-doing and by-trying to solve problems are useful experiences. One example is the attempt of TLG to make its industrial gas supply system more powerful and flexible. Initially, TLG intended to make this change using its own staff, who are capable of mechanical engineering adjustment. After several months of trying, the managers found that it was impossible to change the system without physical knowledge of air flow pressure. Eventually, TLG had to invite people from the MOI Centre for boiler equipment to help, and at the same time, learned new knowledge of boiling system and acquired many skills through working together with these people. In addition, they got very good experience about the need for more specific knowledge to deal with small technical problems.

Table 9.1 Learning mechanisms at TLG

TC	Investment	Production	Minor change	Marketing	Linkage	Major change
Ranking	*no*	*strong*	*strong*	*no*	*no*	*no*
Learning						
By-doing	+	+	+	+	0	0
Prior accumulation	0	+	+	0	+	0
On-the-job training	0	+	+	0	0	0
Off-the-job training	0	+	+	0	0	0
Foreign connection	0	+	+	0	+	0
Information	0	+	0	0	0	0

More recently, learning-by-doing began to occur in investment and marketing. For the first time, without any assistance from external personnel, TLG commenced to expand its production facility and invest in a new subsidiary plant in Haiphong - a town on the east coast 100 km from Hanoi. It took the firm almost two years (1991-1993) to complete investment and start-up activities in this new venture. By making several mistakes and solving difficulties (how to deal with poor physical infrastructure, how to negotiate with local authority, how to recruit and train new workers coming from a harbour area and having less skills in garment, etc.), the firm gained many experiences. Similarly, some new marketing attempts were made by TLG through opening a new business centre and showrooms in Hanoi and some provinces. In the first year, the business centre has lost money. Mr. Ta Anh Khoi, director of the centre admitted:

> We did not make much profits after a year. Our staff have little knowledge and experiences to advertise our products and market them to buyers. They just sit here, watching people passing by. But we learn something from this mistake. Probably from now on they should be more active for marketing and go out to buyers.

These learning-by-doing activities in investment and marketing, therefore, are just the beginning of TLG's learning process and so far, is not enough for them to acquire these TC. Without backing up these efforts with other learning forms such as training or foreign contacts, this simple accumulation just by doing cannot lead to the strong development of investment or marketing capabilities.

The contribution of the various learning mechanisms to TC building at TLG can be seen in Table 9.1.[2]

The case material confirms the importance of absorptive capacity (associated with the passive attitude of firm's managers), without which TLG could not learn more actively from two phases of foreign assistance: the SIDA programme and GunYoung direct investment.

9.1.4 Macro external factors, micro behaviours and learning

The pattern of using learning mechanisms is influenced by external factors and by TLG's interaction with these factors. During the 1970s and 1980s, pre-reform advantages in training and education contributed to the prior accumulation of TLG. It relied heavily on the R&D, education and training system for a free and continuous supply of personnel from higher education, both technicians as well as workers. But the weaknesses of this supporting system (such as poor curricula, the technical bias of training courses and slow and ineffective information flow) led to the firm remaining weak in its non-technical learning. The specific market conditions (i.e, dealing only with CMEA) also prevented the firm from being stimulated to acquire investment and marketing competencies. Regulations of the state governing relations with foreign partners were cumbersome and TLG had difficulty in maintaining flexible relations with its foreign buyers and technology suppliers. This has prevented the firm from pursuing its limited learning opportunities for acquiring knowledge, information, and experience from foreigners.

Reforms after 1986 landed the firm in a new situation. In terms of what it needs to know, there is now a higher demand for knowledge of investment, business administration and marketing. The most important change is that due to the competitive pressure of market changes, TLG has changed its attitude to technical change activity, and its staff has also regained a positive learning attitude. The firm has to do more product modifications which require minor technical change capability. With respect to its learning through prior accumulation, both new opportunities and difficulties have arisen. TLG has to take responsibility for supplying its own skilled garment workers but shortage of funding influences its off-the-job training, since fees for courses have increased. Even when the firm can pay, the existing training curricula is less suitable to addressing new changes. Thus, TLG has had to retrain its educated technical personnel to undertake garment activities, through promoting working experience and providing subsequent training.

In reaction to external problems and being sensitive to long-term opportunities for business,' TLG tried to diversify its activities, its markets, its products and its business relations with partners. This response, although aimed at meeting a business strategy, has also brought new learning and information sources to the firm. Diversifying by developing connections with foreign partners (both Western European and East Asian) has helped the firm to access new information, and to gain new experience. By diversifying its involvement with foreigners, the firm's managers have learned different kinds of knowledge, piecemeal, from different sources. Moreover, the firm started to think more consciously about upgrading its relations with foreign firms from simple subcontracting to a more active role as OEM and ODM. Indeed, by diversifying its involvement with foreigners, the firm's managers has learned different kinds of knowledge, piece by piece, from different partners. For example, TLG's vice-director noted the sort of things that he learned from various companies: shape and colours of high fashion products from German partner, technique of producing jeans and coats from the Swedish; the way of organising a production workshop, planning and running quality control from the Japanese and Korean; and techniques and skills of sewing jackets from the Korean buyer. "We have to listen to them", he said, "and be patient. Then we can learn something different from each of them".

In addition, TLG is trying to find new non-traditional ways of acquiring knowledge and information. Since 1991, the firm has been demanding certain technical qualifications from potential employees. TLG uses an informal network of consultants to obtain necessary experience and information. It has upgraded the activities of its showroom and sales centre to gather market intelligence. And, to improve training (on-the-job and off-the-job), TLG has designed more incentives for those employees who are willing to learn more actively.

Still, TLG cannot so far find sufficiently appropriate solutions to the problems posed by external factors. TLG's managers stressed that this depends on further changes to government policies. Due to weaknesses in the domestic sources of expertise and information for the garment business, TLG has tended to rely more on assistance from its foreign partners.

9.2 Spinning company TG6 (NTC)

9.2.1 The company profile and business context

This company is located outside Nhatrang city of Khanh Hoa province in the central part of Vietnam (about 500 km north of HoChiMinh City). In order to meet Vietnam's need for yarns for weaving plants after the war, MOI contacted Itochu Co. of Japan in 1972 to sign a contract worth 50 millions USD for a turn-key spinning plant of 100,000 spindles, included supervision of installation and training of Vietnamese personnel. The technology is a kind of 'combing and carding independently' which technologically is a semi-modern line in comparison with 'combing and carding together' and is similar in sophistication to European plants (Italian, Swiss and German) of the 1970s. The mill also has a line with Open-End technology which uses rotors instead of looms to make best use of poor quality cotton. The planned operating time of the plant is 22.5 hours per day with three shifts a day and 306 days per year .

In 1992, the company was reorganised as a corporation consisting of three plants: spinning (1,291 employees), weaving-dyeing-garment (700) ,and a services workshop (100). This reflects a downstream shift for the company from producing only textiles to include knitwear and garments. Production of the mill is shown below.

Years	1989	1990	1991	1992	1993
Products					
Yarns (tons)	6,473	6,335	5,641	5,500	6,500
Fabrics (t)	-	-	-	600	600
Garment (pieces)	-	-	-	500,000	1M

NTC's employment changed slightly from year to year as follows:

1987: 2,000 persons; 1989: 1,785; 1990: 1,750;
1991: 1,750; 1992: 2,136; 1993: 2,150; 1994: 2,000.

The structure of the workforce is as follows: in addition to the production staff, 45 people are working in indirect supporting activities such as directorship, financial and accounting tasks. About 20 people are working in three groups specialised in technical (3-4), planning (4) and sales-supply (3) issues. Sixty five people (59 in 1987) have higher education degrees (university graduates, engineers), 120 graduated from vocational technical training colleges and 200 are technicians. The rest are workers who have been recruited during the construction phase of the project and subsequently trained by the Vietnamese and Japanese instructors to run spinning workshops.

Production facilities of the company includes:

- spinning: 100,000 spindles with a designed capacity of 5,100 (expected to be 6,000) tons of yarn per year; Open-End (OE): 1,200 rotors with a designed capacity of 600 to 1,000 tons per year.
- garment, weaving and knitting: designed capacity of equipment is 1,000 tons of knitted fabrics and 2 million pieces of garment per year.
- other equipment for carding and combing, for test and experimental laboratories.

Turnover (in USD):

1989: 6,862,630; 1990: 7,157,420; 1991: 7,427,430
1992: 9,000,000; 1993: 14,000,000; 1994: 17,000,000.

The company began export of yarns in 1983 to the former Soviet Union on the basis of a government trade agreement. During this period, the volume of export was small and quality of yarns was not very high. In 1989 and 1990, due to changes in this market and the start of textile joint venture operations in Vietnam which need yarns for their production, NTC began to sell yarns to these companies with payment made in USD (42% of the firm's total yarn production). More recently yarn product is being exported to other Asian markets like Taiwan and Singapore.

Since September 1992 NTC commenced exporting new products, like knitted fabrics and garment, to Japan and other countries. In 1993, NTC exported 1 million pieces of garment with a value of 2,200,000 USD to Japan, rising in 1994 to 2 million pieces (about 4 millions USD). Japanese long term partner of NTC - Itochu - has contracted to buy back these products after they helped the firm to invest in knitting and garment production activities. In addition, NTC also begins export of 60 new models of garment to France and Italy. This trial effort seems successful in European markets as well.

For NTC's business activities, macro-economic policies are influential, the first of which is the planning and allocation of productive companies in the textile industry. Because of this unique policy (to evenly distribute industrial capacities throughout the country), NTC was relocated to an isolated central province of Vietnam without the necessary infrastructures of roads, a harbour, electricity, storage or communication facilities. The great distance of NTC from HoChiMinh City caused a great deal of problems for the company in maintaining and expanding its business activities. It also created difficulties for gaining access to the industrial support system, with respect to providing training, gathering information and expanding its connections with new foreign partners. Regulations of foreign currency exchange are strict and NTC cannot keep its foreign exchange to satisfy the needs of new business activities - including technical change, repair and maintenance activities.

After the reforms of 1986, and with the increased need of Vietnamese-foreign joint-venture enterprises in yarns, the domestic market became more profitable for NTC. However, the smuggling of yarn from China (an outcome of the inefficient trade and customs policy) has done considerable damage to this business.

In the face of these external factors, NTC managers have made some responses. To secure funding for new businesses, the company has diversified its production by moving to downstream knitted garment products. This is the way to utilise NTC's own yarn products for a more value-added products (e.g., ready-to-wear clothes aimed directly at end users). This move to knitting has also been promoted by the increasing difficulty of doing business in spinning, due to the yarn smuggling problem. Hence, diversification to the new business of knitted garments is quite an important move for NTC. By doing this, it can tap more sources of income and accumulate reserves for new investment choices. The firm can also pursue its technological innovation and learning activities such as hiring experts, inviting teachers and instructors, sending people to courses, etc. In this way, the firm's response to its business problems and its learning efforts are almost the same.

At the same time, to secure better sources of supply, to widen its market channels, and to find the kinds of assistance that it cannot receive from the state, NTC continues to upgrade its long-term relationship with Itochu Co. Having worked with this Japanese trading company for almost two decades, NTC has established a very close and effective relationship that proved helpful in both the starting phase of spinning and the expansion phase of garment production. According to interviews with NTC's managers, the aim of the firm is to become a more equal partner with Itochu, not only in the textile business but also in other types of business in the near future. This may relieve NTC from dependence on serving the unstable needs of the domestic market, especially in yarn products.

However, NTC's isolated location continues to cause problems for the firm, although to a lesser extent than before. The weakness of the labour market still poses a difficulty. To expand production and recruit new workers, without the back-up of the training and research environment in HoChiMinh City, NTC will have to spend a lot of money on training and technical consultancy.

9.2.2 Building technological capabilities

Investment capability

Establishment phase: Since the start, all pre-investment and investment studies were carried out by specialists of both sides. Japanese companies included Itochu Co Ltd, Shin-Etsu Trading Co Ltd and Toyobo Engineering Co Ltd. - experts in engineering, construction and technical services for industrial plants, especially in textiles. Implementation of the project was also undertaken by Japanese experts responsible for choice of technology suppliers, designs of the plant, supervision for construction and installation works, starting up activity, etc. Vietnamese staff participated in some simple activities like construction and installation, but did not play a decisive role.

Mr. Duong Van Khang, director of another large textile plant in Hanoi was recruited as manager of the project (now Director of NTC). However, since the participation of the company's staff in the first phase of investment activities was limited, they got little from the experience, except for some vague idea about new venture investment.

Expansion phase: In 1991, Itochu helped NTC to set up a workshop for production of T-shirts, pullovers and children knitwear for export to Japan and South Korea. In 1992 it exported 1,500,000 pieces of garment (its buyers carry out all marketing and distribution). New products were not only for export but also for sale on the domestic market. Having the largest production capacity for spinning and the most modern technology facilities, NTC could sell its products to all other Vietnamese textile companies, and these products are much in demand. NTC staff are now more active and confident in drawing new investment studies, negotiating with technology suppliers, and looking for other technical assistance such as guidance and support in management issues from local as well as foreign partners. For example, alongside co-operating with Itochu in knitwear production, the company has also co-operated with ThanhCong textile company in HoChiMinh City for technical assistance on how to start and run newly set up knitwear and garment workshop.

The move of NTC from spinning activity to downstream business, like knitting and garment assembly, is a big shift in its orientation. This successful expansion (regardless of initial difficulties) shows the ability of the firm in carrying out investment activity. The company continued to invest in its spinning plant to expand and upgrade the existing production facility. During the past five year, the company has imported two production lines of combing and rotor spinning machines (2 more Open-End machines per year), improved the carding system, added auto splices hand fitting and testing instruments. In 1991, the company imported new equipment for dyeing, knitting and sewing from Japan, Korea and Taiwan (about 2,100,000 USD). Before this, (since 1989) the company had already invested 1,750,000 USD. Although in this period, the company still had to ask partners from outside (both Japanese and local) to assist in certain activities like starting up garment production, clearly its investment skills, experiences, and confidence now are more developed than in the previous phase.

Production capability

NTC staff can handle all production activities including management, maintenance and repair of equipment. The firm's performance has improved steadily in turnover, total volume of products and export. Since the start in 1982, the quality of products has also steadily increased.

In the initial period, the company relied on Polytechnic institute of HoChiMinh City and on technical companies for repair and maintenance of equipment (electrical, mechanical, etc.). Now, the company is more confident in running all production lines and dealing with repair activities by itself. It is observed that all levels of management (directorship, head masters of workshops, heads of divisions and operation groups) know how to run and organise workers at their respective levels. There was no outside permanent consultant to assist with production tasks (neither Japanese nor Vietnamese). When technical problems arose, the firm had a strict rule to follow, relying on local staff competence: workers and heads of units (workshops) have to look into the problem first, then report to technical experts if necessary. Usually, staff of each workshop is able to deal with these problems without help.

Still, maintenance has remained an issue for reasons other than capability. First, infrastructure facilities are poor. Supplied by the local electricity network, the company suffered power cuts during the 1980s for about 5 hours per day, sometimes for 15-20 days consecutively. It had to work 2.5 shifts instead of 3 which seriously prevented the company from reaching its designed capacity. Due to power cuts, some special equipment (such as filter that converts sea water into fresh water) needed for Nhatrang location was damaged. Second, poor supply of cotton material (or of poor quality cotton) caused problems for the operation of the plant. Recently, these problems have receeded through the provision of better infrastructure conditions locally and by the company itself. Third, maintenance problems remain due to shortage of foreign exchange for purchasing spare parts. According to estimates of experts from MOI, in general, 10 USD per spindle is needed annually to maintain and repair (buy part, etc.). That means NTC would need 1 million USD per year. In practice, it received only 100,000 USD from MOI. Up to 1990, due to lack of foreign exchange for purchasing parts, the rate of deterioration of equipment, such as the rotor of OE machines, is quite high. Some parts have to be used much longer than intended (e.g. leather belts of spindles have been used for 3 years instead of 6 months).

Except for the maintenance problem, NTC's personnel have no major problems in operating the production facility. After Japanese experts left in 1982, all production and related activities needed to maintain the project were run entirely by the staff of the company. Moreover, when the newbusiness opened up (garment and knitting) in 1991, after about a year relying on guidance of external consultants (mostly Vietnamese), NTC can now master all these new production processes in knitting and sewing operation.

Minor technical change capability

Since the start of operations, NTC has been able to introduce some minor changes aiming at rehabilitation of old equipment, and improvement of existing production facilities and products. The company has undertaken various small scale projects like manufacturing dust filter, sets of paraffin carding, ball-bearing drying equipment, improving dust-collecting system, etc. All these activities are done by the staff of the company itself without significant help from outside consultants.

Initially in the structure of NTC there was a special technical unit responsible for all technical improvement jobs. After 1989, the firm dissolved this unit and organised technical change activity on an ad-hoc basis. Whenever NTC needs to do some technical adjustment or adaptation, the director set up a group of experts from different divisions and workshops to deal with the problem. The kind of technical change undertaken sometimes involves adjusting elements of imported technology that are not suitable for Vietnamese conditions. An example is the dust-collecting system of spinning workshops. When the Japanese design of this system was brought to Vietnam it turned out not to be hermetic enough to deal with higher air temperatures. Dust was still penetrating into the workshop causing low quality of yarns. In addition, some pipes in this system were not functioning properly. The company had to work out what pipe changes were necessary and devise a method of sealing to help the system become more hermetic. From time to time, in order to save foreign currency, the staff also suggested some local made alternative of equipment like dotting machine to replace imported ones. They handled these minor technical changes with considerable confidence.

Marketing capability

This capability of NTC is nearly non-existent. Since the beginning of operations, types and ranges of products were decided by MOI in agreement with Japanese supplier, and mostly to meet local market needs. Products of high enough quality were bought back by the Japanese supplier or by some Soviet buyers. Thanks to high local demand for these products, the company has been able to sell its yarn products easily, thereby, easing the need for export marketing activities, at least up until recently. As for export markets, some trial exporting was being undertaken by the company, but mostly it relied on the foreign buyers and Vietnamese trading companies of the Ministry of Trade. Thus, the company did not need to acquire any marketing skills.

This situation is starting to change with the move to new garment products. NTC now exports through a co-operative agreement due to limited marketing capability. Itochu Co. is the main buyer of these garment products (80 to 85 % of NTC's total garment production is exported). NTC is able to supply input material from its own yarns, as well as its own management and technical expertise (with the support of ThanhCong weaving company in HoChiMinh City). The buyer provides design, colour, ranges of products and some special equipment which are not available locally. At present, the marketing function belongs to the division of planning, market and export-import. Also, the company has a show-room in joint venture with a district of HoChiMinh City to introduce its products and gather market intelligence from customers, mostly local. Still, this is only the firm's very first step in building up its marketing competence.

Linkage capability

NTC has weak linkage capability. One type is developed mostly with domestic institutions and universities to help the company in its problem solving in both technical and managerial issues. NTC has close co-operation with HoChiMinh City polytechnic institute for training of its staff and other technical assistance services. Because it is considered by many managers in the sector as one of the most modern spinning plants of Vietnam, NTC is even used as the site where technical people come on various study excursions. The RITI and Textile Engineering Factor No.2 of MOI have visited in order to make a survey together with NTC staff, on the different designs of equipment at the mill. The aim was to design, produce or improve similar equipment.[3]

The second type of linkage is with other weaving companies who buy NTC yarns, such as Thanhcong or Phongphu weaving plants in HoChiMinh City. In return for this, they support NTC with technical guidance and some problem-solving, especially in a new activity like garment and knitting production. This linkage has an important role in keeping NTC in touch with the latest developments in HoChiMinh City - the hub of textile industry in Vietnam - at the same time as ensuring it access to this dynamic Southern market.

Internal linkages within the company have been developed closely among its divisions and workshops. After the technical unit was dissolved, staff of the unit became seconded to production and sale units in a more flexible framework. Every year, the firm sent its staff from different divisions to work in its shop and show-room in HoChiMinh City; in this way, the circulation of information between sales and production activities is promoted.

Despite these linkages, NTC still lacks some linkages and information exchange mechanisms with other spinning firms working in Hanoi. One of the reasons is difficulties in communication, due to isolated location of the firm.

Major technical change capability

There was no evidence of capability in major change and design work at NTC. In spite of active minor technical change activities, it is difficult to see how NTC can develop them into a more major change capability, due to many problems, one of which is the weakness of the overall supporting R&D and industrial infrastructure.

9.2.3 Learning mechanisms

Prior accumulation

As a new turn-key project, staff of the company were prepared by MOI rather intensively in order to be able to receive transferred technology. Many managers of the firm come through being transferred (to the newly created project) from other textile plants in order to get to know the technology from the beginning. The most distinguished example is Mr. Duong Van Khang. He was the director of 'March 8' textile plant - one of the largest textile complexes in the North - before being assigned by MOI as NTC director. He brought with him about ten engineers and managers from his old plant as well as other staff. This group of people constituted the first generation of the company's employees working throughout the investment and start-up phases. On the basis of their former experiences, they knew how to run textile production, how to do investment studies and implement investment plans. Although this expertise was geared to older and more simple technology than that of NTC, its staff already had some elements of investment and production capabilities from the start. This prior knowledge was especially helpful for them later, in upgrading investment and production competence during the project's implementation.

The second generation of NTC staff was recruited during the implementation period from different Vietnamese and foreign universities and polytechnic institutes. Mr. Nguyen Thanh Binh, for example, graduated in textile engineering from Lodz University (Poland) and went back to Vietnam in 1978 where he obtained his Vietnamese experience at Hanoi Polytechnic Institute in textile engineering faculty. In 1982 he moved to NTC together with a group of newly graduated engineers of this faculty who became managers of NTC working in different work places. Mr. Nguyen has been promoted to head master of one spinning workshop. In general, they are young, more knowledgeable and educated. Many of them can speak foreign languages (Russian and East European languages such as Polish and German, and more recently English). Compared to their predecessors, they have been much better prepared in modern textile engineering. For example, the first generation like the director is more familiar with Chinese loom technology of the 'March 8' plant. The second generation learned more from the Soviet and quite modern spinning technology of East Germany (combing and carding), and they have a general idea about Open-End technology (non-loom technology based on rotors). Thanks to their formal training, this second generation of managers have contributed significantly to the firm's accumulation of technological expertise. Whenever a need for some minor technical change has arisen, they felt confident to deal with it. However, the lower level technical workforce like technicians and workers, benefited little from prior accumulation mechanism.

As was presented above, this prior learning process for accumulating knowledge and experiences is crucial for investment, production and minor change activities. Also, existing contacts of NTC's staff with their class mates and former colleagues who are working in research institutes, universities and other organisations help them a lot to develop linkage capability. At the same time, there was no marketing knowledge to be accumulated before the start of NTC. Its staff also did not have any experience of major technical change before working.

Foreign connections

Japanese technology suppliers and product buyers are the most active source of learning for workers and technicians. The assistance of the Japanese Itochu Co. can be divided into two main periods. The first period was the setting up of the turn-key spinning plant during 1978-1982. In the framework of this contract, the Japanese supplierd technical assistance for 10 months before and 6 months after mechanical completion of the last unit of the project. To implement the project, about 46 Japanese experts were sent in over 28 months (or 322 person-months) to undertake the following tasks:

Numbers of persons:	Time budget:
general management (1 person)	12 person-months
construction activity (7)	48 person-months

climatic and air conditioning (14)	95 person-months
electricity (independent source of power for emergency lighting) (8)	60 person-months
installation of equipment and start-up (16)	107 person-months

A group of Vietnamese personnel were assigned to support the Japanese experts. They worked together and shared (although informal) experiences. By working side by side with the Japanese, the Vietnamese got first hand experience of how the project was implemented. For example, NTC's staff gained some experience of international purchase and supply of equipment, eventhough they did not take part directly in this activity; by discussing with the Japanese experts, reading blueprint and contract documents, much new knowledge such as this became familiar to them. Thus, by associating with the Japanese since the early days of the project, NTC's personnel had a very good opportunity to learn investment skills. At the top level of management, the director of the plant and others worked together with the Japanese, discussing the implementation plans and time table, solving difficulties in dealing with local conditions. At the lower level, technicians and engineers such as Mrs. Nguyen Thi Ngoc Lien were assigned to accompany and assist Japanese experts in technical issues such as installation of equipment, utility and electricity erection. They got a chance to watch what the Japanese personnel did in reality, to ask them questions regarding how to solve certain difficulties and so on.

More formally, training and technical guidance were also provided by Itochu. Technical assistance for Vietnamese staff was undertaken in two areas. The first batch of knowledge was transferred through technical documentation which consisted of:

- specifications of machines;
- operation and maintenance manual;
- catalogue of spare parts;
- detailed operative conditions;
- standard operating procedures;
- special technical advice.

In production, Japanese Industrial Standards (JIS) and other Japanese practical manufacturing standards were applied. In order to train the Vietnamese staff in spinning production, another group of Japanese experts were sent as technical instructors:

Numbers of persons:	Time budget:
general management (1 person)	6 person-months
utility: mechanical engineer (1)	10 person-months
electricity: electrical engineer (1)	10 person-months
spinning activity: engineer (2)	24 person-months
Total: 5 persons	50 person-months

The working language was English so easing the process of communication, since the Vietnamese staff had some specific Vietnamese-English interpreters working for them, and there were some young personnel who could speak English themselves. There was also a Japanese-Vietnamese interpreter to help get contacts going more smoothly.

In addition to receiving experts, a group of 6 Vietnamese staff were sent to Japan for training one of whom was the director. They spent about 7 months learning how technological processes similar to that of NTC work and how to manage that kind of project. Since Itochu is a trading company, it arranged for this group to spend time in various plants with similar technology provided by Toyoda Co. and Murata Co. At these plants, Vietnamese managers became acquainted not only with production technology but also with other aspects of running the project. For example, they saw the ways Japanese firms organised production management, the ways they organised workers, dealing with discipline and other techniques of human resources management, and incentive system. During these 7 months, they also had a chance to associate with Japanese workers in various social activities and learned about Japanese life and working style, and observe labour relations processes. This trip turned out to be a very important experience for them. As the director said:

> Our Vietnamese proverb - one time of seeing is much better than a hundred times of hearing - is true in this case. I was there, I saw how Japanese did all these things and it's much easier to understand and remember.

Specifically, the reliance on foreign connection in this first period brought more knowledge and experience of production engineering, management skills, and repairs and maintenance. These important elements of production capability were obtained by NTC's staff almost at the start of operations.

Additional investment knowledge arrived with the second period of foreign assistance. In 1991, Itochu Co., at request of NTC, agreed to supply new equipment for knitting and garment production and technical assistance but much less than in the spinning phase. NTC's staff had to be more active in all investment activities through working with suppliers and learning from discussion with them. During this new investment phase, NTC's managers learnt more about starting a new venture.

So far, there is no evidence that other expertise like marketing or technical change has been accumulated by these foreign connections.

On-the-job training

This mechanism has contributed importantly to the accumulation of investment, production and minor change knowledge within NTC. Annually, NTC organises competitions and exams to increase qualification levels of its technical personnel and workers. In order to upgrade their skills, workers have to prepare themselves in theoretical questions and practical training before taking the exams. NTC sometimes held short term training courses (from 10 days to 2 weeks) to prepare workers for the exams, mostly in technical expertise (quality control, trouble-shooting activity). The importance of these courses is to keep workers aware of the need to upgrade their skills on a regular basis. Through this training, knowledge and skills about production management and engineering were provided. For managers and supervisors of workshops, another kind of on-the-job training is provided. Consultants and instructors are invited from MOI to work, teach or solve specific problems on a contract basis. These people, working in a managerial organisation like MOI, have more knowledge and experience in issues like setting up investment plans, applying for credit from financial institutions and banks, or dealing with administrative procedures. Therefore, sometimes they came to solve not only specific technical, but also non-technical problems. There, right on the site of the firm, they taught NTC staff in a semi-informal way. At the same time, others have assisted NTC in technical matters of production engineering and change. When the firm started its new knitting and garment venture, the company invited personnel of Thanhcong textile company from HoChiMinh City to help for a couple of months with start-up operations.

From time to time, researchers from Southern filial of the RITI, HoChiMinh City Polytechnic and Textile Mechanical Factory No.2 have visited NTC and contributed to the consulting and teaching courses. Working together with them in different assigned groups (similar to working with foreigners), NTC's staff learned about production know-how that is not written in any textbook or manual. One example was the manufacturing of 1,200 sets of paraffin carding. While undertaking this task, NTC had difficulties in knowing the exact components of these sets. They contacted researchers from RITI for consultancy. These people together with NTC provided some experimental tests and consequently came up with the most optimal solution. After that, NTC staff knew how to do these tests and similar experiments for other relevant activities next time.

Off-the-job training

More recently, NTC has been exercising this mechanism to a certain extent. The company sends managers for short courses on economic and management issues mostly to HoChiMinh City. These courses are run by HoChiMinh City Economics University and other consulting/training organisations (such as Technology Development Co. belonging to the City's Science and Technology Department) and range from 2-3 days to 2 weeks. They give participants a quick update and introduction to basic ideas on business administration, foreign trade, systems of international payment, project appraisal, etc. More recently, this training has tried to cover marketing issue as well. However, as confessed by both Mr. Nguyen Thanh Binh and Mrs. Nguyen Thi Ngoc Lien, these courses are too theoretical and lack practical usefulness, especially for local Vietnamese conditions.

Information search

This mechanism is not very much used by NTC. The most significant pool of documentation was that collected by the company in the implementation of the spinning project and therefore, it was useful for spinning only. For the next phase, there was little documentation available for NTC on knitting and garment production, from any source. Even Vietnamese sources of information are very difficult for NTC access because of the long distance between Nhatrang and HoChiMinh City where most technical information and documentation are held. In short, NTC acquires information on a very ad-hoc basis, lacking regular access and screening.

Learning-by-doing

Again, it is quite difficult to assess learning-by-doing effort. The fieldwork revealed that this way of learning occurs widely in NTC. In all investment, production, minor change and linkage areas, the firm has been involved in many activities, made some mistakes, repeated again and learned how to avoid these mistakes in the future; each time, the staff learnt something more. Only in marketing and major technical change did NTC not attempt anything significant. One example is how they learned investment capability just by engaging in a new investment project (an expansion). Having been involved and taught by Japanese experts quite actively in the first phase investment for spinning production, NTC managers seem to have known how to do feasibility studies, how to choose equipment and deal with the transaction, installation and start-up. This factor, in addition to shortage of funding for involving more foreigners in the second phase of new knitting and garment business, led them to decide to do this expansion mostly by themselves. The director described their attitudes as:

> We thought that we can do it this time. We learned from Japanese a lot from first time, so it should be easier for us.

He was overly optimistic. When they wanted to choose technology, this was more complicated than it seemed. The types of knitting technology and sewing machines that are suitable for knitted material are many, and range widely in terms of quality, sources of input quality and prices. These issues are more diverse than in the spinning phase and were new to NTC. Although Itochu Co. was asked to help with technology supply and some simple technical assistance was brought in, it was not enough. The scale of Japanese involvement was much less than before and NTC simply did not know what to do next. They tried to install equipment and start production. It did not work properly, there was a high rate of defects. NTC technical staff had to struggle with re-arranging, re-installing, re-test, and even asked for help from Thanhcong textile company in HoChiMinh City who are more experienced in knitting and garment. It took them almost a year to put the new operation in order. From this, they learnt about the need for better preparation in starting any kind of new business.

Table 9.2 Learning mechanisms at NTC

TC	Investment	Production	Minor change	Marketing	Linkage	Major change
Ranking	*strong*	*strong*	*weak*	*no*	*weak*	*no*
Learning						
By-doing	+	+	+	0	+	0
Prior accumulation	+	+	+	0	+	0
On-the-job training	+	+	+	0	0	0
Off-the-job training	+	+	0	+	0	0
Foreign connection	+	+	0	0	0	0
Information	+	0	0	0	0	0

Although now NTC staff is more confident in knitting and garment, they know how difficult it is, if they go further to garment production based on more sophisticated fabrics such as microfiber. If they do expand again, they know from where to start, how to deal with potential problems in a shorter period. Mrs. Nguyen Thi Ngoc Lien said:

> We were over confident. Next time, we have to be better prepared.

The patterns of learning in NTC is given in Table 9.2.

9.2.4 Macro external factors, micro behaviours and learning

Factors of macro-economic policies are the most influential for learning efforts of NTC. The first policy is the planning and allocation of productive forces in the textile industry. It was due to this unique view (to evenly divide industrial capacity throughout the country), that NTC was located in such an isolated place. This policy (related to the investment policy of the industry), caused a lot of problems for the company: poor availability of training; poor sources of information; and inhibiting opportunities to expand its foreign connection to new partners. It seems difficult for all these learning mechanisms to operate, being far from HoChiMinh City where most learning sources are concentrated. Regulations of foreign currency management are strict and NTC cannot keep its foreign exchange to satisfy the need of technical change, repair and maintenance activities. It prevented the firm from being active and self-learning or from having more financial resources for on-the-job training.

A weak labour market factor is another cause of difficulties for NTC in its recruitment efforts and training programmes for newly recruited work force. As a small town, Nhatrang cannot supply a large project like NTC with enough skilled and professional labour as in HoChiMinh City area. The domestic market offers a profitable business opportunity for NTC, but the smuggling of yarn from China, (encouraged by an inefficient trade and customs policy), has done some damage to this business.

As a result of isolated location, other supporting institutions function poorly. The physical infrastructure was badly provided: a lack of electricity; and poor communication and transportation facilities caused many problems for NTC in getting information and attracting more foreign connections. During the 1980s, the supply of cotton imported from the former Soviet Union was of poor quality. Because of this, some attempts by NTC to experiment with production of finer yarns were unsuccessful and eventually discouraged the firm from learning-by-doing through 'trial and error'. The long distance of NTC from HoChiMinh City made it difficult for the firm to get easy access to learning sources for its training activities. Experts from other companies, R&D institutes or

HoChiMinh City polytechnic were usually hesitant to visit the firm, due to the fact that transport to Nhatrang is slow and inconvenient (a bus takes 12 hours to cover this 500 km distance, for example).

Cultural factors have also had some impact on the learning attitude of the work force at NTC. The long period under planned economy and subsidised incentive system made staff of the company quantity rather than quality-oriented. They care more about volume of production and plan implementation than quality and diversification of product range.[4] Some workers do not understand the necessity of quality and don't even bother to think about it. This attitude undermines both on-the-job training and learning-by-doing efforts of workers, in spite of initiatives taken in some areas. In this regard, the attitudes of MOLI and other authorities concerned are also a problem. For them, NTC, with its modern technology from outside sources is doing well enough. Accordingly, in their plans, it does not require further assistance from the authorities which should concentrate on weaker enterprises. This mentality of 'equality' reduced potential help which NTC still needs to receive from these administrative organisations for its learning, in terms of provision of information, investment sources or training opportunities, etc.

As a result, NTC has to face most pressures coming from external factors for its on-the-job, off-the-job training, collection of information and getting foreign contacts.

NTC managers have responded to these factors in various ways. The most visible response is to diversify its business activity from spinning to garments and knitting. In this context, the assistance of its familiar partner, Itochu, was a suitable option. The company has diversified its production by moving to downstream knitting and garment products. By doing so, NTC utilises its own yarn products for more value added products like ready-to-wear clothes aimed directly at end users. This enables the firm to generate more income and accumulate reserves for new investment projects. The firm is also able to benefit from this for its technological innovation and learning activities such as hiring experts, inviting teachers and instructors, sending people to courses, etc. In this way, the fimr's response to problems for business and for learning efforts are almost the same.

As for the problems caused by the poor supporting system, some additional measures were taken. To secure a better source of supply, market channels, and assistance that NTC cannot rely on of the state, the firm continues to upgrade its long term relations with Itochu Co. Having worked with this Japanese trading company for almost two decades, NTC established very close and effective relations that have been helpful in both the starting phase of spinning and the expansion phase of garment assembly. According to NTC's managers, the aim of the firm is to become a more equal partner with Itochu, not only in the textile business but maybe in other types of business in the near future. This may also relieve NTC from depending on the unstable needs of the domestic market, especially in yarn products.

However, there are problems to which NTC cannot find any solution. Its location continues to cause problems for the firm, although to a less extent than before. A weak labour market still poses difficulties. If NTC intends to expand production and recruit new workers, without the backing of the state training and research environment in HoChiMinh City, then the firm will have to spend a lot of resources on training and technical consulting.

By diversifying to avoid the problems facing its business, NTC can in many respects reduce the difficulties of learning, but this might not always be the case. In order to deal with market factors and the difficulties caused by state policies and weaknesses in the supporting infrastructure, NTC is developing its ties more closely with Itochu Co. At the same time, however, the firm is not diversifying its foreign connections to access newer learning sources.

9.3 Some distinct features of two textile/garment firms

Both firms share similar sequences in TC building, with production capability coming first and others arriving later. However, while TLG has acquired only production and minor change capabilities, NTC has also developed investment and linkage capabilities. This TC accumulation pattern is explained by the way the two firms learn. The patterns presented in Tables 9.1 and 9.2 suggest that the firms need to have (i) learning-by-doing as a necessary mechanism, then (ii) at least one other learning mechanism to achieve some degrees of TC. In order to obtain strong TC, they need to use more mechanisms. In the case of linkage capability, both firms used two mechanisms. The main difference is the essential learning-by-doing mechanism used at NTC - which TLG did not try. In TLG, without this learning mechanism, the other two mechanisms of prior accumulation and foreign connection have not proved sufficient for building up the capability. Neither learning-by-doing alone (in TLG), nor off-the-job training without learning-by-doing (in NTC), is sufficiently effective for marketing capability accumulation.

The first distinct feature is the different *use of prior training and accumulation of experience* by the two firms. While NTC can enjoy non-technical investment knowledge brought from other work places by its new director and managers, TLG's managers mostly have technical knowledge suitable for production activity. Thus, prior accumulation has contributed to investment capability in NTC, but not in TLG. Both firms used this prior experience and connections to develop their linkage competence, but with different results: NTC has got this capability whereas TLG has not. This is due to the combined use of this mechanism with learning-by-doing in NTC. The policy of putting experienced managers into NTC from the start has contributed positively.

There is another difference in the way that *training* has contributed to the TC acquisition of the two firms, depending on the *attitude of their managers*. Compared to TLG, NTC managers are more active in maintaining good connections with R&D and training institutions and bringing consultants in to give courses. The attitude of NTC managers, in this respect, is crucial for deciding to what extent the firm uses sources for on-the-job training. Also, concerning off-the-job training, NTC seems to have a more conscious commitment than TLG to sending its staff on courses, in spite of the long distance from HoChiMinh City.

TLG tends to send its people on training courses held by Hanoi polytechnic or university on quality control or textile mechanical engineering. Investment appraisal or marketing courses have only very recently started and do not as yet contribute to the firm's accumulation of non-technical knowledge. Therefore, this mechanism has mainly helped the firm in learning knowledge suitable for production and minor change capabilities. At NTC, training includes knowledge and experience relevant for investment competence. In addition to the technical knowledge that NTC gets from the training programmes of MOI, the company has acquired greater knowledge of economic and business management - mostly from institutions in HoChiMinh City. The availability of more non-technical expertise in HoChiMinh City than in Hanoi is a result of the more favourable historical circumstances of Southern industrial development.

The next feature is in the *use of foreign connections*. TLG used this mechanism mostly to acquire engineering and management experiences suitable for production and minor change capabilities. TLG's heavy reliance on the SIDA programme and its Korean direct investor (contributing to the firm's passive attitude in both pre- and post-reform periods) prevented it from gaining marketing and investment knowledge and experience. In contrast to TLG, and in addition to learning production expertise from Japanese suppliers, NTC has been more active in investment activity while dealing with foreign partners, especially in its expansion phase into the garment business. Due to the prior knowledge accumulation of managers coming from elsewhere, the absorptive capacity of NTC is higher than that of TLG. This explains why, for investment capability, NTC is able to utilise foreign connections more than TLG. This fact suggests that the use of foreign connections to some extent depends on a firm's use of the prior accumulation mechanism.

Honesty and openness are also important attitudinal differences separating the two firms with respect to their co-operation with foreign partners. For example, when Itochu Co.'s managers were asked their general opinion on project implementation, they cited one reason for the successful technology transfer to NTC as the honest attitude of its Vietnamese managers, including the most senior people such as the director, towards the Japanese partners, as compared with other Vietnamese managers. At the same time, not all TLG managers were open-minded towards their Korean partners. Only the Vice-Director and some of his junior managers seemed willing to learn from the Korean experts. Apart from these few people, the impression (from talking to other junior staff) was that there is still a general reluctance to co-operate, on the part of the director and other managers.

In general, the different *attitude to learning* can be understood in the context of the different background of the staff in the two firms. There is more evidence of managers at NTC having an entrepreneurial orientation and a keeness to learn from outside consultants than in TLG. Moreover, the managers of NTC constitute a more coherent and comprehensive group who have been working together, almost since the beginning of the project. Therefore, they are more ready to get on and co-operate, sharing a willingness to ensure the technological progress of the firm. This fact is a reminder that a firm's learning behaviour is influenced significantly by the background of the firms and its managers' attitudes.

Both TLG and NTC face very severe pressure from external factors in their business activity and learning efforts, especially in terms of the macro-economic policies of the state and the supporting system of training, education and R&D and other service institutions. Accordingly, the two firms are pursuing a similar strategy of diversification. However, they differ in the scope of the diversification and therefore in the types of TC they need. TLG diversified its range of products mostly from within garment production, which required almost the same sewing techniques albeit with a need for new finishing skills. NTC diversified into the knitting and garment business and its managers have had to take certain risks to learn the TCs required for products unfamiliar to them. Although it is more difficult, this way of learning-through-struggling with new technological issues has given NTC's managers a reward which TLG does not have: the acquisition of more diversified production skills and new investment competence.

The different strategies of the two firm's are observed in their long-term co-operation with their foreign partners. In upgrading its relations with foreign partners, TLG's managers preferred to expand to new partners (German, Korean, Swedish) for the same depth of relations and learning, while NTC has upgraded its relations with a single partner

(Itochu), to a more intertwined and co-operative link. This difference in pursuing foreign contacts has given TLG more diversified foreign sources from which it can learn minor change and linkage and it reduces its dependence on a single foreign partner. NTC's close relation with Itochu has brought mid-term benefits (more training and consultancy), but in the long run it may make NTC too dependent on this Japanese trading house and thus reduce the chances of finding new learning sources. Interestingly, the too-close relationship of NTC with Itochu turned out to be a disadvantage for learning minor technical change skills. The new turn-key plant seems to raise both psychological and technical barriers for NTC's staff in thinking about changing their technical specifications. The Japanese partner did not undertake any technical change or give advice on this issue, and NTC's employees were unable to learn technical change expertise from their foreign partner. Besides, a dependency may arise in exploiting new market opportunities, and thus prevent the firm from learning from other sources for new marketing knowledge.

In using foreign connections, NTC managers are also sometimes less creative than TLG's vice director - a spin-off from learning from GunYoung workshop in TLG, for example. If NTC can remedy this weakness, the firm may be in a much better strategic position and thus continue its current stronger status of learning TCs as compared with TLG.

9.4 Consumer electronic firm E2 (HAL)

9.4.1 The company profile and business context

HAL was set up in Hanoi at the end of 1984 as a local state-owned enterprise. The company started with about 100 staff, and now has five member enterprises specialising in materials, mechanical engineering, industrial electronics, consumer electronics and repair and maintenance activities. The total labour force is about 500 (on average 40 to 50 per enterprise), including its joint venture subsidiaries. At the outset, HAL produced black-and-white TV sets, simple radio cassettes and some audio equipment. Now, its range of consumer electronics has expanded to include colour TV sets, TV tubes and a sample production of VCRs and hi-fi equipment like karaoke machines.

From the beginning, the company aimed to produce consumer electronics for the domestic market together with some measurement and control equipment. In 1985 HAL chose JVC (Japan Victor Co., a Matsushita company) as a partner in a technology transfer agreement. JVC supplied the complete equipment for assembly lines which could produce colour TVs, radio cassettes and some hi-fi equipment, as well as instruments for testing, measurement and quality control. By 1988, HAL expanded its foreign relations to other Japanese and Korean companies, also on the basis of business contracts which stipulated the transfer of all the equipment for the production lines.

The firm has two lines to produce consumer electronics products from CKD and SKD components, with one line of SKD production to be completed. In co-operation with JVC, it intends to further develop its IKD production capability. The two CKD and SKD lines have capacity for 60,000 machines per year. In agreement with both Japanese and Korean companies, production is split: 85% for consumer electronics; 15% for industrial electronics. HAL's turnover (in USD) has dramatically in only three years: 1992: 8 million; 1993: 13.8 million; 1994: 27.3 million.

Five years after its establishment, the company was still only operating in the domestic market. However, in 1989, it signed a contract with a Japanese company to produce industrial electronic parts for the robotic hands used in NISSAN's car assembly plant in Britain. Production is carried out on the basis of OEM agreements: the design and technical specifications are provided by the Japanese company, while HAL organises the production arrangements and the supply of almost all inputs. However, these products are simple, mostly involving metal-working, and some specific components are still provided by the Japanese partner.[5] The Japanese partner took care of all marketing and distribution activities and the contract marked HAL's first involvement in exporting. For other activities, HAL tried to approach the Soviet and East European markets with consumer electronics products such as colour TV sets and radio cassettes but without meeting any success. It could only occasionally export very small volumes of product. Recently, HAL has tried to explore the possibilities of exporting its products to remote locations in South China where similar Chinese-made products are of lower quality.

In the domestic market, HAL actively co-operated in 1993-1994 with foreign companies, especially Daewoo. The firm has signed contracts to assemble tubes for Daewoo's colour TV sets for export purposes. The project is worth 170 million USD and has involved setting up a plant to produce about 1.6 millions tubes per year, 80% of which are for export. The company is also co-operating with Daewoo to set up a plant to assemble colour TV sets for export in Vietnam (where 70% of the components are to be made locally). In addition, HAL has approached other large firms like French Thomson CSF, and the American companies, Digital Equipment Co. (DEC) and AT&T, in its attempt to pursue its future expansion in the computing business.

Among external factors, the heavy taxation burden receives the most criticism from this company. Its unequal position, as compared with foreign investors, concerning tax rates and incentives make local firms like this one less competitive. For example, while domestic companies have to pay rather high taxes without any exemption period, foreign investors are exempted from tax for a period of four years after profitable production has started. As HAL sees it, this problem makes it less able to accumulate resources for attempting various kinds of new investment.

The lack of long-term policies to develop the electronics industry as a whole also hinders the efforts of this SOE firm to orient itself towards making long-term investments, and it is difficult for HAL to anticipate how it may best co-operate with foreign firms.

State ownership poses its own kind of problem for HAL. Salaries are low and rigidly set. Although there used to be perks attached to jobs in this kind of company - such as housing and social security benefits - these became minimal following the reforms of 1986. The managers of SOEs cannot implement flexible incentive systems, as is possible in private companies. Nor can they regulate themselves financially or in terms of their recruitment or labour practices.

Market problems also cause some difficulties for HAL. The weak development of the domestic market for industrial electronics and computing has led to a poor demand for high-tech products. This situation renders electronics firms like HAL a disincentive to making an effort to produce more sophisticated products. Meanwhile, the consumer electronics market is becoming increasingly competitive.

To lessen the difficulties of generating adequate capital, one of HAL's priorities has been to pursue many different foreign partners. Using the assistance of foreign partners during the initial stage, the firm hopes to accumulate sufficient resources to ensure that they can invest back into their own core electronics activities. Moreover, the aim of the firm is to become more equal with its foreign partners, and, consequently, to become an independent and strong player in the electronics business, both at home and in international markets. Therefore, HAL is attempting to expand beyond electronics into other types of business through its three joint ventures with Daewoo: picture tubes; TV sets and electronic appliances; and a business centre and hotel complex.

To deal with market factors, HAL pursues a mixed approach of diversifying its product range as well as searching for niches that the firm can comfortably enter. While continuing with its production of consumer electronics, the company also actively looks for opportunities to do something quite new, e.g., assembling electronics hands for robots. New products like this may help the firm to exploit a niche market with the Japanese producers and to become part of that particular niched network globally. In addition, the firm is currently searching for new partners (who are not Japanese or Korean) for other higher value-added products.

This represents one way for them to side-step the weak local demand for their high-technology products. Besides, HAL has also approached and held negotiation with other large firms like Thomson CSF (France), American Digital Equipment Co. (DEC), and AT&T for future expansion into computer business.

9.4.2 Building technological capabilities

Investment capability

In the early years, the managers of HAL were not very confident in dealing with investment issues. When the company started, it relied on local experts for financial and economics matters. HAL is one of the first electronics company created by Hanoi city. People working in financial and legal departments of the city assisted the starting process in setting up the firm, dealing with financial accounting and payment, banking and credit system, etc. Also, experts of some research and training institutions like Hanoi polytechnic were invited to take part in investment issues, starting up production lines and dealing with technical problems.

The second phase of expansion in late 1980s and early 1990s brought more new investment practices when the firm began its relation with other firms, like Daewoo. In contracts to import technologies from Japan or South Korea, the company also involved some foreign experts in investment studies. Now, the company is able to make decisions by itself concerning investment plans and implementation of these plans. In some activities, like construction or civil engineering design of its new facilities, it may invite some people from local construction companies to take part.

Although the company still has not fully acquired the competence in sourcing new technologies, it has become more capable of dealing with general investment issues than before. Dr. Hoang Van Nghien, director of the firm, said:

> When working for the first contract with JVC, we need a year to complete feasibility study and investment plan. Now, when we work and develop new activities with Daewoo, we know how to do things and it takes us about one month. We have to be faster and I think we can be so.

The ambition and capability of HAL in investment activities can be seen in its rather aggressive approach to ventures of the latest expansion in co-operating with foreign companies in 1993-1994. It has signed contracts with Daewoo to assemble tubes for colour TV sets for export. The project is for 170 millions USD to set up a plant to produce about 1.6 millions tubes per year, 80% of which are for export. The company has a plan to go further in co-operation with Daewoo, to set up a plant to assemble colour TV sets in Vietnam for export (with 70% of components to be made locally).

Production capability

When HAL began operation, the company needed the support of other local companies, research institutes, universities such as Hanoi Polytechnic and the National Centre for Scientific Research (NCSR). In addition to providing equipment for assembly, foreign technology suppliers assisted the company to accumulate its first knowledge and experience in the management and operation of production facilities. Under the supervision of JVC quality control is carried out strictly in accordance with procedures using appropriate measurement equipment, etc.), as well as other maintenance and repair activities. After two years, HAL has become confident in handling all its production lines, maintenance and repair activities, without regular help from foreign experts. Presently, the company has a special unit to take care of quality control. This unit introduces quality standards to different production units of the company and oversees implementation of these standards. Thanks to these measures, the quality of consumer electronics, such as TV sets or audio equipment, is equal to that of South Korean or other Southeast Asian products. In industrial electronics, HAL's quality is regarded by the Japanese contractor as acceptable.

Although having a production capability did not lead to the export of consumer electronics, its accumulation did play an important role later when the company shifted to production of industrial electronics for export. The production of new products requires almost the same skills and techniques: welding operations, placing components, testing and organising component supply, and the same technical standards of precision and miniaturisation. Therefore, the skill and knowledge acquired by HAL's staff in assembling TVs and hi-fi products has accelerated the firm's ability to assemble industrial electronics parts in this new venture.

Minor technical change capability

Minor change capability developed along with the accumulation of production capability. In assembling consumer electronics, HAL has introduced some minor changes to upgrade products or improve production processes: it changed aspects of assembling radio cassettes and TV sets (procedures, schemes), replacing components in order to multiply utilities or make them more suitable for use in Vietnamese conditions (poor infrastructure: electricity, transport, housing, stores facilities, less stable power supply).

With video tapes coming from different countries using various transmission standards (NTSC for Japan and the US, PAL for Europe and

ASEAN countries, and SECAM for France and Soviet block countries), Vietnamese consumers prefer to have a multi-system TV and VCR set that is compatible with all of these. In order to sell modified TVs and VCRs, HAL replaces parts of the original design with new components and parts.

HAL has also changed the rate of labour use to suit the capacity of Vietnamese workers. For example, while the length of a shift for Japanese workers is 8 hours, because lower productivity (due to poorer health and lower wages) the shift length for Vietnamese workers has been adjusted to only 6 hours (a similar adjustment exists in Thailand, where there is a 7 hour shift using the same assembly technology). Since the production design of the foreign suppliers did not deliver the expected productivity, production lines were rearranged after which productivity almost doubled.

Starting from small changes, HAL now began new and more changes of product design and production. After some years of passively importing semi-complete technologies, it commenced to design its own production lines. The firm purchased new equipment and parts from various foreign sources and put them together into new assembling facilities; technology suppliers, both local and foreign, were now less involved than before. Going further toward technological innovation and change activity, HAL now participates in one of the projects of the state research programme on developing IKD component production in Vietnam.

Marketing capability

This capability is still very weak. The firm is oriented only to the local market where it has been opening 11 shops or show-rooms in big cities and provinces to introduce its products and take care of maintenance and repair services. As for foreign markets, due to still limited export activities, marketing activity has only recently been instigated. The company has also explored marketing its industrial electronics products through its partner in Japan. By participating in subcontracting for a company in Japan, HAL used this contact to enter the Japanese market indirectly. It then set up a joint-venture office, Yokohanel (with Yokohama city), in the beginning of 1992. With this office, HAL tries to develop not only its marketing activities for existing products but also keeping an eye out for potential partners and markets for new products. Nevertheless, an overall marketing capability is still absent in HAL.

Linkage capability

HAL has close relations with sources of research and technological intelligence, like Hanoi Polytechnic or NCSR. Forms of co-operation range from signing contracts to solve technological problems of the company to long-term consultancy agreements. For example, the company has had to import tin for its welding equipment for sometime and this caused the dependency on foreign sources (Japanese or Korean). To solve this problem, HAL, in co-operation with a research institute, tried to produce welding tin locally. After a successful experiment, the company can now supply itself with this material. In general, the services of these research institutes and technical companies could serve the needs of HAL well, but they are not regular and systematic. HAL also has relations with some other local firms, but these links still lack any long-term commitments to co-operate. Linkage among different divisions of HAL (e.g technical division is co-operating with production and sales divisions) is organised under the supervision of the director. Linkage of the company with foreign suppliers and buyers is also quite well developed. HAL's relations with JVC were fruitful in creating the initial capabilities. It then developed further linkages with other Japanese and Korean companies, such as NEC, Daewoo, Samsung and Lucky Goldstar (LG Group).

Major technical change capability
According to HAL's assessment, it has taken some first steps towards acquiring this capability. It has a specialised unit for R&D (15 persons) reporting directly to the director, and is responsible for the introduction of new changes and improvements. Despite its name, the R&D unit has been doing more technical improvement than research, although recently HAL has started to engage in research effort.[6] These minor technical changes contributed considerably to the firm's earnings. In the long run, these activities could help the firm prepare for further and more research activity, and which might lead to significant innovation. However, these change activities are still more minor than really radical, in terms of the taxonomy of major technical change (ie the ability of the firm to introduce new in principle products and process technology). So far this capability does not exist in the firm.

9.4.3 Learning mechanisms

Foreign connections
This is the most frequently used learning mechanism at HAL. In the start up period, JVC was the main supplier of technology including training for HAL's assembling activities; JVC engineers and technicians went to Vietnam to give instruction and supervise production lines. Later on, they visited the firm on a regular basis (periodically 2-3 experts visited for a couple of weeks to a month). This direct assistance occurred during the first two years of co-operation. Within the framework of this contract, different groups of Vietnamese engineers and technicians also went to

Japan for training. These trips were repeated (with 4-5 persons per trip) with a duration ranging from some weeks to one month. JVC had also arranged for Vietnamese trainees to visit various manufacturing facilities. As a result, these persons learned how to run assembly lines with similar production technology. More importantly, they learnt the whole business culture of JVC like organising work places, dealing with training of workers, linking one workshop with others in information flows.

These trips to Japan continued up until recently, becoming more of an experience exchange (exhibition, study tours, etc.), with the topics expanding from merely technological issues to international transaction and marketing. This first wave of foreign assistance helped HAL a lot in its initial accumulation of knowledge and experience. By 1987, after 2 years working together with JVC, HAL acquired some competence in production activities. To a lesser extent, JVC personnel were also involved in preparation of some investment studies, shared working experiences with HAL through informal discussion, and sometimes gave advice to HAL's managers.

Since 1988, HAL has developed relations with new foreign partners. When the company began relations with Korean firms, in particular with Daewoo, this learning by co-operating with foreigners got a new stimulus. Currently, Daewoo is working very closely with HAL in three new joint ventures, Daewoo has a 75% stake in each case. The first project is for Daewoo-Hanel Co. to start a 233 millions USD plant to produce TV sets, refrigerators and other appliances for export. Korean experts also came for several months to assist HAL with preparation of feasibility studies and other construction, erection, start up activities. The second joint venture is the construction and operation of the Dae-Ha Business Centre on the outskirt of Hanoi; building a hotel, two high-rise appartment building and shopping complex, amounting to 250 ı million USD. Although this joint venture is far from electronics business, HAL managers can learn a great deal in investment and expansion skills, especially on how to deal with procurement, international shipment of goods and other issues of large scale project management.

The third joint venture (with Orion Electronics Co., a subsidiary of Daewoo) contributes the most to learning in electronics for HAL. The two sides set up a 170 million USD plant Orion-Hanel, to produce TV picture tubes, part of which would enable HAL to produce TVs for itself. This plant started production by the end of 1994 intending to produce 1.6 millions tubes per year of which 1 million is for colour TVs, 600,000 for black and white TVs, and computer making. 80% of products are for export and the rest for local use.

In the joint venture agreement, Orion Co. Ltd transfers technology and supply equipment for HAL, of which the most important ingredient for learning is a training programme, to be divided into two phases. In the first phase, 72 engineers and technicians went to Korea to learn about the production of tubes, technology handling and other production management issues. This group of personnel learned rather more technical knowledge and at a higher level of qualification compared to the group of Vietnamese personnel trained in Korea in the second phase. For the first time many HAL managers got a chance to learn experiences directly, at a large and comprehensive foreign production plant. Thanks to this training, HAL's staff got an overall technological landscape for working with Daewoo, providing a very crucial background to starting the plant. In addition, they also learned basic Korean and something about Korean culture.

In the second phase, about 20 Korean engineers came to Vietnam for equipment erection works and provided instruction and general guidance. At the same time, workers of the joint venture were sent to Korea for training in running production facilities: assembling tubes and dealing with other operations. These workers were divided into four groups and sent at different times to Korea, each time spending three months there. To comment on this training provided by the Korean partner, Mr. Binh from sales and international transaction division, said:

> Before this training, we knew more or less about electronics technology. Through working with JVC, we already learned many technological skills. But the knowledge of running production plant on such a large scale we never had. This massive training giving us a fresh idea in a complete programme is unique. Moreover, some knowledge in management is quite new for us.

All these efforts have produced a complete working team for the joint venture, ensuring that all people involved in the production have a general idea of tube making and can handle their relevant working positions properly. Moreover, HAL learned from its foreign partners how to link different workshops of the same plant to produce the final product.

In the interaction with foreign partners, HAL even invited foreign engineers (Japanese and later Korean) to give them advice on making technical improvements. Although officially, foreign experts were not assigned to help HAL with technological change, informal discussion and talk sometimes helped managers by giving them a clearer idea of technical issues, such as the whole concept of Japanese quality management.

As shown here, foreign connections play a crucial role in HAL's learning for investment, production, minor change and linkage capabilities. To a lesser extent, the company has also tried to acquire marketing knowledge through intensity of foreigners' visits. Every day, the firm meets no less than 2-3 delegations of businessmen from different companies and countries. The director set up a secretary group, who have to write down all questions that visitors ask during the discussion, their proposal, suggestions, conclusion, etc. These transcripts are later analysed by the firm as it tries to identify what foreign businessmen want and what they expect from HAL and Vietnamese producers, as well as what the market wants. As Dr. Hoang Van Nghien mentioned:

> We learned a lot by doing this analysis, especially for finding new production tendencies or information about market perspective, potential niche product, etc. that sometimes they (foreigners) told us during our meeting.

Moreover, he compared and cross-checked information given by different groups of businessmen, and try to combine them in terms of reaching some conclusions.

At the same time, HAL approached Yokohama City to create Yokohanel Business office in Yokohama. The aim of this initiative is for HAL to have an on-the-spot point for gathering marketing intelligence and business opportunities. Through establishing this office, the firm got a good picture about the development of industrial electronic companies and the market perspective in Japan. More recently, the opening of a similar office in Hanoi (aimed at serving Japanese businessmen) is being considered. However, these efforts are just beginning so that the firm cannot be said to have acquired a fully developed marketing competence.

Looking at the development of HAL's relations with foreign partners, the dynamics of learning activities can be seen as follows. First, the company expanded its links with foreign partners, from having only JVC to having a more diversified source of learning. While Daewoo has become the most important partner, HAL still continues its relations with other Japanese and Korean firms (Samsung, NEC, etc.). Second, the format of relations has changed from being simple and passive subcontracting, to a more equal partnership. The range of products has also moved from simple black and white TVs to colour TVs and other audio equipment, and on to complicated industrial electronics. As for technological learning, the firm began from having simple technical assembling knowledge and has moved on to non-technical experiences in investment and management issues.

Prior accumulation

Initially, the firm was started by a group of 5 scientists and their 13 employees, who moved from the department of radio-electronics engineering of Hanoi Polytechnic to set up a new production unit at the request of Hanoi city committee. Dr. Hoang Van Nghien, the director of HAL, was the Dean of this department. The other staff were researchers and lecturers working in this department or other institutes and universities before Dr. Nghien invited them to work at HAL. They had already accumulated deep academic knowledge on electronics technology before moving to the firm. Although this technical knowledge and experience are more academic, they still provide many advantages when working on problems of production and minor technical change. Also, HAL recruited many engineering graduates polytechnics and universities in Vietnam and abroad (Hungary, Czechoslovakia, East Germany). Thanks to this, HAL staff have developed very strong links (formal and informal) with classmates working in Hanoi Polytechnic, University, and other R&D institutes. Relations with Hanoi polytechnic even helped in the forming of an agreement where the two organisations train more practical engineers (from 3 to 5 years of education) than usual, using HAL as a practical experiment base. In this way, the firm is able to train and get access to newly graduated engineers in accordance with its needs.

This prior accumulation helped HAL to gain many aspects of production, minor change and linkage capabilities. As for investment activity, some cadres of the brought with them knowledge when they moved from financial or planning departments of the City council. This way of recruitment also helped to ease the firm's efforts in dealing with investment problems. So far, none of HAL's staff have brought with them any prior accumulated capabilities in marketing or more radical technical change.

The changing dynamics of learning is also seen in modes of prior accumulation. In the first 4-5 years, prior accumulation mostly relied on massive recruitment of young engineers and graduates from universities and polytechnics. More recently, the firm has adapted its recruitment and pursuit of prior accumulated skills by applying specifically designed programme that are more selective in gathering practical knowledge and skills.

Off-the-job training

Training of engineers and technical cadres has received special attention. To increase general knowledge of manufacturing, or specific techniques in assembling, the firm regularly sends its staff on various short courses. More systematically, it has a contract with Hanoi polytechnic for long term co-operation in engineering education. This programme is for practical engineers and is intended not only for new graduates, but also for those workers and technicians of HAL who have ambitions to become engineers. The advantage of this training is that students can use the firm's facilities to practise their skills with theoretical back up, and later, these skills will be used directly for the firm's benefit. Similarly, HAL sometime sends its workers on training courses offered by the vocational school of the Ministry of Industry, mostly for mechanical and electrical engineering.

Concerning non-technical learning, HAL managers are eager to fill the gaps in their knowledge of investment, business administration and other economic topics. The director spent one year on a course on how to manage business of the firm. He said:

> I was from an academic environment, surely I did not have enough knowledge of doing business. Therefore, I had to spend the whole year to learn a new subject: how to do business. Fortunately, my friends and colleagues from Hanoi Economics University helped a lot.

Not only the director, but other managers of HAL also took these courses following the plan set up by the firm to re-educate all managers. The firm signed a contract with the Economic Management School of Hanoi to teach all staff who hold positions of workshop supervisor and above. These managers spent 6 months at school learning production management and business management techniques, including human resource management and accounting. They also studied investment issues such as how to do an investment survey; feasibility studies, how to calculate cost/benefit analysis, and how to deal with international transactions. After exams, the firm divided them into those suitable and unsuitable for promotion in the future. In using this incentive, the firm tried to make its managers take part seriously and actively in the courses.

Although off-the-job training has been useful for developing the capabilities of managers and workers across many topics (investment, production and minor change), little was gained through these courses for acquiring other capabilities, like marketing or linkage. It is understandable since off-the-job training courses usually have a more short term perspective, aimed at solving more urgent and day-to-day problems of the firm's activities. In recent years one change that can be seen in off-the-job training programmes is the shift in content from technical to more non-technical subjects.

On-the-job training

There was surprisingly little of this in HAL. So far, the only courses organised were for technical workers, given by instructors invited from Hanoi polytechnic. These courses are very short, lasting only 2-3 days if held formally, or they can be small sessions where people give instruction and discussion of relevant problems directly related to daily production operation, e.g how to deal with material supply or replacement. Occasionally, even foreign language courses such as English have been provided.

Information search

HAL's managers know very well the importance of these as a source of learning. Dr. Hoang Van Nghien himself and other managers took part very actively in academic and non-academic meetings, workshops, seminars, exhibitions, etc. The purposes of this activity is expressed rather clearly by the company's director:

> Electronics is high-tech industry and it is changing very fast, if not by days then by months. You have to know about these changes. If you don't, you'll be out of this business.

Existing friendships and relations between HAL's managers and external colleagues help to maintain a flow of new information on recent changes occurring in production and research environment elsewhere.

One of the ways to get access to information and enhance linkages with R&D institutions, universities and other consulting organisations is to participate in research programmes funded by external agencies. Conferences, seminars, workshops and discussion between HAL's managers and researchers in these programmes give them a lot of information on trends in technology development, difficult problems and the market perspective, locally and internationally. This new source of intelligence is especially useful for the firm in its future production plans and searching for co-operative links with potential partners, in and outside Vietnam.

By involving in these research efforts, HAL can greatly upgrade its technological knowledge and experience, especially in production and linkage activities, and to develop its relations with foreign sources of information. This active involvement, is actually not very common among the majority of consumer electronics firms, which have less opportunities to work side-by-side with R&D institutes. The academic background of its senior management staff, and active by-doing and other approaches means that this firm is most likely to have major technical change capability in future.

Learning-by-doing

This mechanism has supported the development of all capabilities, except for major technical change, where HAL has just begun to undertake the first activity. In initial investment activities, it had to go through many trials and errors. After the early years of learning from JVC, HAL attempted to launch their own investment by choosing technology from Japanese and German suppliers, and putting them together as its own design of production lines. By the end of the 1980s, the firm was trying to replace its passive purchase of turn-key project by a more active involvement using local personnel capable of contributing to the development of technical blueprints and schemes.

In the 1990s, active learning through doing various practical efforts by HAL occurred as well. As the local partner in joint ventures with Korean partners, the firm had to be responsible for all activities relating to the Vietnamese side: dealing with authorities, asking for land using right, clearing up all procedures for construction, transporting equipment, purchasing local inputs and material, etc. By doing all these tasks in combination with some consultation from its foreign partners, HAL acquired a better idea of what should be done, how to do it, what could go wrong and why, and how to avoid mistakes next time.

According to the planning and financial department, in order to obtain an investment licence for HAL's joint venture with Korean companies, they had to revise investment documents and application papers more than ten times. This long and hard work was exhausting, but really useful for their own learning. This active learning-by-doing and by-trying in combination with a foreign connection, turned out quite helpful for the company. Thus, HAL has experienced the necessity of combining different learning mechanisms with active by-doing.

Similarly, HAL engaged in various production and minor change activities and learned through these efforts. The R&D unit of the firm, while adopting some technical improvements, found that they were capable of changing some assembling operations as well as carrying out minor technical replacements that improved products and productivity. From each foreign partner, the company has learned something useful. By combining them, some of HAL's TV products now have features and specifications that are better than some foreign made products. More importantly, some of this technical upgrading was not passed on to foreign partners. The director said:

> These new things are our assets that we acquired through our very hard and long way of trying.

HAL is also able to gain many new experiences through trying to upgrade its linkages with external sources of research competence as well as its internal linkages.

The director has quite a clear appreciation that although learning-by-doing is necessary (especially for simpler tasks), learning-by-interacting is even more important. For workers, formal training should be short, concrete and geared directly to their daily skills. Overly wide and general courses for workers should be avoided. On the other hand, technicians and engineers should have at least some formal training programmes in both technical and non-technical knowledge.

The use of learning mechanisms in HAL is presented below. As can be seen here, learning-by-doing occurs in almost all activities, but HAL has only acquired four capabilities. It is still inexperienced in marketing and, so far, even its foreign connections are not proving sufficient for acquiring this capability. This lack is compounded by the absence of any formal training being undertaken by the firm. Foreign connections, extended from JVC to Daewoo, is the mechanism most used by HAL and is deployed quite creatively by HAL's managers. This may explain why HAL is one of the few firms able to utilise this mechanism for acquiring a technical change capability. As for prior accumulation, the background of HAL's managers as former scientists has contributed not only to strong linkage capability but also to high absorptive capacity which is useful for utilising foreign connections in a more active way.

Table 9.3 Learning mechanisms at HAL

TC	Investment	Production	Minor change	Marketing	Linkage	Major change
Ranking	*strong*	*strong*	*strong*	*no*	*strong*	*no*
Learning						
By-doing	+	+	+	+	+	0
Prior accumulation	+	+	+	0	+	0
On-the-job training	0	+	0	0	0	0
Off-the-job training	+	+	+	0	0	0
Foreign connection	+	+	+	+	+	0
Information	0	+	0	0	+	0

9.4.4 Macro external factors, micro behaviours and learning

Macro policies and market factors are the most influential of the external factors on the learning activities in HAL. The strict regulations which apply to an SOE's financial management reduce speed and flexibility in using resources for technological innovation activities. The difficulty of doing business without first having a strategic view of the whole sector also hinders the efforts of this SOE firm to orient itself to long-term on-the-job and off-the-job training programmes. Similarly, HAL has difficulty in organising its learning through foreign connections over the long run, due to the state's confused industry development policy. The weak domestic market for industrial electronics and for computing business also conspires to reduce HAL's active self-learning attempts. The firm's willingness to try to produce more competitive products - implying the need to master more TCs - is jeopardised by a lack of market motivation.

HAL's managers have reacted in various ways in facing problems caused by macro policy factors. It continued to rely on its strong relations with the supporting system to solve the problems of training and information gathering. The firm tries to use more non-fee training activities, such as exchange programmes with other Vietnamese production units, companies, and research institutes. This also applies to exchange of information and documentation. HAL also tries to use existing strengths by combining its resources. For example, the older generation's experiences and younger personnel's knowledge can be shared and exchanged by working together.

Differentiation of relations with foreign partners remains one of HAL's priorities. Experience has shown that by co-operating with various partners at the same time, the firm can gain varied knowledge and experiences. Moreover, the aim of the firm is to become a more equal partner in its relations with foreign companies, and consequently, an independent and strong player in electronics business, both at home and in international markets. In pursuit of these aims, HAL tries to expand beyond electronics to other types of business through its three joint ventures. Using the resources of foreign partners initially, the firm hopes to accumulate more resources that can then be invested back into its core electronics activity.

To deal with the market factor, HAL has a somewhat different approach. This is a kind of mix between diversification of products and searching for 'niches' that the firm can enter. While continuing to pursue with the production of conventional consumer electronics, the company also looks for opportunities to do something quite new: assembling of electronics hands for robots. This new product may help the firm to enter a niche via relations with the Japanese producers, and to become part of a network of these producers world-wide. In addition, the firm is currently searching for new business partnerships for other higher value added products. Its current negotiation with AT&T and DEC are quite promising, offering an involvement in the computer and telecom businesses. It is one way to avoid weak local demand for high-tech products.

Although the state ownership problem is much more difficult to deal with, HAL has tried to give employees more incentives to work with a long-term commitment to the firm. The sale of its plastic factory subsidiary is an example. When the firm sold its share to employees, they were very positive and bought a large part of the 55,000 shares of this polystyrene packaging factory (at a price of about 10 USD each). This first experience of privatisation of an SOE may help the firm (and other firms as well) to look forward to the long term.

HAL's responses to external factors also contribute to shaping its TC acquisition and learning. As mentioned in the last section, diversification into new business areas and specialisation in niched products (like robotic components) are HAL's main strategies. The firm needs to acquire TCs such as how to invest in new business or engage in large-scale production. Moreover, the specialisation strategy in particular requires specific knowledge of robotics assembly. Although encountering few problems with the industrial support system (thanks to good informal connections, a strong background in R&D and high absorptive capacity), HAL still has difficulty in acquiring marketing and investment competence, and it looks to its foreign partners to complement its dearth of non-technical knowledge. Besides, there is a desire to explore more business opportunities and to secure its funding. All these factors encourage HAL to forge closer links with foreign partners; the foreign connections mechanism is one of the most important learning devices of the firm. The behaviour of this firm is, thus, the joint outcome of external constraints posed by investment policy and market factors and of its reactions to these constraints.

The interviews reveal that the interaction of HAL's managers with their environment is crucial to how the company uses its available learning mechanisms in the most effective way.[7] However, the role of the government in implementing policies which are suitably supportive to encourage the firm further in its learning efforts is no less important. So far, HAL's experience reveals that the Vietnamese government does not yet have a suitable selective policy to support the learning efforts of electronics firms.

9.5 Computer firm E3 (3C)

9.5.1 The company profile and business context

3C was established in 1989 as a private share-holding company in Hanoi by scientists who had moved out of state-run R&D organisations or companies. The company started with 15 people who mainly worked in a Hanoi office. At the start, the company had 17 shareholders: scientists and engineers educated in the former Soviet Union or East European countries. By contributing their own money or borrowing from relatives and friends, the founding shareholders had raised an initial capital of about 25,000 USD. The Director had worked for many years in banks and trade and financial organisations. The Vice-Director and the Chairman of the Governing Board were both scientists who had worked in Vietnamese and foreign-owned organisations before setting up the firm. After about two years, the company had grown to about 50 staff. 3C now has four main units in Hanoi, HoChiMinh City, and two overseas offices in Moscow and Singapore.

At the outset, the company had established that the computing market in the Soviet Union was huge but disorganised; that buyers there did not demand high quality from computing products; and that a close relationship between customers and producers was lacking. Imported computers were not 'Russianised', it was difficult for Russian users to handle the Latin script of the typical imported keyboard, and there was no system of maintenance or repair available. All these shortfalls pointed to an excellent opportunity to do business in Russia. 3C has designed a model 3C-286 specifically for sale in the Soviet market, which includes a main board, a keyboard, and a Russian-tailored software package. This solution was granted a patent by the Vietnam National Office of Industrial Property.

The production location for these computers was planned to be in Vietnam, but it turned out to be too expensive (it would have needed about 200,000 to 300,000 USD to install the necessary production line). 3C hired a Singaporean company to assemble the model using Singapore core hardware. 3C's managers learned of potential Singaporean partners in 1988, and by 1989 - almost immediately after the firm's establishment - had initiated a co-operative deal with a Singaporean partner. This decision addressed their need to find good technological facilities and to begin manufacturing at a reasonable cost. They could thus avoid setting up a more expensive plant within Vietnam, and they were confident of the mutual benefits accruing to themselves and their Singaporean partner as they had established rather good personal relations with them.

Thus, from the beginning, 3C had a very specific orientation: to supply one product to one designated market. The initial efforts of the firm were geared to exploiting the unique opportunity offered by the huge market they had identified in the former Soviet Union. This way of starting business, therefore, depended on their possessing some initial knowledge assets and this, in turn, strongly influenced how the firm proceeded to accumulate TCs later.

Since 3C started as an export-oriented company, the production performance of the firm can be judged through its export results. From 1989 to 1991, on average each year 3C exported about 1,000 sets of PCs. In 1990-1991, the turnover of company was 4 million USD. After its exports fell following the collapse of Soviet market, 3C began to turn to the domestic market, although it still retains its relationship with its Singapore partner for selling PCs and providing computing services. By now, the company only exports on a fairly modest scale. There have been some recent attempts to export products to markets in Cambodia, Southern China and the Eastern European countries, but without any great success. The volume of products for trial export remains negligible.

At this stage, 3C's activities have shifted to engaging in newer ventures, though it continues to maintain its computing business both in software and hardware provision and in other industrial electronics services. Its first effort to expand into non-computing activities was to produce specialised equipment such as electronic balance and data-transfer blocks for use in industrial projects. It also became involved in providing maintenance services for medical equipment such as ECGs (electrocardiographs) and in supplying telecommunications videotext for use in remote provinces (i.e., designing software for district-level broadcasting stations which carries text over satellite television transmissions). The company is also active in non-electronics businesses such as bio-chemistry, construction and even the garment industry. By taking this task, 3C aims to accumulate sufficient financial strength and investment skill to enable it to return, in the long run, to its core computing activities. An embryonic form of venture capital to serve technological innovation can be seen in 3C's non-electronics activities; this company has invested in well-tested innovations which are owned by other firms that lack the initial capital to proceed any further with their development.

Among the problems posed by external factors, the most significant for this company, is that private companies cannot compete with SOEs on equal terms; they are subject to higher tax rates levied on their sales and their financial systems are more strictly monitored by the authorities. In general, 3C argues that it has to face greater difficulties than the SOEs in doing business. The well-known discrimination against private entrepreneurship makes it more difficult for them to accumulate financial reserves. Another difficulty is related to market activity. The firm currently finds it difficult to export and although the domestic market is expanding, it is still rather small and disorganised. Infrastructural systems, both physical and legal, also create difficulties for the firm, especially as its access to these systems is not as favourable as it is for the SOEs.

In response, 3C has diversified its activities beyond computing as it tries to accumulate financial reserves from non-computing business to subsidise new investment in the development of software products. The firm is thus using diversification not only to develop new markets and products, but also to maintain its old market. After the collapse of the Soviet market, the firm had to cease trading in this area for some time, although it has continued exploring the options for new business opportunities in this market. A new approach that 3C is exploring is to review how it may conduct its business more flexibly. Instead of just selling PCs, the company now also acts as a middle-man in arranging business deals. It first looks for potential customers, and than finds the money to finance the deal - arranging payment on behalf of those organisations which lack this kind of capability. Also, instead of transferring goods back to Vietnam, the company involves other partners from third or fourth countries to arrange for payment in the form of goods that bring the best results. Thus, by acting as the broker in tri-partite international contracts, 3C continues it activities in Russia.[8]

In addition, 3C is attempting to exploit other computing niches, replicating its strategy for its initial PC production project, although it has been less successful this time round. It does not yet have sufficient marketing knowledge to engage in the international sale of software packages. The marketing expertise required for entering the Soviet market is not relevant for entry into other markets. In general, without a change in government policy, this company continues to wrestle with a number of problems which they have not yet been able to solve or side-step.

9.5.2 Building technological capabilities

Investment capability

At the beginning of its computer production, the company got some support from outside consultants in preparing its investment plans. Managers of the firm, especially Mr. Bui Huy Hung - director - had very close contacts with people working in the State Planning Committee, State Commission for Pricing, and Hanoi City Council. He asked them to assist in the first phase of setting up the company, and to provide the initial business contacts. Investment feasibility studies were being undertaken mostly by the staff of the company, with some assistance from these external consultants. 3C negotiated with its Singaporean partner on choice of components, parts, and other suppliers and also took part in some production management activities.

Investment experiences of 3C have been further developed through other local electronics businesses. One example is the production of electronics balances which were tried by some research organisations and industrial enterprises. Unfortunately, during 8 years, these research activities did not bring any practical results. The Union of enterprises for new product and new technology (LICOSA - one of the organisations involved in this programme) has suffered severe financial difficulties. LICOSA owned the design of the new product but could not commercialise it. Managers of LICOSA sought help from 3C which by this time had accumulated good financial reserves from sale of computers to the former Soviet Union. 3C helped LICOSA to repay its debts and finance product development, and in the launching of a new electronic balance product. The product was also patented in Vietnam and 3C got the commercial rights to the product. Since then, this product has been sold widely to many customers in the provinces.

3C has also invested in other electronics products like ECG or telecom activities, although on a smaller scale. In these cases, 3C provided not only technical assistance but also financial resources as seed money or advanced investment. This way of doing business is quite a new phenomena in Vietnam. By offering large sums of money and technical assistance with a focus on commercialisation of existing technology or know-how, 3C became a source of not only capital, but also expertise on how to commercialise and market new products. Thus, 3C is among the first Vietnamese companies to be involved in venture capital activities.

This new and embryonic form of venture capital for technological innovation can also be seen in 3C's activities in non-electronics business. 3C owns 60% of a joint venture BCE (Bio-Chemical Enterprise) to produce products based on bio-chemistry technologies developed by the National Centre for Scientific Research (NCSR). These technologies are varied: using domestic ingredients such as herbs to stimulate growth of household animals like pigs, and the production of a supplementary substance for concrete material used in construction industry. 3C has 71% of Hong Bang (HB) company, which specialises in architecture, design, construction and property development. The firm also holds 10% of MTT (fashion garment) and 67% of a tourist company to develop a lake resort complex. Although these new investments are non-electronic, 3C has practised its investment skills, learnt lessons along the ways to becoming more capable of dealing with new investment issues.

Initially, 3C had little general investment knowledge in computing, except in relation to specific product for specific market. Step by step, it acquired a lot of general knowledge and experiences of starting a new venture, dealing with investment and sourcing activities which in turn, helped the firm in its new electronic business. As a result, 3C is now confident enough to invest in venture capital activities, in both electronics and non-electronics areas.

Production capability

By relying on the Singaporean sub-contractor producer, 3C has no need to set up production facilities and develop production expertise, and therefore has no capability in producing computers; the management of production; quality control and packaging were carried out by the Singaporean contractors. All computer products were shipped (by air freight) directly from Singapore to Moscow. The 3C office in Moscow took care of after sale maintenance and repair services for these products. Its office in Singapore only supervised the last stage of quality control. Recently, 3C became involved in other local production activities, but still its production skills are limited.

Minor technical change capability

Initially, 3C's production rested on minor technical change activity. By studying the existing model of Singaporean machines, 3C re-designed and adapted it to suit Russian customers. The company changed the structure of the old model, adding some components (random access memory, or RAMs), and redesigned and created a new keyboard with Russian alphabet. 3C also had to design a Russian version of software to be used with this new "Russian" machine, which was called 3C-286. To maintain this minor change activity, 3C invested in two divisions, one specialised in hardware and the other in software development.

In software, 3C created 3C-SOFT Centre with 30 engineers and other experts in computer science, specialising in the development of software packages. This centre has good technical facilities: 386 and 486 IBM compatible PCs, other automated office equipment such as laser printers, scanners, colour photocopiers, etc. The cost of this centre is about 300,000 USD, working conditions are quite good and people receive a good salary (about 250 - 300 USD per month) compared to average level of 150-200 USD in other industrial companies. In addition, about 20% of sales of any software go to staff who are directly involved in producing this software product.

After producing the Russian software for 3C-286, the Centre has continued working on other software aimed at both domestic and export markets. One of the products - TINCO (Tutor for Intelligent Computing) - is a software for engineering calculation and mathematics tasks which can be applied in many industrial projects as a computing 'toolbox'. Initially in 1991, this software was made in MS-DOS 3.0 version, but with the introduction of the Windows programme, TINCO became more difficult to sell. 3C-SOFT had to change and adapt this software to a new version that could be used in Windows. In 1992, 3C-SOFT introduced Personnel Image Database System, which is a multimedia management system for companies to store both full-colour images and text in an electronic database.

The Centre also has designed some specific software for using as cognitive tools in using Vietnamese fonts for computer desktop works such as 3C-SCRIPT. In 1993, 3C-SOFT designed a Vietnamese version of Windows 3.1 called VietWind, and has sold this product widely in Vietnam. Moreover, against a background of severe piracy of computing software, 3C added a 'hard lock' to prevent hacking of this software.

3C introduced VNij in 1995 which is a software designed by Cadpro - an associated group of 3C - for word processing in Vietnamese. This is the first programme that allows easy communication between computers using different Vietnamese fonts. Its also has a spelling check facility. Among other things, one important feature is that VNij can operate in various Windows application including Microsoft Word, CorelDraw, etc. On average every two years 3C has introduced a new software product for sale in the domestic market. Some products, such as TINCO, were also sold on a trial basis in France and Germany.

3C also has a hardware centre of 8 persons co-operating through a network with many others working in different institutions. Besides research activities, this group also takes part in maintenance and repair work in Moscow on a regular basis. More recently, this hardware centre started to work in other electronics activities, such as providing maintenance and repair services for cardiological equipment, or control equipment for electrical kilns in the production of brick and construction material, etc.

The activities of these two centres has relied mainly on graduates recruited from the computer science and electronics departments of Hanoi's polytechnic and other foreign institutions. Under the guidance and lead of the firm's managers, who are themselves experienced scientists, young employees have a chance to learn new knowledge and experiences. More importantly, in the environment of a private company they have a free hand to develop their ideas into commercialisable products, can expect to be remunerated in accordance with their performance.

Judging by its hardware and some software products, 3C can be considered as one among a few (4-5) leading computer companies in the whole country. Unlike other firms assembling products through joint ventures with foreign producers, often without any change to the foreign model, the most distinguished feature of 3C is that the firm produced its 3C-286 model for the Russian market by changing, improving, and adapting an old model. So far, not many companies in Vietnam can do this.

Marketing capability

Similar to minor change capability, 3C has been obtaining its marketing knowledge and experience since the beginning of the firm, using this experience to capitalise on computer sale. The company organised its marketing activity through both its official and personal contacts. Its office in Moscow, in co-operation with Vietnamese trade representatives, played quite an important role during the end of the 1980s and beginning of the 1990s in the regular gathering of marketing intelligence. This office gathered information about defects of products, trends, and customer requirements to guide changes in computer design. To serve this need, 3C had stores of parts and even complete PC sets in Moscow to supply or replace defected machines for customers.

Among marketing activities, one noteworthy feature is 3C's ability to deal with hard currency payment procedures. By the end of 1980s, Soviet buyers had little or no hard currency to pay 3C for its computer products. Instead, they agreed to pay 3C in goods and commodities such as steel, construction material, cotton and iron, other consumer goods, etc. The firm sold these goods to Vietnamese wholesalers for local currency, then exchanged it for hard currency coming from Vietnamese import-export companies that had a surplus of US dollars. This mechanism has helped 3C to secure dollar reserves to do business with the Singaporean partners. But, in order to pursue this mechanism, they needed some specific knowledge and practical experiences of the Soviet business situation, Vietnamese connections, and international market, including shipping and freighting issues. By the end of the 1980s, only a few companies had this "business know-how" to deal with Soviet buyers. 3C was also able to gain advantage by entering the computer business earlier than its competitors.

This unique marketing know-how, however, seems no longer valid following the radical changes in the Soviet market. Almost all interviewees at 3C agree that the unique experience they have gained from the Soviet market may not be so relevant in other international markets. Nevertheless, experiences and knowledge on how to deal with marketing and international payment problems are valuable for the company. The company has some marketing capability, although this marketing activity is unique and the company has been experiencing more problems in recent times.

Linkage capability

This capability is strong in all three aspects of linkage. The overall picture shows that 3C has obtained close links with the whole industrial and R&D system, the most important ingredient of linkage competence. The company has close relations with a wide network of collaborators working at many local research institutions and universities such as the Institute of Mathematics, Institute of Information Technology (IOIT), Hanoi Polytechnic, etc. At the same time, 3C assisted IOIT in its sales effort. This institute designed a software called Ador, a programme that enables an optical scanner to recognise text and translate it into computer data as a file. In 1992-1993, this Ador programme went on sale (together with some 3C's products, like TINCO or 3C-SOFT) in France and Germany.

3C also collaborates with local companies such as FPT (computer), and LICOSA (electronics for printing and other services). This form of involvement allows 3C's staff to maintain an operative relationship with the business community in Vietnam to share jobs or to do joint development.

Internally, 3C has very strict regulations about circulating job positions and information flows. Every 6 months, for example, personnel of the hardware centre have to replace their colleagues who are stationed in the Moscow and Singapore offices to keep them closer to production or market activities. Similarly, personnel of the software and other units have to exchange information, suggestions and planning, at an internal roundtable organised by the director. By doing so, 3C tries to ensure that all new information or related market trends are quickly circulated among its staff.

Major technical change capability

Although 3C pursued a lot of research-related activities and did introduce some new products, these products were largely adaptations and modifications of existing foreign made models. 3C-286, for example, is a version of a Singaporean machine adaptated to satisfy Russian customers. Other software products were designed by 3C staff, but most of them, except for TINCO, are "Vietnamisation" of existing Microsoft products.

Economically, the production of 3C-286 is significant for the firm's business, but, technologically, the firm did little to change the computer's design, approrpiate to the minor technical change category. Similarly, 3C's software products were simple adaptations. Although TINCO is a new product, it used the same principle of software design (as Mr. Van Son, expert of Software centre admitted) adapted for a new purpose. Thus, it is reasonable to consider 3C's R&D activities as just taking its first steps towards major technical change.

9.5.3 Learning mechanisms

Prior accumulation

This seems to be 3C's most important learning mechanism. Starting as a group of scientists and private entrepreneurs, the company has relied entirely on its staff's existing knowledge and expertise, at least initially. Fortunately, before setting up their company, most of 3C's managers had worked in various government and private companies and organisations, accumulating a very good knowledge base and pool of experience. The director of 3C worked many years as a senior expert in the foreign economic relations department of the State Planning Commission, and at the State Committee for Pricing. He also worked as secretary for some ministers, including the minister of foreign trade, after being educated in financial and economic issues in the former Soviet Union. He speaks Russian fluently, knows the Soviet market very well, has strong connections with Soviet business, and was one of the very first persons to conceive of selling computers to Soviet market.

Mr. Nguyen Quang A, chairman of the governing board and Nguyen Minh Song, vice director, were educated in Hungary in computer sciences. Mr. Quang A obtained his Doctorate and Professorship, worked in Hungary for some years and was chosen as a member of the Hungarian Academy of Sciences. After coming back to Vietnam in the mid 1970s, both of them worked for the Military Technological Research Institute (Ministry of Defence). During this period, although the institute was one of the top priorities of the government, by the end of 1980s working conditions had worsened through necessary financial cuts. Mr. Quang A was invited to work in Hungary as a visiting scholar but he decided to stay on, quitting the military institute, and went to work for the General Department of Electronics Industry. In this capacity, he was assigned as Director of GenPacific, the first joint venture between Vietnam's electronics industry and Bull.S.A of France, to produce computers in Vietnam. This was a very good preparation for him to create his own company, which he did in 3C. 3C's vice-director also followed a similar path, but instead of working for a Vietnamese non-military institution, he went straight to work for GenPacific, then moved together with others to 3C. By the time they came back from Eastern Europe, these scientists had accumulated a very good and deep knowledge of electronics theories. This knowledge and information took on a more practical orientation when they worked for the Military Technological Institute, where they tried to deal with the sample production of electronics products like transistors and components, etc.

While the head of the governing board and vice-director had more technical expertise that was necessary for minor change capability, the director had more business knowledge and marketing experience. This period can be considered as the first phase of knowledge accumulation by these people in minor change and marketing activities (with a focus on the Soviet market). To a lesser extent, they acquired some investment, production, and linkage knowledge as well.

The second phase of prior accumulation occurred when all of them moved to work for GenPacific (E5 in this study). As a joint venture, this company specialises in computer products and services, both for export to the Soviet Union and for the domestic market. In the directorship of GenPacific, and working alongside French partners, were Mr. Nguyen Quang A as general director, Mr. Nguyen Minh Song as director of Hanoi office and Mr. Bui Huy Hung as assistant to general director in charge of dealing with the Soviet market. This was a valuable learning period (1988-1989) enabling them to upgrade their knowledge and experience. In investment activity, they learned from their French partners about how to start a joint venture, prepare investment studies, and conduct the implementation phase. Moreover, because one member of the governing board of the joint venture was a French lawyer, they learned a lot about the international and legal dimension of investment activities in the Western environment.

Since GenPacific was producing computers in Vietnam, these persons had a very rare opportunity to see and learn how production is run, what were the difficulties of operating this business, especially in Vietnam, and how a French multinational like Bull dealt with these problems. They were involved in production operations such as assembling, quality control test, organisation of production lines, dealing with supply, maintenance and repair activities, and packaging. When products were shipped out of the workshop, they had to look after delivery and sale activities, mostly for export to Soviet market, and had got an opportunity to experience various kinds of problems in marketing.

They furthered their own existing knowledge on electronics during this period, learning more about the technology of PC assembly, particularly of Bull's machines, and also about how to link business internationally, and information circulating with foreign partner's headquarters - Bull S.A. in France.

By working for GenPacific, all of these persons, in fact, were trained in the practical problems of doing business. Their minor change capability was upgraded from theoretical to more applied electronics knowledge and geared directly to PC assembly. Investment knowledge was upgraded almost from nothing to doing business internationally and starting a joint venture project. Marketing experience expanded to include Western techniques while still using their unique know-how on doing business in the Soviet market. In linkage knowledge, they learned about internal and international relations of a joint venture company. Experience in all these activities gave them confidence as they moved out from GenPacific to set up 3C. This can be seen through their own assessment as Mr. Nguyen Quang A said:

> We learned a lot from the French. In our governing board there were two Frenchmen (one of them was Mr. Pascal, Bull's regional director for Asia Pacific), who were experts in international business. When we worked for the benefit of the same company, they did not hide anything from us. In many cases, they opened our eyes to the outside world.

One contributing factor is that GenPacific invested a lot in training its staff. This joint venture sent its personnel to training courses in France for different periods with total training expenses amounting to about 200,000 USD in 2 years. At the same time, Bull sent some French experts to assist the joint venture with operating the assembly line. Sometime, they stayed for about 6 months. All these activities at GenPacific certainly gave these persons a great opportunity to learn about the computing business before they became managers of 3C.

With accumulated knowledge and experience, the founders of 3C could be called the 'first-tier' learners who benefited from training and working before the start of the firm. To continue this tradition, 3C tries to recruit and rely on young and talented individuals, newly graduated from Hanoi University and polytechnic or institutions abroad (Hungary, former Soviet Union). These persons are the 'second-tier' of learning-by-accumulating knowledge prior to working for 3C.

Every year, 3C offers 9 scholarships for the best students in universities and polytechnic institutes who are involved in research activity. By doing so, 3C tried to engage selected students in its research even before graduation, after which the firm can recruit them and sign a preliminary contract for three months. If everything goes well, these students may get a permanent job with 3C. In this way, the company is creating for itself a fresh and ready-to-use source of young, dynamic and talented graduates who continuously feed its knowledge accumulation.

The prior accumulation mode of learning has changed from period to period and brought to 3C knowledge in minor change, marketing and then investment and linkage experience. First, it happened in the academic environment of higher education abroad and research activity in Vietnam. Then, it was continued through working experiences in a joint venture company. The content of learning also developed from those aspects suitable for minor change and marketing capabilities (that helped it to seize the unique chance of business) to the practicalities around the investment competences needed in the expansion phase.

Foreign connections

The connection with Bull.S.A continued even after the 3C managers left GenPacific, but since they are no longer members of the joint venture, their contacts with the French members of GenPacific have become less co-operative. However, 3C did not limit itself to Bull. After starting up, 3C's managers began to build new contacts with Singaporean companies, with whom they made contact through trade fairs, workshops, and exhibitions since 1988. Through the assembly operation that the Singaporean firm performed for 3C (3C-286), the company learnt knowledge which was different from the Bull joint venture experience: for example, how to produce rather cheap Southeast Asian computers (cost cutting through saving raw material, input and component sourcing).

Similar to investment activity, 3C's managers could no longer learn market competence from the French after quitting GenPacific. 3C has recently made new connections with some American companies newly arrived in Vietnam like Digital Equipment Co. (DEC), IBM, and Apple in the beginning of the 1990s. Of these, 3C is to be DEC's sale representative in Vietnam, responsible for machine sales, provision of equipment and software package, and maintenance, repair, and guarantee services related to DEC's activities in Vietnam. This contact has brought 3C a very good chance to keep up-to-date with the computer business. 3C's vice-director said in the latest interview in 1994:

> Computer business is changing very fast. With Bull, we learned technology of 1980s, with the Singaporean, we learned about low-cost and cheap models of Southeast Asian standards. But to learn more world class business, not to say about technology of 1990s and beyond, you have to be with American. Fortunately, we are with them now.

Learning through working together with foreign partners at 3C was used both as prior accumulation and as an on-going activity. Although foreign connection mechanism contributed to all investment, marketing and production activities, the firm only acquired investment and marketing capabilities. It can not acquire production capability just by having contacts with foreigners, without any other learning mechanisms being used. The case shows that the changing pattern of using foreign connections (moving from French to American) can help the firm to upgrade its technological expertise from knowledge of the 1980s to that of the 1990s.

Information search

This is also one of the active learning mechanisms at 3C. As mentioned above, one of the strengths of 3C is its wide range of connections with people working in many R&D institutes, universities, etc. developed even before the start of the firm. This network is a lively source of information, documentation and many informal consulting opportunities for 3C to draw on. The overall impression from talking with various managers is that 3C makes intensive use of its informal relations with researchers and staff of other organisations. One example is that half of those working in 3C-Soft are not 3C's staff but come from the IOIT, Hanoi polytechnic, or other competitors computing companies. They may stay for a few hours to some days, just to use 3C's facilities. Mr. Van Son at 3C-SOFT Centre explained this situation:

> They came here just to use our Centre which is among the best equipped, for free. Most of the time, they used for their own things: something urgently to do, or just playing games. But sometimes, we asked them a few things, or suggested to do something together. And they did this also for free.

In fact, this 'barter' approach of informal relationship with its informal club atmosphere has attracted many people to 3C: scientists who have talent, knowledge, expertise but lack facilities and a conducive working environment. In many cases, they moved from just 'hanging around', to working for 3C in many projects.

This mechanism not only helped 3C to learn knowledge of minor technical change (in some instances, rather advanced expertise can be helpful for even major technical change capability) and linkage, but marketing capability as well. 3C's managers are members of different associations or clubs: club of company' directors, club of private entrepreneurs, Vietnam Chamber of Commerce and Industry, Vietnam Union of Science and Technology Associations, Vietnam Informatics Association. These connections help them to take part in different exhibitions, fairs, meeting, workshops. Still, more important are 3C managers' personal contacts and friendships with people working in Ministry of Finance, Ministry of Planning and Investment, Ministry of Trade. Through these connections, 3C upgraded its existing expertise in marketing. It can be said that this network of personal contacts and relations was, and remains, 3C's main conduit of information collection.

On-the-job and *off-the-job training*
Surprisingly, learning through methods like sending people on training courses did not exist at 3C. During the three years (1992-1993) that this study lasted, there were no training courses organised by 3C for its staff. Also, none of its personnel (almost all of them have university degrees) have been sent on courses to increase their qualifications. The reasons for this could be twofold. One is that the training resources of the firm are limited (it is a small private firm). Second, and because of that, the firm's managers maybe deliberately exploiting the existing academic strength of its staff, rather than developing it further.

Learning-by-doing
Almost all activities were undertaken quite actively by its staff, except for the production of computers. In investment, 3C was heavily involved in all kinds of pre-investment and investment studies, preparation of feasibility studies, and dealing with starting up activities of the firm. Although knowledge and experiences which 3C's managers had previously accumulated were very valuable for them, it was not enough. When they started the firm, many problems arose and they have to learn how to deal with these, through their own trial and error. One problem was the establishment of a private company. At the time when they tried to create 3C, there were not many private companies in existence. The legal framework was poor. In 1988, they submitted documents to Hanoi City's authority for the establishment of a private firm. It was refused. It took them almost a year of hard study to find a way forward. They found that they had to use Vietnam Informatics Association as a sponsor to create their firm. Thre were other problems. As a private firm, they had many difficulties dealing with foreign economic issues, including the hiring of a Singaporean manufacturer to produce computers. Again, they had to try hard to find appropriate partner, and mode of operation. To describe this step-by-step trying, the firm's director said:

> With all experiences we had from GenPacific and other organisations, we were confident. When we began our own business, something turned out new and quite different from the things we knew. No one taught us how to run a private firm. So many pressures, so many new problems... But we had to accept this and carry on. It took time, but we learned a lot. Now, we know how to expand to garment or construction business, how to take and give shares in the new share holding companies. And if we decide to go into East European market for computing, we know more or less how to start a plant in Czechoslovakia.

This learning-by-doing or it could be called "leaning-by-struggling to get things done" also occurred in marketing activities. Prior accumulated experiences and knowledge of the Russian market helped 3C a lot in selling its computers to the former Soviet market. When it produced software, things became very different. 3C tried hard to sell these products to some neighbouring countries by showing them at computer fairs and software exhibitions (in Thailand, Hong Kong, Singapore). It even tried to market these products (TINCO) to Western countries like Germany and France. Despite these efforts, its success was limited. Numbers of sold copies were insignificant. After a couple of years of marketing software, the lesson they got is not surprising, but important as the vice-director mentioned:

> Software is very special product. It's tough for us to sell. You can design something, but sell it is 10 time more difficult. You cannot compete with big players like Microsoft. They are Kings in this business. In order to sell, you need a network of advertisement, sale, after-sale and standardisation services. We do not have anything like that. But we can try to become part of this big players' network. Find a niche, and try to get a piece of this. That is the only way.

It seems that 3C learned this lesson quite well. They have dropped the idea of exporting its own software by itself. Instead, it has moved to working with an international network of firms specialising in the sale of software. Vietnamisation of software to serve the domestic market is one of the niches they have found, and software subcontracting is being discussed with Microsoft and Oracle.

Although 3C's learning-by-doing in minor technical change and linkage activities are not as clearly seen as in investment and marketing, this mechanism was also used. The modification of computer hardware to suite Russian customers brought 3C many practical experiences in adaptation technique. In designing software, the first test of 3C's capability was adaptation of the English version for the Russian market. They have obtained some small "know-how" in this adapting process, and this success led the firm to its next venture with more confidence and less time consumption. To modify Windows to Vietnamese version, 3C needed about 4-6 months (compared to about a year to prepare Russian software) thanks to the use of this know-how. 3C also started its first effort in learning major technical change, through producing an industrial software package for the domestic market, and doing some research on mainframe computing. But this effort is still very new and its impact on learning is yet quite limited.

A full picture of 3C's use of learning mechanisms for its TC accumulation is given in Table 9.4. Prior knowledge and experience accumulation and collection of information are the most important learning mechanisms for 3C. Foreign connections have contributed significantly to TC accumulation while training mechanisms have not been used at all.

Table 9.4 Learning mechanisms at 3C

TC	Investment	Production	Minor change	Marketing	Linkage	Major change
Ranking	*weak*	*no*	*strong*	*weak*	*strong*	*no*
Learning						
By-doing	+	0	+	+	+	+
Prior accumulation	+	0	+	+	+	0
On-the-job training	0	0	0	0	0	0
Off-the-job training	0	0	0	0	0	0
Foreign connection	+	+	0	+	0	0
Information	0	0	+	+	+	+

There is an explanation for why training mechanisms have not been deployed. In 3C, prior accumulation is one of the most important mechanisms for gaining knowledge of minor technical change and marketing, and the recruitment of researchers and engineers plays a crucial role in this regard. This emphasis on previous accumulation suggests that this firm is over-reliant on this mechanism since it provides no further training for its staff. Although a lack of funding and of sufficient state support for private firms constitute part of the reason for this situation, 3C's over-emphasis on using prior experience may also be a contributory factor.

3C's profile also highlights the significance of the barter approach (i.e., using informal and personal relationships) to ensure access to information and technological expertise. Indeed, the difficulty of learning-by-doing (in marketing software products, for instance) means that this mechanism is not at all straightforward, but involves active trying and struggling.

9.5.4 Macro external factors, micro behaviours and learning

As for difficulties in learning activities, 3C's managers reported the weakness of the supporting system as the most serious problem. The domestic network of R&D institutes and universities are not capable enough in supporting the firm in its innovation and learning activities. These problems are varied: lack of modern facilities for providing training and experiments, and the curricular of training and education programmes is unsuitable for the needs of the computer business. The way research programmes and co-operative relations are organised and structured does not encourage scientists to cooperate with 3C in formal contracts. One possible reason is that computer scientists graduated from different schools and countries and worked in different organisations; the tendency toward competition is obvious. At the same time, given the funding shortage and bureaucratic funding application, relations between different groups of scientists sometimes can be rather negative and intense. Many education courses have not provided practical training. All these have prevented 3C from using more formal learning mechanisms such as sending its staff for different kinds of training beyond university degrees. This also explains why 3C did not use any formal training mechanism. Information sources necessary for upgrading its knowledge in high-tech areas such as computing are also limited.

3C sees the infrastructure, both physical and legal as a big problem for its training. One example is the production of the VietWind software. When 3C began to sell this product to Vietnamese buyers at a cost of about 100 USD per copy, in very short time the company found that its product was being copied by computer users. As noted earlier, the firm had to put an extra hard-lock on this software. Nevertheless, some expert users are able to break this lock after using the product for a while. Although this product was registered with the National Office of Industrial Property, there are no effective measures to protect 3C from piracy. This situation is widespread, affecting many other products as well (most of which are foreign made). This explains the reluctance of foreign firms (American firms, for instance) to co-operate with 3C in long-term software development. Without this co-operation, it is difficult for 3C to learn the skills of minor technical adaptation and improvements from foreign sources.

It would be unfair to say that 3C faces only negative factors from the supporting system. In fact, even as a firm set-up privately, it has enjoyed many positive factors of the system. The founders of 3C got training abroad and worked in these R&D institutions for many years. They acquired much knowledge during the 1970s and 1980s thanks to this system. Also, the continuous recruitment and accumulation of knowledge and experiences at a later stage of 3C's development was helped mainly by the resources of the supporting system.

Policy factors are criticised by 3C's managers as being not favourable for a private company in its learning efforts. The well-known discrimination towards private entrepreneurship makes it more difficult to accumulate financial reserves for learning. At the same time, public sources of training and expertise are very limited. As 3C's managers mentioned, these difficulties prevented them from using off-the-job training mechanism: no funding, and no available free courses from the state. Moreover, 3C's unequal position as a private company, and the unstable future prospects of the private sector, may lead to the reluctance of foreign companies to cooperate more closely with the firm.

Market factors have a significant impact on the learning activities of 3C. In a market open to competition, searching, establishing and using foreign contacts for learning have all become more costly and difficult. Domestically, the company has problems in developing its co-operative efforts with other companies; undermining the scope for its off-the-job training. Also, its own learning-by-doing efforts are affected by a weak domestic electronics market. At the same time, market changes have also given 3C something positive. Opening up the Vietnamese and international markets to each other, and the integration of Vietnamese companies with regional and international networks, has led to more open and transparent information flows. As a company working mainly with information storage and processing, these conditions are certainly important advantages that 3C can now enjoy.

One cultural factor has had a strong impact on learning in 3C. When researchers from many institutes work together, there is always a psychological problem: their uncooperative attitudes to working for the same software product. Because of this, 3C has had problems when it tried to rely on these scientists for off-the-job training and collecting information.

As discussed earlier, 3C has responded to its external environment and these responses have influenced how the firm has proceeded up its TC acquisition learning curve. Diversification both within and beyond electronics is one of 3C's main strategies for developing its business. This strategy requires that 3C acquire new kinds of knowledge and experience about, for example, entering new markets. By moving from a Singaporean partner (a suitable relationship for producing PCs) towards forging new links with advanced US firms for doing software business, 3C hopes to diversify its foreign learning sources as well. Hence, diversification represents more than the attempt to accumulate additional financial resources for business activities; it also becomes a means to support learning and innovation efforts. In trying to deal with problems like the poor system of support and discrimination against private companies, 3C tends to seek out alternative business, leading it to explore even more foreign connections. Joining a larger network of software producers is another approach. Again, to identify a niche market and to specialise in a niche product is not only a business strategy, but also a crucial solution for augmenting the firm's knowledge and experience. Moreover, this might help the firm to overcome the problem of protecting its industrial property rights.

Although these reactions seem quite workable in the short term, 3C may encounter more difficulties in the years to come. Until now the firm has relied too heavily on its existing competence, accumulated long before the firm starting trading. This prior experience accumulation has helped 3C to gain an edge by winning huge profits in the Soviet market from a very unique business. But without any kind of training (on-the-job or off-the-job), the company will find it difficult to maintain its level of expertise in the fast-changing computing business.

As the firm's diversification strategy has also involved it in a shift away from its core computing business, this will have an impact on the extent to which the firm can deepen its technological competencies. Whether 3C can maintain its role in the high-tech computing business in the future remains to be seen. At the same time, as a private company, the firm can do nothing about state policies. This factor must be addressed at a level higher than the individual firm; it demands new government policies.

9.6 Some distinct features of two electronics firms

While HAL has production capability and no marketing expertise, one of 3C's most valuable assets is its marketing skill although it has no production competence. This difference can be partly explained by the general situation of the electronics industry in Vietnam. But, in addition, the explanation lies in the specific circumstances of the firms where 3C intentionally did not try to produce its own products, but relied on its previously accumulated marketing and minor technical change capabilities for starting up in business. This is quite a unique feature compared to other computing companies in this study.

The HAL case study also suggests that the company probably has the potential for major technical change capability because of its good minor change capability, its academic background, its initial steps in R&D activity and its active collection of information. The director of the firm also has a very clear vision about training programmes and has concrete plans to enhance his engineers' knowledge. 3C's ability to develop major technical change on the basis of its quite good minor change capability remains to be seen.

One of main features of both firms is that they both benefited from using prior accumulation of knowledge and experience. Their managers came from a *research background*, which helped them acquire the minor technical change capability and to develop their linkage capability. The same can be said for investment knowledge and experience, since both HAL and 3C employ experts either from Hanoi City or from financial and trade ministries. The two firms use collection of information to differing extents. HAL used this mechanism only to learn production and linkage, while 3C used this mechanism more efficiently for marketing, linkage and even technical change capabilities (although it could acquire only minor change and not major change capability). Interestingly, this difference can be understood as a *spin-off of R&D development* in the electronics industry. Because research activities take place much more actively in computer sciences than in consumer electronics, 3C was able to utilise this factor as a strength: ensuring better access to information and documentation, and greater availability of research experts who could act as consultants for the firm.

Both firms have relied heavy on foreign connections although this has led to different results, mainly with respect to marketing capability which 3C has acquired but HAL has not. The valuable time spent at GenPacific and collaboration with DEC have contributed to the marketing capability of 3C's managers. Although HAL has had an active approach towards learning from foreigners, this had been geared more towards acquiring technical knowledge, with marketing efforts still being too new to have achieved any significant results. It seems that in 3C, its director's previous experience of working in financial and banking circles better prepared that firm to absorb the new knowledge provided by the foreign partner than was the case with HAL's director who was just a scientist.

Both firms used learning-by-doing in *combination* with other learning mechanisms which, as discussed earlier, is a must for their TC accumulation. 3C's lack of involvement in production has prevented the firm from learning this capability through learning-by-doing, in spite of its co-operation with a Singaporean partner.

The extent to which the firms combined their learning-by-doing with other mechanisms also differs. As mentioned above, in HAL learning-by-doing is supported by more mechanisms than in 3C for most TCs, except marketing. Although HAL's managers initially relied on prior knowledge and experience and on foreign connections, at a later stage they continued to upgrade their capabilities by intensive on-the-job and off-the-job training programmes. This *continuity by provision of training* did not occur in 3C and this factor plays a large role in positioning HAL as having more formal knowledge of investment and production activities. As for international marketing, if HAL can continue its creative attempt to learn this capability through learning-by-doing and using foreign connections more vigorously for export links, it is very likely that it can catch up and even surpass 3C in the long term.

Both HAL and 3C have diversified beyond electronics into other businesses in order to secure more financial and technological resources. They have also both attempted to specialise in a niche area of business: industrial electronics and customer-led software production. So far, HAL seems more successful than 3C in its diversification and niche-entering strategies, the main reason being that the two firms have faced different external environmental problems relating to their background: the issue of ownership, and the technological area in which they are specialising.

Due to *different ownership*, 3C has had to face many more government policy problems than HAL, of which discrimination against private enterprise is the most serious. Although up to very recently both firms have enjoyed the advantages of the supporting system for their prior accumulation, the unequal playing field offers HAL more favourable conditions than 3C in doing business. Specifically, HAL has easier access to financial resources and it can more easily use facilities and forge contacts with foreign partners in investment ventures. This difference explains why HAL has been involved in many more investment projects than 3C over the last four years. As a 'pet' company of Hanoi City, HAL has a better business future than 3C, a small private company.

These differences have shaped the manner in which the same macro-environment has nevertheless had differing impacts on firms' learning. First, because of different ownership, more learning sources are available to HAL than to 3C, and HAL enjoys easier access to expertise and knowledge sources. Unlike 3C, HAL has few problems in getting access to the learning sources provided by the supporting system. Taking into account that R&D and training activities in computer sciences are more active than in consumer electronics, the problems of 3C are even more stark. As a result, 3C has little opportunity to deploy any training mechanisms, and the firm has also less credibility in developing foreign connections and collecting information. Because of this, 3C's managers choose not to pursue training courses and this may well lead to a serious weakness with respect to its ability to maintain its learning efforts as mentioned above.

Second, both firms encounter the learning problems caused by policy factors, albeit in opposing ways. While HAL can enjoy the many advantages of being an SOE, 3C sees the inequality applied against private companies in many incentive regimes as a barrier to learning. In the meantime, HAL complains about the restrictions on SOEs that a private company does not have to face (concerning financial management, taxation, labour policy, etc.). The firm does not even see state ownership as an advantage but as a difficulty (as given in section 9.4). However, in my view, HAL enjoys more advantages than disadvantages with respect to its ability to learn as compared with 3C. The kind of difficulties that 3C deals with are much more serious and systemic than the problems facing HAL.

The *business areas* of the two firms are different (consumer and computer electronics) and they have differing access to market opportunities. For HAL, the local market of consumer electronics is more developed but rather saturated. The computing market is undeveloped and weak. In the meantime, export markets for both consumer and computer electronics are fairly inaccessible. As a result, although both firms tend to forge links with foreigners as a way to bypass market barriers and to access more learning sources, these foreign partners differ depending on which area of business is under discussion (Asian firms for consumer electronics versus US firms for computing).

An overall comparison between these two firms reveals the different extents to which they react to learning difficulties, with HAL displaying more conscious learning efforts. Although the different ownership backgrounds and business areas are crucial in shaping the whole context for their learning, the *role of managers* is also very decisive. HAL's managers seem to be able to better utilise their firm's advantages (being state owned, for instance) to build long-term plans for learning. One indication of this is the continuous attempts by HAL's managers to support their previously acquired competence by sending their people off to gain new knowledge and skill; something not seen at 3C. Although HAL and 3C have both diversified their connections with foreign companies, diversification is stronger and more vigorous in HAL. The move from JVC to Daewoo, followed by the expansion to their Japanese robotics producer and other Korean partners, provides an example. Hence, the specific management practices within each firm contribute importantly to their learning behaviour.

Several issues have been seen from the cases' experiences. The factors of the supporting infrastructure such as the research background and the spin-off from R&D activities (especially in electronics) is crucial. It has even led to the higher absorptive capacity of firms like HAL, a pre-condition necessary for fully utilising other mechanisms like foreign connections. The availability (or not) of suitable learning sources in the supporting system is also important in shaping whether or not firms can acquire new non-technical knowledge. This factor explains the difference outcomes from using prior accumulation in TLG and NTC.

Next to amplify the findings in previous chapters, case studies show that the ways companies specialised or diversified (within the scope of their traditional activities as in TLG, or beyond them as in NTC), and whether with one partner (Itochu) or with many, affected their accumulation of competence. In addition, the background of the firms, their historical circumstance, and managers' backgrounds, all play an important role in micro-macro interactions. One of the most distinct features to emerge from these cases is the role of managers in enabling learning efforts (or not). This feature affects how firms use training to support other learning mechanisms. Instead of being mere passive receivers of external impacts, firms actively respond through their managers' actions. Even within the same macro environment, firms take different management strategies which, in turn, leads to different outcomes for learning attempts and TC accumulation. This can be seen most clearly between TLG and NTC in developing their business, acquiring technology and accessing market channels.

Discussed cases point to the role of government in creating favourable conditions for learning to take place, through conducive policies; through the supporting infrastructure; and through how it deals with issues like ownership. The specific current history of as a transitional economy also emerges as an influential factor in Vietnam. These issues are discussed in the next chapter.

Notes

1. These workers are mostly young women of 18-22 years old, coming from families which were involved in various kinds of small scale sewing and cloth-making for self-use or sale at local markets. In this setting, it was old type manual sewing machines (not electrical) that gave these women the first idea of sewing technique. Although this small scale activity is quite popular in cities and small towns, the production is fragmented, not co-ordinated and people are not familiar with industrial standards.

2. In the Tables 9.1 to 9.4, a (+) means the learning mechanism has been used to accumulate corresponding TC, a (0) means it has not been used.

3. For example, a study on manufacturing Open-End technology had been undertaken. This specific technology was produced by Japanese manufacturers on the basis of Czech patents. The advantage of the technology is its specification to use poor quality cotton for spinning. The research group studied in details the design of this equipment, unpacked the machine and looked at how it worked, and from which parts it was made. They then tried to produce similar parts with the aim of assembling the same sort of machine. If successful, this could be a great solution for

textile plants because they could use poor quality cotton, and save foreign exchange (no need to import these machines). Unfortunately, when the group wanted to make some important parts of the machine (mostly rotating and whirling parts requiring very precise mechanical engineering operations), none of the existing Vietnamese mechanical engineering facilities could meet their requirements in terms of precision and technical standards, and they had to drop this idea of imitation. This was a first attempt at reverse engineering in textiles. But, due to weaknesses of mechanical engineering capability in the country, this attempt failed. This experience shows that without the development of related industries such as mechanical engineering, attempts by the textile industry to upgrade and learn technologically have been easily frustrated.

4. In another study to evaluate technology transfer projects, of which NTC was one, I had a chance to know of this problem from both Japanese and local experts working in MOI. Some instructors from Itochu, for example (in interview as with technology suppliers) mentioned difficulties when they have to discuss with workers on-site about upgrading product quality.

5. The name of this new Japanese partner was not disclosed during interview for competitive reasons.

6. One example is a project to research the possibility of produce IKD components in Vietnam. This project is a stimulus for the firm to develop further from lower level of CKD and SKD production to higher level.

7. By co-operating with various partners at the same time, HAL's managers can gain varied knowledge and experience and then subsequently recombine them in ways most useful to them.

8. One of possibilities that 3C is now considering is to open a production facility in Czechoslovakia, where the import of SKD components is tax free. From this assembly facility, the firm may be able to serve its market in the former Soviet Union and in other countries as well. According to the firm, this strategy may carry some advantages. Setting up a business (sales offices, shops, service centres or assembly facilities) is easier and cheaper in Eastern Europe than it is in Russia, and the business environment is also more stable and safe. In addition, this strategy means that the firm can utilise the existing academic strengths of Eastern European organisations. Meanwhile, the firm's Russian business has shifted towards non-computing activities. For example, in 1992 3C signed a deal worth more than 3 million USD for selling garment products there. It is also involved in financial brokering such as arranging financial exchanges and transfers for Vietnamese organisations operating in Russia. The firm stands to gain about 20% of its total exchange from this kind of business.

10 Learning and technological capability in a developing and transitional economy

10.1 The relationship between TC accumulation and learning

10.1.1 Limitations of technical change and marketing capabilities

The first research question of this study was to examine which TCs have been obtained by the firms. It can be said that most of the TCs developed by the firms in this study belong to the start-up level of functions, comprising operational capabilities, or the capacities to use a technical system (Bell and Scott-Kemmis, 1985b). The technological change capabilities of the firms in this study are not very developed, and certainly far from being the innovative (or innovation) capabilities (Baranson & Roark, 1985; Westphal et al, 1985). Few firms seem able to conduct institutional search for innovation and/or basic research as defined in Fransman's taxonomy (1984). In particular, this finding is rather similar to the experiences of Korea as a NIC, where production and investment capabilities were more developed than innovation capabilities (Westphal et al, 1985). However, this study shows more concretely which TCs are being acquired by the firms. Among technical change capabilities, the majority of Vietnamese firms in this study have developed minor technical change capability geared to improvements, adjustment and adaptation of technology, whether process or product. The major technical change capability, involving R&D or design has been much less developed. Only a few firms such as TG4 after long experience of engaging in minor technical changes, took the first steps towards attempting any major technical change activities. This feature is not specific to Vietnam, but is rather common in developing countries where major technical change activities are out of reach.

Another distinct finding in this study is the much weaker development of non-technical compared to technical competence. For example, compared to production and minor technical change capabilities, investment and, to a larger extent, marketing capabilities were less in evidence. This point is rather important since in many industries, marketing has proved to be a crucial competence if a firm is to be competitive, in domestic as much as export markets. Similar findings can be found in other studies of software and computing (Ernst & O'Connor, 1993; Katz, 1987b), and the fashion garment industry (Lall & Wignarajar, 1994). Studies of other developing countries show that this is mainly due to the difficulties experienced by specific industries. For instance, in the computer software industry, internal and external barriers[1] cause problems for firms in exporting and in learning marketing. In the top-end garment industry, such as high fashion, similar problems exist: the dominance of some selective top fashion designers in the international market, the rapid change of product trends, the high cost of activities to support the design, etc. (Mytelka, 1991).

However, in the case of Vietnamese firms, this problem is even more systemic. There is a lack of marketing competence in almost every Vietnamese firm, regardless of which industry is under discussion. Firms working in low-value product areas, like spinning or weaving, and in consumer electronics all lacked marketing capability, even for the domestic market. When it comes to the export market, the problem is even more severe. As a result, it would be fair to say that weaknesses in marketing capability are inherent to Vietnam's condition, not only as a developing country, but also as a country whose economy has had a history of being centrally planned. Similar findings emerge from other studies of transitional economies (Radosevic, 1993; Balasz, 1995). This weakness is also apparent in other non-technical knowledge areas like business management, and economic analysis of investment activities such as cost/benefit analysis and feasibility studies. The lack of competitive pressure and the slight regard for performance in terms of quality all contributed to firms having no need to develop this kind of non-technical competence in the pre-reform period before 1986. During this period, when a subsidised and passive mentality among producers was dominant, awareness of marketing - in particular, recognition of the importance of this activity for both sales and innovation - was absent. The whole business culture in pre-reform firms can be regarded as lacking market consciousness and incentive motivation.

After reforms, the weaknesses of training and education facilities in offering firms non-technical knowledge was another serious constraint. Thus, the cause of the underdevelopment of non-technical expertise shifted from a lack of desire to develop it, to the lack of facilities to learn it (in terms of access, sources of expertise, and experience) and non-technical capabilities continue to be weak. Since these capabilities are still underdeveloped among the Vietnamese firms of this study, this issue is very important for both firms' managers and policy-makers.

10.1.2 Patterns of learning

Second research question concerns the learning mechanisms used by firms in the two industries to accumulate their TCs. As shown earlier, the types of knowledge needed partially shapes the forms of learning mechanisms used. This section specifies the rough proximity of different learning mechanisms to the various kinds of knowledge firms need to learn.

The pattern of using learning mechanisms has been examined in Chapter 7. The *learning-by-doing* mechanism is central to the TC accumulation of firms, occurring in all firms of this study. The practice of Vietnamese firms indicates that this learning mechanism is a must for firms to obtain TC - whatever capabilities are being developed. However, learning-by-doing may sound too general, failing to capture the different nuances of this activity that emerge within the differing circumstances of the firms. In his study of Celltech, Dodgson (1992) called learning-by-doing 'learning-by-solving' the technical problem. Von Hippel & Tyre (1995) referred to learning-by-templating. In the Vietnamese firms, this mechanism was a process of trial and error; learning by trying to get things done. In some cases, firms' efforts to try something, adjust and then try again were so lengthy and painful that Fleck's (1991) term "learning by struggling to get it to work" is very relevant. In other words, the important implication is that learning-by-doing is not simply the act of just-doing-the-thing, but the whole painful process of making a conscious effort to try something in order to get some technology (process and product) to operate as wished. Without these conscious and constant attempts at adjustment for better results - what Bell (1984) calls learning-by-changing - the simple and passive repetition of functions by the firms has less importance for TC accumulation.

The findings also show that no firm can obtain a TC simply through deploying the learning-by-doing mechanism alone. Most use other learning mechanisms to supplement learning-by-doing.

The importance of *previously accumulated knowledge and experience* in facilitating the process of learning gives support to the notion of absorptive capacity suggested by Cohen & Levinthal (1990). Still, the importance of this capacity does vary in relation to different types of knowledge. Most prior knowledge came through two types of recruitment: new graduates from universities and experienced managers from other organisations and firms. Depending on the specific background of the graduates or the experienced new recruits, the absorptive capacity of the firms is likely to support one type of knowledge over another. As shown earlier, recruitment by the firms mostly introduced people with technical backgrounds. This is an obvious outcome of the situation where R&D institutes, universities and colleges mainly run courses in technical subjects and can supply firms with people having engineering skills. Similar technical biases also exist in the recruitment of people who worked elsewhere as engineers or scientists (e.g., in firms whose directors have technical and engineering backgrounds (see cases of TG6, E2 and E3 in Chapter 9). It has been impossible to recruit graduates having non-technical backgrounds due to the lack of training courses in subjects such as business administration, marketing, and economic or investment analysis. These are all poorly developed in Vietnamese universities and colleges. The recruitment of managers only introduced non-technical experience to a limited extent. Nonetheless, the majority of firms in this study were unable to find people with skills and experience suitable for their business, especially in the post-reform period. Few firms were able to recruit managers with the financial and management experience of someone like E3's director. Hence, this bias of technical over non-technical prior knowledge and experience can be attributed to the kinds of knowledge and experience imparted by training institutions and other organisations. The nature of this knowledge, in turn, is the result of policies in training and education development; the Vietnamese context before reform did not place a high priority on the provision of non-technical knowledge. So far, the recruitment of people with previously accumulated expertise is more useful for acquiring technical competence in production or technical change.

The evidence of the firms in this study also confirms that *training* (on-the-job and off-the-job) can greatly enhance the TCs of firms. As Enos (1991) mentions, the effects of on-the-job training seem to be substantial. Indeed, this learning mechanism, which is mostly informal, is important for supplementing formal education to upgrade the TC of the firms.

Learning through *foreign connections* is one of the most significant mechanisms used by the firms in this study. Though, the foreign connections mechanism was less helpful for learning technical change and marketing than for other capabilities. This finding is rather similar to those of some other studies on the textile and electronics industries of developing countries. For instance, Lall and Wignaraja (1994) found that German involvement in the garment industry of Sri Lanka did not lead to the development of higher level capabilities in the local firms. Both forms of German involvement (subcontracting and direct investment) stressed the efficient utilisation of imported technologies rather than the development of independent design and process capabilities in the local partners. As a result, the foreign connection proved necessary for starting up some technological capabilities, but was not sufficient for upgrading these TCs. A similar study by Mytelka (1992) of the textile industry in the Ivory Coast found that reliance on foreign companies did not help local training and that, due to a preference for using expatriates rather than local staff, no learning took place.

In a more optimistic study, Ernst (1995) shows that Korean electronics firms used their connections with foreign companies to learn important knowledge, during the initial period, about investment and production activities. In some cases they could even learn adaptive engineering skills, but they still could not learn about major technical change nor develop their own R&D competence. Evidence from other developing countries suggests that this situation is typical when using foreign connections for technological learning. The Vietnamese firms in this study seem to be in a similar situation. Although it may be likely that foreign partners hesitate to help Vietnamese firms develop their relationship beyond simple subcontracting, there are also some other reasons for this problem on the part of Vietnamese firms. So far the evidence does not permit us to conclude that this is a conscious strategy deployed by foreign companies in Vietnam.

Another point is the importance of *informal networks* based on personal relations and contacts among the firms for collecting *information*, *documentation* and offering consulting services. The significance of networking is widely recognised. Examples include Mytelka's (1993) survey of Latin American networking, and a study of global networking by Japanese electronics firms (Baba & Hatashima, 1995). Most of these studies present networking as a *formal* relationship between organisations and firms or between the personnel of these organisations. There is no doubt that formal networking can be crucial in technological learning. However, these studies are not explicit enough regarding the extent to which informal networking among actors (subcontractors, suppliers, buyers and producers) contributes to such learning. The informal dimension of networking can help the flow of technological knowledge and experience, though this has not received as much attention.

In the Vietnamese firms of this study, networking contributed to the flexibility of production organisation, where many big firms (most are SOEs) subcontract their work to a network of small private and household companies in order to fulfil their workload more quickly using a less rigid organisation of jobs. Informal relationships are also vital for the accumulation of those technological knowledges which help firms to overcome some of the difficulties of the formal R&D, training and education system, both before and after reforms. This feature of informal networking has been observed among industrial firms and R&D organisations in other countries, such as those of Central and Eastern Europe (Balazs et al, 1995) and of the former Soviet Union (Shaw, 1995) in their transition to market economies. This observation highlights the specific character of centrally planned economies, where formal and rigid relationships, cumbersome regulations, and a lack of incentive systems inhibits dynamic and efficient innovation activities. As a result, bureaucratic structures are by-passed as actors use their informal networks to learn from each other. An illustration of this was where E3's director used his informal connections to do business in the former Soviet Union. He secured a unique financial arrangement thanks not only to his know-how, but also to his know-who knowledge of the Ministry of Finance, and of various banks. It seems that these case studies provide new evidence on the significance of collective networking efforts in the TC building of firms in developing countries, especially through the channels of informal networking.

10.1.3 The relationship between learning mechanisms and TC building

One part of second research question is to examine the contribution of each learning mechanism to different types of TC. The relationship between learning mechanisms and TCs can be seen by looking more specifically at each mechanism and its use in accumulating each TC.

First, *learning-by-doing*. Despite the difficulty in assessing this mechanism, the experiences of firms in both the textile/garment and electronics sectors have confirmed that for most types of TC, this mechanism exists in all firms with TCs. No firms have TC that did not use learning-by-doing. It seems quite obvious that any firm wishing to accumulate TC in any function must practice and gain experience through trial and error. By operating machines and checking certain technical functions, most firms learn to identify and solve problems by making improvements. Similarly, they learned by-doing various tasks of investment, undertaking technical change activities or developing linkages. The use of active learning-by-doing (through struggling or trying as discussed in the last section) in Vietnamese firms is rather similar to the learning mechanisms presented in Lapid's (1994) study of layers of learning, and in Von Hippel & Tyre's (1995) work on templating, where problem identification and solution-finding are done through practical tests, checking and problem-solving. Thus, the argument given by Rosenberg (1982) that doing or using is necessary (due to the complexity and unpredictability of interactions between the product and its use environment) is also borne out by Vietnamese firms.

Among learning mechanisms to support learning-by-doing, *prior accumulation of knowledge and experience* seems to emerge as the most important mechanism for almost all firms in both sectors. Formal training and work experience accumulated elsewhere play an important role, although there is a bias toward technical knowledge. The prior accumulation mechanism - despite being present in almost all TCs - is not as important for marketing and major technical change capabilities, especially in textile/garment firms. The reason for this is simple. The lack of marketing awareness, the technical orientation of Vietnam's education system and the way that ministries support industry contribute to this bias in the accumulation of TC among firms. In addition, these factors could not satisfy firms' needs for specific non-technical learning such as are required to deal with economic and investment issues.

Foreign connections is the second most important mechanism of learning. The case evidence in the study shows that in both sectors, this mechanism is mainly used for building capabilities in production, investment and linkage, but contributes little to marketing capability. Also few firms were able to learn technical change and innovative competencies from their foreign connections. These findings are similar to other studies on the East Asian economies of South Korea, Hong Kong, Singapore and Taiwan (Hobday, 1995b; Ernst, 1995). These studies recognise the importance of foreign connections for learning, and at the same time point out the limited learning provided by foreign connections for developing major technical change capability. As Bell & Pavitt (1993) suggest, although in general international technology transfer can be of significant help to firms in developing countries in building up their TC, with some exceptions (e.g., East Asian firms) the utilisation of foreign connections through international transfer tends to help the expansion of production capacity rather than the building of TCs. This study of Vietnamese firms confirms this observation. Moreover, while East Asian firms (e.g., in Korea) seem able to learn minor technical change from their foreign connections, most Vietnamese firms are still unable to do so.

According to Lall (1993a), foreign investment is not always geared to transferring innovation capability; indeed foreign firms tend to base such capability in their home countries. While this may partly explain the absence of R&D and design capability in the Vietnamese firms in this study, it cannot explain the weakness of using foreign connections for learning even minor technical change. Local efforts at R&D and technical improvement activities are not very effective and there is a lack of a dynamic linkage between the S&T infrastructure and industry - a common feature of centrally planned economies (see Balazs et al, 1995). Despite this, many firms in this study were still able to learn minor technical change skills from non-foreign sources. At the same time, only a few firms with conscious strategies and capable managers knew how to utilise foreign contacts for learning technical change (i.e., E2, E10, E11 and TG14).

As a result, it can be said that the weakness of Vietnamese firms in using foreign connections for learning technical change is related first of all to the limited abilities of Vietnamese firms to adopt the necessary strategies and measures to utilise their foreign contacts. Similarly, the study shows that the majority of firms found it difficult to use foreign connections for learning marketing. Only those firms who know how to devise flexible strategies and techniques (like E2's ability to combine various foreign sources) can learn marketing experience from their partners.

In both sectors, a similar relationship exists between TC and *training* mechanisms (on-the-job and off-the-job), offered by the S&T, training and education system. Unlike foreign connections, these mechanisms do contribute to building up minor technical change capability, in addition to production and investment capabilities. The results of this study are rather similar to the findings of other studies regarding the role of training and education programmes in accumulating TC in developing countries. As noted by Bell & Pavitt (1993), there is little information about the use of learning mechanisms such as training for TC accumulation in most of developing countries (with the exception of some NICs in East Asia and Latin America). This study of Vietnamese firms contributes to filling this gap in our knowledge. For example, the study of East Asian late-comers (Hobday, 1995a and 1995b) does not provide a concrete illustration of how firms use training courses to support foreign connections, which was the study's main focus. In contrast, my study shows concretely what kinds of training courses Vietnamese firms use, in what format, for how long and for what type of TC. By focusing on these questions, the study is able to reveal, for example, the absence of local training mechanisms for Vietnamese firms to learn marketing and major technical change capabilities.

One interesting contrast is found between the Vietnamese experience and the findings of another study where, surprisingly, formal technical training was found to have a negative influence on TC accumulation. Massaquois (1995) shows that in the case of the informal sectors in some African countries (Kenya and Sierra Leone), many specialised training centres use expensive imported machinery, producing an undesirable 'demonstration effect' in the trainees which leads to excessive capital intensity. In contrast, the training facilities available to Vietnamese firms were less modern than the production facilities. Although this can cause other problems (a lack of practical experience, for instance), training programmes in Vietnam do not have the above mentioned undesirable effect on learning. Another reason for this difference is that in the above-mentioned African countries, training courses were related more to small-scale firms operating in informal sectors. These activities were not massively organised as in the case of

Vietnamese SOEs, and tended to be isolated from other industries which are more obsoletely equipped. The point to be emphasised here is that in spite of the deficiencies in the training and education system, training courses still have an important effect on the learning efforts of Vietnamese firms. This point confirms the known importance of training and education in other East Asian countries, mostly for the acquisition of technical knowledge and, more recently, non-technical knowledge.

The dominance of technical knowledge (capabilities in production, minor technical change, and linkage) can also be seen in the case of *information* and *documentation* collection in both sectors. The only difference between the two sectors is in the area of non-technical learning. While textile/garment firms use this mechanism for learning about investment but not marketing, electronics firms tend to learn more about marketing and nothing of investment.

Drawing on earlier discussions on the strengths and weaknesses of each learning mechanism and their associations with various TCs, some general features of these learning mechanisms may be identified. Prior accumulated knowledge through recruitment is the most important mechanism for active learning. This provides the firms' personnel with the initial assets to climb up the learning curve, together with the absorptive capacity (Cohen & Levinthan, 1990) to know what to learn next, and how. Foreign connections are more helpful for learning investment and production capabilities and less so for technical change. Among the two training mechanisms, on-the-job training seems to serve better for learning the routine skills of production and minor technical change capabilities, while off-the-job training seems to support the learning and updating of knowledge that is newer to the firms. For instance, the firms could not acquire much expertise in investment and marketing through recruitment or on-the-job training, but relied instead on off-the-job training, such as short-term courses, seminars or workshops.

The use of learning mechanisms depends on the availability of particular types of knowledge from these mechanisms (technical versus non-technical). Since the learning sources available to Vietnamese firms are more competent in providing technical knowledge and experience like production or minor technical change, firms tend to use mechanisms (such as prior accumulated learning, training and information and documentation) more for acquiring technical expertise than non-technical expertise. In the case of foreign connections, the firms use this mechanism for non-technical learning like investment (and in some cases, also marketing). This depends both on the ability of firms to utilise their foreign connections, and on the actions of the foreign partners. As a result, when asking the question "what learning mechanisms are most suitable for which TC?", the question "what knowledge and expertise are offered to firms, and how do they utilise what is on offer?" comes into focus. In turn, this question leads us to consider the activities of the R&D, training and education infrastructure - indeed, the whole external environment of learning - as well as the strategic behaviour of the firms in their environment. This latter focus reveals that, the use of learning mechanisms depends not only on the availability of relevant knowledge, but also on the types of knowledge (TC) firms want to acquire. These TCs can be the outcome of the aims which firms want to pursue (e.g., commercial objectives, strategic directions, etc.), and, these aims are likely to change over time. As can be seen in Chapter 8, the overall external environment conditions the strategic responses of firms. These responses then shape the firms' TC needs and, accordingly, their use of appropriate learning mechanisms. Hence, the importance of the external macro-environment and its interaction with the strategies of firms is a central issue in understanding the relationship between learning mechanisms and TC.

Thus, the relationship between using learning mechanisms and TC accumulation in Vietnam can be presented as a two-way connection. First, the issue of which knowledge is to be learnt is important. The question of what to learn (i.e., whether technical or non-technical knowledge is required) suggests how it may be learnt (i.e., by means of which mechanisms), provided that firms have their own conscious strategies for utilising these mechanisms. Second, the availability of learning mechanisms (i.e., which learning mechanisms are offered by the supporting system, or by the national system of innovation) has an important influence on the kind of knowledges that can be learnt. Firms face difficulties in learning a specific knowledge like marketing, if it is not available from any source. Taking into account the notion of learning as the means to accumulate TC suggested by Bell & Pavitt (1993), the relationship between learning and TC could be schematically represented in Figure 10.1.

In Figure 10.1, the *purposes* of learning (which TCs firms need to acquire) depend on the macro-environment and the strategic directions firms take in this environment (e.g., whether to export or not; whether to diversify products and markets or to just concentrate on a few specific things, etc.). The macro environment and firms' strategies should decide the *means* for, and the *activities* of, learning: what learning mechanisms can be, and are being, used by firms. These factors are varied, and depend on firms' formation, the industry, and the ownership of the firms. In other words, it depends on firm-specific conditions. As a *result* of learning, some TCs (or knowledge) accumulated by the firms may, or may not, be the same as those they had originally anticipated.

Figure 10.1 tries to present the preliminary sequence of actions in the learning process. However, learning might not have such a straightforward linear pattern. It is, rather, a constantly changing process. Although it is very difficult to distinguish clear-cut patterns of interaction within this relationship, one thing is certain. The conditions of the macro-environment and firms' behaviour are major determinants of the suitability of particular learning mechanisms for accumulating certain TCs. This could also be termed more fully as "conditional suitability".

Despite these difficulties, according to experience of firms, some patterns in the combination of learning mechanisms can be found, and these are centred around certain TCs.

10.1.4 The combination of learning mechanisms

As mentioned above, it is difficult to provide a ready-made recipe as a way of bench-marking firms' learning activities. For example, it is not simply a case of stating which learning mechanisms firms have to use in order to achieve what kinds of TC. Still, some points can be specified as the results of my empirical studies. First, the need to combine various learning mechanisms in order to acquire a TC has been observed in the study. However, when it comes to the more concrete issue of which combinations are best, few studies have been done. Many unanswered questions remain such as "what is the necessary rate of combination?" (i.e., how many learning mechanism are sufficient to learn a certain TC) or "in what patterns are learning mechanisms combined? and for which TC?".

The results of this study can straight-away answer the first question about the rate of combination. As mentioned in Chapter 7, the general picture is that textile/garment firms need at least two extra interactive learning mechanisms in addition to learning-by-doing to acquire a TC. As for electronics firms, at least three extra mechanisms are required. These additional mechanisms tend to be prior knowledge accumulation and foreign connections. Other mechanisms are less frequently present. The differences between the sectors are probably due to the specific nature of electronics as a more knowledge-intensive industry than textile/garments, and it therefore requires more learning mechanisms to obtain a particular TC. However, when it comes to only firms having strongly developed TC, the rate of using learning mechanisms is much higher, ranking from 3.2-3.3 for linkage capability to 5.17-5.5 for production capability in both sectors.

Regarding the patterns of combination of different learning mechanisms to accumulate certain technological capability, the task becomes more complicated. The practice of TC acquisition among Vietnamese firms shows combinations involving not only learning-by-doing with other mechanisms, but also of various non-doing-based mechanisms. *Investment* and *production* capabilities are accumulated mostly through a combination of prior knowledge, back-up from foreign partners, and then off-the-job training (for investment only) or on-the-job training (for production only). This pattern is similar for both textile/garment and electronics firms. Prior accumulated knowledge supports the initial effort, while foreign connections place the firms on a more substantial footing. Still, relying on foreign connections seems too passive and therefore, training courses (on-the-job or off-the-job, depending on the TC) update expertise and enable the learning to become more independent of foreign sources.

Prior knowledge continues to support *minor technical change* capability, but it is combined with training and information collection (for textile/garments) or with training and foreign connections (for electronics). While training and information collection serve as ways of updating knowledge, foreign connections play little part in helping firms to learn minor technical change capability. The exception here is a few electronics firms, which are able to learn something from foreign partners for this TC (e.g., E2, E10 and E11), thanks to the special relationship of the Vietnamese managers with their foreign counterparts (especially in E2).

To learn *marketing* competence, the firms use prior accumulation in combination with either off-the-job training (in textile/garments) or information collection (in electronics). Some electronics firms have added foreign connections as well. Although firms have a tendency to make little use of foreign connections in learning marketing, some electronics firms did consciously use their foreign partners for this end. Firms in both sectors use similar combinations of mechanisms for learning *linkage* capability. In addition to prior accumulation, they use information collection to develop and maintain their network of relations. Electronics firms can combine these with foreign connections.

The patterns of combining learning mechanisms presented here suggest a probable guideline for firms. As emphasised before, however, this is not a recipe which guarantees that a firm following this combination will acquire an appropriate TC. The possible universality of these findings (if there is any) demands further comparative research across many firms and countries.

10.2 Sequential features of TC building and learning dynamics

As part of the first research question on patterns of TC accumulation, the study confirms the sequential nature of TC development. The majority of firms commence the process of TC building at the level of simple kinds of production capability, then move on to acquire the further capabilities of minor technical change or investment.

The sequence differs across sectors and sub-sectors and also across firms, depending on firm-specific characteristics such as ownership, circumstances of operation and establishment, etc. In textile/garment companies, for instance, the sequence of TC accumulation depends on the ownership of firms, with SOEs having accumulated TCs gradually while private firms have, so far, had much less time to accumulate their TCs. In electronics firms, differences exist between computing and consumer electronics companies.

At the same time, differences between the two sectors in the sequence of TC building is related to the interaction of the firms with their external environment. In some specific conditions, it is not necessary for firms to begin with production capability; several capabilities may come together. The cases of private firms TG8 and TG9 in the post-reform period illustrate this 'jumping in' pattern, as we saw how they accumulated various TC at the same time. Similarly, electronics firms (most are private like E3 and E4) show that coming from within R&D, the personnel of these firms can go straight to various kinds of activities with little or no production capability. This by-passing of the production mode of starting a firm result from some special conditions, e.g., R&D-based activities and experience of personnel and unique start-up circumstances. However, these cases provide the exception to the overall pattern of sequencing. Comparing the findings of this study with the model of East Asian late-comer firms (Hobday, 1995b), we can see that this jumping-in mode of Vietnamese firms does not offer an instance of a leap-frogging pattern where a firm can cut short its learning path and accumulate TCs in a less gradual way. In fact, most Vietnamese firms still exhibit the same pattern of learning: they start with well-proven and mature technologies and then "move back" - to use Hobday's (1994) term - to more untested and newer technologies. The second research question is also addressed by the findings of this study, which supports the key characteristics of learning such as learning is not costless and automatic. Firms' experience shows that learning is not one-go switch but an on-going accumulation process from nothing to something and, further still, from something simple to something more complex requiring additional knowledge contents. The cumulative pattern of the technological learning escalator (Bell, 1984) found in this study is similar to the generally observed pattern of learning among firms in other developing countries, especially in East Asia (Ernst, 1994 & 1995).

The dynamic nature of learning (changing over time in terms of its sources, mechanisms and content) is also found in this study. For instance, the Vietnamese firms started with learning-by-doing, prior accumulation of knowledge and some simple training. Information collection and other on-the-job training came later. In using foreign connections, firms moved from a simple subcontracting format to an OEM mode of relations; sources of learning also changed from the Soviet Union and Eastern European countries to the EU and Asia-Pacific countries. The content of learning also expands over time.

The changes in learning taking place in Vietnamese firms are similar to those found in some other empirical studies, such as the study of East Asian firms by Hobday (1995b) who identifies the changing nature of both learning content and learning mechanisms over time. Although this model of export-led technological learning for late-comer firms suggested that the sequencing of learning starts with mastering simple tasks and with complex learning and R&D coming later (Hobday, 1995b), in addition, within this pattern, some exceptional new start-up firms may jump in at an advanced level, missing out the early stage of innovation. These experiences are somewhat similar to the case of E3 in my study when the firm jumped directly into producing PCs and software.

The third research question of this study is to consider why firms accumulated their TCs using the learning patterns they did. The findings of Chapters 6 and 7 revealed what kinds of TC firms acquired, and through which patterns they learned. The reasons behind the similarities and differences of TC accumulation, for example, are attributed mainly to two factors: ownership of the firms in textile/garment industry, and historical establishment features across the two sub-sectors in the electronics industry. The concept of a national system of innovation (NSI), in the experience of this study, can be observed through the activities of various macro-policies exercised by the state, the emergence of competitive pressures on firms both locally and in export markets, and the activity of the supporting infrastructure, etc.

10.3 Vietnam's context: a developing and transitional economy

Many of the features specific to Vietnam, not only as a developing country, but also as an economy in transition from being centrally planned to being more driven by market forces, have already been presented in Chapter 5. The reforms initiated in 1986 and which continued until the beginning of the 1990s, affected all social and economic aspects of the country. The change to the external factors after reform became one of the most important influences on the business activities and learning efforts of the firms.

10.3.1 The influence of the macro-environment on business and learning

Macro economic policies of the state are always central to discussions on external environmental factors. These external factors are discussed as supply-side and demand-side factors, comprising policies of the state, the functions of market factors, and the activities of the S&T and education infrastructures. All these factors are undoubtedly important in understanding the learning process in TC accumulation. Nonetheless, most studies do not provide an answer as to which factors are most influential on which types of learning. Although these studies specify the impact of these factors on either the general performance of firms or on their innovation activities, they do not cross-check each factor against various forms of learning. Therefore, the findings of this study represent a further step in specifying the influence of external factors on firms' learning processes; they help to show more clearly what hinders or facilitates learning by means of ranking those influences in terms of their effects on forms of learning. My data presents the firms' perspectives on the influence of external environmental factors on business activities in general, and on learning activities for TC accumulation in particular. The findings in Chapter 8 report that the influences are almost the same for both doing business and for learning activity, in terms of the type of factor and of the ranking of groups of factors. State policies and the supporting system emerged as the most influential.

Table 8.1 presents the influences on business, while Table 8.2 offers an overall picture of the influence each group of factors has on different learning mechanisms. Some tendencies have emerged from these tables. *Policy factors* such as policies of the state on taxation, financial, banking and labour issues, and management regulation influence almost all learning mechanisms for both sectors. These factors have a mostly negative effect on the business and learning activities of the firms: they have the effect of imposing funding shortages, cumbersome regulations, and an overly strict labour management practice, just to name a few. The *supporting system* - R&D, training and education institutions; the activities of other support and service organisations governing issues on standardisation, metrology and industrial property rights; and legal and physical infrastructures - has a considerable influence on training (on-the-job and off-the-job), and especially on information sources. This is to be expected since training courses, provision of documentation, information collection and consultancy depend directly on the expertise and activities of the R&D, training and education organisations. This system helps firms to accumulate their initial technological knowledge through recruitment and training. However, the main characteristics of the system (e.g., poor curricula for training workers, and the lack of a dynamic linkage with industry) make it less effective in helping firms use learning sources.

One interesting finding is that *market factors*, like the change of the market structure and the pressures of domestic and international markets, are not considered by companies to be as negatively influential on learning as macro-economic policies and the supporting system. There might be an explanation for this finding. Although the influence of market factors on general business activities of the firms are severe, at the same time they also create many opportunities for firms to learn TCs, in terms of new learning sources and formats, mostly coming from foreign partners in the EU and Asia-Pacific markets. Surveys of firms' opinions show that although the opening of markets has created difficulties for firms in adjusting their activities, at the same time the changes have had positive impacts on firms' learning. The benefits that firms gain from market changes are greater than the problems they also bring in their wake. Considering the benefits versus difficulties, the firms tend to criticise market changes less than other external factors. This factor, in any case, has a significant impact on learning and TC accumulation in the Vietnamese context. The majority of firms in the study are involved in export activities and depend very much on foreign partners as learning sources. Therefore, as market factors change, most firms in both sectors feel that their learning through foreign connections are being influenced by these changes. *Social* and *cultural factors* have similar influences on both sectors: the special mentality and learning traditions of the Vietnamese have an impact on on-the-job training and learning-by-doing mechanisms.

10.3.2 Features of Vietnam's transitional economy: the impact on learning

First, about changes in the *industrial infrastructure*. The heritage of the command economy has had both positive and negative influences on learning activity. Prior to reforms, the free, regular and subsidised supply of new university recruits, educated workers and other technical staff were significant sources of learning for firms. Continuous support received from state campaigns to promote learning was another strength. At the same time, the weaknesses of the pre-reform period such as limited market access (only the CMEA countries were accessible) and the deficiencies of training and education programmes are well-known. Similarly stemming from the heritage of a centrally planned economy, other problems associated with the pre-reform period - the lack of an incentive system; a lack of concern about the quality dimension of performance; the passive subsidised mentality of producers; and the absence of any market awareness - are common among industrial firms.

With the transition to a market economy, things changed. R&D, training and education were liberalised and became more dynamic, thanks to the entrepreneurial attitude introduced into the system by the reforms. This has meant that more learning resources have become available to firms. Many scientists have even moved out of state organisations to set up their own technical institutions, thus providing firms with additional expertise and skill. In some cases, they have become the owners of newly set-up firms. The creation of spin-off companies from R&D and education institutions is characteristic of many other transitional economies in China (Gu, 1996), and in Central and Eastern Europe (CEE) (Balazs, 1995; Mosoni-Fried, 1995). This has had a positive influence on these firms' ability to learn: a good deal of expertise has been accumulated by staff even before they start trading.

Not all the reforms to the industrial infrastructure have had a positive impact on learning. In particular, the R&D, training and education system is now less supportive of industry than it used to be. Poorly equipped, and enjoying even fewer state subsidies, the system has become outdated and is inefficient at serving industry. Although Vietnam's S&T system is still intact, its state funding has been cut and many research institutes must supplement their funding with contracts. When they fail to win research contracts, R&D institutes now have to rely on providing various kinds of service. This has significantly diminished the scientific expertise as well as the potential learning resources of R&D institutions. This trend is mirroring the experience of the CEE countries as they shift their R&D towards the downstream activities of the spectrum (Radosevic, 1993). In addition, Vietnamese firms no longer have access to free education and training for their personnel.

The reforms of the transitional period, as Vietnam's experience shows, have brought both good and bad times for firms in utilising the industrial supporting infrastructure. This situation echoes that of other countries who are also moving from a centrally planned to a market economy. For instance, Shaw (1995) shows the difficulties experienced by Russian industries in securing financial support for R&D to develop new competence, even in such a prestigious industry as aerospace. In China, the problems within the R&D, training and education system and with its relation to industry, are similar to those of Vietnam (Baark, 1994; Zhang & Reeve, 1995; Jamison & Baark, 1990). For instance, Gu (1996) emphasises that the new technology enterprises forming China's computing industry are spin-offs from the restructuring of R&D institutions. The innovative potential of Chinese S&T personnel is limited by both political compromise and the inertia of the economic system (Baark, 1994).

In the CEE countries, the same situation can be seen. Before the changes, the R&D system was also structured, like Vietnam's, into three separate parts: academic, universities and industrial branch sector institutions. Links between these three areas are fragmented. There is only a slight liaison between S&T and industry. Marketing and business interests are largely notable for their absence (Balasz et al, 1995). This system is inefficient and weak. Due to its rigid structure and the formal barriers of the planning system, people have devised ways to get around the system, e.g., relying on extensive informal networks. This way of communicating has helped them to get things done. Like Vietnam, the CEE countries are also experiencing many radical changes to the R&D and other supporting infrastructures for industrial firms. New problems have emerged in the transition, such as lack of capital and tax incentives for new ventures (Balasz, 1995). The creation of spin-off companies from R&D institutions can also be seen in many CEE countries, such as Hungary (Mosoni-Fried, 1995) and the Czech Republic (Muller, 1995).

In the context of reform, what are the observed *similarities* and *differences* between Vietnam and these other transitional economies? One similarity is that the lack of any overview in co-ordinating R&D activities has led to poorly co-ordinated government strategies (Balasz, 1995). This problem is especially evident in Vietnam's electronics industry which does not have a coherent industrial strategy. Another similarity is the preoccupation of industrial firms with short-term issues (Balasz et al, 1995) which is common for the majority of Vietnamese firms. Not many firms in my study could demonstrate that they had developed a long-term strategic perspective.

Informal networks of connections are another important issue for learning in Vietnamese firms. Also discussed elsewhere is the importance of small private firms which serve as subcontracting networks for larger firms (usually SOEs) in implementing large contracts. But it is necessary to emphasise the role of personal networking in building TCs in the firms. This factor plays a pivotal role for using learning mechanisms (prior accumulated relations, training and information sources) to accumulate various kinds of TC. One of the main reasons firms use informal links so extensively is the heritage from the command economy where formal contacts were rigid, cumbersome, and slow to react to the needs of industry. In many cases forming such contacts was even illegal.[2] This situation is quite common in other Eastern European countries and in countries of the former Soviet Union, as Balasz et al (1995) note.

Before the reforms personal networking did, of course, exist in Vietnam as elsewhere. In the CEE countries, the transition has disrupted those informal links which previously had helped to get things done (Balasz et al, 1995). However, in spite of the loss of many old contacts (people moving to new jobs or losing old ones), these networks still have some relevance. People in the CEE countries have learned to use informality - to trust friends more than bureaucrats - and new start-up firms thus tend to rely on family support rather than bank credit for capital. As a result, informal relations between people have re-emerged as a way of getting things done even after reform, although to a lesser extent.

This kind of relationship is still working in the Vietnamese context. During the reform period, the use of learning mechanisms such as information, documentation and consulting services have became even more heavily dependent on this kind of informal connection. Informal networking in Vietnam takes two main forms. One is non-political; it concerns connections among classmates, former colleagues, friends and relatives. The other has more political links where party connections are used by informal groups and factions within the party and the administrative organisations. Other forms of informal networking (e.g revolving around religion, race, cultural tradition or habit) are almost non-existent in Vietnam. The experience of Vietnamese firms shows that personal and informal contacts have not been greatly disrupted by reforms. Unlike the CEE countries, they did not submerge only to re-emerge later. In Vietnam, they have simply always been operating. The first reason for this is that the political structure of institutions (i.e., the leading party) is still in place. In spite of the reforms, old connections (both party and non-party) have not been disrupted, rather they have adjusted to the new conditions of a market economy. A second factor behind this continued informal link is the mentality of Vietnamese staff. For a long time now, they have not been in the habit of using consultancy services, seeing that occupation as an untrustworthy one. The only mechanism for creating confidence and credibility is the personal trust built up over a long period through very informal social relations. The continued reliance on this old way of working seems common to many other post-communist and transitional economies, but seems stronger in Vietnam's case.

Another difference is the *more active role of government* in Vietnam as compared with other CEE countries in supporting the formation of new entrepreneurial enterprises like science parks, technology parks and professional associations. In the CEE countries, these efforts are undertaken by individuals and research organisations, while in Vietnam and, to a similar extent, in China (see Gu, 1996), government has been more involved in initiating these activities. Again, the explanation lies in the fact that the whole political and administrative system in the CEE countries has been shaken to its roots, while in Vietnam and China it has not.

Having discussed the features of transitional economies and compared them to Vietnam, one should bear in mind that, in many ways,

Vietnam is not easily comparable to these other countries. There is a fundamental difference between Vietnam and these countries: while resembling the CEE countries and the countries of the former Soviet Union in that they all share a history of communist political ideology, Vietnam is far less developed industrially. Economic transition in the former countries came about as a result of, and together with, radical political changes. This is not the case in Vietnam. In this sense, China shares more similarities with Vietnam, although the huge scale of the Chinese economy makes further comparison difficult.

As a result, Vietnam is a *unique developing and transitional economy*. While retaining a political structure which has not been dismantled, profound economic changes have taken place. In comparison with other transitional countries, Vietnam is unique in terms of its low level of industrial development and its slower pace of reforms. At the same time, compared to other developing countries in Southeast Asia, it has a more bureaucratic administrative structure and has less market awareness of the whole socio-economic system. One can note that in this unique context, there are some features that resemble those of other transitional economies, and some of other developing countries. These characteristics are sometimes the same for both types of countries (for instance, the importance of various external environmental factors on learning and TC acquisition), but more often they are different.

On the one hand, the commonalties between Vietnam and other transitional economies (such as the weaknesses in learning non-technical knowledge, the limitations on marketing capability, the lack of consciousness about product quality and qualitative performance) are less apparent in developing countries. Developing economies typically have had more exposure and access to the market pressures of the international economy. The problems of formerly centrally planned economies (both before and after reforms) are surely unique to those countries; they are not problems that are shared by other developing economies.

On the other hand, features such as the limitations on technical change capability, and the weakness of domestic R&D in providing technical expertise for technological absorption and adaptation, are more often observed in developing (mostly non-NIC) countries than in the CEE countries, where the NSI has accumulated a relatively good industrial basis for innovative activities. Similarly, the weakness of foreign connections in helping local firms to learn technical change and marketing can be seen quite clearly in the experiences of Vietnam and also in some developing countries (Lall & Wignaraja, 1994), while that difficulty is less obvious in the CEE countries.

Since not enough empirical studies have been conducted, it is difficult (and beyond the scope of this study) to comprehensively compare the characteristics of developing and transitional countries in their technological development paths.[3] Nonetheless, one thing is clear. Vietnam exhibits features of both developing and transitional countries. Some features are similar and exist in both types of country. Some even apply to all economies, e.g., the importance of informal networking for innovation activities. As for other features, these differ among the two types of country. In consequence, the way these features blend in Vietnam suggests that Vietnam experiences most of the difficulties of both developing and transitional economies. Still, some features of Vietnamese reforms which seem a disadvantage, in fact turned out to be an advantage for R&D. For example, the slower pace of political change in Vietnam (in governmental, political and administrative structures) as compared with the CEE countries, seems to have prevented Vietnam's NSI from free-falling into chaos as has happened in some CEE countries. Paradoxically, after some years of abandoning subsidies for education and training, the role of government in this respect is now being reassessed. The East Asian belief that developing countries require their governments to play a strong hand is returning to Vietnam also.

10.3.3 The opening up of export markets and the emergence of local markets

The transitional period has brought many radical changes. Market changes have brought Vietnamese industry to meeting the needs of their users and have shaken Vietnamese firms out of their long period of inertia, bringing them closer to buyers, especially for export products. Given the newly-created market pressures, the firms in this study have had to change their business activities and this, in turn, is changing their learning behaviour.

The importance of a competitive environment, or competitive pressure (Fransman, 1995), and of market factors (Lall, 1994a; Dalum et al, 1992) is obvious. Fransman (1995) observes that as a source of competitive pressure, export markets can be very important. He compares Japan, where exports tend to be the *result* of the accumulation of competencies, with Korea and Taiwan, where export activities are the *cause* of the accumulation of competencies. These notions are not new. However, when looking at the role of market changes in the Vietnamese situation, some points can be noted. As case studies reveal, export activities and a closer orientation to export markets have increased the level of technological capabilities within the firms involved. Similar findings can be seen in other studies of Thailand (Poapongsakorn & Tonguthai, 1998), Malaysia (Kassim & Salleh, 1994) and Indonesia (Wie & Pangestu, 1998). Hence, Vietnamese industrial firms - as late-comers - tend to follow a pattern similar to other small NICs in South East Asia; this pattern also resembles that found in Korea and Taiwan.

Experiences of Vietnamese firms also show that a firm can acquire advanced technological skills yet still to remain at an early stage of marketing competence. While most of the firms achieved at least an average level of skill handling process technologies (process adaptation and incremental improvements) and product technologies (reverse engineering and prototype development), their marketing activities still remain at an early stage of development (i.e., simple OEM and sub-contracting). This is understandable since Vietnamese firms have accumulated certain technological rather than marketing skills in advance of their ability to develop markets. Indeed they have not accumulated any marketing competencies in preparation for competing in a market economy. However, it is because marketing experience is new and rare among Vietnamese firms, that their new access to international markets becomes even more significant.

The recent changes in Vietnam have not only opened up export markets, but have also introduced new opportunities to exploit the domestic market. Although in general the purchasing power of the population is still weak, it is increasing rapidly and newly-created local businesses make firms more aware of competition. New actors in the domestic market (e.g., private firms and firms enjoying foreign investment) create stronger competitive pressure. Companies must now take active measures to improve their product quality, range and specification. At the same time, new business opportunities force firms to innovate just to keep up with the new requirements of the market; they must continually adjust their mode of production if they are to hit the moving target of what to produce and how to produce it. Thus, together with new export markets, the emergence of a local market is a new feature of Vietnam's transitional period, and is proving critical for learning and TC accumulation as new challenges and opportunities emerge.

10.3.4 The changing and contrasting role of the state

With respect to the effects that the transitional period has had on the industrial supporting infrastructure, one question comes into focus. In considering the balance between the positive and negative aspects of reforms in R&D, training and education on the learning activities of firms, one should look at the role of the government in supporting these activities (or not) through subsidies and other intervention measures.

When reforms leading to the market economy were initiated, some economists of Vietnamese studies argued that the government should no longer play a dominant role. Indeed, in economic theory, a belief in the powerful role of markets and a commensurate reduction in the need for government intervention has been widespread in political and economic circles. Against this view, Lall (1994a) criticises approaches that minimise not just the role of technological activity in developing countries, but also the need for policies to support, protect and induce such activities. He goes further to emphasise the crucial role that government policies must play to promote technological development. Similarly, Bell & Pavitt (1992) emphasise the importance of government in market economies, where the administration supports technological accumulation through investment in education and training. According to them, an effective education and training policy must be designed to promote learning, and to create change-generating human resources. My aim here is not to engage in the debate as to whether government intervention is good or bad, but merely to point out that - even in a market economy - government intervention remains important. Its role seems even more significant in the transitional economies of Eastern Europe, China and Vietnam. In this period, when the old structural and institutional framework is undergoing radical change, and a new one is still absent or nascent, the guiding and co-ordinating role of government looks irreplaceable.

What can the experiences of my case studies contribute to this debate? Chapter 8 suggests that the majority of the firms still advocate a certain role for government in supporting their TC accumulation. Two main groups of external factors (macro-policies and the functions of the supporting infrastructure) are the direct outcome of government actions. It is important too devise macro-policies (for trade, financial, banking and labour affairs) that support a market economy not only for aiding the general business performance of firms but also augmenting technological learning and TC accumulation. Furthermore, the activities of the whole industrial infrastructure (R&D, training, education and other services organisations) have, until recently, been managed by the government; it lies beyond the capacity and resources of any single firm to address or reform that infrastructure.

Given the importance of government, the question here is to what extent it is important and what specific modes of intervention would prove more beneficial? Should the government (continue to) subsidise some of the internal activities of firms, e.g., providing them with free education, research services or the like? The evidence of my case studies indicates that some activities provided by the national system of innovation are beyond the resources of any single firm - or even a group of firms - to supply alone. Only government has the resources to deal with macro problems, such as providing training facilities for both vocational training and higher education. The same can be said for S&T, especially for funding large-scale and complex research programmes. Here, although I entirely agree with Justman & Teubal's (1995) point on the catalytic role and stimulating influence of government, I would be more reluctant to revoke all subsidisation of R&D as they advocate. The role of government should go further than just guiding activities. Government should concentrate on measures (such as funding policies, tax incentives and banking and labour management regulations) that help firms to learn, and help them to conduct their businesses more effectively. Moreover, government subsidy is still necessary to help firms generate technological capabilities through underwriting some specific activities such as training, especially in primary, secondary and technical vocational schools and for some strategic R&D.

One further consideration is the need for a *holistic view of the industrial supporting infrastructure* in Vietnam. The problems of input sourcing, the dependency of both textile/garment and electronics firms on other industries (e.g., mechanical and chemical) all point to the interrelatedness of industries (Rosenberg, 1982). This infrastructure includes not only R&D, education and training activities but also other types of activity such as industrial services in standardisation, metrology and quality control, the legal and institutional framework and the creation of associations and other new organisational forms of innovation promotion like S&T parks, etc. All these elements constitute the national system of innovation which governments can help to develop and promote. In addition, the government has a crucial role to play in bridging this system with the socio-economic environment of the country so as to create favourable conditions for these institutions to interact with industry. So far, these important measures have not yet been put in place in Vietnam. The opinions and the practices of firms indicate that, on the one hand, the Vietnamese government still seems unable to create a sufficiently favourable macro-environment or to enact sufficiently conducive policies to promote technological learning in industrial firms. Despite the reform, the grip of government remains hard with respect to many business activities of firms (especially private ones). Firms feel that government over-intervenes in this area. On the other hand, the firms also indicate that they feel under-protected by state policies and that the NSI does not promote their efforts at technological accumulation.

The reason for over-intervention is that the government believes that, even in transition to a market economy, it still needs to retain a certain level of control over industry. In large part, this belief is based on the political motives of the government to exercise control over most societal activities. Moreover, the negative attitude towards private firms exists within the context of a government fear that the private sector could over-run the economy, which would be dangerous for socialist development. Concerning the second phenomenon (under-protection and lack of promotion), the government feels it does not have enough resources to continue subsidise for the sake of economic reform (budgetary and trade balance deficit problems, etc.). Adding to the confusion, in certain circumstances, the government simply lacks the information necessary for taking effective action. The absence of a long-term strategic view is the outcome of this factor. As a consequence, the Vietnamese government is now in the situation of controlling its industries without promoting them. One solution to this dilemma is for the government to selectively intervene utilising its scarce resources wisely. So far, no decisive and clear intentions of the government can be seen in the selectivity of its actions.

The experiences of the firms in my study also point to another important role for government, i.e., its co-ordinating role in supporting, linking and guiding the learning efforts of different firms to create their TCs. The evidence for this argument is the strong need felt by Vietnamese electronics firms for a coherent, long-term policy designed and supported by the state to develop the whole sector. Electronics firms in this study are facing enormous problems in orienting their learning efforts because there is no long-term and consistent strategy for developing the sector. This can be considered as one of the specific features of Vietnam's transition to a market economy. After some years of reform, with the government loosening its grip on firms, firms miss the traditional forms of support offered by the state (regardless of how weak and uncomprehensive this support used to be) and now they want it back. This phenomenon of wishing to revitalise state involvement coincides with the drift away of state control in favour of market forces.

Another issue is the *scope and scale of the government's intervention* in supporting firms' technological learning. Advocating the importance of industrial policy in his critique of the World Bank study, Lall (1994b) argues that government intervention should be selective, and should be separately specified for each industry to ensure efficient resource allocation. Uniform protection is not equally effective for every industry. In garment assembly, where the learning period is relatively brief, protection may not be necessary. For complex activities, where learning takes years or even decades, protection is more crucial.

In the case of Vietnamese industries, as shown above, it is clear that the government cannot, and should not, be involved in all kinds of intervention into all activities. Due to its many commitments and its limited resources, it cannot subsidise everything. On the other hand, it should step back from intervening in the daily internal affairs of firms. The necessity for selective intervention is obvious. Nonetheless, there is not enough data to establish what form of deliberate and selective state intervention there should be in either of the two industries considered in this study. It seems that they continue to face the macro-economic constraints after reform as they did before, and must continue to rely on the same industrial supporting infrastructure. The strengths and weaknesses of the two industries are broadly similar albeit with a few differences. Still, there are some policy measures being differentially applied to the two industries (e.g., the tax rates imposed on imports). If we can find instances where different treatments are being meted out to the two industries, it seems likely that these rest on spontaneous selectivity rather than on harmonised and co-ordinated policy-making. Further, there is little evidence of government selectively applying measures to each sub-sector (garment v. textile; consumer electronics v. computing). However, looking at criteria like the support different industries receive from R&D organisations, it can be said that the textile industry has got more and earlier support than the garment industry. The same can be seen in the electronics industry, where computing activities tend to receive more attention then consumer or industrial electronics in terms of training, research and education facilities and promotion. Whatever differences exist within sub-sectors, these are rather fragmented and do not form part of a coherent and co-ordinated state intervention policy.

What now characterises government intervention in Vietnam is simultaneous over-intervention and under-protection. Those activities that firms want greater personal control over (e.g., management and salary regulations) are subject to quite considerable state control. Conversely, those functions that require state support (e.g., education, training and support for research and technical development) are left to companies to tackle alone as best they can. In the firms' view, this is a situation of "both redundancy and shortage". Governmental action (or lack of it) with respect to technological learning is thus another feature of Vietnam's transitional economy. The selectivity of government intervention in this case (intervening more heavily in firms' economic affairs than in industrial support activities) creates an undesirable balance in the view of the firms interviewed.

Another feature of the government's role is its attitude to state-owned enterprises (SOEs) and the public sector. The experiences of the reforming economies of Eastern Europe and the former Soviet Union illuminate the weaknesses of SOEs as compared to private businesses in sustaining economic competitiveness. This can lead to the extreme assertion that SOEs have no future in a market economy - a view especially prevalent among Vietnamese policy-makers and research circles - with the implication that everything should be privatised. However, some recent outcomes of reforms in many Eastern European countries, and in China and Vietnam show that state-owned firms have significantly improved their performance while remaining under public ownership. This evidence thus contradicts the assertion that it is impossible to reshape SOEs without the incentives provided by private ownership (McMillan, 1995). Similarly, this study reveals that although the majority of SOEs are in bad shape, some SOEs can remain rather competitive providing their managers adopt suitable policy measures and strategies. The existing competitiveness and technological learning of SOEs such as E2, TG1 and TG6 (although differentially successful) provides the evidence to support this point. The significance of this observation is that, helped by the necessary support from the state, the strategies exercised by certain managers in some SOEs are important for learning and TC acquisition.

Nonetheless, there are some basic differences separating SOEs and private companies. These, in turn, lead to different learning behaviours and TC accumulation abilities.

10.3.5 State and private ownership

The history of Vietnamese industrial development shows that government support is preferentially offered to SOEs at the expense of the private sector. In some transitional economies like Russia and China, similar discrimination against the non-state sector can be found (McMillan, 1995), with the exception of a few pet companies as joint ventures with foreign firms (whose local partners are SOEs). This discrimination against Vietnam's private sector causes many problems for doing business as a private firm (Beresford, 1989). In technological terms, the influence of these activities on the accumulation of TC is severe. One consequence is that SOEs have much greater access to industrial support than private companies do. This, together with differential access to financial resources and credit, provides SOEs with indisputable advantages over competing private firms.[4] The discriminatory external environment leads to different patterns of TC accumulation and learning. The sequence of TC building in the textile/garment sector differs depending on type of ownership. The relaxed attitude to investment activity, and a lack of competitive pressure - a pressure which is pivotal to TC building (Fransman, 1995; Bell & Pavitt, 1993) - caused the SOEs to fail to acquire investment and marketing capabilities. On the other hand, the 'production first' attitude contributed to the sequence where such firms tend to learn production capability initially. As for private firms, by setting-up after 1986, TG8 and TG9 followed a very different sequence of TC creation. This is largely explained by the difference in ownership. Private companies must begin with some capabilities and cannot rely on the technical expertise of R&D institutions which SOEs usually can. In most cases, private sector firms have to face more severe problems in pursuing learning efforts.

Nonetheless, the SOEs have their problems too. In the transition period, Vietnamese SOEs face serious competition from private enterprises, especially those that can enter joint ventures or can make significant contacts with foreign partners (Moghadam, 1994). In order to react to the changes wrought by the reforms, SOEs must also radically improve their management expertise. While enjoying favourable conditions, SOEs managers enjoy fewer decision-making freedoms. Also, some SOE directors see public ownership as an eternal safety net; they feel no particular incentive to secure the long-term viability of their firm, especially as their retirement package is poor. As a result, both publicly- and privately-owned firms encounter distinct problems as a direct result of the ownership issue - albeit that those problems differ between them.

The cases in my study confirm that SOEs face different pressures and so learn technological capabilities differently than private companies do. Taking into account that competitive pressure has such an important impact on the competence-building of many East Asian countries (Westphal et al, 1985; Amsden 1989; Fransman, 1995; Wade, 1990), and the notion that external pressure can influence the learning behaviour of firms, the issue of ownership (as one element of external environmental pressure) might not be unique to Vietnam's economy but may exist in other countries as well.[5] However, this notion could be specific to Vietnam in one sense. It would appear that the private sector in Vietnam is subject to greater surveillance and control than is the case in most other developing countries (including those whose economies are in transition) and the specific differences in opportunities and behaviours of the two types of firm seem more acutely drawn. The study reveals that the influence of the ownership issue in Vietnam is more pertinent to the textile/garment industry than it is to the electronics industry. Although ownership differences do exist among electronics companies (due to the different start-up conditions between consumer electronics and computing companies), patterns of TC accumulation and learning differ between these two electronics sub-sectors rather than being explained in terms of the ownership variable. As a result, the ownership issue in the electronics sector hides beneath the more obvious differences in the trading conditions of the two sub-sectors. The features separating the textile/garment and electronics sectors and those separating the two electronics sub-sectors will be addressed in the next section.

The nature of firm ownership, then, is one of the key factors influencing the business and technological learning of firms. This finding is somewhat different to that given by Enos (1991). According to Enos, the ownership status of the competent firm seems to matter not at all, whether private or public. Although he emphasises the *indifference of competent firms*, it seems that he does not give enough emphasis to how ownership may affect attempts at competence-building. Furthermore, Enos stresses that internal affairs are more significant for competence-building than external factors. He focuses on the competent firm's ability to attract skilled and motivated staff, its stability, its training opportunities, its access to learning and its raison d'être. Nonetheless, in my view, all these internal matters are influenced significantly by external factors such as state policies which, in turn, are not uniform for firms under different kinds of ownership. Here, the close interaction of internal and external factors becomes significant. External factors present firms with both opportunities and hurdles. How to overcome the hurdles and take advantage of the opportunities then depends on each firm's specific behaviour. At this level, managers' actions and strategies really matter. In order to help firms respond to external factors - and because the ownership issue clearly does affect a firm's ability to learn - the state must devise promotional policies which are suitable for both types of firm. A specific policy geared for the private sector might be needed (Massaquois, 1995) because managers of private firms face different commercial conditions than do managers of SOEs (Mytelka, 1985). In this context, policy intervention by the Vietnamese state to promote learning and TC accumulation should also be selective across the two types of ownership.

10.4 Sectoral perspectives: some comparisons

In this section, differences between the two sectors are examined in order to evaluate whether the role of government is identical in both, and to assess whether there is any need for different policy measures to be devised for each. This study can offer valuable insights in this respect, without underestimating the similarities between the two sectors. Although the firms are similar in the type and extent of TCs being developed (more of production, investment, minor technical change and linkage, less of marketing, and almost nothing for major technical change capabilities), they follow quite different sequences across the textile/garment and electronics sectors. The sector-specific focus of innovation discussed elsewhere by Bell and Pavitt (1993), Katz (1987a) and Pavitt (1984) offers a useful theoretical background for evaluating my findings.

Pavitt's work (1984) on the sectoral pattern of technical change deals mainly with innovating firms. In addition, however, we find sectoral differences not only in relation to innovative activities but also to TC accumulation and learning. The experiences of the Vietnamese firms in my study show that across the textile/garment and electronics sectors, the patterns of TC accumulation differ, both in terms of TC types acquired and in their accumulation sequence. For each industry, the firms also display differences in the pattern of using learning mechanisms. However, these differences do not apply to all features of TC accumulation and learning.

In an extended work on sectoral variation, Bell & Pavitt (1993) identify five sectoral categories that capture many of the different paths towards technological accumulation. The two industries in my study fall into two of those categories. The textile/garment sector is, in these terms, supplier-dominated, while the electronics sector is science-based. In their work, Pavitt (1984) and Bell & Pavitt (1993 & 1997) outline some of basic innovative features of these two sectors. In the supplier-dominated textile sector, firms have a high degree of dependence on external sources for process technology and a relatively small level of activity devoted to product innovation; a relatively small average size; technological diversification is mainly vertically into production technology with very little movement into other product markets. In contrast, science-based electronics firms make a relatively high contribution to their own process technology and a high proportion of product innovation that is used in other sectors. They are relatively big, and conduct most of their technological diversification non-vertically.

It is impossible to comprehensively compare all these features in this analysis due to a lack of sufficient evidence (and it was not, in any case, the main purpose of this study). Nonetheless, based on the experience of case studies, I can observe those sectoral differences which relate directly related to a firm's ability to learn a TC. Concerning technical change activities in textile/garment firms, these are mainly minor improvements in and modifications to production methods or associated inputs. Some firms improve their product technologies but these are mostly modifications of existing models. Changes of production organisation also occur in textile firms. No firm in the study was able to engage in major technical change. Electronics firms, in contrast, prioritise product specification over technical change activities. Fewer electronics firms rearrange their production processes.

The argument of Bell & Pavitt (1993) and Pavitt (1984) on the way firms diversify their activities are less clearly seen in my study than other criteria of comparison. Vietnamese textile/garment firms tend to diversify their production activities vertically but not into non-textile business areas: textile firms work downstream towards knitting and garments, while some garment firms do the reverse. Electronics firms tend to diversify their activities into new areas or products which concentrate around electronics: industrial electronics, computer services in banking and financial services. There is also some diversification into tourism or construction, but these are exceptions which reflect Vietnam's particular national context.

My findings differ from Pavitt's (1984) in one respect. According to Pavitt (1984), textile firms tend to be small while electronics firms are big. In my study, this was not the case. Most of the older textile/garment firms are large (with more than 1,000 employees), while electronics firms are small or medium-sized, and are more recently established. Dependence on the mechanical engineering and chemical industries to complement technological innovation is evident in both the textile and the electronics sectors.

With the exception of firm size, these observed features seem to support arguments that sectors differ from each other, although there is a less clear-cut pattern in the case of Vietnam. While the textile/garment sector - "supplier-dominated" in Pavitt's terminology (1984) - developed its TC in a traditional way, firms in the "science-based" electronics sector developed their TC more from their R&D activity. The creation of electronics firms by scientists from academic circles can be considered as a diffusion of R&D activity into a more technology-driven kind of enterprise. The comparison made here is based on the learning and TC accumulation efforts of the firms, while the notion of sectoral differences suggested by Pavitt is addressed at understanding the innovation activities of firms in more industrialised countries. Whether this explains the weak similarity with Vietnamese firms (in addition to the specificity of Vietnam's conditions) remains a question to be explored further.

The differences between the two sectors in using learning mechanisms, as argued by Lall (1993b), Preverez & Shohet (1995) and Andersen (1992), can also be seen in my study. Electronics firms - being located in the sector most closely linked to the R&D, training and education base of the country - have less problems than textile/garment firms in using prior accumulated knowledge as a learning mechanism. Further, the two sectors deploy different combinations of learning mechanism for acquiring minor change and marketing capabilities. The main difference is the greater use electronics firms make of foreign connections. Indeed Bell & Pavitt (1993) also consider that science-based firms are more likely to use foreign contacts given the relative strength of research scientists and engineers in such firms. Differences can also be seen between sub-sectors. Although differences in the pattern of TC accumulation are not so clear-cut between textile and garment firms, they are rather marked between consumer electronics and computing firms, which follow distinct sequences of TC accumulation.

As Cooper (1995) notes, the concept of innovative competition better characterises the electronics sector, but is less relevant to understanding the traditional profile of the textile/garment sector. Therefore, the ways that firms in these two sectors compete with other firms, link up with foreign partners and create new firms differ, and this factor provides us with a better understanding of firms' behaviours. The superior use made by electronics firms of links with foreign partners can also be explained by the conscious strategic behaviours of their managers; in general, they are more dynamic and efficient than their counterparts in textile/garment firms. This, in turn, helps those managers to make better use of their foreign contacts for learning marketing. Thus, the question of firm-specific strategies remains important.

10.5 Firm-specific features, their strategies and learning: Vietnamese experiences

In this study firms differ both in terms of their historical emergence (e.g., history of establishment, ownership, etc.) and in terms of the personalities and backgrounds of individual managers. Firms in the textile/garment industry differ in their TC building patterns with respect to their ownership status as opposed to their sub-sectoral location. These findings echo the conclusions of African (Mytelka, 1985) and Greek (Tsekouras, 1995) studies of firms, where firms are understood to differ in their learning behaviours to become technologically competitive on the basis of managers' actions. Similar evidence of the importance of managers' activity (i.e., the significance of a firm-specific factor) can be found in Katz (1987a), Rhee et al (1984) and Laurence (1980).

Moreover, even when firms have many things in common (whether in terms of technological behaviour or TC building patterns), case evidence shows that each firm is still unique in its actions. The cases of HAL and 3C or of TLG and NTC are examples of how firms in the same sector nevertheless adopt their own unique 'special techniques' for learning TCs. It seems that the specificity of TC accumulation at the level of the firm is more pertinent than any sector-level specificities. These 'special techniques' (or technological learning behaviours) are, in fact, the strategies firms deploy - with various degrees of clarity and vigour - to respond to external factors.

Having recognised the importance of firms' specific strategic approaches to learning and TC acquisition, the next question concerns the strategies of the Vietnamese firms in this study adopted in response to changes they experienced in the external environment. Although firms can respond to the influence of external factors (e.g., policy factors, market factors and supporting infrastructure and social-cultural factors) both through conscious strategies, and through ad-hoc tactical manoeuvres, in general, responses can be grouped into three types.

The first trend is the *diversification* of business development during the transitional period, when firms tried to diversify their products, markets and business relationships. To respond to limited market opportunities and increased pressure, companies (especially in the textile and garment sector) tried to increase their product quality, expand their product range and strengthen their business relationships with foreign buyers. In addition, the textile companies - TG3, TG4, TG5 and TG6 - re-oriented themselves to selling in local markets by rearranging their core activities to include knitwear or garment production. This tendency towards market and product diversification has led to another tendency to diversify business linkages with foreign partners in order to secure access to almost everything: capital, technologies, markets, supplies of materials, expertise, etc. Diversification can be understood as the response firms make to the changing (and problematic) supporting infrastructure. For private companies like TG8, TG9 or E8, diversification is synonymous with their survival strategies; it is the means by which they can acquire new technologies and sales channels. Being forced by the desperate need to tap alternative resources (of finance, knowledge or technology), these firms pursue the diversification strategy as a deliberate action.

Specialisation - increasing their competitiveness in niche markets through niched products or services - defines the strategic behaviour of some firms. Companies seek to augment their product quality; the efficiency of their business organisation; their investment in R&D activities; their systematic training efforts by means of both formal programmes and on-the-job training; and the quality of their staff through special recruitment campaigns. Some companies move quite consciously to higher value-added products or they try to enter niche markets. Examples in this study include the attempts to enter high fashion design (TG4 and TG5), software production for specific users (E3 and E4), and industrial electronics in robotics (E2). Some companies - like E3, which for some time individualistically tried to sell specialised software - have realised that it is a very tough business, and that it is better to join a network of international specialist software producers and sellers. Being a small part of this network is more productive than working alone in the market place. Some computer companies, in addition to continuing their business in the former Soviet Union, are trying to link up with more powerful foreign partners to produce parts of their product package. By doing so, they have access not only to new technologies, but also to new markets and to some crucial material inputs.

Through a lack of long-term strategies for development, and insufficient support from the state, firms are *regrouping* and *consolidating* their common activities. There is evidence of joint efforts and new associations which lobby for change in government regulations, incentives, and in the accessibility of market intelligence. It should be noted here that although (selective) efforts to join forces constitutes third type of company response to external conditions, any collective such activity being pursued irrespective of whether the company is diversifying or specialising.[6] In the main, there are two different strategies adopted by firms.

Studies of types of business strategy have identified various groups of strategic options. For instance, Gemunden and Heydebreck (1995) identify five clusters of business strategic stances: the technological leader, the customer-focused developer, the cost leader, the specialiser and the dissipater. Among these groups, the cost leader stance most resembles the diversification strategy of Vietnamese firms. Firms occupying this position offer customers a wider range of products than any other type of company. Cost leaders try to diversify their products by copying and modifying other producers' products, and can achieve a high level of novelty. Vietnamese firms adopting a diversification strategy also modify many foreign products to diversify their product range, and the low price of products is also important, especially among textile/garment companies. Although the names are similar, the specialiser group of companies - which sell products that offer little opportunity for differentiation through superior quality - is not similar to the specialisation strategy of the firms in my study. Unlike the specialiser cluster, i.e., firms that rarely undertake any development activities at all, some Vietnamese companies are adopting a specialisation strategy geared to offering niche products to niche markets. In order to do so, they have to develop customer-oriented solutions to meet the specific needs of a single customer or of a small niche. This feature suggests that firms pursuing a specialisation strategy in my study more resemble the customer-focused developer group.

The diversification strategy is also common in other developing countries (Mytelka, 1991). The diversification tendency in Vietnam, however, exists not only in products, but also in markets, and in the ways of doing business. Some firms in the study, especially in electronics (e.g., E2, E3 and E4) even try to diversify across the borders of their traditional sector. This is due to the reforms where - cut off from state subsidies and with limited sources of finances and technologies, etc. - firms have to struggle to find solutions to their market constraints. Still, this diversification strategy, as Ernst (1995) shows through the experiences of Korean companies, can have a negative effect on TC accumulation in the long run.[7] In the case of Vietnamese firms, the diversification of products and markets can bring new income and reserves, and new business opportunities and markets.

In the context of developing countries, Kim (1990) - on the basis of Korean experiences - divides firms' strategies into two types: apprentices and imitators. Depending on financial resources, size and the organisational ability of managers, firms may adopt an aggressive technological strategy which leads them either to become apprentices or imitators. Small firms like E2 or E3 which both pursue aggressive strategies resemble the imitator type. Through a process of imitative learning, these firms have been trying to add their own technical improvements to existing foreign products (e.g., the change of TV set specification). Reverse engineering (done by technically competent individuals who come mainly from an R&D environment) is a common activity in these firms. TG6 is an apprentice type of firm; it has relied on foreign technologies from the outset and has assimilated these technologies and learning through training mechanisms. Having said this, I should emphasise that not all these firms fall strictly into one or other category. There is no distinct demarcation between firms. Although primarily located within one category, a firm may also possess features which are associated with the other category.

What influence can these strategies have on the technological learning of the firms? The learning process is shaped by the combined impact of external and of internal factors such as the strategies of the firms (Saviotti, 1992). This interaction has several kinds of influence on learning and TC accumulation. First, it *determines the purpose of learning*. Depending on the strategy adopted, firms set different priorities on acquiring particular TCs and this affects their pursuit of skills, knowledge and experience through learning activities. Dodgson (1992), in his study of Celltech, notes that this firm gradually shifted its learning focus from R&D skills, to manufacturing competence and then to marketing functions. In my case studies, learning activities (as the means to achieve TCs) have changed since the pre-reform period when there was no need to learn marketing. Now, in the reform period, as firms adopt diversification strategy, they need to learn knowledge suitable for this strategy, such as marketing in diversified markets. The evidence show that most of the study firms are following this strategy and some of them have successfully acquired the TC necessary for this strategy.

The number of firms embarking on a specialisation strategy are fewer. Some companies, such as E2 and E3 in electronics or TG4 and TG14 in textile/garment, have taken their first step towards specialisation in producing niche products for niche markets. These firms have one thing in common. They diversified from traditional products (or markets) to new ones so as to gain access to better financial resources and to further their learning. On this basis, they then selected new activities and new niche products (consumer electronics to robotics in E2; PC assembling to software in E3; ordinary weaving and garment products to high-quality microfibre in TG4; and high-fashion for top quality markets in TG14). Up to now, this combined strategy of both diversification and specialisation seems to be working for these firms. However, in the long-term, if they pursue both diversification and specialisation strategies - especially diversification across sectoral boundaries - they may encounter problems. For instance, in the case of E3, the specialisation strategy may be suitable for producing software for niche markets. The export of niche products is appropriate for firms engaged in exporting software from developing countries and may have a larger impact than other strategies on learning and building up TC (Correa, 1995). However, the on-going diversification of E3 beyond electronics to construction and real estate may divert the firm's resources and energy away from upgrading its specialised products. Similarly, in the case of E2, the first step of specialisation in robotics parts to serve Japanese components and parts suppliers is a positive one to enter a niche market and become part of an international production network. On the other hand, E2's joint venture with Daewoo in providing hotel and business services signals that the firm may move further away from its core electronics activities, for the sake of new business opportunities and financial gains.

As can be seen here, firms adopt strategies in response to macro external factors, and this has led to particular types of knowledge and TC being acquired. The purpose of learning, hence, is the outcome of the interaction of firms' business strategies with those macro factors.

The second influence of the interaction is on *the enrichment of learning sources of firms*. The practice of the firms here shows that as an outcome of diversification strategy, Vietnamese firms are able to find more learning resources, and to access new technological experience and expertise. The textile/garment companies diversifying from upstream to downstream product areas, and from CMEA markets to EU and Asia Pacific markets, all point to this. Similarly, electronics firms' diversification from consumer electronics to industrial electronics (such as E2) are further examples of how firms can learn more technological skill and knowledge through diversification. Nonetheless, where some firms diversify beyond the boundaries of their traditional sectors, the impact on learning might be negative in the long run (fragmentation of activities; lack a sufficient concentration of technological strength). This situation is similar to that mentioned by Ernst (1995) with respect to Korean companies, where the over-diversification of chaebols like Samsung or Daewoo reduces the ability of these firms in deepen their technological competence. For learning activities and technological deepening to take place, firms should concentrate on differentiation within a (limited) range of products and activities rather than diversifying to numerous types of business. At a later stage, when resources and expertise permit, some of them may choose to adopt a specialisation strategy which may have a greater impact on the technological deepening process.

The main implication of this discussion is that - depending on the context of macro factors (pre-reform or post-reform) - firms may have different requirements for learning and different means to achieve that learning. In this framework, learning and TC acquisition are shaped in accordance with the strategic behaviours of firms in doing business and with the interaction between these behaviours and external factors.

The last point to mention in this section is that learning - as the means to achieving certain TCs required by specific business strategies - could be a strategy in itself (Coombs et al, 1992b). This notion is strongly stressed by Teece et al (1990) and Dodgson (1992). Such a strategy places great emphasis on the creation of new dynamic capabilities through the firm's learning process. It is beyond the purposes of my study to comprehensively examine the business strategies of study firms. However, it would be fair to conclude from this study that the learning activity of firms is closely intertwined with their strategic behaviour. This relationship is also partly presented in Figure 10.1 on the learning-TC relationship. In this figure, the activities of learning (i.e., which learning mechanisms are used by firms) are decided by the strategic behaviour of firms (managers' actions, for instance). In addition, the purposes of learning (i.e., which TCs are needed by firms) are also conditioned by macro environmental factors and the business strategies of the firms.

The process of TC accumulation and learning in Vietnam bears the characteristics of both a South East Asian developing country and a transitional economy. Some of these characteristics are similar, but most are different. On the one hand, as a developing country, Vietnam suffers from the weakness of the industrial infrastructure, and the deficiencies of R&D and training organisations together with their isolation from industry. On the other hand, like other transitional economies, it faces difficulties such as the lack of competitive pressure and marketing awareness; the absence of exposure to competition in global markets; and imperfect market structures and legal and institutional frameworks. These factors - combined within one country - create additional problems for Vietnamese firms in accumulating their technological competence. They combine to produce a weak industrial system, which is unable to support adequately firms' attempts at learning how to handle technical change. Indeed, the poverty of actual experience; the limited access to sources which may enable firms to learn marketing expertise; the technical bias of knowledge; and the lack of a long-term strategy for learning, are all the direct outcome of this unique context. Thus, these problems are often more serious in Vietnam than in other countries.

Comparing the two industries, some main differences are found. First, with regard to the sequence of TC accumulation, jumping-in patterns are more evident in electronics than in textile and garment firms, the latter having making more traditional and gradual progress. Second, electronics firms use more foreign-related and R&D-based learning mechanisms than do textile and garment firms. Third, consumer electronics and computing follow different patterns of TC accumulation. The reasons why textile/garment and electronics firms vary depending, respectively, on the issues of ownership and sub-sectoral location are mainly due to the firms' origins; macro-environment factors; and managers' strategic responses those environmental factors. Variations from the general pattern of TC accumulation and learning can be explained by closer examination of firm-level activities. To respond to the influence of environmental changes, the Vietnamese firms in this study have adopted two main business behaviours: diversification (undertaken by the majority of firms) and specialisation (undertaken by a few). Affected by each of these strategies, the use of learning mechanisms by firms has varied. In the main, Vietnamese firms have been able to acquire TCs more suitable for diversification than for specialisation strategies, the latter being more critical for technological deepening. More broadly, the process of TC accumulation and learning in Vietnamese firms is the outcome of micro-macro interactions between firms' outside environment and their reactions to this environment. The experience of Vietnamese firms can be quite usefully applied to policy-making in other countries which are in a similar economic and political situation.

Notes

1. These problems are high quality standards, shortages in qualification or lack of methodologies, poor infrastructures, the small domestic markets of developing countries, the lack of support for accumulating financial resources, and the dominance of US producers in an international market which is highly competitive (Correa, 1995).

2. Until reforms, the contracts between R&D organisations and industrial firms in Vietnam were not allowed by law.

3. One of the few comparative studies available is the work of Henderson (1996). This study finds some similarities between Eastern European and East-Asian countries such as the role of the state, a weak secondary association, the role of education and training, and similarities in economic coordination and income inequality. As for differences, these include the role of trade unions, the nature of economic and administrative bureaucracies, the function of the rule of law, family and kinship relationships, issues of development versus restructuring, differences of geo-politics, location in the world economy and systemic changes. According to this work, Vietnam and China float between these two poles. However, this study focuses on political and economic issues, rather than on technological orientations.

4. The difference between SOEs and private firms refers not only to (discriminatory) state policies and access to the supporting infrastructure. It also encompasses issues of management style, work conditions and labour standards as found by the study of WIDER/UNU (Moghadam, 1994).

5. We find different learning behaviours among Indian firms depending on whether they are publicly or privately owned enterprises (Deolalikar & Sundanam, 1983), and Argentinian firms under different kinds of ownership adopt different attitudes to risk-taking (Lucangeli, 1983).

6. Almost all firms adopting one or another strategy have recently consolidated (some of) their activities in response to the increasing pressures from the external environment.

7. According to Ernst (1995), octopus-like diversification across sectoral boundaries prevents continuous long-term accumulation and development of TCs for a given set of products. It may also lead to a neglect of selective and gradual product differentiation within a given product category, as well as a neglect of technological deepening.

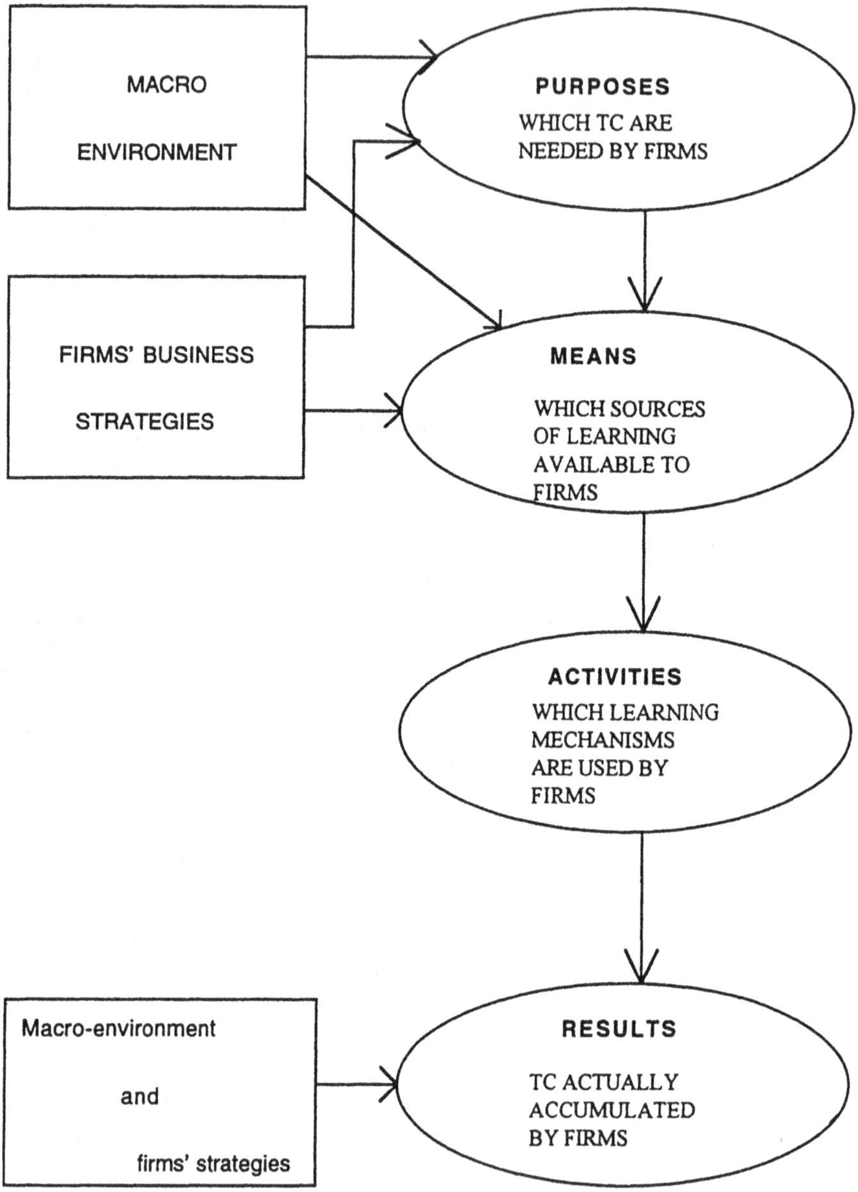

Figure 10.1 Learning - TC relationship

11 Conclusions

This book examines the learning process and TC accumulation of selected firms in the Vietnamese textile/garment and electronics industries. By conducting interviews and case studies of 24 firms, the study looks at several issues.

11.1 Some new evidence for innovation studies

The book confirms the findings of various well-known studies on innovation, by providing additional empirical evidence from Vietnam.

With respect to the first research question, features such as the unevenness and the sequencing of TC accumulation, together with the firm-specificity of this accumulation, are seen throughout the firms' experiences. The sequence of TC accumulation tends to begin with production and minor technical change capabilities, subsequently moving on to others. The extent of TC accumulation is uneven; production, investment and minor technical change are more developed than other capabilities. Proposition suggesting that patterns of TC accumulation are different in different sectors has also been confirmed by the differences found between textile/garment and electronics firms.

The examination of the second research question, on the nature of learning and the relationship between learning and TC accumulation, has confirmed that learning is neither costless nor automatic. Its cumulative and dynamic nature are clearly observed in the learning patterns of Vietnamese firms. The experience of Vietnam's firms also shows that learning is a gradual rather than a leap-frogging process. The evidence also supported the need for conscious investment efforts in learning, whereby they combine active learning-by-doing with different learning mechanisms for the acquisition of various TCs. In addition, firm-specific (and to a lesser extent, sector-specific) features of learning have been shown to exist. Proposition that different learning mechanisms are used for accumulating different TCs, has been supported by Vietnamese empirical experience as well.

Based on the findings of this study, it appears that, whilst firms need to engage in learning efforts in order to build up their TCs, the precise deployment of learning mechanisms may differ across different contexts. As Cooper (1991) and others similarly argue, this study implies that the generally well-established concept in innovation studies of TC and learning activities may commonly be applied to firms in different countries, including the applicability of the concept to the case of developing countries.

However, because learning is localised in accordance with various contexts, the patterns of learning may differ depending on the macro environmental conditions which pertain in any given context. Learning must be a firm-based effort and it is influenced by the strategies adopted by firms. Therefore, learning patterns differ among firms even where those firms operate in the same environment.

In examining the third research question concerning the reasons behind patterns of TC accumulation and learning, this study also supports the argument about the importance of macro environmental factors on firms' business and learning activities. The more interactive macro-micro link, and its influence on firms' learning and TC acquisition as suggested by some propositions is a new finding elaborated by this research. Moreover, the influence of each group of macro factors, and the extent of this influence in the specific context of Vietnam, also constitutes new evidence which this study has explicated.

The main new findings of the study are summarised below.

- *TC accumulation in Vietnamese industrial firms:*
  among TCs, technical change (major technical change, in particular) and marketing capabilities are less developed than others due to a lack of competitive pressure, and a consequent lack of a need to engage in marketing or to innovate products in terms of range and quality.

- *The nature and mechanisms of learning :*
  - among learning mechanisms, active learning-by-doing is necessary to achieve a TC, but is not in itself sufficient.
  - learning through foreign connections, in Vietnamese firms, is weak for acquiring marketing and technical change capabilities, due to the ineffective utilisation of these connections by Vietnamese firms themselves and very likely a lack of readiness by foreign partners to help in this area.

- *The relationship between learning and TC:*
  - there seems no clear-cut linear relationship between the use of learning mechanisms and TC accumulation which is universal regardless of circumstances.
  - as a result, learning must take place and be examined in a specific context: decisions of what learning is appropriate for acquiring which TCs, and by means of which learning mechanisms, tend to vary across different contexts (of firm, period and sector).

- *The unique context of Vietnam:*
  - the joint interaction of both macro environmental factors and firm-level micro factors is an important influence on learning and TC accumulation.
  - personal networking is crucial in the Vietnamese context for learning and, even following the reforms, remains more significant that is the case in other Central and Eastern European countries.
  - the government plays a contradictory role. It over-intervenes in industrial activity in some respects yet it simultaneously offers inadequate support for other activities. There is little evidence of selective intervention.
  - ownership is an important issue for learning and TC accumulation. There is a tension between private and state ownership.
  - firms' strategies such as diversification and specialisation in niche products in response to influences of macro factors are important determinants of the learning process and TC accumulation.

11.2 TC accumulation and learning mechanisms

Depending on the context of different firms (i.e., the strategies they follow, what they want to produce, and for which market), they need different types of TC and therefore, adopt different ways of learning. Each context determines the precise TC needs of the firm and this, in turn, leads to their using different learning mechanisms. As a result, because of the localised specificity of learning activity - and in contrast to the universality of the *need for learning* - there might not be a single universal *pattern of learning* which describes all contexts.

Although the notion of combining different learning mechanisms is not new, this study has extended this notion into a more concrete finding. Learning mechanisms have to be combined in multiplicity, albeit that the learning-by-doing mechanism remains the single most used device. Again, next to this need to combine learning mechanisms - which is quite universal across various firms, sectors and countries - the patterns of combination vary depending on background. The use of learning-by-doing, for instance, has to be backed up with at least two other mechanisms in textile/garment firms, and with more than two in electronics firms, if they are to acquire a TC. As for developing strong TC, firms need to use nearly all six learning mechanisms in both sectors.

For each of the six learning mechanisms, there are some relevant findings. First, even though the learning-by-doing mechanism requires less investment from firms than other mechanisms, it still has to be actively and consciously pursued by them if they want to learn anything. The notion of learning-by-struggling or learning-by-trying (Fleck, 1991 and 1994) is evident in many firms. Furthermore, most firms acquiring TCs have experienced a painstaking and long process of tests and checks, where they make errors and continuously adjust their activities to address such errors. The suggested active notion of learning-by-doing in the taxonomy for this study has worked well. Rather than just by-doing (or by-using) technology once the technological system has been set in place, learning-by-trying has to take place even prior to this, and becomes evident in the process of installing the new system.

Concerning the use of foreign connections, this book shows that Vietnamese firms have difficulties in using foreign connections to learn technical change capability for two reasons: the ineffective utilisation of this mechanism on the part of Vietnamese firms themselves, and the likelihood that foreign partners not willing to help them in this area. The implication of this is that the learning mechanism through foreign connection is not the one-for-all solution for the technological accumulation of developing countries. Firms should not passively rely on this mechanism, but should try to exploit this connection more consciously and creatively. The contrasting examples of TLG with its quite passive attitude towards using foreign connection and HAL which very actively tries to learn from foreign companies illustrate this point.

Whilst using learning mechanisms such as training, information collection and search, documentation and consultancy services, the practice of firms in this study reveal the significance of personal networking and of relationships between people working in different organisations. In many cases, personal relationships contribute a firm's ability to learn those skills and knowledges which formal relationships cannot provide them with. The extensive reliance of electronics firms HAL and 3C on this informal network of connections confirms this claim. In particular, the way 3C uses informal relations for learning knowledge through a "barter arrangement" - to use Faulkner & Senker's (1993) term - reveals its importance both to this firm and to other similar firms, which lack alternative resources for acquiring new knowledge and information.

Although, as noted above, the cumulative sequence of learning is not a new finding, one element this study reveals - matching that found by Hobday (1994 and 1995b) and Ernst (1995) in NICs - is that leap-frogging cannot replace the hard slog of learning if TCs are to be accumulated even by late-comer firms. The gradual learning process starts with the acquisition of simple skills, first on mature products and well-established technologies (through subcontracting and OEM arrangements), and then moves on to engaging in more complex tasks, working on newer products and process technologies in ODM arrangements and beyond. There are several reasons for why this long and hard road towards learning must be travelled, all related to the nature of knowledge accumulation, and to the conditions of developing countries. Knowledge is complex, cumulative and tacit; it takes times to learn; it is specifically located in the sense that it must accord with particular contexts; and its acquisition requires that organisations have absorptive capacity - a capacity which is limited in the case of firms in developing countries which cannot learn different kinds of complex knowledge all at once. The implication of this finding is that learning is not a quick and easy activity. Firms must devote many inputs to achieve their learning purposes. Those who might attempt to leap-frog or to take short-cuts have to take this feature of learning into account. This may provide quite an useful lesson for many Vietnamese companies - or other firms operating in similar economies - in considering scenarios for their industrial development.

11.3 Learning and TC accumulation relationship

One of the important research questions of this study (the examination of the relationship between learning mechanisms and TC) was a novel concern in this area. The purpose of this book in linking these aspects was to find out if there is any relationship between them, and if there is, what the nature of the connection is.

The overall answer to this question is that, it looks like that there might exist a relationship between learning and TC accumulation and they influence each other: by using certain learning mechanisms, one can acquire certain TCs. However, this study has found that this relationship might not be universal across developing countries, but more specific to Vietnam (or similar conditions). There is no clear-cut linear relationship between TC accumulation and learning; they are intertwined with each other.

By exploring how learning mechanisms and TC acquisition relate to each other with respect to the frequency of use made of particular mechanisms, the study has also identified some concrete ranking of learning mechanisms in relation to their contribution to TC accumulation. Active learning-by-doing is the most used mechanism, followed by accumulation of prior knowledge through recruitment.

Another important learning mechanism is training, and the study found that training in Vietnam tends to have a technical rather than a non-technical orientation. As a result, it may be possible to provide some recommendations about what learning mechanisms should be used for accumulating which TCs. However, these recommendations cannot suggest a universal pattern suitable for all firms, because conditions vary from context to context. For instance, depending on a firm's background and on the type of TC to be accumulated, there can be different (successful) ways of combining learning mechanisms. Thus, the relationship between the use of certain learning mechanisms and the accumulation of particular TCs needs to be considered in the context of specific firms. Outwith this context, the relationship becomes quite vague and indeterminate.

This conclusion points to another question. Is it possible - or even necessary - to make the relationship between TC accumulation and learning more clear-cut and, by so doing, provide firms with a kind of model of learning? The answer to this question seems to be mixed. On the one hand, it is both possible and necessary to examine the relationship between learning mechanisms and TCs in the context of one firm in a specific industry or country. From this, one can provide some bench-marking and some recommendations based on the 'technological health' of that particular firm - something akin to a management consultant's assessment of the 'business health' of that firm. More concretely, by assessing a firm's problems over the course of a particular period of its development, some desirable goals might be nominated for special attention. Under this kind of analysis, a firm might be usefully advised on which TCs to accumulate, and which specific know-how and skills it should set about acquiring, in accordance with the business orientation and the priorities of that firm. And accordingly, which learning mechanisms are most likely to achieve this objective.

On the other hand, this study reveals that it is extremely difficult to offer a universal prescription for different firms in the same industry, or the same country, because of the firm- and sector-specificity of learning and TC accumulation. Moreover, it might not be useful to attempt this exercise. This suggests that further examination is required on the question of TC and its relationship with learning to see how this relationship might vary in various contexts.

11.4 The impact of the macro-micro link and Vietnam's unique context

The importance of external influences and internal responses

This study has investigated the research question of the impact of macro-micro factors' interaction on learning. The main findings support propositions that learning activity is the jointly-shaped outcome of both sets of factor. Neither macro nor micro level factors have separately influenced the learning process of the firms. An important contribution of this study is its empirical evidence of the activities of Vietnamese industrial firms.

Macro policies of the state are the most influential external factors on all learning mechanisms used by Vietnamese firms. The deficiencies of the industrial infrastructure have a significant influence on training mechanisms, and on the search and collection of information by firms. The change from a command to a market economy, which is the crucial element in Vietnam's transition, is having a significant influence on the way firms do business, learn knowledge and become more competitive. In reacting to these influences, the study suggests that there might be an interesting link between business behaviour of firms and the kind of knowledge necessary for them, the way they search for TCs, and the learning mechanisms they adopt for this purpose.

In addition to features similar to other transitional economies in Central and Eastern Europe, China or the former Soviet Union - such as the phenomena of spin-off companies, of the lack of a strategic long-term view of development, and of the existence of informal networking - the transitional period in Vietnam also shows some other specific features. One of these is that informal networking in Vietnam has survived almost intact from the pre-reform period, and continues to play a greater role in the learning process of firms than in most other Central or Eastern European countries. The mixture of characteristics of both a developing country and of a transitional economy leaves a unique imprint on the ways that Vietnamese firms operate and on how they learn technological expertise.

The role of the state

In the transitional period, the question of the role of the state emerges as an important issue in relation to learning activity. In common with other former centrally-planned economies, the state's role has traditionally been perceived as dominating Vietnam's society and economy. However, this study shows the contradictory role of the state in Vietnam: it has over-intervened in the daily business of the firms, and at the same time not offered sufficient support in creating an environment conducive for learning and TC accumulation. This role can be described as one of controlling without promoting industrial and technological development.

Although the role of the state for learning and TC accumulation is necessary, it has to be selective and it must be favourable for doing business. In the case of Vietnamese industrial firms, there is little selective intervention as yet, at least in the form of explicit promotional policies such as tax rate reductions and exemptions, adjustable financial incentives, or flexible regulations on labour use and recruitment, etc. The criticism mounted by the firms in this study about the lack of an efficient trade management system which could help them deal with smuggling problems, is one example of the shortage of protection measures for domestic industries. The observed phenomenon of rolling back the state seems unique in Vietnam's case but is understandable in the context of the search for suitable models for industrial and technological policies. Here, Vietnam's similarities with the East Asian NICs - where the state plays a strong and successful role in promoting economic growth and technological development - is quite attractive to Vietnam. This situation is rather different from that of the transitional economies in Central and Eastern Europe where the whole structure of state administration has changed so radically that the current wisdom is that the role of the state should be as minimal as possible or, in some cases, should be totally redundant.

The ownership issue

In the context of Vietnam, the question of ownership also becomes important for learning and TC accumulation. In countries where state and private ownership coexist within a well-established and transparent legal framework, this issue is not so crucial. Given the context of Vietnam where the state has an anti-private attitude, the tense competition between these two forms of ownership has been pushed to the limit. The inequality within the competitive environment creates various kinds of problems for firms - especially privately-owned ones - in exercising their business as well as in engaging in their learning activities. That private firms have less access to R&D, training and education facilities, are subjected to stricter financial and tax regulations, and have more limits placed on their opportunities to use bank credits are just some examples of this discrimination. While both private and state-owned firms have their own problems, this factor strongly influences their learning. As a result, it might be necessary to devise suitable policies and measures to support learning and TC accumulation for differentiated ownership within the framework of selective intervention for different sectors, which might be a concern peculiar to Vietnam. However, this depends largely on the government's orientation towards supporting firms under different kinds of ownership.

One interesting finding of this study is that SOEs in some specific conditions - for example, ones which are sufficiently supported by the state, pursuing the correct strategies and being properly steered by capable managers - can become good learners, and achieve positive performances in holding or increasing their competitive position. This finding is quite contrary to the traditionally poor image of SOEs in a centrally-planned economy. This is not to suggest that the perception of SOEs as being ineffective should be overturned wholesale but that, given the right conditions, SOEs can be successful as private firms. Still, SOEs such as HAL or NTC in this study are exceptional: their managers are quite capable of devising creative learning techniques and have adopted an active approach in utilising learning mechanisms. Again, the importance of the strategic behaviours undertaken by these firms' managers is noteworthy.

Firms' strategies are key

As the other half of the macro-micro link, the strategic responses of firms to external pressures are crucial for how they proceed in doing business, and for their TC accumulation and learning. The study has identified two main types of strategy that firms pursue: diversification (undertaken by the majority of firms) and specialisation (undertaken by a few), despite the difficulty of distinction between them. Although there are other strategies available, like exporting or exploiting the domestic market, actual observed strategies tend to concentrate around the two aforementioned choices (one question could be an interesting further exploration is that depending on the type of strategy, firms may require different types of TC). These tendencies are the main responses of firms to changes in the macro external environment. Most of the firms following the diversification strategy are intent on maintaining their business performance in a more difficult situation. The few firms adopting specialisation are seeking to gain more value-added in their activities, and they are aiming at bettering their performance in the long run. Because no attempt has been made to deal with these strategic issues exclusively, the study is not in a position to provide a more specific comparison between these two strategic behaviours. However, these two tendencies can be regarded, respectively, as a strategy for survival and a strategy for growth. They each require different types of knowledge, and different levels of knowledge complexity and range.

The issue of differentiation versus specialisation may have a significant implication. It is suggested by Ernst (1995), and supported by this study, that first of all firms need to concentrate on differentiating their products and services within a chosen and limited range of activities, rather than diversifying into too many types of business. Only later, when resources permit, can some firms adopt specialisation strategies on the basis of their accumulated and core technological knowledge. This gradual approach should ease the strain on firms' learning processes. Examples of firms which have adopted both strategies show that they are currently performing well (e.g., HAL and 3C aiming at niche products, and NTC's diversification beyond knitting), although in the long run, this may not remain the case. Some companies are diversifying beyond their traditional product areas. Even firms aiming at specialisation have shown some signs of pursuing both strategies at the same time (e.g., HAL's joint venture with Daewoo in the construction business, or 3C's non-electronics activities). These activities may weaken the ability of those firms to concentrate their resources for technological deepening as Ernst (1995) found in the case of Korean firms. The diversification strategy, if it is over-done, could eventually have negative impacts on the learning activities of firms.

Whatever strategies firms pursue, the attitude of managers to learning is crucial for upgrading their knowledge. The passive attitude of TLG's managers cause difficulties for them in using foreign connections more effectively, which may be attributed to the subsidised mentality generated by the old centrally-planned economy. In the meantime, NTC's managers have a more active approach to risk-taking (e.g. trying to get their new knitting technology working) and, as a reward, they have learnt investment capability where TLG has not. The continuous efforts of HAL's managers to organise training mechanisms to support their previously accumulated knowledge while 3C's managers have omitted to do the same thing may give the former learning advantages over the latter. The earlier mentioned 'special technique of learning' - the ability to know how to exploit learning opportunities in the most effective way - is mostly associated with the role of a firm's personnel: its managers, technicians and workers. Thus, "learning how to learn" is also influenced by firms' strategic behaviours. This supports the notion of "learning to learn" which depends on previously accumulated learning, i.e., the knowledge and experience gained by firms' personnel over a learning curve. After each period of development, staff know more about how to learn and how to alter their learning formats and sources.

As mentioned, the above issues may also exist in other countries, whether developing or transitional or both. In Vietnam, they have been seen quite distinctly and carry implications for policy-making at the national level and at the level of the firm.

11.5 Policy implications

There are some implications and recommendations for policy-making in terms of improving learning and TC accumulation at the firm level.

11.5.1 From the perspective of firms

It is obvious that firms should clarify what they need to learn and how they need to learn it, depending on their business orientation and strategies. As a coherent part of their business plan, firms have to identify what is required for each period and specific context and which kinds of knowledge they are searching for, and then decide on how to acquire this knowledge and bend their learning efforts accordingly. Instead of learning on an ad-hoc basis, this activity should become a key and permanent means for firms to become more competitive. A conscious approach to investing in, planning and organising learning activities is necessary for learning to take place in firms.

The role of managers is important if they want their firms to be competitive. They should be creative in devising their own "special learning technique" which suits their own context (this context can vary greatly), in order to fully exploit all the learning sources and opportunities available to them. More concretely, firms have to institute a plan of action for using each learning mechanism, for each period. They must consciously pursue learning-by-active-doing (or struggling) and they must train their staff and maintain their access to - and effectively utilise - R&D expertise and the S&T infrastructure. They have to combine learning-by-doing with as many other learning mechanisms as possible. They should also utilise their existing linkages and networks, both formal and informal. Indeed, firms should continue to promote their informal connections (such as class mates, alumni clubs, family relations, etc.) in support of their goals.

In the main, Vietnamese firms are probably still not active enough about augmenting their learning activities. In many cases, they tend to look to government to take the lead and they wait passively for governmental measures to be taken. My argument is that the government should play a role (as discussed below), but that firms should also be more active in taking the lead. They should introduce new initiatives in their relations with the government concerning policies conducive for learning. For example, they should submit proposals to government, and organise lobbying pressures in order to obtain regulations in their favour. The establishment of the Associations of the garment industry and of the electronics and informatics sector is a step in the right direction, but attempts of this kind should be even more vigorous. In any case, firms have to prepare themselves for doing business, learning, and upgrading their TCs without expecting too much from the state. As marketing is one of the weakest capabilities, and there is a lack of training courses providing this kind of knowledge in Vietnam, firms should learn more by-doing. Firms have to throw themselves into the market place; their managers and personnel should be more entrepreneurial and creative in learning from marketing experiences.

To side-step the serious funding shortage, firms need to devise flexible mechanisms for learning which do not require heavy levels of funding, e.g., the "barter" or exchange of knowledge and training courses, and the organisation of mutually beneficial services. Among TCs, major technical change and marketing capabilities are less developed than others. In order to further develop these TCs, Vietnamese firms need to take some concrete actions. The recruitment of young graduates from available courses in non-technical subjects such as marketing is useful, but is hindered by the relative dearth of such courses. Therefore, this learning mechanism should be complemented by recruiting experienced staff from other organisations - especially from R&D and administrative institutions like ministries and banks. Moreover, firms should invest step-wise, setting up special units to take care of R&D and major technical change activities. This can also be done for marketing by creating a network of shops, showrooms and sales offices, both locally and abroad. More importantly, the function of these units should be reviewed regularly to draw necessary lessons for improvement (on the basis of marketing audit, for example).

The utilisation of foreign connections is especially important for Vietnamese firms and they should be more aware of the advantages and disadvantages of this mechanism. Vietnamese firms need to be more active in this respect. They need to stop relying passively on "receiving" knowledge and substitute that passivity with conscious "intelligence gathering" (by which I mean consciously seeking out experience, information, skills, and know-how) while working with their foreign partners. The experience of HAL and of some other consumer electronics firms in using their foreign connections purposefully may provide other firms with a useful model of how to proceed. It is important to put people working closely with foreign partners right from the start of the project, in order to gain insight into the 'nuts and bolts' of the technology, and to prepare vigorously for the day when the foreign experts are no longer available to them. Firms should seek joint implementation of different kinds of technical improvements, using this as a chance to learn the ways foreign companies handle technical change activity. The practice adopted by some electronics firms (E2, E10 and E11 in this study) provide examples of this behaviour. The firms can do the same thing for learning marketing skills. By becoming part of a larger network of producers and suppliers, such as that of the Japanese electronics giants in East and Southeast Asia, firms may be able to learn more about marketing. Firms such as E3, TG14, TG5 and E2 have began to do this. Different foreign sources could be used in combination to create new learning expertise. In textile/garment firms, the strength of European partners in design and fashion trend-setting should be complemented by the advantages proffered by Asian companies in terms of their work organisation and management techniques. The experience of some consumer electronics firms such as E2 and E10 in combining Japanese, Korean and Chinese sources of technological expertise also provide a good example.

Vietnamese textile/garment firms tend to place more emphasis on changing their process rather than their product technologies. They need to learn the design skills that are crucial for product innovation. In order to do so, they may have to be more active in developing their relations with foreign partners beyond simple subcontracting. One improvement would be to better utilise the services of local R&D institutions such as RCGI or RITI, including embarking on joint research projects with these institutes to resolve their technical problems.

Pursuing a consistent strategy is necessary for the deepening of technological competence. Vietnamese firms should distinguish between which of their actions contribute to meeting their long-term strategy, and which only meet their tactical or short-term ends. The selectivity and flexibility in changing their business orientation may need to be done more cautiously to avoid fragmenting their limited resources and efforts. The too-wide diversification of so many firms into businesses unrelated to their core activities (e.g., into construction and tourism) should be seen as tactical manoeuvres to solve short-term problems, but not as meeting long-term strategic goals.

11.5.2 From the government's perspective

For learning within firms to take place, their own efforts are not sufficient. Support and intervention measures by the government are also necessary. As the policy-maker, the government should create the general framework for industries to develop - a framework which includes regulations relating to macro economic stability and the generation of socially-favourable conditions e.g more business friendly attitudes of government officials, especially toward private entrepreneurship. Among other things, the government should create more conducive conditions and provide more learning resources for firms in R&D, training and education. Possible initiatives include promoting technological development by issuing S&T policies for the whole country, devising plans suitable for each sector and providing incentives for firms to do business and to learn.

The government's catalytic role in guiding and co-ordinating the activities of firms and other organisations is important. A necessary set of governmental tasks includes the reorganisation, funding and co-ordination of R&D institutes, training schools, and other educational organisations to ensure the effective functioning of the whole industrial supporting infrastructure. The government should enhance activities which support standardisation and quality control and establish or subsidise information and documentation centres and industrial property offices. Also, the government should take care to create an effective legal and institutional framework for industrial activities. Moreover, even in the transition to a market economy, the government should continue supporting - even subsidising - crucial activities for firms' learning such as education, training, and strategic R&D. The experience of industrialised countries shows that, even in a market economy, the government should play an active role in these activities. This approach also lends continuity to the heritage of the socialist period in Vietnam, but in a more effective and selective way.

On the basis of these general points, what can be said for government's role in the Vietnamese context? First, the contradictory role of the state should be changed to support firms' activities. The role of the state should be redirected towards selective intervention. The government should intervene less in the daily business activities of firms, and at the same time, be more supportive in creating conditions conducive to firms' activities.

More specifically, it should revise its banking, financial, trade, investment, labour and management policies to help firms in general, and augment their scope for learning in particular. For instance, it should abolish the situation where firms prefer to trade rather than to produce locally (mostly in electronics) since, currently, the import tax on components is too high and the tax on complete products is not high enough. The import-export taxation system should be revised and updated flexibly (but not too frequently). The system of financial management, foreign currency management, taxation, accounting and credit - especially for long-term technological innovation and learning purposes - should be reformed. Banking procedures must be reformed more radically to smooth the business of firms, by imposing a less rigid and cumbersome structure for lending for the purposes of technological innovation and learning. Labour and immigration regulations could be improved, allowing firms more freedom to develop their human resources (e.g., whom and how to recruit or sack, how to organise training activities, whom to invite in or to send abroad for co-operation, etc.). Trade management and custom regulations have to focus more strictly on solving the smuggling problem which is very serious for both the textile/garment and the electronics sectors. Some of these specific policies would have a direct impact on the learning activities of firms. For example, more liberalised regulations on labour and recruitment could make it easier for firms to use prior accumulated knowledge. Some other policy changes, like financial incentives that lead to the availability of new resources, can have an immediate impact on doing business, while having a more indirect influence on the learning process.

Second, state support for the whole industrial infrastructure in both the textile/garment and electronics industries should be continued after reforms. Some initiatives are needed for both industries, while others are more peculiar to one or other industry. One example is that textile/garment firms are less supported by R&D activities than are electronics firms. This could be changed by reforming the R&D system, making RITI and RCGI closer to the needs of firms in specific industries. In particular, upgrading RCGI's research activity could significantly enhance the fashion and design capabilities of garment firms. The legal system should be more transparent and should be sufficiently consistent that firms have time to readjust their activities accordingly. Improvements to the industrial supporting infrastructure should include the physical infrastructures of information, telecommunications and transport. The need for improvements stretches beyond these particular two industries, to the development of other related industries such as mechanical engineering, plastic, chemical and packaging industries without which both the textile/garment and electronics industries experience difficulties.

The government should embark on creating a long-term policy and development strategy for both industries. This is crucial. Although firms have to decide on their own plans and strategies by themselves, without a long-term view of the industrial and technological development of the whole country, it is difficult for the firms to orient themselves and to devise the moves they need to make accordingly. This factor is important for both private companies and SOEs, although SOEs are more dependent on this set of policies being put in place since they are directly controlled by the state and depend on the state budget for implementing their long-term investment plans (including their training and learning goals). So far, the electronics industry in Vietnam has not had any sound long-term development strategies and this creates great problems for firms. Co-ordinating the sector can be pursued through the improving state electronics research programmes in such areas such as information technology, or in promoting the activities of the Vietnam Association of Informatics.

In the textile/garment industry, the Association of garment industries for example, could be made responsible for managing and overseeing the chaotic competition among local subcontractors. The curricula of vocational schools and training centres should be upgraded to meet the requirements of a market economy and the increasing need for appropriately skilled workers. Universities and other higher education institutions could train more personnel for new professions such as garment fashion design. Research institutions serving the textile/garment sector should be reorganised to suit the newer needs of that industry.

In electronics and computing, some specific measures can be suggested. Training programmes of universities, vocational schools and training centres should be reorganised to offer courses with a more practical orientation, updated and augmented by the knowledges necessary for operating in a market economy like business administration, investment and marketing. Research institutes such as VIELIN, IMET and IOIT should be restructured and geared more to serve the practical needs of firms. Issues of protecting industrial property rights, and of standardisation (very important for computing and software development) should be addressed more vigorously by government organisations like the Ministry of Science, Technology and Environment.

The problems of ownership should be dealt with more consistently. Only in a non-discriminatory environment can healthy learning take place. Therefore, the government should treat firms under different ownership equally. This does not contradict the selective intervention principle applied to differences between sectors.[1]

One point relates to both firms and government organisations. Firms and other actors involved in learning activities (e.g., government agencies) have to work together through dialogue to devise the most appropriate recommendations for learning to take place, such as strategies of firms and conducive macro-policies of the state. The results of my interviews with external organisations show that these organisations tend to see the same things differently, based on different facts and figures. As a result, they act quite differently from each other, sometimes blaming each other and wasting scarce resources. The S&T department of the Ministry of Industry and industrial associations have an important role to play in organising this dialogue.

11.6 Further research agenda

The results of this study provide a basis for future research in the field.

11.6.1 TC accumulation and learning

The first area concerns the evaluation of TCs. Some other studies have shown that there is not usually enough evidence to assess the status of firms in accumulating TCs (Viana, 1984). The question remains unanswered of how to accurately judge the TC accumulation of firms when they are using, creating and dealing with different types of technology. Whether the concept of 'learning to learn' (Lall, 1993b), and assessing whether a firm has acquired that ability, can lead to a new kind of TC needs to be addressed further. The difference between production capacity and technological capability - as Bell & Pavitt (1993) have mentioned - may also be further addressed.

A relationship between specific TC and learning mechanisms found in this study of Vietnamese firms might not applicable to other conditions. Thus, it could be worthwhile to explore how this relationship varies in different contexts. Perhaps this issue can be addressed in more detail. For example, some questions can be explored to find out more about the importance of each learning mechanism to each TC: which learning mechanisms contribute more to the different levels of TC development? what kinds of combination are best? and for what type of TC? and under what conditions? etc. Although the academic value of this research could be important, it would be quite a difficult topic to study because of the intertwined nature of the learning and TC relationship.

Another issue concerns the sequencing of TC accumulation, that is, the possible contribution of previously accumulated TCs to other TCs which are accumulated later. In this area, the concept of path-dependency could be developed more specifically to study TC accumulation.

11.6.2 The perspective of developing countries

There are some research possibilities related to the context of developing countries. Given that the current conditions of most developing countries differ from those of the decades when Japanese and other late-comer NIC firms learned their technological capability (Bell & Casiolato, 1993; Bell & Pavitt, 1993), a study of how current conditions help or hinder learning is worthwhile. Is there any possibility for the developing world to learn and catch up in today's fiercely competitive international markets? Is the theory of a window of opportunity (Perez & Soete, 1988) still applicable to the present development of poorer countries? What are the conditions necessary for catching-up to happen? And what are specific implications for the technological development of developing countries?

The role of the state in developing countries in supporting TC accumulation and learning is an issue that would benefit from further discussion. In order to learn some lessons, evidence which demonstrates that poorly thought-out policies (such as over-protection or overly liberal attitudes) have an impact on learning (Bell & Pavitt, 1993) can be examined through analysing less successful cases. The role of the state in exercising selective intervention (Lall, 1993a) is usually an important issue. But in terms of how this selective intervention should be implemented in practice, more specific questions can be investigated such as how different interventions affect different industries, or how firms under different forms of ownership may not be competing on a level playing field (as we saw in the case of Vietnam). Although these questions have been dealt with to some degree in the context of other countries, more specific research on countries like Vietnam could be a further step. Also, the argument that protection is sometimes not sufficient for dealing with macro external factors (Bell & Pavitt, 1993) begs the question of what else is required if firms are to learn.

Another direction is to examine more specifically the models or approaches suggested by other authors, e.g., the stages of development model as providing the scenario for developing countries (Lee et al, 1988) or the model of gradual learning suggested by Hobday (1995b). Are these models applicable to all other late-comer countries? If they are, under what conditions do those models work? Is the pattern of gradual learning universal, or is there any possibility of leap-frogging? Again, if leap-frogging in learning is sometimes possible, what conditions are necessary for this to occur? This research could be very useful to late-comer countries as they develop scenarios for catching-up and competing equally with developed economies. The ways that Vietnamese computing firms started their business - by directly jumping into some activities - suggest that there might be some chance to do this, if the context is right. Some questions can be further addressed, such as whether leap-frog learning and the jumping-in pattern are the same phenomenon or whether they are different things? Is the notion that engaging in software activity in Vietnam may be the means for electronics firms to catch up in the sector generally a feasible strategy? Can Vietnamese electronics firms rely on the relative strength of Vietnamese academic achievements in mathematics and computer science to advance the industry? Under what conditions might this be possible? Can Vietnamese electronics or garment companies become part of a larger network of producers, suppliers and subcontractors (Baba & Hatashima, 1995; Mytelka, 1993) and thus learn more successfully in the long run?

The issue of firms' strategic interaction with external environmental factors is crucial. Besides diversification and specialisation as observed in Vietnamese firms, there are other strategies for responding to external factors and these are addressed in business and management research. However, when it comes to learning and TC accumulation, this issue can be examined more specifically. For instance, concerning the diversification of firms, what are the advantages and limitations of diversification? Will the difficulties of technological learning experienced by Korean chaebols in adopting diversification (Ernst, 1995) be replicated in other contexts? What are the implications for countries like Vietnam?

Other research questions can also be further investigated. Some examples are the issue of foreign firms' role and the role of TNC (UNCTAD, 1991); the issue of ownership, of local versus foreign-owned companies (Enos, 1991; Lall & Wignaraja, 1994; Mytelka, 1992; Fransman, 1985; Lall, 1994b); and of private versus state-owned enterprises. Although all these research areas have been addressed to a certain extent in many studies, more empirical studies could contribute to our knowledge of technical change, especially in the context of late-comer non-NICs which are currently enjoying less favourable conditions than previously.

11.6.3 The perspective of transitional economies

Many of the key issues for transitional economies mentioned in Chapter 10 so far remain unresolved.[2] The various ramifications of reform, which define the current confused status of many transitional economies, are enormously complex. It is reasonable to point to some issues relating to the technological development of these economies. One interesting question could be the issue of the "big bang" approach to reforms versus the gradual approach of instituting piecemeal adjustments - in Haggard et al's (1996) terms - as in the cases of Russia and the Central and Eastern European countries on the one hand versus the cases of China and Vietnam on the other, in order to assess the affect each of these approaches have on learning and TC accumulation. Other questions concern the changes to the R&D system and the S&T infrastructure in transitional economies following reforms. What is the role of the R&D community in facilitating learning and TC accumulation in industrial companies? What is the impact of reduced state funding on this system? What are the changes in human resource development in R&D institutions and what influence do such changes have on learning sources for industries? What contribution can R&D personnel make to firms, in the general terms of their knowledge, skill and experience and in the particular terms of the phenomenon of spin-off companies?

The question of networking is important and should be further addressed. How does informal and formal networking compare, and what is the relationship between formal and informal patterns of networking? Do party (communist) connections still influence whether and how TCs are accumulated in the industrial firms of transitional economies?

In addition to comparing European and Asian modes of reform, among the Asian transitional economies further comparisons might be made between Vietnam and China. Concrete issues which might be explored more thoroughly include: macro policies versus the role of micro institutions; the shaping influence of state and administrative hierarchies; the importance (or not) of party versus non-party connections; the role of research think tanks; the role of civil society; and the effect that personal networks, trust relationships and family ties have on industrial development, learning and TC accumulation. Are they similar to the East Asian patterns observed in Korea, Taiwan, or Singapore? What are the outcomes when the features of a transitional economy are combined with a specifically Asian route towards development? These issues may become more actual in the context of latest economic and structural problems all over East and Southeast Asia.

The list of potential research questions to be addressed could be enlarged to encompass the development of the national system of innovation, and the technological activities in industrial firms. Whatever research agenda is taken, future research could enrich our knowledge of technology and development studies, could contribute to our understanding of transitional economies, and could offer key insights into the combined effect of different contexts which are the new phenomenon of the 1990s.

Epilogue

As this book ends, there is a feeling that it has produced more questions than answers. No research is perfect, and this study is no exception. However, some findings of the study can serve as a stepping stone to further research which deals with the learning process and TC accumulation.

One point is certain. Learning is the means by which companies and nations acquire the technological capabilities which are so necessary for their long-term economic growth and development. One question posed by Clark (1985) in a review on learning studies is whether this new tradition of learning studies, initiated by Arrow and continued by many authors, informs the formation and implementation of S&T policy? My study adds one more voice to the answering chorus: yes, it does, and it should have more impact on the agenda of S&T studies in general, and on S&T studies of developing countries in particular.

Vietnam as a developing country has recently embarked on a road of reforms in the transition to a market economy. Some economists tend to argue that Vietnam might become another economic tiger in Asia, whilst other say it might not. This remains to be seen. One question concerns the path of technological development in Vietnam: will Vietnam repeat the success of other NICs in becoming a learning nation and in accumulating TCs for the purposes of economic growth? There are some signs that this learning process is on-going in Vietnamese industries. Regardless of which direction the country takes, one condition is necessary for a prosperous future: Vietnamese firms and policy-making organisations have to work together to promote the learning process at all levels to achieve the technological competence that will help Vietnam move into the 21st century.

Notes

1. The role of private enterprises as the engine for economic growth in many economies is well-known. However, the role of private and state enterprises in Vietnam's economic development depends on the political orientation of the government - an issue which is beyond the scope of this book.

2. For a more detailed overview of these issues - in particular of those questions relating to R&D activity in Central and Eastern European countries, see Balazs et al (1995).

List of appendices

17. Appendix 5.9 Employment in electronics industry

18. Appendix 5.10 Export of electronics industry

Appendix 4.1 Criteria for being qualified as having technological capabilities (check-list)

A company can be considered to have TC if it can do certain activities as follows

1. Investment capability (new investment project, or for substantial expansion of existing old projects during the last 5 years)

1.1 Pre-investment phase

- preparing the economic-technical feasibility and pre-feasibility studies
- choosing the firm to do these studies
- site selection
- start of offshore investment venture (if there is any)

1.2 Project execution phase

- choosing the design and types of machinery and technology suppliers
- negotiation of contracts/bargaining for suitable transfer conditions
- designing the plant (engineering)
- preparing the order books (sourcing)
- plant construction: link to suppliers, contractors and other services for construction, installation
- production start-up, arranging some training from machinery suppliers
- recruitment of work force

2. Production capability 3 types of activities to be carried out on the daily basis:

2.1 Production management

The company knows how to operate machines, equipment, how to organise and control (monitor) production processes and interactions with upstream, downstream and ancillary activities.

2.2 Production engineering

The company can do:

- machinery adjustment to produce designed products

- raw material control
- production adjustment and scheduling, modify plant lay-out
- trouble shooting
- quality control: test products for quality standards

2.3 Repair and maintenance of physical machines, equipment

3. Minor change capability Adaptive engineering/organisational adjustment to be carried out systematically (monthly and/or quarterly, annually) such as:

- modify machinery to do more functions (tasks) or do the functions better or faster, more effectively
- substitute components or inputs material
- adjust production process accordingly for different (new) products
- modification and redesign products, change structure to make them more improved: functions, quality, to add new features and elements, for marketing purposes (easier to sell or with higher prices)
- change of product mix (assortment, move to upstream or downstream products)

4. Marketing capability. Company has TC if it can do by itself almost all following activities regularly (on the monthly basis):

- gathering marketing intelligence to find out trends, structure, etc of markets
- collecting information about competitors, suppliers, buyers
- establishment of international and local distribution channels and provision of customer services (sales and after-sales services)
- set up its own representative/branch offices abroad for dealing with export activities

5. Linkage capability. A firm can have TC if it has at least 2 of following 3 types of activities to be implemented regularly (1 and 3, or 2 and 3):

5.1 Linkages within the firm

- sharing information/interactions among different division and business functions (R&D, design, engineering, procurement, production, marketing, sales and customer services)
- rotation of personnel/exchange of experiences

5.2 Inter-firm linkage

- exchange of information with suppliers, procurement of material,

parts and components, services
- sharing marketing and distribution activities
- sharing and joint development of R&D results, product design and production technology

5.3 Links with S&T infrastructure

- to get available pool of human resources, to use new R&D results and technology development, expertise
- to have close relations with R&D units (formal or informal with persons)

6. Major technical change capability. If a company can do following activities in a planned and conscious pattern (to be reviewed and implented annualy) by its own staff, it has this TC:

- design new products which require new machinery or tooling
- develop new process engineering
- choose new machinery, equipment, organise the purchase of these inputs
- have programme or activities to develop local component supplies
- introduce new applied and/or basic R&D results which can be patentable

Appendix 4.2 Degree of TC acquisition

Criteria	Autonomy	Regularity	Extent of tasks performing
Degree of TC			
Strong	Total by themselves	Day-to-day plans and routine	All tasks and functions
None	Reliance on outsiders	Rarely No plans	Very few functions

The intensity of activities is not compatible to those of global companies, but mostly to regional standards of firms in South East Asian countries like Thailand, China, Indonesia.

Appendix 4.3 Learning mechanisms

1. *Learning-by-doing*: learning through doing different kinds of functions, before and after the technology is installed in the company.

2. *Learning by accumulating previous knowledge* (or Prior accumulation): through recruitment from universities, R&D institutes, or from other workplace, companies, organisations.

3. *Learning by on-the-job training*: through training courses and programmes organised with people keeping their jobs, usually on the site of the company.

4. *Learning by off-the-job training*: formal training courses, workshops, seminars, etc. organised when people are sent for certain period of time and usually off the site of the company (in R&D institutes, schools, colleges, etc.)

5. *Learning through foreign connections*: all forms of learning with the involvement of foreign partners, including training, technical assistance, provision of information, documentation and consultancy.

6. *Learning through searching information, documentation*: mostly by searching and using sources of information, documentation and other consultancy services locally.

Appendix 4.4 Groups of macro external factors

1. *Government policies, laws and regulations* concerning:

- Financial and banking issues
- Investment issues
- Trade issues
- Management issues
- Labour issues
- Industrial property right and technology transfer issues
- Other regulations implemented by the government

2. *Market factors*: structure, scale and scope of market activities for both local and export market; other specific market practice.

3. *Factors of supporting system*: activities of the whole industrial infrastructure including R&D institutes, training and education

organisations, industrial services such as standardisation, metrology, quality control, information and documentation, library services, consultancy, etc.

4. *Socio-cultural factors*: specific factors related only to the country's conditions in terms of historical tradition, cultural habits, social context, etc.

Appendix 4.5 List of companies, dates of interviews and names of interviewees.

A. North:

Textile/garment:

TG1: Thang Long garment company (or TLG)
(18.7.1992; 1.8.1992; 11.9.1992; 7.10.1993; 19.3.1994)

TG2: Doximex (17.9.1992; 29.1.1994)

TG3: Hanosimex (14.9.1992; 9.11.1993)

TG10: Chigamex (15.10.1993; 22.10.1993; 30.11.1993)

TG12: Textile company 'May 19' (3.12.1993; 11.12.1993)

TG13: Thanglong knitwear company (1.12.1993; 10.12.1993)

Electronics:

E1: Viettronics Dong Da (27.8.1992; 10.9.1992; 21.1.1994)

E2: Hanel (27.7.1992; 9.10.1992; 14.12.1993; 5.4.1994)

E3: 3C (26.8.1991; 31.1.1992; 28.7.1992; 19.9.1992; 23.10.1993)

E7: VESCO (20.10.93; 24.12.1993; 20.1.1994; 29.1.1994)

E8: Nam Mon private Co. Ltd. (20.10.93; 25.12.1993; 7.4.1994)

E9: Vietnam Informatic Company (VIF) (15.1.1994; 6.5.1994)

B. South:

Textile/garment:

TG4: Thanh Cong textile company (23.9.92; 16.11.1993; 1.3.1994)

TG5: Legamex (1.11.1992; 10.11.1993)

TG6: Nhatexco (NTC) (5.5.1987; 6.10.1992; 28.9.1993; 9.3.1994)

TG7: Coats Tootal Phong Phu joint venture (6.11.1992; 8.3.1994)

TG8: Hong Ngoc garment Co. Ltd. (1.3.1994; 10.3.1994)

TG9: Huy Hoang garment Co. Ltd. (14.11.1992; 7.3.1994)

TG14: Viet Tien garment export-import company (9.3.1994; 11.3.1994)

TG15: Giditex Co (25.2.1994)

Electronics:

E4: SCITEC (24.9.1992; 2.3.1994)

E5: Gen Pacific joint venture (7.9.1992; 3.3.1994)

E10: Viettronics Thu Duc (5.3.1994; 7.3.1994)

E11: Viettronics Tan Binh (3.1994; 8.3.1994)

Appendix 4.6 Questions used in interviews with companies.

A. Company's profile and basic data.

- Name
- Date of establishment
- Ownership
- Location
- Creation of the firm: background
- Historical and educational background of respondents (managers, engineers, etc.)
- Employment
- Main products/services
- Forms of foreign/domestic technology sources
- Productivity
- Turnover
- Quality of main products (increase/decrease in specific features, change of design and diversification of product assortment)
- Export performance.
    + share of export as percentage of total production
    + main products exported
    + main markets, change of markets, products, types of cooperation with foreign partners.

B. Accumulation of technological capabilities and learning.

1. Does the company have a plan or strategy (in terms of consciousness of its managers, for example) for acquisition of *investment capability* as abilities to acquire information, skills and knowledge, competence in activities such as follows?

- Pre-investment activities:
    + pre-feasibility and feasibility studies,
    + site election, scheduling of investment to the search for sources of technology
    + negotiation of contracts and bargaining for suitable transfer conditions
- Project execution activities to establish or expand facilities:
    + civil engineering and associated services
    + selection and procurement of equipment
    + detailed engineering
    + training and recruitment of the workforce, start-up operations

More specifically, what did they do in these activities, what they can do now which they could not do before, when did they start to do these?

2. The same question for *production capability* which includes:
    - Production management:
        + organisation and control of the production process and its interaction with upstream, downstream activities
    - Production engineering:
        + raw material control, production scheduling
        + quality control
        + trouble-shooting
    - Repair and maintenance activities

3. *Minor technical change capability*:
    - Adaptive engineering: minor adjustment and incremental improvements in production process
    - Other organisational adjustments

4. *Marketing capability*:
    - Acquisition of market knowledge and intelligence
    - Ability to set up marketing divisions locally and overseas, penetration of new markets, changes of market shares

5. *Linkage capability*:
    - Ability to transfer of technology within a firm to manage interactions and information-sharing among different divisions and business functions such as R&D, design, procurement, engineering, production, marketing, sales and customer service
    - Inter-firms linkages: procurement of materials, parts and components and servies, exchange of information with suppliers, sharing of marketing and distribution activities, sharing of other knowledge and joint development activities
    - Linkages with the country S&T infrastructure:
        + to attract, absorb and upgrade the availale pool of human resources
        + to screen and scan new technology development
        + to establish close interactions with applied and basic science

6. *Major technical change capability*:
    - R&D activities at different levels.

7. Could they get mentioned skills, knowledge, competence of investment activities by simple participating in these investment activities? And how firms get knowledge, information?

- what exactly new knowledge or skills firm can get which they did not know before?

8. Could they accumulate these skills, knowledge in production activities by operating production facilities? How it can be described?

9. The same question to be asked for minor change capability.

10., 11., and 12. for other capabilities.

13. Could firms get these skills, knowledge, competence in investment activities by formal activities inside the firms and by interacting more actively with actors and organisations outside firm? And how?

- by what mechanisms such as various kinds of training, hiring local and foreign experts, signing contracts, participating in cooperation contacts, subcontracting, joint venture, technology transfer agreements, etc?
- who taught staff of the firms? for how long? when?
- who gave the firms documentation, learning material, brochure, if any?
- are there any guidances from anybody?

More specifically, each of mechanism will be divided into more detailed activities. For instance, training activities can have various modes and duration: off-the-job (domestic and overseas), on-the-job overseas, on-the-job with or without foreign assistance, few months (one to 4-5 months), one year programmes, more than a year, etc. The same can be applied for hiring and other forms of interacting.

14., 15., 16., 17. and 18. will be asked similarly for other capabilities. However, depending on each capability, more details will be put in the question. For example, for minor change capability, question will include elements of conscious and formal changes at the firms to pursue this accumulation as:

- organisation of improvement activities
- setting up of technical divisions for this purpose
- sending people for training courses
- signing contracts with consultants and R&D institutions, universities, etc.

C. Differences in firms and sectors characteristics and learning.

1. What differences the company has in comparison with other companies in the same sector in terms of ownership (state, private, cooperative, joint venture) and size (large, small, medium) and other features, etc. How these factors affect the learning activities of the firms (as mentioned in questions 7 to 12 and 13 to 18) and why?
   - easier or more difficult to invest in R&D or training?
   - sequence of learning for certain capabilities?
   - ability to respond flexibly to external factors?

2. What differences the company has in comparison with other companies in another sector in terms of type of activities and other specific features, if any? How these factors affect the learning efforts (as mentioned in questions 7 to 12 and 13 to 18) by firms positively and negatively and why?
   - any sector-specific features to make firms more difficult (or easier) in their learning
   - are sequences of accumulation of technological capabilities different for two sectors? and why?

D. Learning and macro-environment factors.

1. Which factors are favourable or constraints/barriers/obstacles for company in doing the activities mentioned in questions 7 to 18 in terms of government related policy dynamics, such as:
   - orientation of development and investment policies
   - trade policies
   - investment priorities
   - financial and monetary policies
   - other policy changes

   How these factors influenced the learning activities of firms and why?

2. Which factors are favourable or constraints/obstacles for company in doing the activities mentioned in questions 7 to 18 in terms of macroeconomic stability like:
   - inflation rate
   - exchange rate
   - others.

3. The same questions will be asked at firms for other macro-environmental factors with more details for each of group of factors such as market factors: existence and activities of capital and labour market, structure and size of market, etc.

4. R&D and education infrastructure systems:
   - availability of R&D skills, training programmes, educational facilities
   - activities and development of consultancy, standardisation and other organisations of industrial supporting systems

5. Other social, cultural and historical specific factors:
   - tradition of industrial development
   - tradition of study and willingness to learn
   - existence or lack of disciplines, social order, mentality

6. More concretely, how do these factors influence (positively or negatively)? And why?

   - can firms get support from this system? in what ways?
   - which organisations (ministries, universities, R&D units, etc.) prevented or contributed to the firms' learning process, and how?
   - how the existence or lack of certain external supporting organisations contributed or hindered learning afforts of firms?
   - how one or another policy prevented firms from doing certain learning? or forced firms to do so?
   - how various mechanisms and regulations, law, policies created favourable (or unfavourable) atmosphere for firms to carry out learning efforts?
   - what attitudes or tendencies in firms' behaviour did these factors shape?

Appendix 4.7 List of interviews of external organisations: names of interviewed persons and dates of interviews.

A. North:

Ministry of Science, Technology and Environment (MOSTE)

1. Mitec Inc. & Institute of microelectronic technology (IMET) (22.2.1994)

2. Department for Industrial Property (1992-1994)

Ministry of Heavy Industry

1. S&T Department (23.2.1992; 3.2.1994)

2. VEIC (18.10.1993)

3. VIELIN (Vietnam institute of electronics and informations)(19.1.1994)

Ministry of Light Industry (MOLI)

1. Textimex (14.10.1993)

2. Confectimex (15.2.1994)

3. Research centre for garment industry (RCGI) (15.2.1994)

4. Research institute of Textile Industry (RITI) (20.1.1994)

5. Information Centre (many times during 1992-1994)

Others

1. Vietnam Association for Information Processing (VAIP)(15.7.1992)

B. South:

1. Polytechnic University of HCMC (4.3.1994)

2. Swiss-AIT management program in Vietnam (25.2.1994)

3. People's committee of HCMC. Department of Industry (24.2.1994)

4. Economic and Industrial consultants company ECO Ltd., Management Training Center MTC (26.2.1994)

5. The technical professional school HCMC (24.2.1994)

6. United Association of Industrialists HCMC (26.2.1994)

7. Chamber of Commerce and Industry HCMC (26.2.1994)

8. Institute for Economic Research (IER) (24.2.1994)

9. Department for S&T of HCMC (23.2.1994)

Appendix 4.8 Questions used for interviews with external organisations

1. General data on development and activities of the organisations:
   - staff
   - main activities, functions
   - orientation
   - historical background, etc.

2. Do they have any conscious plan, strategy to develop technological competence of the sector concerned?
   - plans of action
   - research programmes
   - training programmes
   - development of S&T information and documentation units
   - development of other industrial supporting units such as consultancy, standardisation, quality control, technical services, etc.
   - brief historical background of these plans, programmes and activities

3. Do they have relations, linkages with companies and how these relations take place in practice?
   - any services they provide for firms?
   - any coopration programmes like trouble-shooting, technical assistance, guidance?
   - any training and education courses provided?
   - how many and for how long these programmes have been undertaken? for how many persons? for what kind of staff of the firms? for what type of firms?
   - other supporting activities?

4. For what type of learning activity/mechanism firms tend to rely most on external organisations? in what stage of capabilities accumulation? and why?
   - training
   - R&D
   - technical assitance services
   - others

5. What are the main obstacles to improve relations with the firms:
   - lack of financial sources of firms to pay for services? surplus or shortage of other resources?
   - unfavourable general environment of doing business?

- lack of necessary policies of the government?
- poor infrastructure?
- lack of willingness and initiatives from the firms themselves to learn?
- others?

6. Is there any difference among firms of different sectors in their efforts to get relations with external organisations for learning purposes? and why so?
   - more active/passive attitude and behaviour
   - more availability of financial sources
   - existing rate of skills of firms' staff
   - specific features of sector: some regulations which another sector does not have

7. Any other comments or reasons why one or another firm can not have good cooperative relations with interviewed organisations?

Appendix 5.1 Specifications of textile/garment industry

Activity	Equipment	Capacity (per year)	Quality
Spinning	900,000 spindles	90,000 tons	10 Nm - 102 Nm
Weaving	43,000 machines	450 - 500 M metters	n.a
of which:			
SOEs	14,200 looms		
non-state	29,000 looms		
Dyeing & finishing	n.a	450 M metter	all kinds of fabrics print on flat screen, roller printing machine
Knitting	n.a	14,900 tons	n.a
of which:			
circular machines		13,550 tons	
warp machines		1,400 tons	
Garment	49,000	93 M pieces	n.a

Source: Textimex, Confectimex. 1994

Appendix 5.2 Numbers of enterprises in textile/garment industry industry

I. State sector

Year	Textile	Garment
1980	166	59
1985	113	67
1986	116	70
1987	118	72
1988	121	77
1989	131	85
1990	118	96
1991	112	99
1992	110	92
1993	106	93
1994	100	101

II. Non-state sector

Year	Total	Cooperative	Private	Small & handycraft units
		Textile		
1990	-	1,224	17	35,107
1991	36,348	739	16	45,324
1992	46,082	474	83	45,088
1993	-	298	83	57,067
1994	-	165	99	57,067
		Garment		
1990	-	296	26	38,976
1991	39,298	287	28	39,895
1992	40,210	262	114	38,554
1993	-	89	147	36,324
1994	41,000	77	383	32,539

Source: Statistics Yearbook. Hanoi. 1992.1993-1994

Appendix 5.3 Employment in textile and clothing industries (in thousand persons)

	Textile			*Garment*		
Year	Total	State	Non-state sectors	Total	State	Non-state sectors
1980	n.a.	80	n.a	n.a.	25.8	n.a
1985	476.9	103.2	374.6	112.8	30.4	82.4
1986	446.1	104.7	341.4	128.0	35.5	92.5
1987	493.9	110.4	383.5	131.6	38.1	93.5
1988	481.0	115.5	365.5	184.4	47.9	136.5
1989	370.1	103.8	266.3	167.7	49.2	124.8
1990	306.5	104.2	202.3	136.4	54.9	81.5
1991	300.7	98.4	202.3	145.4	63.9	81.5
1992	370.0	103.8	266.0	164.0	75.7	88.2
1994	400.0	n.a	n.a	165.5	75.5	90.0

Source: Statistics Yearbook. Hanoi. 1980-1992; 1993-1994

Appendix 5.4 Textile/garment production in Vietnam

Years	Fibres	Fabrics	Garment
	('000 tonnes)	(mln.metters)	(mln.pieces)
1957	n.a.	67.0	n.a.
1960	10.4	89.7	4.4
1965	12.7	100.3	7.9
1968	n.a.	83	n.a.
1970	n.a.	89	n.a.
1972	n.a.	73	n.a.
1974	11.5	95.8	17.2
1975	13.0	164.6	19.1
1976	35.5	218.0	n.a.
1978	38.0	320.	n.a.
1980	29.3	175.3	69.2
1981	31.0	179.2	52.7
1982	36.0	238.0	55.3
1983	44.8	307.0	74.1
1984	53.0	367.1	70.7
1985	51.3	374.3	73.6
1986	53.0	357.0	102.3
1987	57.0	361.0	n.a.
1988	62.0	384.0	109.9
1989	56.4	337.3	114.6
1990	58.3	318.0	125.3
1991	40.0	280.4	106.1
1992	44.0	272.0	104.0
1993	38.0	215.0	91.0
1994	44.4	228.1	121.0

Source: Statistics Yearbook. Hanoi. 1992, 1994

Appendix 5.5 Export of textile and clothing in millions roubles and USD (1991 and 1992 in USD only)

Year	Total value	Clothing	Cotton and peco yarns (in tonnes)
1980	52	44	5,300
1981	47	39	2,961
1982	62	52	4,887
1983	76	66	5,028
1984	85	74	6,800
1985	93	81	6,300
1986	93	74	4,900
1987	91	60	6,200
1988	132	99	7,300
1989	193	140.4	7,300
1990	210	178.1	n.a.
1991	132	93	n.a.
1992	145	119.2	n.a.

Source: Statistics Yearbook. Hanoi. 1992

Appendix 5.6 Export structure of textile and garment industry in 1991 - 1992 (in %)

Products	1991	1992
Cotton yarn	6.6	0.7
Polyester yarn	3.54	0.5
Fabrics	7.85	10.47
Other text. products	11.54	6.11
Garment	70.41	81.75
Garment parts & material	0.06	0.475
Total of textile & garment	100.0	100.0

Source: Statistics Yearbook. Hanoi. 1993.

Appendix 5.7 Destination of garment export in 1986-1990 and 1991-1992 (in %)

Year	Total	East European & Soviet Union	Market economies
1986-1990	100	95	5
1991	100	60.3	30.7
1992	100	42.4	57.6

Source: Statistics Yearbook. Hanoi. 1993

Apendix 5.8 Number of enterprises (for both electronics and electrical industries)

Year	State sector		Non-state sector	
		Cooperatives	Private	Small & handicr. units
1985	79	n.a	n.a	n.a
1988	75	n.a	n.a	n.a
1989	76	n.a	n.a	n.a
1990	61	109	14	5,186
1991	60	89	13	5,462
1992	67	49	10	1,244
1993	62	43	36	1,244
1994	59	14	42	2,209

Source: Statistics Yearbook. Hanoi. 1992.

Appendix 5.9 Employment in electronics and electrical industries (in thousand persons)

Year	Total	State sector	Non-state sector
1985	28.0	19.1	8.9
1988	31.9	21.0	10.9
1989	29.5	18.9	10.6
1990	30.5	18.0	12.5

Source: Statistics Yearbook. Hanoi. 1992

Appendix 5.10 Export of electronics industry (in USD)

Products	1991	1992
Office machines & parts	1,111,350	266,218
of which PCs	805,805	139,407
Telecom & audio-visual products	3,076,419	1,327,348
of which:		
colour TV	134,100	923,453
radiocassetes	782,840	42,000
black/wh. TV	n.a	219,360
Parts & comp. for audiovisual equipment	1,008,067	249,314
other parts & comp.	2,952,704	15,570

Source: Trade Statistics Yearbook. Hanoi.1993

Bibliography

Ahmed, Q. (1981) Accumulation of technological capability and assimilation of imported industrial production system in the cotton textile industry in Bangladesh. *Absorption and diffusion of imported technology*. Proceeding of workshop. IDRC.

Alic, J. (1995) Organizational competence: know-how and skills in economic development. *Technology in society*. Vol.17. No.4.

Amsden, A. (1989) *Asia's next giant. South Korea and late industrialisation*. Oxford University Press.

Amsden, A. (1994) Why isn't the whole world experimenting with the East Asian model to develop ? Review of the East Asian Miracle. *World Development*. Vol.22. No.4.

Amsden, A. & Kim, Linsu. (1986) A technological perspective on the general machinery industry in the Republic of Korea. in Fransman, M (Ed.) *Machinery and economic development*. Macmillan.

Andersen, E-S. (1992) Approaching national system of innovation in Lundvall, B-A. (Ed.) *National System of Innovation. Towards a theory of innovation and interactive learning*. Pinter. London.

Arrow, K. (1962) The economic implication of learning-by-doing. *Review of Economic Studies*. Vol. 29. p.155-173.

Asia-Pacific Centre for Technology Transfer (APCTT) (1988). *Technology policies and planning. Socialist Republic of Vietnam*. Country study series. Bangalore.

Baark, E. (1991) The accumulation of technology: capital good production in developing countries revisited. *World Development* . Vol 19. No7.

Baark, E. (1994) Technological entrepreneurship and commercialisation of research results in the West and in China: comparative perspectives. *Technology Analysis and Strategic Management*. Vol 6. No 2.

Baba, Y. & Hatashima, H. (1995) Capabilities transfer in the Pacific Rim nations: the case of japanese electrical and electronics firms. *International Journal of Technology Management.* Vol.10. No.7-8.

Balazs, K. (1995) Innovation potential embodied in research organizations in Central and Eastern Europe. in Balazs, K, Faulkner, W & Schimank, U. (Ed.) "The research system in post-communist Central and Eastern Europe" EASST Special Issue. *Social Studies of Science.* Vol.25. No.4.

Balazs, K, Faulkner, W & Schimank, U. (1995) "The research system in post-communist Central and Eastern Europe" EASST Special Issue. *Social Studies of Science.* Vol.25. No.4.

Baranson, J. & Roark, R. (1985) Trends in North-South transfer of high technology in Rosenberg & Frischtak (Ed.) *International technology transfer*. Praeger.

Batchelor, J., Donnely, T. & Morris, D. (1995) Learning in support of lean supply chains: customer-supplier relationship and the learning organisation. in Bennett, D & Stewart, F. (Ed.)*Technological innovation and global challenges*. Proceeding of the European conference on management of technology. Aston University. Birmingham.

Bell, M. (1984) Learning and the accumulation of industrial technological capacity in developing countries. in Fransman, M. & King, K. (Eds.) *Technological capability in the Third World.* Macmillan.

Bell, M. & Hoffman, K. (1981) *Industrial development with imported technology: a strategic perspective on policy.* SPRU.

Bell, M. & Scott-Kemmis, D. (1985a) *Training and the acquisition of technical knowledge*. SPRU working paper No.4.

Bell, M. & Scott-Kemmis, D. (1985b) *Technological capacity and technical change: case studies*. SPRU working paper No.6.

Bell, M., Scott-Kemmis, D. & Satyarakwit, W. (1980) *Learning and technical change in the development of manufacturing industry: a case study of a permanently infant enterprise.* SPRU.

Bell, M., Scott-Kemmis, D. & Satyarakwit, W. (1982) Limited learning in infant industry: a case study. in Stewart, F & James, J. (Ed.) *The economics of new technology in developing countries*. Frances Pinter. London.

Bell, M., Ross-Larsson, B. & Westphal, L. (1984) Assessing the performance of infant industries. *Journal of Development Economics*. No 16. pp.101-128.

Bell, M. & Pavitt, K. (1992) Accumulating technological capability in developing countries. *Proceeding of the World Bank Annual Conference on development economics.* World Bank.

Bell, M. & Casiolato, J. (1993) *Technology imports and the dynamic competitiveness of Brazilian industry: the need for new aproaches to management and policy.* Report for the Estudo da competitivedada da industria brasileira. SPRU.

Bell, M. & Pavitt, K. (1993) Technology accumulation and industrial growth: contrasts between developed and developing countries. *Industrial and corporate change.* Vol 2. No.2.

Bell, M. & Pavitt, K. (1997) Technological accumulation and industrial growth: contrasts between developed and developing countries. in Archibugi, D. & Michie, J. (Eds.) *Technology, globalisation and economic performance.* Cambridge University Press.

Bennell, P. (1984) The utilisation of professional engineering skills in Kenya. in Fransman, M. & King, K. (Eds.) *Technological capability in the Third World.* Macmillan.

Bennett, D. & Stewart, F. (Ed.) (1995) *Technological innovation and global challenges*. Proceeding of the European conference on management of technology. Aston University. Birmingham.

Beresford, M. (1989) *National unification and economic development in Vietnam.* Macmillan.

Bessant, J., Caffyn, S. & Gilbert, J. (1996) Learning to manage innovation. *Technology analysis and strategic management.* Vol.8. No.1.

Boisot, M. (1995) Is your firm a creative destroyer ? Competitive learning and knowledge flows in the technological strategies of firms. *Research Policy.* No 24.

Buttinger, J. (1982) *A dragon defiant. A short history of Vietnam.* David and Charles. Newton Abbot.

Chudnovsky, D. (1986) The entry into the design and production of complex capital goods: the experience of Brazil, India and South Korea. in Fransman (Ed.) *Machinery and economic development*. Macmillan.

Clark, N. (1985) *The political economy of science and technology.* Basil Blackwell.

Cohen, W. & Levinthal, D. (1990) Absorptive capacity: a new persepctive on learning and innovation. *Administrative science quarterly.* Vol.35.

Coombs, R., Saviotti, P. & Walsh, V. (Ed.) (1992a) *Technological change and company strategies: economic and sociological perspectives.* Hartcourt Brace Jovanovich Publishers.

Coombs, R., Saviotti, P. & Walsh, V. (1992b) Technology and the firm: the convergence of economic and sociological aproaches? in Coombs, R., Saviotti, P. & Walsh, V. (Ed.)*Technological change and company strategies: economic and sociological perspectives.* Hartcourt Brace Jovanovich Publishers.

Cooper, C. (1991) *Are innovation studies on industrialised countries relevant to technology policy in developing countries ?* UNU/INTECH. Maastrict. December.

Cooper, C. (1995) Technology policy and industrialisation policy in the global economy in Heeks, R (Ed.) *Technology and developing countries. Practical applications, theoretical issues.* Frank Cass. London.

Correa, C. (1995) Strategies for software exports from developing countries. *World Development*. Vol.24. No.1.

Dacy, D. (1986) *Foreign aid, war and economic development. South Vietnam, 1955-1975.* Cambridge University Press.

Dahlman, C. (1984) Foreign technology and indigenous technological capability in Brazil. in Fransman, M. & King, K. (Ed.) *Technological capability in the Third World.* Macmillan.

Dahlman, C. & Fonseca, F. (1987) From technological dependence to technological development: the case of the USIMINAS steel plant in Brasil. in Katz (Ed.) *Technology generation in Latin American manufacturing.*

Dalum, B., Johnson, B. & Lundvall, B-A. (1992) Public policy in the learning society in Lundvall, B-A. (Ed.) *National System of Innovation. Towards a theory of innovation and interactive learning.* Pinter. London.

Dang Ba Lam, Nghiem Xuan Nung & Sloper, D. (1995) Research activities and higher education. in Sloper, D. & Le Thac Can (Ed.) *Higher education in Vienam. Change and response.* Institute of Southeast Asian Studies. St. Martin's Press. Singapore.

David, P. (1975) *Technical choice, innovation and economic growth.* Cambridge University Press.

Deolalikar, A. & Sundanam, A. (1983) Technology choice, adaptation and difussion in priavte- and state-owned enterprises in India. in James, J. (Ed.) *The technological behaviour of public enterprises in developing countries.* Routledge.

Dickson, K., Coles, A.M. & Lawton-Smith, H. (1995) Learning from experiences: lessons in managing inter-firm R&D collaboration. in Bennett, D. & Stewart, F. (Ed.) *Technological innovation and global challenges*. Proceeding of the European conference on management of technology. Aston University. Birmingham. UK.

Dodgson, M. (1992) Strategy and technological learning: an interdisciplinary microstudy in Coombs, R., Saviotti, P. & Walsh, V. (Ed.) *Technological change and company strategies: economic and sociological perspectives.* Hartcourt Brace Jovanovich Publishers.

Dosi, G. (1984) *Technical change and industrial transformation: the theory and application to the semiconductor industry.* Macmillan.

Dosi, G. (1988) Sources, procedures and microeconomic effect of innovation. *Journal of economic literature.* Vol.26. No.3.

Dosi, G. & Soete, L. (1991) Technological innovation and international competitiveness. In Niosi, J. (Ed.) *Technology and national competitiveness. Oligopoly, technological innovation and international competition.* McGill-Queen's University Press.

Dosi, G. (1995) Technological and industrial dynamics. *Options*. Summer issue. IIASA. Laxenburg. Austria.

Duiker, W. (1983) *Vietnam. Nation in revolution.* Westview Press.

Enos, J. (1958) A measure of the rate of technical progress. *Journal of Industrial Economics*. No 6.

Enos, J. (1991) *The creation of technological capablity in developing countries.* Pinter.

Enos, J. & Park, W.H. (1988) *The adoption and diffusion of imported technology. The case of Korea.* Croom Helm.

Erber, F. S. (1986) The capital goods industry and the dynamics of economic development in LDC: the case of Brazil. in Fransman (Ed.) *Machinery and economic development*. Macmillan.

Ernst, D. (1994) *What are the limits to the Korean model ? The Korean electronics industry under pressures.* A BRIE research paper. The Berkeley Roundtable on the International Economy. UC Berkeley. Berkeley.

Ernst, D. (1995) *Technology management in the Korean electronics industry: achievements and new challenges.* BRIE. UC Berkeley. Paper presented at 3rd international ASEAT conference. Manchester. September.

Ernst, D. & O'Connor, D. (1989) *Technology and global competition: the challenge for newly industrializing economies.* OECD. Development Centre. Paris.

Ernst, D. & O'Connor, D. (1993) *Competing in the electronics industry - the experiences of NIEs.* OECD. Development Centre. Paris.

Ernst, D., Ganiatsos, T. & Mytelka, L. (1997) (Eds.)*Technological capability building and export success: cases from Asia.* UNCTAD Report.

Ernst, D., Ganiatsos, T. & Mytelka, L. (1998) (Eds.)*Technological capabilities and export success in Asia.* Routledge.

Faulkner, W. (1993) *Conceptualising knowledge used in innovation: a second look at the science-technology distinction and industrial innovation.* Edinburgh PICT working paper No.43. Edinburgh University.

Faulkner, W. & Senker, J. (1993) *Policy and management issues in company links with academic and government laboratories: a cross-technology study.* Edinburgh PICT working paper No. 48. Edinburgh University.

Fforde, A. & Paine, S. (1987) *The limits of national liberation. Problems of economic management in the DRV.* Croom Helm.

Fforde, A. & de Vylder, S. (1989) *Vietnam: an economy in transition.* SIDA. Stockholm.

Fforde, A. & de Vylder, S. (1996) *From plan to market. Economic transition in Vietnam.* Westview Press. Boulder. Colorado.

Fleck, J. (1991) *Innovation during implementation: configurations and CAPM.* Paper at ESRC/DTI research initiative on new technologies and the firm and technology group conference. University of Stirling. School of Management. No.2.

Fleck, J. (1994) Learning by trying. The implementation of configurational technology. *Research Policy.* Vol 23. No.11.

Fransman, M. (1984a) Technological capability in the Third World: an overview. in Fransman, M. & King, K. (Ed.) *Technological capability in the Third World.* Macmillan.

Fransman, M. (1984b) Some hypotheses regarding indigenous technological capability and the case of machine production in HongKong in Fransman, M. & King, K. (Ed.) *Technological capability in the Third World*. Macmillan.

Fransman, M. (1985) Conceptualising technical change in the Third World in the 1980s: an interpretive survey. *The journal of development studies.* Vol. 21. No.4.

Fransman, M. (1986a) International competitiveness, international diffusion of technology and the state: a case study from Taiwan and Japan. in Fransman (Ed.) *Machinery and economic development*. Macmillan.

Fransman, M. (1986b) (Ed.) *Machinery and economic development*. Macmillan.

Fransman, M. (1986c) *Technology and economic development.* Wheatsheaf books.

Fransman, M. (1990) *Market and beyond.* Cambridge University Press. Cambridge.

Fransman, M. (1991) What we know about the Japanese innovation system and what we need to know. In Inose, H. et al (Eds.) *Science and technology policy research. What should be done? what can be done?* Mita Press. Tokyo.

Fransman, M. (1995) *Competitiveness and the importance of technology, competence, and strategy at enterprise and national levels: an interpretive survey of literature on developed and less developed countries.* Japanese European Technology Study (JETS) Institute. Mimeo.

Fransman, M. & King, K. (1984) *Technological capability in the Third World.* Macmillan.

Freeman, C. (1987a) Technology policy and economic performance. *Lessons from Japan.* Frances Pinter. London.

Freeman, C. (1987b) Technological innovation, long cycles and regional policy. in Chapman & Humphrys (Ed.) *Technical change and industrial policy.* Basil Blackwell.

Freeman, C. (1988) Japan: a new national system of innovation. In Dosi , G. et al (Eds.) *Technical change and economic theory.* Frances Pinter. London.

Frischtack, C. (1994) Learning and technical progress in the commuter aircraft industry: an analysis of Embraer's experience. *Research Policy.* 23.

Gemunden, H. & Heydebreck, P. (1995) The influence of business strategies on technological network activities. *Research Policy.* 24.

Girvan, N. (1983) *Technology policies for small developing countries. A study of the Caribean.* Institute of social and economic research. University of West Indies.

Gourevitch, P., McMillan, J., Schoepflin, H. & Liem Le (1994) *Vietnam in transition: macro and micro views of economic prospects and choices.* Report of the Vietnam Pacific project. Graduate School of International Relations and Pacific Studies. University of California. San Diego.

Grabher, G. (1993) (Ed.) *The embedded firm. On the socioeconomic of industrial network.* Routledge.

Gu Shulin. (1996) The emergence of new technology enterprises in China: a study of endogenous capability building via restructuring. *The journal of development studies.* Vol 32. No 4.

Haggard, S., McMillan, J. & Woodruff, C. (1996) *Trust and search in Vietnam's emerging private sector.* Mimeo. Graduate School of International Relations and Pacific Studies. University of California. San Diego.

Hartley, K. (1965) The learning curve and its application to the aircraft industry. *Journal of industrial economics.* No 3.

Henderson, J. (1996) *Looking East ? Industrial transformation in Eastern Europe in the light of the East Asian experience.* Speech made at business seminar series. Department of Business Studies. Edinburgh University. March.

Hewitt, T. & Wield, D. (1996) Technological capability and competitiveness - two needs that defy measurement. *UNIDO. 30 years of industrial development. 1966-1996.* UNIDO and International System of Communication Ltd. London.

Hiebert, M. (1993) Chain lending. Informal credit fills void left by Vietnam's bank. *Far Eastern Economic Review.* March 4.

Hirsch, W. (1963) Firm progress ratio. *Econometrica.* No 4.

Hirshleifer, H. (1962) The firm cost production, a successful reconstruction. *Journal of Business.* No 7.

Hoang Ngoc Nguyen (1990) Economic renovation in Southern Vietnam. Challenges, responses, prospects. Paper presented at the Conference on Doimoi, Vietnam's economc renovation policy and performance. ANU. Canberra.

Hobday, M. (1993) Export-led technology development in the four dragons: the case of electronics. *Development and change.*

Hobday, M. (1994) Technological learning in Singapore: a test case of leapfrogging. *Journal of Development Studies.* Vol.30. No 3.

Hobday, M. (1995a) *Innovation in East Asia: the challenge to Japan.* London. Edward Elgar.

Hobday, M. (1995b) East Asian latecomer firms: learning the technology of electronics. *World Development.* Vol. 23. No 7.

Hollander, S. (1965) *The sources of increased efficiency: the study of Du Pont rayon plant.* MIT Press.Cambridge. Massachusetts.

ILO (1994) *Vietnam: labour and social issues in a transitional economy.* East Asia multidisciplinary advisory team. Bangkok.

Imai, M. (1986) *Kaizen: the key to Japan's competitive success.* McGraw-Hill. NewYork.

IMF (1991) *Vietnam recent economic changes*. Washington.D.C.

Jamison, A. & Baark, E. (1990) *Technological innovation and environmental concern: contending policy models in China and Vietnam.* Research Policy Institute. Discussion paper No 187. Lund.

Justman, M. & Teubal, M. (1995) Technological infrastructure policy (TIP): creating capabilities and building markets. *Research Policy.* Vol 24.

Kassim, H. & Salleh, I. (1994) Technological dynamism behind Malaysia's successful export performance. in Ernst, D., Ganiatsos, T. & Mytelka, L. (Eds.)*Export performance and technological capabilities - lessons from East Asia.* UNCTAD. Geneva.

Katz, J. (1984a) Domestic technological innovation and dynamic comparative advantage: further reflections on a comparative case study program. *Journal of development economics.* Vol.16. No.1.

Katz, J. (1984b) Comparative advantages of Latin American metalworking industries. in Fransman, M. & King, K. (Ed.) *Technological capability in the Third World.* Macmillan.

Katz, J. (1985) Domestic technological innovation and dynamic comparative advantages: further reflection on a comparative case - study. in Rosenberg, N. & Frischtak, C. (Ed.) *International technology transfer*. Praeger.

Katz, J. (1987a) Domestic technology generation in LDCs: a review of research findings in Katz (Ed.) *Technology generation in Latin American manufacturing industries. Theory and case studies concerning its nature, magnitude and consequences.* Macmillan.

Katz, J. (1987b) (Ed.) *Technology generation in Latin American manufacturing industries. Theory and case studies concerning its nature, magnitude and consequences.* Macmillan.

Katz, J., Gutkowski, M., Rodrigues, M. & Goity, G. (1987) Productivity and domestic technological search efforts: the growth path of a rayon plant in Argentina in Katz, J. (Ed.) *Technology generation in Latin American manufacturing industries. Theory and case studies concerning its nature, magnitude and consequences.* Macmillan.

Keesing, D. & Lall, S. (1992) Marketing manufactured exports from developing countries: learning sequences and public support. in Helleiner (Ed.) *Trade policy, industrialization and development: new perspective.* Oxford. Clarendon Press.

Kim, L. (1980) Stages of development of industrial technology in a developing country: a model. *Research Policy.* 9.

Kim, L. (1990) Korea: the acquisition of technology. In Soesarsto, H. & Pangestu, M. (Ed.) *Technological challenge in the Asia-Pacific economy.* Allen & Unwin.

Kline, S.J. & Rosenbeg, N. (1986) An overview of innovation. in Landau, R. & Rosenberg, N. (Eds.) *The positive sum strategy.* Academy of Engineering Press.

Kogut, B., Shan, W. & Walker, G. (1993) Knowledge in the network and networks as knowledge. The structuring of new industries in Grabher, G (Ed.) *The embedded firm. On the socioeconomic of industrial network.* Routledge.

Lall, S. (1982) *Developing countries as exporters of technology. A first look at the Indian experience*. Macmillan.

Lall, S. (1984) Export of technology by newly industrialising countries. An overview. *World Development.* Vol.12. No 5/6.

Lall, S. (1985) Trade in technology by a slowly industrialising country: India. in Rosenberg, N. & Frischtak, C. (Ed.) *International technology transfer*. Praeger.

Lall, S. (1987) *Learning to industrialise. The acquisition of technological capability by India.* Macmillan.

Lall, S. (1990) *Building industrial competitiveness in developing countries*. OECD. Development centre Studies. Paris.

Lall, S. (1992) Technological capabilities and industrialization. *World Development.* Vol.20. No.2.

Lall, S. (1993a) Technological development, technology impact and industrial strategy: a review of the issues. *Industry and Development.* No.34. UNIDO. Vienna.

Lall, S. (1993b) Policies for building technological capabilities: lessons from Asian experiences. *Asian Development Review*. ADB. Vol.11. No.2.

Lall, S. (1994a) Technological capabilities in Salomon, J-J., Sagasti, F. & Sachs-Jeantet, C. (Eds.) *The uncertain quest. Science, technology and development.* UNU Press.

Lall, S. (1994b) Industrial policy: the role of government in promoting industrial and technological development. *UNCTAD Review 1994*. Geneva.

Lall, S. & Wignaraja, G. (1994) Foreign involvement and garment exports by developing countries. *Asia-Pacific Development Journal.* Vol.1. No.2.

Langdon, S. (1982). *Indigenous technological capacity in Africa: the case of textiles and wood products in Kenya.* Paper to international workshop on facilitating indigenous technological capacity. Centre of African Studies. Edinburgh University. May.

Langdon, S. (1984) Indigenous technological capability in Africa: the case of textiles and wood products in Kenya. in in Fransman, M. & King, K. (Ed.) *Technological capability in the Third World*. Macmillan.

Lapid, K. (1994) *Externalities and learning patterns during the innovation process: a case study of cross-learning in a electronics firm*. The Jerusalem Institute of Israel Studies. Research report No17.

Lapid, K. (1995) Cooperation within successful innovation processes: industrial learning patterns. in Bennett, D. & Stewart, F. (Ed.) *Technological innovation and global challenges*. Proceeding of the European conference on management of technology. Aston University. Birmingham.

Laurence, P. (1980) *Managers and management in West Germany.* Croom Helm. London.

Lazerson, M. (1990) Subcontracting in the Modena knitwear industry in Pyke, F, Becattini, G & Sengenberger, W.(Ed.) *Industrial districts and inter-firm cooperation in Italy*. ILO. Geneva.

Lee, J., Bae, Z. & Choi, D. (1988) Technology development processes: a model for a developing country with a global perspective. *R&D management.* Vol.18. No 3.

Le Thac Can & Sloper, D. (1995) Higher education in Vietnam: the door opens - from inside. in Sloper, D & Le Thac Can (Ed.) *Higher education in Vienam. Change and response.* Institute of Southeast Asian Studies. St. Martin's Press. Singapore.

Lucangeli, J. (1983) Technological behaviour of Argentine public enterprise: the case of Yacimientos petroliferos fiscales. in James, J. (Ed.) *The technological behaviour of public enterprises in developing countries.* Routledge.

Lundvall, B-A. (Ed.) (1992) *National System of Innovation. Towards a theory of innovation and interactive learning.* Pinter. London.

Lundvall, B-A. (1993) Explaining interfirm cooperation and innovation: limits of the transaction-cost aproach in Grabher, G (Ed.) *The embedded firm. On the socioeconomic of industrial network.* Routledge.

Malecki, E. (1991) *Technology and economic development. the dynamics of local, regional and national change.* Longman scientific and technical.

Malerba, F. (1992) Learning by firms and incremental technical change. *The economic journal.* Vol.102. July.

Marr, D. (1981)*Vietnamese tradition on trial, 1920-1945.* University of California Press.

Marr, D. & White, C. (1988) (Ed.) *Postwar Vietnam: dilemmas in socialist development.* SEAP. Cornell University. Ithaca.

Massaquoi, J. (1995) The effect of some sectoral development policies on technology. The case of the informal sector in Heeks, R. (Ed.) *Technology and developing countries. Practical applications, theoretical issues.* Frank Cass. London.

Maxwell, P. (1981) *Technology policy and firm learning efforts in less-developed countries. A case study of the experiences of the Argentine steel firm Acindar S.A.* DPhil Thesis. SPRU. Sussex University.

McMillan, J. (1995) *Markets in transition.* Symposium address at the seventh World congress of the econometric society. Tokyo.

Mensch, G. (1975) *The technological stalemate*. Ballinger. NewYork.

Metcalfe, S. & de Liso, N. (1995) *Innovation, capabilities and knowledge: the epistemic connection.* Paper presented at 3rd international ASEAT conference. Manchester. September.

Mlawa, H. (1983) *The acquisition of technology, technological capability and technical change: a study of the textile industry in Tanzania.* DPhil Thesis. SPRU. Sussex University.

Mody, A., Rajan, S. & Jerry, S. (1991) Keeping pace with change: organisational and technological imperatives. *World Development.* Vol.20. No.12.

Moghadam, V. (1994) *Market reforms and women workers in Vietnam: a case study of Hanoi and HoChiMinh City.* UNU WIDER. Working paper No 116. July.

Mosoni-Fried, J. (1995) Industrial research in Hungary: a victim of structural change. in Balazs, K, Faulkner, W & Schimank, U. (Ed.) "The research system in post-communist Central and Eastern Europe" EASST Special Issue. *Social Studies of Science.* Vol.25. No.4.

Mowery, D. & Rosenberg, N. (1989) *Technology and the pursuit of economic growth.* Cambridge University Press.

Muller, K. (1995) Changes on the "bordelines" between research and industry following economic transformation in the Czech Republic. in Balazs, K., Faulkner, W. & Schimank, U. (Ed.) "The research system in post-communist Central and Eastern Europe" EASST Special Issue. *Social Studies of Science.* Vol.25. No.4.

Mytelka, L. (1985) Stimulating effective technology transfer: the case of textiles in Africa. in Rosenberg, N. & Frischtak, C. (Ed.) *International technology transfer*. Praeger.

Mytelka, L. (1991) New modes of competition in the textile and clothing industry: some consequences for the Third World exporters. in Niosi, J. (Ed.) *Technology and national competitiveness. Oligopoly, technological innovation and international competition.* McGill-Queen's University Press.

Mytelka, L. (1992) Ivorian industry at the cross-road in Stewart, F., Lall, S. & Wangwe, S. (Eds.) *Alternative strategies in Subsaharan Africa.* Macmillan.

Mytelka, L. (1993) Rethinking development. A role for innovation networking in the "other two-thirds". *Futures.* 7/8.

Myung Rae-Cho. (1994) Weaving flexibility: lasrge-small firm relations, flexibility and regional clusters in South Korea in Pedersen, P., Sverison, A. & van Dijk, M. (Eds.) *Flexible specialization. The dynamics of small scale industries in the South.* Intermediate Technology Publication.

Nakaoka, T. (1987) On technological leaps of Japan as a developing country. *Osaka City University Economic review.* 22.

Nelson, R. (1987) Innovation and economic development: theoretical retrospect and prospect. in Katz, J. (Ed.) *Technology generation in Latin American manufacturing industries. Theory and case studies concerning its nature, magnitude and consequences.* Macmillan.

Nelson, R. (1988) Institutions supporting technical change in the United States. in Dosi, G. et al (Eds.) *Technical change and economic theory.* Frances Pinter. London.

Nelson, R. & Winter, S. (1982) *An evolutionary theory of economic change.* Cambridge. The Belknap Press of Harvard University Press.

Nguyen Ngoc Ngoan (1992) 'To develop electronics there should be harmonised coordination'. *Liberated Saigon*. 19 September.

Nguyen Quy Son (1992) General context and some activities of Vietnam Association of Informatics. *Proceeding of third informatics week.* Vietnam Association of Informatics. Hanoi. July (in Vietnamese).

Nguyen Thi Tri, Pham Quang Sang & Sloper, D. (1995) Physical facilities and learning resources. in Sloper, D & Le Thac Can (Ed.) *Higher education in Vienam. Change and response.* Institute of Southeast Asian Studies. St. Martin's Press. Singapore.

Nguyen Truong (1974) *Role of public enterprises in national development in South Vietnam. Problems and prospects.* Regional Institute of Higher Education and Development. Singapore.

Nohria, N. & Eccles, R. (1992) (Eds.) *Networks and organizations: structure, form and actions.* Harvard Business School presss. Mass.

Ostry, S. & Harianto, F. (1995) The changing pattern of Japanese foreign direct investment in the electronics industry in East Asia. *Transnational corporation.* Vol.4. No.1.

Ozawa, T. (1980) Government control over technology acquisition and firms' entry into new sectors: the experience of Japan's synthesis fibre industry. *Cambridge Journal of economics.* 4.

Patel, P. & Pavitt, K. (1992) The innovative performance of the world's largest firms: some new evidence. *The economic of innovation and new technology.* 2.

Pavitt, K. (1984) Sectoral patterns of technical change: towards a taxonomy and a theory. *Research Policy.* Vol.13.

Perez, C. & Soete, L. (1988) Catching up in technology: entry barriers and windows of opportunity. in Dosi, G., Freeman, C., Nelson, R., Silverberg, G., & Soete, L. (Eds.)*Technical change and economic theory.* Pinter. London.

Phan Dinh Dieu (1992) Some suggestions about national policy to develop information technology in our country up to the year 2000. *Proceeding of third informatics week.* Vietnam Association of Informatics. Hanoi. July (in Vietnamese).

Poapongsakorn, N. & Thongudai, P. (1998) Technological capability building and the sustainability of export success in Thailand's textile and electronics industries. in Ernst, D., Ganiatsos, T. & Mytelka, L. (Eds.) *Technological capabilities and export success in Asia.* Routledge.

Polanyi, M. (1966) *The tacit dimension.* Routledge. London.

Porter, M. (1990) *The competitive advantage of nations.* Macmillan. London.

Post, K. (1989) *Revolution, socialism and nationalism in Vietnam. Vol. 3. Socialism in half a country.* ISS. Dartmouth.

Powell, W. & Brantley, P. (1992) Competitive cooperation in biotechnology: learning through networks in Nohria, N. & Eccles, R. (Eds.) *Networks and organizations: structure, form and actions.* Harvard Business School Presss. Mass.

Preverez, M. & Shohet, S. (1995) *New knowledge: production v diffusion; town v gown.* Paper preasented at 3rd International ASEAT Conference. Manchester. September.

Pyke, F., Becattini, G. & Sengenberger, W. (1990) *Industrial districts and inter-firm cooperation in Italy.* ILO. Geneva.

Radosevic, S. (1993) *Eastern European science and technology capabilities during the transition: a provisional assessment of effects and prospects.* Paper to the conference "The role of S&T policy in economic transformation programs with particular regard to East-Central Europe and the former Soviet Union". Lyon. December.

Ranis, G. (1995) Another look at the East Asian miracle. *The World Bank Economic review.* Vol 9. No 1.

Rhee, Y. W., Ross-Larson, B. & Pursell, G. (1984) *Korea's competitive edge: managing the entry into world markets.* Johns Hopkins Press. Baltimore.

Robert, J. (1973) Engineering consultancy, industrialisation and development. in Cooper (Ed.) *Science, technology and development. The political economy of technical advance in underdeveloped countries*. Frank Cass. London.

Rosenberg, N. (1976) *Perspective on technology*. Cambridge University Press. Cambridge.

Rosenberg, N. (1982) *Inside the black box. Technology and economics.* Cambridge University Press. Cambridge.

Rosenberg, N. (1990) Why do firms do basic research (with their own money)? *Research Policy.* 19.

Rosenberg, N. (1994) Path-dependent aspects of technological change. *Exploring the black box. Technology, economics and history.* Cambridge University Press.

Saviotti, P. (1992) *On the economics of expertise and the expertise of economics.* Paper presented at PICT workshop on exploring expertise. Edinburgh. November.

Senker, J. (1992) *The contribution of tacit knowledge to innovation.*. Paper presented at PICT workshop on exploring expertise. Edinburgh. November.

Senker, J. & Faulkner, W. (1992) Industrial use of public sector research in adavanced technologies: a comparison of biotechnology and ceramics. *R&D Management.* 22 (2).

Shaw, B. (1995) *The restructuring of the national technological innovation system within the Russian aerospace industry.* Paper presented at 3rd international ASEAT conference. Manchester. September.

Sloper, D. & Le Thac Can (Ed.) (1995) *Higher education in Vienam. Change and response.* Institute of Southeast Asian Studies. St. Martin's Press. Singapore.

Spender, J.C. & Di Bello, L. (1995) Constructive learning: a simulation approach to developing the workplace skills for implementing complex industrial systems. in Bennett, D. & Stewart, F. (Ed.)*Technological innovation and global challenges*. Proceeding of the European conference on management of technology. Aston University. Birmingham.

Spoor, M. (1988) 'State finance in the socialist republic of Vietnam. The difficult transition from state bureaucratic finance to socialist economic accounting'. in Marr, D. & White, C. (Eds.) *Postwar Vietnam: dilemmas in socialist development.* SEAP. Cornell University. Ithaca.

Stewart, F. & James, J. (1982) *The economics of new technology in developing countries.* Frances Pinter. London.

Teece, D., Pisano, G. & Shuen, A. (1990) *Firm capabilities, resources and the concept of strategy*. CCC Working paper. No. 90-8. Center for research in Management. UC Berkeley.

Teece, D., Miller, K. & Melcher, R. (1992) The Partners. *Business Week.* 10/2.

Teitel, S. & Sercovich, F. (1984) Latin America. *World Development* Vol.12. No5/6.

Teubal, M. (1984) The role of technological learning in the exports of manufactured goods: the case of selected capital goods in Brasil. *World Development.* Vol.12. No 8.

Teubal, M., Halui, N. & Tsiddon, D. (1986) Learning and the rise of Israel's exports of sophisticated products. *World Development.* Vol.14. No12.

Tornquist, D. (1991) *Vietnam.* Flint River press. London.

Tran Ngoc Ca & Le Dieu Anh (1998) 'Technological dynamism and R&D in the export of manufactures from Viet Nam'. in Ernst, D. et al. (Eds.) *Technological capabilities and export success in Asia.* Routledge.

Tsekouras, G. (1995) *Formulating "core competencies" in a less developed country*. Paper presented at 3rd International ASEAT conference. Manchester. September.

UNCTAD (1990) *Transfer and development of technology in the least developed countries: an assessment of major policy issues.* Geneva.

UNCTAD (1991) *Technology selection, acquisition and negotiation.* Papers of a seminar organised by Islamic Development Bank and UNCTAD. Geneva.

UNIDO (1989) *Vietnam's industrial development - an assessment.* Vienna.

UNIDO (1990) *Microelectronics and information technology in Vietnam. An overview.* Vienna.

UNIDO (1991) *Vietnam: industrial policy reforms and international co-operation.* Industrial development review series. Vienna.

UNIDO (1994) *Economies in transition: restructuring of large-scale industries.* Europe programme. Country strategy and programme development division. August. Vienna.

UNIDO/UNDP (1994) *Electronics and information technology in Vietnam.* Report of project DP/VIE/89/002.

Viana, H. (1984) *International technology transfer, technological learning and the assimilation of imported technology in a state-owned enterprise: the case of direct reduction in SIDOR steel plant in Venezuela.* DPhil Thesis. Sussex University.

Vietnam Association of Informatics (VAI) (1990) *Proceeding of second informatics week.* HoChiMinh City. August (in Vietnamese).

Vo Nhan Tri (1988) Party policies and economic performances: the second and third five year plans examined. in Marr & White (Ed.) *Postwar Vietnam: dilemmas in socialist development.* SEAP. Cornell University. Ithaca.

Vo Nhan Tri & Booth, A. (1992) *Recent economic development in Vietnam.* SOAS working paper No.7. London University.

Von Hippel, E. (1982) The consumer-active paradigm for industrial product generation. *Research Policy.* 11.

Von Hippel, E. & Tyre, M. (1995) How learning by doing is done: problem identification innovel process equipment. *Research Policy.* 24.

Vu Cao Dam (1992) *Vietnam's science and technology on the way of democratisation.* Paper presented at 4S/EASST conference. Gothenburg. August.

Vu Cao Dam, Tran Ngoc Ca & Nguyen Thanh Ha (1991) *Evaluation of technology transfer to Vietnam.* A final report . ISM/RPI joint project. ISM. Hanoi.

Wade, R. (1990) *Governing the market. Economic theory and the role of government in East Asian industrialization.* Princeton University Press. Princeton.

Westphal, L., Rhee, Y. & Pursell, G. (1981) *Korean industrial competence: where it came from.* World Bank. Staff working paper no. 469. Washington, D.C.

Westphal, L., Rhee, Y., Kim, L. & Amsden, A. (1984a) Republic of Korea. Export of technology by NICs. *World Development.* Vol.12. No 5/6.

Westphal, L., Rhee, Y. & Pursell, G. (1984b) Sources of technological capability in South Korea. in Fransman, M. & King, K.*Technological capability in the Third World.* Macmillan.

Westphal, L., Kim, L. & Dahlman, C. (1985) Reflections on the Republic Korea's acquisition of technological capability. in Rosenberg, N & Frischtak, C (Ed.) *International technology transfer*. Praeger.NewYork.

Wie, T.K. & Pangestu, M. (1998) 'Technological capabilities and Indonesia's manufactured export.' in Ernst, D., Ganiatsos, T. & Mytelka, L. (Eds.) *Technological capabilities and export success in Asia.* Routledge.

Wong-Seng Hon (1992) Exploiting information technology: a case study of Singapore. *World Development.* Vol.20 No.12.

World Bank (1993) *Vietnam in transition.* East Asian Division.

Zhang Jianshin & Reeve, N. (1995) *Toward the 21st century: China's economic development, technological innovation system and programmes.* Paper presented at 3rd International ASEAT Conferrence. Manchester. September.

Index

For Product Safety Concerns and Information please contact our EU representative GPSR@taylorandfrancis.com Taylor & Francis Verlag GmbH, Kaufingerstraße 24, 80331 München, Germany

Batch number: 10726009

Printed by Printforce, the Netherlands